The Literary Impact of
The Golden Bough

BY JOHN B. VICKERY

The Literary Impact of

The Golden Bough

PRINCETON UNIVERSITY PRESS

PRINCETON, NEW JERSEY

Published by Princeton University Press, Princeton, New Jersey
In the United Kingdom: Princeton University Press,
Guildford, Surrey

LCC: 72–4049
ISBN 0–691–01331–4 (paperback edn.)
ISBN 0–691–06243–9 (hardcover edn.)

Publication of this book has been aided by
a grant from the A. W. Mellon Foundation

This book has been composed in Linotype Janson

Printed in the United States of America
by Princeton University Press
Princeton, New Jersey

First PRINCETON PAPERBACK printing, 1976

Preface

The general nature of this study is substantially indicated by its title, which though somewhat cumbersome is also clear. It may, however, be useful to amplify the implications and assumptions that it possesses for the organization of the book. The first point, which at initial glance may seem trivial, has to do with the choice of "impact" rather than "influence" in the title. The intent was to convey a concern with literary forms, figures, and motifs that is both broader and rather less precise than that traditionally exhibited in older studies of literary influence. To look for an exact and single source of most literary images and ideas or to seek an exact congruence between the latter and the former is in the majority of instances to search for a chimera. The artist's mind is chameleon-like, and to trace his memories, impulses, and past thoughts with any precision requires more rigorous psychological techniques than are currently available. Consequently, the relationship assumed in this study between Sir James Frazer and modern writers is as much that of ancestor to descendant as that of lender to borrower. At the same time, the delineation of direct borrowing is made in those specific instances that evidence seems to warrant.

Because Frazer and *The Golden Bough* antedate the writers on whom the impact is made, the book naturally begins with various aspects of his greatest work. Chapter one examines *The Golden Bough* in relation to its age and attempts to show how in summing up many strands of nineteenth-century thought it embodied the dominant intellectual tradition shaping the modern spirit. To this end, the chapter focusses on Frazer's relation to the nineteenth century's rationalism, historicism, evolutionary ethic, and mythological imagination. In chapter two the emphasis shifts to *The Golden Bough* itself and in what its major ideas and central thesis consist. Here, no effort whatsoever has been made to do anything other than set forth as clearly and economically as possible the controlling concepts of the book's third edition of twelve volumes (1907-1915). The drawing of dazzling implications or

v

the formulating of ingenious hypotheses from Frazer's material
has been resolutely, though reluctantly, eschewed. Instead a
more modest goal is pursued, namely, that of determining what
exactly *The Golden Bough* said on those diverse topics which
were to fascinate so many modern writers. Readers who are already familiar with Frazer's work may pass over this chapter with relatively few qualms. Those who are not will find it a
convenient summary and useful aid to appreciating the distinctive uses made of *The Golden Bough* in twentieth-century
literature.

Chapter three sketches in admittedly incomplete fashion the
extent to which Frazer's views were diffused throughout the humanities and social sciences. The aim is to suggest in a general
manner the inescapable nature of Frazer's point of view and emphasis for the creative artist whatever his dominant interests.
This chapter moves steadily toward disciplines more closely related to literature and in so doing prepares for the more exclusively literary issues of later chapters. Chapter four addresses
itself to the distinctive verbal texture and structure of *The Gold-
en Bough* with a view to explaining why Frazer's study rather
than other anthropological works achieved the dominant literary
impact that it did. This literary reason for *The Golden Bough*'s
eminence is intended to augment rather than replace those historical and intellectual reasons adduced in earlier chapters.

In the course of its consideration of the style, structure, and
genre of Frazer's most famous work, this chapter illustrates the
affinities between *The Golden Bough* and specific artists and
texts. The next chapter continues this emphasis but with greater
weight given to the variety of strategies by which poets and novelists assimilate *The Golden Bough* to their individual attitudes
and preoccupations. The writers touched on here are not those
dealt with in detail in the balance of the book nor are they more
than a fraction of those who warrant treatment were this study
to be exhaustive and hence as long as *The Golden Bough* itself.
Nevertheless, they suffice to suggest major areas of impact as well
as the diversity of uses to which artists have put Frazer.

The remainder of the book is devoted to chapters probing in
some detail the intellectual, thematic, and formal impact of *The*

Golden Bough on William Butler Yeats, T. S. Eliot, D. H. Lawrence, and James Joyce. Though the treatment of these authors necessarily varies—between, say, chronological and thematic approaches—the general method does not, in any substantial fashion. In the case of each author, consideration begins with the available evidence of his familiarity with *The Golden Bough* as indicated in essays, letters, and the like. So far as possible the date of acquaintance is established, at least within reasonable bounds, with a view to determining the works subject to Frazer's impact. In some instances, such as that of Yeats, works published prior to unequivocal familiarity with *The Golden Bough* are discussed. The aim here is to note other interests which might have contributed to the author's receptivity to the motifs and images elaborated by Frazer.

Following this, the chapters adapt themselves to the contours of the individual author's work. In the case of Yeats and Eliot, the approach is almost exclusively chronological. Obviously, however, not all their works or phases receive the same measure of attention since their concern with *The Golden Bough* fluctuated through the years. On the other hand, the chapters on Lawrence assess Frazer's impact thematically and by selective attention to representative instances of genres. And finally, with Joyce the approach is both chronological and thematic with the emphasis falling on the three works of extended prose fiction. In the case of each author, conclusions about their thematic and technical deployment of *The Golden Bough* are developed throughout their individual sections rather than incorporated in separate chapters. On similar grounds, a concluding chapter summarizing the findings of the study as a whole is foregone. Prolonged involvement with the topic has made it clear that the individual authors' responses to Frazer's impact are so diverse and multiform as to defy easy much less valid classification.

For permission to incorporate materials from periodical and other publications I am indebted to the following: a shorter version of Chapter IV as " 'The Golden Bough': Impact and Archetype" in *Virginia Quarterly Review*, XXXIX (1963), 37-57; a shorter version of Chapter V as "Mythopoesis and Modern Literature" in *The Shaken Realist*, eds. M. J. Friedman & J. B. Vickery, Louisiana State University Press, 1970; a portion of Chapter VI as "Three Modes and a Myth" in *Western Humanities Review*, XII (1958), 371-378; a portion of Chapter VII as "T. S. Eliot's Poetry: The Quest and the Way," *Renascence*, X (1957-58), 3-10, 31, 59-67; portions of Chapter IV, VI, and VIII as " 'The Golden Bough' and Modern Poetry" in the *Journal of Aesthetics and Art Criticism*, XV (1957), 271-288; a portion of Chapter IX as "Myth and Ritual in the Short Fiction of D. H. Lawrence" in *Modern Fiction Studies*, V (1959), 65-82, by permission of *Modern Fiction Studies*, © 1959, by Purdue Research Foundation, Lafayette, Indiana. I am also indebted to the American Council of Learned Societies for support in beginning the study and to Purdue University for XL grants and to the Committee on Research of the Academic Senate of the University of California at Riverside for Research and Opportunity Fund grants that enabled the completion of the project.

Permission to quote from T. S. Eliot, "Choruses from 'The Rock,' " *Collected Poems, 1909-1962* has been granted by Harcourt, Brace Jovanovich Inc.

From *The Collected Letters of D. H. Lawrence*, ed. by Harry T. Moore. Copyright 1932 by The Estate of D. H. Lawrence, 1934 by Frieda Lawrence, Copyright 1933, 1948, 1953, 1954 and each year © 1956–1962 by Angelo Ravagli & C. M. Weekley, Executors of the Estate of D. H. Lawrence.

Reprinted by permission of the Viking Press, Inc.

Contents

The Literary Impact of
The Golden Bough

CHAPTER I

The Golden Bough
and the Nineteenth-
Century Milieu

[I]

In the seventy-five years since *The Golden Bough* first appeared, it has become one of the most influential works in the twentieth century. What is most striking is the depth to which it has permeated the cultural strata of our time. In literature alone it touches nearly everything, from the most significant to the most ephemeral works. At one end of the spectrum is its well-known importance to works like *The Waste Land* and *Finnegans Wake*; at the other extreme is its perhaps largely unsuspected impingement on serious minor fiction like *Devil by the Tail* and *The City of Trembling Leaves*, prize novels like *Tower in the West*, and even Raymond Chandler detective stories. Between these two poles *The Golden Bough* also asserts its role in the very shape and texture of the middle ground composed of genuine but less celebrated works of art. Without it such diverse works as David Jones's *The Anathemata*, George Barker's *Calamiterror*, Ronald Bottrall's *Festivals of Fire*, T. Sturge Moore's Biblical drama, F. L. Lucas' First Yule poem, and the novels of Naomi Mitchison, John Cowper Powys, and Robert Graves would be immeasurably different in outlook as well as style. We find that it has even played a controlling role in at least one television program and engrossed a movie star like the late James Dean.[1] Such random

[1] The television program was a 1964 production of the *Naked City* series which opened with a quotation from *The Golden Bough* concerning the sacred king and his ritual sacrifice and then sought to apply this to the scapegoat humiliation and suffering of a professional football player. James Dean claimed to have studied *The Golden Bough* and the Marquis de Sade in

soundings reveal its presence at every cultural level from the most exalted to the most trivial.

The Golden Bough is both the most encyclopedic treatment of primitive life available to the English-speaking world and the one that lies behind the bulk of modern literary interest in myth and ritual. These were subjects that engrossed William Butler Yeats before the turn of the century as much as they do writers today. As Lionel Trilling has recently remarked, "perhaps no book has had so decisive an effect upon modern literature as Frazer's."[2] To assess the nature, forms, and extent of that impact is the purpose of this study, but to do so some knowledge of *The Golden Bough* itself is necessary. This includes not only the controlling ideas and form of the book but its cultural content as well. It is, of course, a truism that any work is the product of its age. Nevertheless, this is particularly true of *The Golden Bough*, for it sums up so many strands of nineteenth-century thought and feeling. Catching up as it does many of the scientific, philosophical, historical, and artistic emphases of the age, it is a subtly persuasive form of the loose, variegated, and often contradictory intellectual tradition that shapes the modern spirit.

Frazer brought together the major elements of that tradition with such astonishing and subtle power that *The Golden Bough* became a central focus for the many divergent forces struggling to evolve a distinctive twentieth-century temper. This chapter examines in turn Frazer's reflection and adaptation of the nineteenth century's rationalism, historicism, evolutionary ethic, and mythological imagination. Focus and emphasis are sought by relating Frazer to such representative figures as John Stuart Mill, Matthew Arnold, T. H. Huxley, Ernest Renan, and John Ruskin. While scarcely more than a sketch of an intricate subject and voluminous age, it should nevertheless indicate why Frazer's importance was inevitable. He drew together the central strands of thought and feeling in the age, but in an undoctrinaire manner.

---

connection with the minor show-business figure Vampira and what he took to be obsessive Satanic forces. See Hedda Hopper & James Brough, *The Whole Truth and Nothing But* (New York: Doubleday & Co., 1963), p. 171.

[2] Lionel Trilling, *Beyond Culture* (New York: Viking Press, 1965), p. 14.

Consequently, his readers, both original and later, found his ideas and sentiments to be meaningful encounters with their own current problems and experiences rather than merely records of obsolete and tedious arguments or views. In so doing, he inadvertently but powerfully conveyed a sense of the continuity of dilemma and temper obtaining between the nineteenth and twentieth centuries.

At the same time, Frazer also suggested something of how the various intellectual facets of the age fit together. In a way not apparent in the more powerful or sustained thinkers of the period, Frazer shows us the rational, evolutionary, historical, scientific temper conspiring with as well as opposing the imaginative, spiritual, irrational, myth-making impulses of mankind. On the surface, such positions as Mill's rationalism, Arnold's historical sense, and Huxley's scientific and evolutionary outlook seem to be largely antipathetic to the passion for classical and other mythologies felt by nineteenth-century artists and their readers. The former appear grounded in factuality and precision, while the latter ostensibly aspire to the fanciful and conjectural. But actually, viewed in context, all these factors converge on an impulse toward the release and expansion of the mind beyond the confines of a constricting dogmatism. The age itself was not so aware of this convergence. As a result, its members frequently talked as though the role of reason was the elimination of fancy, that of history the dispensing with myth, and that of science the displacement of religion.

What *The Golden Bough* implicitly shows us is that the interest in myth—which extends throughout the entire century, and beyond—became a viable power in the creative world only when the full significance of mythic activity was revealed by the new forms of science and history. It is perhaps not too much to say that without Darwin and the evolutionary perspective, the German historians and Biblical scholars, and the commonsense logic of minds like Mill and Huxley, myth would have remained an airy fancy with no social or psychological relevance to modern man. Frazer's great merit was that he could absorb the relevant training and views of his time, bring them to bear on subjects like myth and ritual, and convey his views to the world at large in a language that neither obscured nor oversimplified them. Without him, the literary concern with myth and related matters would have been substantially different, if indeed it had existed at all. And without the intellectual milieu outlined in the following pages, Frazer too would have been far different than he was and perhaps considerably less significant. Indeed, *The Golden Bough* represents in an almost unique fashion the fusion of an individual author with the temper of an entire age. Later, in the twentieth century, under the growing impact of such forces as Nietzsche's *Birth of Tragedy*, Jung's archetypal psychology, and Bergson's and James's locating of the religious impulses in human emotions, myth for the creative artist and his audience largely pulled free of these rational and scientific underpinnings. But because Frazer remained undogmatic, *The Golden Bough* continued as the artist's vade mecum to myth.

Broadly speaking, the intellectual tradition that shaped Frazer encompassed two chief strains, one looking essentially to the future, the other to the past. The former was the source of major advances in science, radical attitudes in politics, and positivistic philosophical principles. The latter, on the other hand, subsumed political conservatives, religious traditionalists, and historical antiquarians. Though diametrically opposed in beliefs and assumptions, the two nevertheless were not so violently hostile as they frequently were in Europe proper. This was largely because of a firmly ingrained moral attitude common to both, which cut across intellectual lines. *The Golden Bough* aptly exemplifies the fruitful interchanges of the two tendencies, for, though scientific and mildly Liberal in outlook, Frazer also invested enormous time and energy in researches that steadfastly looked to the past for its data and perspectives.

To our twentieth-century notion of science, geared as it is to mathematical formulae, intricate experiments, and concepts that either flout or beggar common sense, the aligning of Frazer with science seems curious and unlikely. Yet like Darwin and Freud, though less emphatically, Frazer thought of himself as a scientist, as one for whom truth and fact were not only accessible but ultimate values. For him, science was perhaps less a refined methodology than a general temper and stance toward the nature of knowledge and the conditions of ignorance. In his Preface to the third edition of *The Golden Bough*, for instance, he clearly feels that while striving for a deliberately artistic form he has also preserved "the solid substance of a scientific treatise."[3] It was as "a contribution to that still youthful science" of anthropology that he offered the second edition to the reading public.[4] And a few pages later he faces the prospect of destroying long-established beliefs possessed of numerous "tender and sacred associations" and concludes: "Whatever comes of it, wherever it leads us, we must follow truth alone. It is our only guiding star: *hoc signo vinces*."[5] Thus, Frazer clearly links himself to the great intellectual development of modern times—the rise of science—that extends back to the sixteenth and seventeenth centuries where the scientific intellectual first emerged as a type.[6]

[II]

While Frazer has affinities with the general scientific temperament of modern times, he also embodies qualities that are even more peculiarly representative of nineteenth-century England. He came too late in the age to be subjected to the full weight of Evangelicalism. Yet there is a sense in which his scholarly vigor, dedicated to the exploration of strange and barbarous customs in often graphic detail, is a latter-day recapitulation of G. M. Young's thesis that "Victorian history is the story of the English mind employing the energy imparted by Evangelical conviction to rid itself of the restraints which Evangelicalism had laid on their senses and the intellect; on amusement, enjoyment, art; on curiosity, on criticism, on science."[7] Even after the deaths of Wilberforce, Hannah More, and Charles Simeon, Cambridge remained a center of Evangelicalism. Thus, by the time Frazer was a member of the university, Evangelical drive and energy

[3] Sir James G. Frazer, *The Golden Bough*, 3rd ed. (London: Macmillan, 1911), I, viii. Subsequent references will be abbreviated to *GB*.

[4] *GB*, I, xxiv. The term "science" is repeated in the next sentence of this passage also. Cf. *GB*, III, viii.

[5] *GB*, I, xxvi.

[6] Lewis S. Feuer, *The Scientific Intellectual* (New York: Basic Books, 1963), p. 7.

[7] G. M. Young, *Portrait of an Age* (Oxford: Oxford University Press, 1936), p. 5.

had been transformed without being dissipated into the more secular Victorian belief in hard work and the active life. Like Samuel Butler and William Morris he is the embodiment of Victorian intellectual dedication in its late form. What distinguished Frazer from the early, less imaginative stress upon self-application, dictated as it was by economics and the social drive to succeed, was his post-Darwinian feeling that there was nothing higher or more rewarding than a life dedicated to working, however humbly, toward the extension of human knowledge. When *The Golden Bough* likens traditional beliefs to a strong tower sheltering man from life and reality, a tower to be breached by "the battery of the comparative method," it typifies the very mood evoked in *Windyhaugh* (1898).[8] The "drudgery" of "a long and patient study of primitive superstition" is more than compensated for by "the extent of the intellectual prospect which suddenly opens up before us."[9] It affords "a greater panorama" even than that "revelation" experienced by "classical scholars at the revival of learning."[10] That this attitude is genuine and not merely rhetorical is attested to both by Frazer's voluminous correspondence with other investigators and by his detailed footnotes, which scrupulously acknowledge information made available by others.

Another aspect of the Evangelical tradition discernible in Frazer provides a bridge to his affinities with Utilitarians like Bentham and James Mill. By his shocked and deeply moved recognition of the savagery and cruelty men have historically visited on one another, Frazer revealed how he shared in both movements' common humanitarian regard for their fellow man. Frazer's concern for the pitiful struggles and suffering of mankind throughout history could not compare in immediacy with the characters of Dickens or George Eliot. It did, however, build on those cultural predispositions established by literature in the middle of the century. From the outset his style stamped him as a literary artist. Hence he was able to convey humanitarian attitudes through the longer and more abstract vista of history because his readers intuitively felt his work to be literature. As a

[8] *GB*, I, xxvi. [9] *GB*, I, xx. [10] *GB*, I, xxiv–xxv.

result they were predisposed to regard it as a likely and admirable medium for the expression of man's tenderer feelings.

His strongest link with the Utilitarian tradition is, of course, his preference for a philosophical outlook that is at least loosely rationalistic in character. Frazer was no philosopher, but insofar as he thought about such matters his temper was substantially that of John Stuart Mill not only in its inherent rationalism but also in its ultimate willingness to allow the claims of the emotions. The very year that Frazer entered Trinity College, Cambridge, Mill's *Three Essays on Religion* (1874) appeared posthumously. They possess several features which point up the kinship of the two men. For instance, the second essay finds that the institution of religion is socially and morally useful to mankind, a view that is qualifiedly entertained in *The Golden Bough* and more emphatically implied by the main argument of *Psyche's Task*. Here both Frazer and Mill affirm beliefs in terms of social and psychological utility and not of objective truth. And in the first and third essays there is a dramatic instance of the struggle the reasonable and tolerant mind undergoes in the search for truth. Mill hovers between thinking that there is and there is not evidence for belief in a personal deity kindly disposed toward man just as Frazer oscillates from volume to volume over his views on euhemerism. In both we see the same kind of temper at work. Their common ground is less the uncertainty over a particular issue than the habit of recognizing and giving due weight to the evidence bearing on the issue. Some may find this a "retreat from rationalism"; others may be more inclined to regard it as a stubborn disavowal of secular dogmatism.[11]

What Frazer, then, has in common with the greatest of the Utilitarians is the ideal of the open, flexible mind, of reason as man's best hope for reaching the truth and solving his problems. Like Bentham, who adapted the critical temper of Hume and Voltaire to nineteenth-century needs, Frazer sought to scrutinize all evidence and authority with the eye of reason. He could, of course, sharply define the limits of his interests, as when

[11] The phrase cited is from G. Himmelfarb, *Victorian Minds* (New York: Knopf, 1968), p. 151.

9

he refused to read Freud or any reviewers of his work. Yet within those limits Frazer showed an enviable tolerance for views other than his own as well as a scrupulous regard for the due weight of all evidence whether it fitted his thesis of the moment or not. His handling of the rival theories of Mannhardt and Westermarck concerning the significance of fire-festivals is a particularly good example of his prevailing attitude. Such an attitude, however, is not one simply shared coincidentally or through deliberate emulation. Rather it is part of a slowly gathering tradition in the middle years of the century of which Mill was but a single instance.[12]

As the century wore on, historical relativism began to emerge as a powerful intellectual force. It is one of the great merits of *The Golden Bough* and its author that they should have survived (with neither apparent corruption nor reaction) the refined and sophisticated scepticism that made up part of the tone of the 90s and the Edwardian Age. In thus maintaining the spirit of free inquiry mingled with a tough-minded caution about theories and ideas, *The Golden Bough* preserved the intellectual gains first established in the 60s without dissolving them into a facile expression of either the *toute comprendre* view or the debunker's disavowal of any and all truths. Doubtless a large part of the credit for this can be traced to Frazer's involvement in the tradition of Cambridge rationalism in which, as Noel Annan has remarked, "ideas were hammered into principles to be judged empirically" and "talking for effect" was rejected in favor of "studies which are precise and yield tangible results."[13]

Since he shared its general feeling about the capacities and uses of the human mind, especially the rational faculty, it is not surprising that he should also have reflected the idea of progress articulated by this tradition and much of the age at large. G. M. Young has observed that in general the thought of early Victorian England was controlled by the notion of progress, whereas that of the later period felt the impress of the concept

---

[12] An instructive illustration of this aspect of the nineteenth-century temper is Gertrude Himmelfarb's discussion of Walter Bagehot, pp. 220-235.

[13] Noel Annan, *Leslie Stephen* (Cambridge: Harvard University Press, 1952), p. 132.

of evolution.[14] For Frazer the two ideas existed together though not in the crude or simple forms that led certain thinkers of the age to use them to justify the extremes of laissez-faire. Thus, in the Preface to the second edition of *The Golden Bough*, Frazer exults in the opportunity afforded the modern historian to trace the fortunes not merely of a single race or nation but "of all mankind, and thus enabling us to follow the long march, the slow and toilsome ascent, of humanity from savagery to civilisation."[15]

Frazer, writing in the 90s and later, did not have the easy and rather complacent certitude about progress prevalent in the early years of the century. Unlike Paine and Godwin, he had no revolutionary flush of conviction that the ideal society can be impelled into existence by sheer concentrated will power directed to a social blueprint. His was rather a qualified, even a somewhat jaded, version of the position advanced by Carlyle, Macaulay, and the early Mill of the 1830s, which saw a greater age of achievement and belief just beyond the present one. In the 1850s and after there was a kind of rapt conviction and looking forward to the coming age in which doubt and uncertainty would be eliminated. By Frazer's time this had become a requisite hope rather than an optimistic assumption. *The Golden Bough* makes progress dependent neither on the application of scientific methods nor on a metaphysical conviction of progress as a law of the universe. Instead, its notion of progress we might more nearly call "humanistic." Progress must occur largely because the alternative is unthinkable and man will not permit his own annihilation or disintegration. Such a view is clearly different in kind from the determinism of Marx and the tragic stoicism of Freud; its tradition is that of Darwinian humanism as espoused by Huxley rather than Spencer. And in some ways, notably in his efforts to strike a balance between competing views of social reality, Frazer recalls too the stance of Malthus. Both countered perfectibilitarian ideals with hard warnings drawn from the grim evidence afforded by the scrutiny of particular ancient and primitive societies. Where they differ, of course, is in Frazer's refusal to adopt the intoxicating dispassionateness of cultural laissez-faireism.

[14] Young, p. 108.   [15] *GB*, I, xxv.

By 1890 the positivist temper of English thought was firmly established. As a result, *The Golden Bough* reflects a more tentative, uncertain, and cautious faith in progress. At the same time, more than earlier Victorians he took the future and man, not the past and God, as his postulates and hopes. It is to the future that Frazer repeatedly looked for whatever value his work is to have. With this he provided a transition from the assured conviction of necessary progress held by the early Victorians generally to the humanistic caution and hope of later thinkers. At the same time it would not do to make this break appear sharper than in fact it is. As early as 1838 Thomas Arnold perceived an "atmosphere of unrest and paradox" in the age. Similar remarks betray the development of a spirit of uncertainty of intellectual belief, which was the first dim realization that the old absolutism was no more.[16]

In sum, Frazer represents that point in the development of the idea of progress at which the distinctively twentieth-century attitude begins to appear. For him its antecedents were also its culmination in the long curve of history. *The Golden Bough* at no point reflects the enthusiasm of, say, Macaulay for "natural" progress or for its unqualified social and industrial manifestations, but it does stubbornly cling to the empirical evidence of its occurrence. In a sense, we might also say that Mill and Macaulay, on this point, constitute the two halves of Frazer's interests and style. On the one hand, there is the vision, almost rhapsodic in tenor, of man's stubborn movement toward the realization of a better world. In *The Golden Bough* this emerges largely through the author's point of view. He implies that one major function of this retelling of primitive customs is to show us how far man has come and how reasonable and sensible we and Frazer are by contrast. It is far from irrelevant that Frazer's greatest work should begin its initial chapter with an epigraph from Macaulay's poetry. On the other hand, there is the harsh evidence from contemporary savage tribal behavior and urban civilized violence

---

[16] Arnold's remark is cited in W. Houghton, *The Victorian Frame of Mind 1830-1870* (New Haven: Yale University Press, 1957), p. 8. See also W. L. Burn, *The Age of Equipoise* (New York: Norton & Co., 1964), pp. 59, 72.

alike to remind us that man is very far indeed from substantial moral and intellectual progress. *The Golden Bough* documented the primitive barbarism, while the age itself recorded the contemporary equivalent in such things as the Corn Law riots, the appalling living conditions of the urban slums, the Hyde Park riots of 1866, and the Dock Strike of 1889. The repugnance felt over these latter expressions of savagery led Frazer, like Mark Rutherford, to regard civilization as no more than a thin veneer over an inferno of primitive terrors and passions.[17] This aspect of human history is powerfully registered by Frazer's laconic, documentary understatement which catches the controlled, unemotional use of fact that dominated the Utilitarian attitude of John Stuart Mill and his father.

[III]

In addition to his rationalism and faith in progress, Frazer shared in another powerful Victorian tradition. It forms a central part of that "amazing capacity for detachment" evinced by the Victorian age, particularly from the 50s and 60s on. Nowhere is this capacity better indicated than in *The Golden Bough* where Frazer imperturbably contemplates the destruction of his own theories he has so voluminously enunciated. In this sense his work forms a late but vital aspect of what John Morley called "dissolvent literature." These were books whose immediate effect was most often to call religious faith into question either directly or implicitly. If the years from 1880 to 1914 form an interregnum between the Victorian and modern ages, an interregnum framed by Mallock's and Hulme's distinctive brands of scepticism,[18] then *The Golden Bough* may legitimately be seen as both contributory to and representative of this diversified and growing iconoclasm.

This emerges strikingly when we recollect the varieties of dissolvents that helped establish a context for *The Golden Bough* in

[17] See Young, p. 26; cf. Leonard Woolf, *Sowing: An Autobiography of the Years 1880-1914* (London: Hogarth Press, 1960), p. 56. For a similar contrast between surface joy and urbanity and subterranean anguish during the Edwardian and pre-World War I eras in Europe, see Gerhard Masur, *Prophets of Yesterday* (London: Weidenfeld & Nicholson, 1963), p. 35.

[18] Raymond Williams, *Culture and Society, 1780-1950* (New York: Columbia University Press, 1958), p. 161.

the minds of thoughtful Victorians. Such works ranged themselves along a broad spectrum. Some exercised their dissolving
role from a position sympathetic to religious belief. Others were
consciously and passionately antagonistic to it. Still others were
more detachedly aware of the possible effects on religious
thought and feeling. At the furthest remove were those whose
subject and treatment precluded the explicit consideration of
religion. And even within these groupings different emphases
developed. Thus, the *Life* of Joseph Blanco White (1842) is significantly different from such a study as Francis Newman's
Phases of Faith (1842). The first records a devout mind's pere-
grinations through three faiths. The second expresses the desire
for a kind of synoptic or eclectic religion based on the most valuable aspects of the known historical religions at the same time as
it criticized Christian dogma. Yet each reflects the determined
groping of the mind toward something other than that with
which it began and different from the prevailing orthodoxy.

In the case of Harriet Martineau, on the other hand, there is
no groping of the mind. Instead, her *Letters on the Laws
of Man's Social Nature and Development* (written with H. G. At-
kinson in 1851), which attained a phenomenal success and noto-
riety, advances a militant agnosticism. Her anticipation of
Frazer's ideas, if not his tone, is frequently striking. For her
Christians are "the adherents of a decaying mythology" and are
guilty of "following the heathen, as the heathen followed the
barbaric-fetish."[19] One of the most influential books in eroding
the faith of the educated man was, according to John Morley,
W. R. Greg's *Creed of Christendom* (1854).[20] Like Newman's
Phases of Faith, though more thoroughly, it continued the tradition of Coleridge, Alexander Geddes, Connop Thirlwall, Charles
Hennell, and Thomas Arnold. Contributing importantly to his
book's success was Greg's greater willingness to conciliate the
devout. Where Francis Newman was almost pugnaciously

---

[19] Miss Martineau's comments are cited in Houghton, p. 53.

[20] For contrasting views of Greg's importance, see Burn, p. 274 and
Annan, p. 156n. and p. 160n. The publishing history of this book seems,
contradictorily enough, to lend support to both views. It took twenty-two
years for it to achieve two editions. But between 1873 and 1883 it went
from three to eight editions.

rationalistic and insistently opposed to all orthodoxies, Greg appraised with a more commonsensical shrewdness what he could venture to say and what his audience could venture to hear. At the same time, he also had the advantage of being able to draw on a broader range of German Biblical scholarship. Charles Hennell's *Inquiry concerning the Origin of Christianity* (1838), for instance, was written in virtually total ignorance of the Continental "higher" criticism. Greg, on the other hand, benefitted from the translations of De Wette, Strauss, and others that had become available in the meantime. Despite or perhaps because of his career as a businessman and civil servant, he sought, as he did in his later *Rocks Ahead* (1874), to submit religion to a keen but practical intelligence.

The whole analytic study of mankind, which had its real efflorescence in the nineteenth century, took its initial orientation from Utilitarianism, the classical economics of Malthus and Ricardo, and associationist psychology. In the 50s, however, other, even stronger forces were making their presence felt as dissolvers of dogmatism and the constrained, impoverished intellectual traditions of the middle class which had dominated England for much of the century. Prominent among these was the revolution in history, which soon extended to other related disciplines. Under the impetus of German scholars like Barthold Niebuhr, Philipp Boeckh, and Leopold von Ranke, history claimed a factual solidity that seemed to rival the findings of Lyell and other geologists. In general, their greatest contributions lay in their efforts at strictest objectivity, their concentration on primary authorities and documents, and their formulation of the science of evidence. Such methodological power naturally encouraged emulation. In England George Grote and Cornewall Lewis typified British adaptations of this trend. Their work on early Greek and Roman history was, in some ways, even more scrupulous in its identification of the truly historical than that of their German masters. Grote's *History of Greece* (1846) particularly helped prepare the ground for *The Golden Bough* in two major ways. First, it attempted not only to discriminate history from legend and myth but also to attend seriously to the nature, causes, and functions of myth. Second, Grote, like Frazer, preferred to make his destructive attacks on established traditions by strategies of analogy and suggestion rather than in sustained assaults.

Sir Henry Rawlinson's decipherment of cuneiform in the 1830s inaugurated the tracing-out of Near Eastern cultures. Thereafter, the new historical attitudes and methods inevitably were extended from Greece, Rome, and Europe to Semitic and Near Eastern studies generally. At the middle of the century Georg Ewald's *History of the People of Israel*, which began to appear in translation in 1867, scandalized the devout. Within a bare twenty years it was outdated as a result of the work of Abraham Kuenen, the Dutch theologian, the Germans Wilhelm Vatke, Graf, Reuss, and above all Julius Wellhausen, whose *History of Israel* (1885) was the apex of the movement. The so-called Graf-Wellhausen Documentary hypothesis achieved a general currency that extended far beyond individual, widely scattered scholars. According to this hypothesis and its arrangement of the historical evidence, it appeared, for instance, that the books of the Bible accepted as genuine were confusingly arranged, that the priestly code was later than the Prophets, and that most of the Psalms were later than either.

Biblical scholars in England rapidly absorbed the lessons of the German historians. Once having done so, they were quick to pass them on to their English readers. David Strauss's epochal contribution to New Testament scholarship, *Das Leben Jesu* (1835-1836), was translated by George Eliot less than a dozen years after it was first published. It saw the Gospel narratives as preeminently myths and sought to isolate their underlying historical truth from any and all forms of supernaturalism. According to Benjamin Jowett, the celebrated classicist and translator of Plato, Strauss's work was very much a part of the Oxford climate by 1844, and it may well have been known even earlier.[21] James Anthony Froude, the historian, was particularly imbued with Strauss's views so that his biography of St. Neots, written for Cardinal Newman's *Lives of the Saints* series, echoes the mythical theory of miraculous narratives.

[21] A. W. Benn, *History of English Rationalism in the Nineteenth Century* (London: Russell and Russell, 1962), II, 38-40, 82. Benn was first published in 1906. See also Himmelfarb, p. 241.

Strauss's book was followed in 1850 by R. MacKay's *Progress of the Intellect*, which brought the Biblical criticism of the Tübingen school originated by Ferdinand Bauer to a wide English audience. As if to ensure that it received the widest possible hearing, George Eliot took care to review it at length in the *Westminster Review*. Her readers would naturally assume the subject's importance, for as Basil Willey has remarked, "no one was more thoroughly abreast of the newest thought, the latest French or German theory, the last interpretation of dogma, the most up-to-date results in anthropology, medicine, biology or sociology."[22] Of even greater intrinsic importance than MacKay was the figure of James Martineau who in singular fashion managed to combine radical views on Biblical scholarship with cautious, even conservative, opinions on ethics. In 1853 his essay "Creeds and Hierarchies of Early Christianity" was published in the *Westminster Review*. Though far less vociferous in its support of Tübingen views than MacKay's book, it nevertheless provided a remarkably detailed exposition and defense of Bauer's theory. A few years later the most celebrated instance of the Higher Criticism made its appearance. Bishop Colenso's *The Pentateuch and the Book of Joshua Critically Examined* (1862) argued that many of the statements found in the Bible were untenable by modern critical standards. The really significant point established by his work was the relevance of so-called uncivilized thought and lower cultures to the most cultivated and sophisticated theological, philosophical, and historical viewpoints. Thus, in a modest and oblique way he adumbrated the shattering implications later thinkers were to find in *The Golden Bough*.

All of these and many more were influential in creating a scholarly climate of greater objectivity that perforce dissolved much of the age's spiritual dogmatism and parochialism. None, however, was more important in shaping the direction and cast of Frazer's mind than William Robertson Smith. Not only was he Frazer's friend and mentor (touchingly remembered in *The Golden Bough*'s Prefaces), he was also the most profound and important advocate of Wellhausen's opinions in Scotland and

[22] Basil Willey, *Nineteenth-Century Studies* (London: Chatto & Windus, 1955), p. 205.

England.[23] Through him Frazer obtained a clear view of both Continental Biblical scholarship and the historical method in general. Together they suggested the possibilities for comparative research in anthropology and religion. A similar model long admired by Frazer was the French savant Ernest Renan, who too followed Wellhausen in his approach to Jewish history. Frazer seems almost an English Renan, so close do the two men appear at a number of points both in outlook and in reputation. Both found in their early days an interest in the more serious aspects of life, which later developed into a preference for an existence organized around studious retirement and peaceful reflection. The primary effect of the combined forces of religious doubt, philosophical scepticism, philological science, and the comparative historical method was to make both men staunch rationalists for whom unalloyed truth was the ultimate goal. Both employed the full arsenal of nineteenth-century rationalism against beliefs which threatened to impede the progress of science and the movement of man to a new plateau of understanding. For Renan, the supernatural was "that strange disease that to the shame of civilization has not yet disappeared from humanity."[24] *The Golden Bough* modulates this irreverent Gallic irony into a more discreet and covert critique. Nevertheless, Frazer is equally emphatic in eschewing miracles and other violations of natural law.

Growing out of their common rationalism were a number of other ideas they shared. One of the most important of these for the nineteenth century as a whole (as Comte, Hegel, and others suggest) was the tracing of man's cultural evolution through three distinct stages of mental progress and psychological change. Renan's stages of Syncretism, Analysis, and Synthesis remind us of Frazer's three Ages of Religion, Magic, and Science as much as of Comte's stages of Religious, Metaphysical, and Positive Society. A concomitant of this likeness was their feeling that

[23] In addition to giving popular lectures developing Wellhausen's views, Smith, as general editor of the *Encyclopaedia Britannica*, afforded Wellhausen the opportunity to appear in its pages and so to reach the English reader directly.

[24] Ernest Renan, *Essais de morale et de critique* (Paris: Michel Levy, 1859), p. 48, cited in translation by Irving Babbitt, *The Masters of Modern French Criticism* (New York: Houghton Mifflin, 1912), p. 267.

the comparative method revealed the pervasive unity of all systems of things whatsoever. Both were especially struck by the
essential similarity in the workings of the human mind throughout the world and by recurring enactments of ancient patterns
of behavior. They even hit upon the same ritual figure to focus
their views. Renan's *Le prêtre de Nemi* (1885) anticipates *The
Golden Bough*'s use of the same drama of unceasing assassination
by but a few years.

Perhaps because of the similarity of their ideas, they shared
the same scholarly role and their major works the same inherent
structure. Each possessed an apparently effortless mastery of
complicated sources and data. As a result they were able to convey an astonishing amount of information in a prose that always
seemed to retain the pace and interest of narrative rather than
the uniformity of exposition. It was this trait as much as anything,
perhaps, which permitted both men to set before the general
reading public materials, topics, and problems hitherto reserved
for theologians and historians of religion. And in their endeavor
to do so, each invested his major work with an essentially bifocal
quality that mirrors one of the modern world's enduring dichoto-
mies at the same time as it creates one of modern literature's most
resonant and flexible perspectives. Albert Schweitzer inadvertently pointed to their similarity in this regard when he remarked
of Renan: "He professes to write a scientific work, and is always
thinking of the great public and how to interest it. He has thus
fused together two works of disparate character. . . . In this double character of the work lies its imperishable claim."[25] Out of the
conflicting claims of science and art, both Renan and Frazer created the multiple possibilities of verbal or aesthetic distance so
that irony is neither linguistic nor existential but embraces both
in a variegation at once ceaseless and luminous.

Nowhere does their resemblance to one another appear so
powerfully as in the dominant mood each evoked through his
carefully controlled and polished style. Irving Babbitt declared
that Renan had "nearly all the qualities of a great artist" and particularly "a special gift for surrounding science with an atmos-

[25] A. Schweitzer, *The Quest of the Historical Jesus*, tr. W. Montgomery,
2nd English ed. (London: A. & C. Black, 1911), p. 191.

phere of religious emotion." In this way he created for his readers "the pleasant illusion that, after all, they are making no serious sacrifice in substituting science for religion."[26] Frazer did not share Renan's continuing sentimental attachment to Christianity. Yet he did have the same stylistic gift for creating scenes and reflections that echoed sonorously with a plangent regard and tender regret for the human condition. Pity mingled with affectionate but dispassionate regard is a recurring mood in *The Golden Bough*, and pretty clearly Renan constituted an influential model for it. Both joined with John Ruskin and, even more, Matthew Arnold in contemplating man's origins, development, and prospects with a "sad lucidity of soul" that made the elegiac attitude and the grand style both inevitable and appropriate.

To follow the historical curve from Biblical scholars to someone like Matthew Arnold and then on to Frazer is to grasp the precise relationship in which *The Golden Bough* stands to this particular segment of the dissolvent critical forces of the age. Lord Annan has remarked that "the new scientific treatment of evidence put Biblical history outside the orbit of any but professional scholars, and as a result bewildered and enraged the mass of the clergy in mid-Victorian England."[27] Frazer in *The Golden Bough* and, in this instance, even more appositely in *Folk-Lore in the Old Testament* was clearly a professional scholar. But it is also true that his treatment of evidence was not nearly so rigorous or sceptical as that of the German historians. He frequently relied on missionary reports for evidence about primitive beliefs and practices and at times seemed to accept them fairly uncritically. And yet Frazer's amassing and handling of comparative evidence drawn from a wide variety of sources was in the general tradition of the historical approach. At the time he was writing, his evidence appealed to the specialist, who could best interpret and use it. Thus, though Frazer lacked the methodological sophistication of Biblical and historical scholars, he was still very much a part of their tradition. In all probability it was

---

[26] Babbitt, p. 260.

[27] Noel Annan, "Science, Religion and the Critical Mind," in *1859: Entering An Age of Crisis*, eds. Appleman, Madden, Woolf (Bloomington: Indiana University Press, 1959), p. 34.

this mediate position coupled with his lucid, graceful style and sense of literary structure that enabled Frazer to transmit the views and attitudes of the professional to the wide audience he reached with *The Golden Bough*.

In this he complements Matthew Arnold almost exactly. Where Arnold approached the problem with his literary talents preeminent and his historical knowledge more or less submerged, Frazer provided the opposite emphasis. Together they saw the issues as entailing a cultural crisis and, perhaps even more important, felt that they could and should bring these to the attention of the literate public in a comprehensible and persuasive manner. With Renan and many of the other great scholars of the century, they felt that one of the scholar's chief obligations was "the transmission of knowledge to interested persons, some of whom may have become interested because the scholar himself knew how to win them to his subject."[28]

Darwin and the evolutionary outlook had a powerful effect on the sense of history in the whole second half of the nineteenth century, and provided the basic framework for Frazer's rationalism, perfectibilitarianism, and historicism. This, however, does not mean that *The Golden Bough* relies on such Darwinian notions as the survival of the fittest or natural selection, much less the more recondite laws of variation. Frazer was neither a conservative apologist for laissez-faire social attitudes nor a meliorist trusting absolutely in the progressive workings of evolutionary natural law. Of all evolutionary thinkers he was perhaps closest in position to the later Huxley. "The Struggle for Existence in Human Society," significantly enough, appeared shortly before Frazer was to publish the first edition of *The Golden Bough*. And some of Huxley's remarks in *Science and Christian Tradition* convey the general tenor of Frazer's view as accurately as his own. In the pages of both men we find recurring notes of the inexorability of change and the ubiquity of wanton destruction and suffering. These create a mood that amalgamates a stoical melancholy, a kind of quietistic mysticism, and a bitter hostility for the world into a brilliant mirror of the *Zeitgeist* shared with Arnold,

[28] R. Chadbourne, *Ernest Renan as an Essayist* (Ithaca: Cornell University Press, 1957), p. 49.

Fitzgerald, and Hardy. Both see human history as a record of "infinite wickedness, bloodshed, and misery." But where Huxley recognized that, logically speaking, it is as possible for evolution to move in a retrogressive direction as in a progressive one, Frazer was inclined to take a slightly more absolutist view of the law of human development. *The Golden Bough* yields to no book of the last two centuries in its sustained and graphic indictment of human folly and barbarism, yet it presents them more as vestigial remnants than as evolutionary responses to be deplored. It aspires to reveal necessary patterns and sequences in social and historical development. Thus, Frazer's effort to trace universal Ages of Magic, Religion, and Science which could not have been ordered differently and which must necessarily culminate in the rational scientific habit of thought is clearly absolutistic in outline.

What qualified this absolutism in Frazer, however, was the uncertainty, growing since the 70s, as to whether any particular formulation of such laws is accurate or exact. Hence he assumed the existence of absolute laws but generally was hesitant about claiming to have discovered any of them. Such tentativeness stemmed in part from the sheer number of competing theories in most intellectual areas. In addition, the gigantic increase in scientific and historical data inundated the age and left it floundering in quagmires of inferences and implications. Men like Spencer and Buckle had developed laws of human development with full confidence in their correctness and as a result had blurred the line between fact and hypothesis. Frazer, on the other hand, is never, or rarely, dogmatic in the high Victorian manner. His more characteristic utterances are tentative and guarded:

> Thus on the whole I cannot but think that the course of subsequent investigation has tended to confirm the general principles followed and the particular conclusions reached in this book. At the same time I am as sensible as ever of the hypothetical nature of much that is advanced in it. It has been my wish and intention to draw as sharply as possible the line of demarcation between my facts and the hypotheses by which

I have attempted to colligate them. Hypotheses are necessary but often temporary bridges built to connect isolated facts. If my light bridge should sooner or later break down or be superseded by more solid structures, I hope that my book may still have its utility and its interest as a repertory of facts.[29]

Because Frazer was more cautious, the laws he sought to enunciate are based on a commonsense empiricism and rational probability of a psychological order. When Frazer formulates a law of thought or offers an explanation of primitive belief or custom, he does so in terms of what seems feasible and likely to the ordinary intelligent and sensible individual. At the same time, the simplicity of his formulations is balanced by the elaborateness and the complexity of his materials and evidence. Thus, *The Golden Bough* both contributed to and reflected the intellectual confusion and uncertainty of the age. The flood of fact and example unleashed on its readers could not help but add to their sense of being lost in a world they never knew or made. This was intensified too by Frazer's habit of entertaining several alternative hypotheses, such as those he formulated on totemism, the merits of each of which he explored in detail without arriving at a definitive position. His own vacillation from one view to another is charted in the three editions of *The Golden Bough* as well as in individual volumes.[30]

In the last years of the century this kind of uncertainty was crystallizing into a doubt as to the mind's ability to find the truth or even to solve practical problems. Actually, *The Golden Bough*

---

[29] *GB*, I, xix-xx. This passage is from the Preface to the Second Edition of 1900.

[30] A noteworthy instance is his theory linking the crucifixion of Christ and the rituals of the mock king of the Sacaea. It formed part of the text in the second edition but in the third is reduced to an appendix with the following prefatory note: "the hypothesis which it [the theory] sets forth has not been confirmed by subsequent research, and is admittedly in a high degree speculative and uncertain. Hence I have removed it from the text but preserved it as an appendix on the chance that, under a pile of conjectures, it contains some grains of truth which may ultimately contribute to a solution of the problem" (*GB*, IX, 412, n.1). The scholarly apotheosis of this habit is, of course, the four volumes of *Totemism and Exogamy* (London: Macmillan, 1910), which reprint each of Frazer's successive statements on the subject before propounding his most recent and extensive treatment.

catches the age at the exact point when Victorian doubt was set-
tling firmly into modern scepticism or relativism. Like the Victorians generally, Frazer never denied that the mind can reach
the truth even though the accretion of the necessary knowledge
is a slow and tedious operation. Yet at the same time his tone suggests that the way in which we achieve a new understanding of
present dilemmas is largely a mystery. He implies that perhaps
in some unforeseeable, miraculous fashion someone in the future
will be able to master and utilize the quantities of data he has
amassed.

Qualified as was Frazer's belief in the idea of absolute
law, nevertheless, it was a factor in his thought. That man moves
progressively from barbarism and savagery to a civilized culture,
that the evolution of religion and society generally is basically
similar everywhere in the world, that the human mind operates
in accord with fixed laws, that the customs and convictions of
man can be arranged in chronological order, and that variants
from the norm of a particular evolutionary stage are to be explained as survivals from an earlier state—all these were substantially unquestioned laws in Frazer's eyes. They constituted
a description of a natural order in human society analogous to
that discovered by Newton in the physical world. Yet because
engaging in thought for its own sake meant not straying very far
from "facts" Frazer's general propositions, axioms, or laws are
more flexible and less obtrusive than those enunciated by other
writers for whom evolutionary ideas were less an ambience than
a dogma.

As a result, though Frazer always esteemed Darwin, he owed
less to that great scientist's specific ideas than to his attitudes, implications, and style. While it may not be deliberately emulative,
there is, nevertheless, a startling parallelism in the two men's sedulous avoidance of controversy. The same is true of their concentration on data rather than speculative generalizations and their
patient search for the truth. Even their literary styles, artfully
fusing modesty of statement, humor, irony, and eloquence into
a powerful instrument of imaginative and rational persuasion are
similar.

This is not to say, of course, that Darwinian concepts do not figure in *The Golden Bough*. To take but an instance, Frazer held that man abandoned magic as a form of thought and action when he discovered that it did not work and was endangering his existence. This is, in a sense, a sociological extrapolation from the evolutionary view that living things engage in a struggle for existence in which the fittest survive as a result of their superior adaptation to environment. Frazer, however, did not treat this as a thesis to be proved so much as a necessary, because true, perspective on the world and the movement of human affairs. As a result, the most striking consequences of Frazer's evolutionism are of a larger and looser order than those issuing from conscious and specific influence. By its very nature the evolutionary point of view focussed on the lower or less developed forms of nature. *The Golden Bough* epitomizes this position in human and societal terms by its concentration on primitive societies as providing the explanation for current modes of life. Thus, Frazer could trace sophisticated religious concepts such as incarnation and immortality to primitive mimetic rituals and misconceptions about natural phenomena, both of which were based, he said, on a faulty psychology of association. As we have seen, by the 60s England was experiencing an intellectual emancipation which left open many things that hitherto had been unquestioned. Frazer and the other classical anthropologists made dramatic contributions to one aspect of this emancipation, in what G. M. Young calls the shift from the statistical to the historical age. In the latter, ideas as well as institutions were explained by reference to their origins and their future estimated in the light of their past character.[31]

What was particularly distinctive about this genetic approach of the nineteenth century was that it operated in dizzyingly expanded spatial and temporal terms. Geologists like Lyell, paleontologists such as Falconer, and evolutionists like James Prichard and Sir William Lawrence, as well as Darwin, established the scientific trend whose effect was drastically to revolutionize

---

[31] A. W. Benn, writing almost at the time the third edition of *The Golden Bough* was about to appear, suggested that it might well constitute late nineteenth-century England's most original contribution to knowledge. See II, 459, also 470, 472, 476.

man's sense of the pertinence of space and time to himself.[32] A gigantic new temporal order emerged in which the human being was a tiny, recent element of not overwhelming significance. When, however, the biological revolution of Darwin was extended to anthropology and prehistory by the work of men like McLennan, Tylor, and Frazer, the effect was to make man important in a way that he was not for geology.

The result was a new humility in the face of a dynamic nature whose future might or might not contain a place for mankind. There also emerged an intensified sense of the continuity of human life and institutions which, under the circumstances, made all their specific forms of pressing interest. Frazer's dominant impression of time seems to have been that of a "long march," a "slow and toilsome ascent" to a new renaissance of knowledge. The effect of *The Golden Bough*, however, is not simply that of admiration for the hard-won gains achieved by the human race. Despite twentieth-century theorists of historical cycles like Spengler and Toynbee, the dominant characteristic of time since Darwin has been its unidirectional, irreversible quality.[33]

The Golden Bough contributed to this sense of the ongoingness of time and to the expectation of novelty even though it was consciously directed to showing how the present is determined by the past, how the uniqueness of Christianity is dissolved in its emergence from primitive fertility cults. As we watch the seemingly endless round of dying and reviving gods move across Frazer's pages, time, history, and human life appear to be on the verge of being drawn into a static cycle. Frazer did find the meaning of the present in the past and seems to imply that true novelty is ultimately impossible. Nevertheless, his work always carries in it a sense too of the precariousness of the past, of its inevitable erosion by the advancement of time and mortality, which are inexorably changing all that they touch. Societies, beliefs, and ideas that were alive for many of Frazer's sources are

[32] Cf. G. P. Gooch, "Historical Research," in *Recent Developments in European Thought*, ed. F. S. Marvin (Oxford: Oxford University Press, 1920), p. 141.

[33] See Loren Eisley, *Darwin's Century* (New York: Doubleday, 1958) pp. 330-331.

already only historical data in *The Golden Bough*, snatched by good fortune and herculean labors from oblivion. Here and there vestigial remnants dot the cultural horizon to underscore what has vanished. As a result, *The Golden Bough* stands as a last great landmark of man's effort to encompass his past in some approximately total form. It signals the end of Victorian encyclopedism, which was the age's unconscious response to the concept of time inaugurated by the Darwinian revolution. But just because it is the last of this order it implicitly defines the need for a new mode of coping with onrushing time.

Strikingly enough, it does so through what we might call its spatial dimensions. Frazer's assiduous use of the comparative method led his readers to an apprehension of the striking diversity of values and beliefs existing in human societies. Because the late nineteenth century saw clearly that it itself marked the transition from agrarian to industrial society it was easier to be concerned with other, vastly different societies, as *The Golden Bough* was. In this even history cooperated, for two-thirds of the last quarter of the century saw conservative and therefore basically imperialistic governments ruling England. As a political and social force imperialism obviously contributed to increased familiarity with remote and primitive countries. And this familiarity was celebrated in literature by men like Kipling, Rider Haggard, Robert Louis Stevenson, and G. A. Henty. Geographical areas which began as markets and fields for investment soon became opportunities for travel and sources of knowledge.

What was true at first hand was even more broadly so at the remove afforded by works like *The Golden Bough*. To see strikingly different cultures possessed of legal systems, moral codes, devoutly worshipped religions, and similar institutions and to note that each in its way was flourishing or capable of doing so was to be driven relentlessly toward cultural and social relativism. Thus *The Golden Bough*'s exploration of the patterns of ancient life made its readers more aware of the specific character of their own society as well as of its roots in earlier, primitive worlds. For instance, Frazer's attention to the tribal sense of community came at a time when urbanization had permanently destroyed England's sense of community. Indirectly, therefore, he contributed to the age's growing nostalgia for village life by giving the impulse an enormous historical perspective. The history of mankind—the chronicle of its passage from pastoral nomad to urban cipher—appeared as a kind of secular expulsion from the garden of nature and redemption a reversion to the primitivistic. D. H. Lawrence affords the crucial literary example of this process. In effect, *The Golden Bough* implicitly raised the issue of self-definition at a time when historical and cultural pressures were beginning to impress it directly on the very nerve ends of individual men and women.

[IV]

Frazer's role in focussing the backward gaze of his time leads us to a vital and as yet unconsidered aspect of his participation in the milieu of the nineteenth century. Hitherto, the stress on his rationalism, evolutionism, and historicism would seem to ally him firmly with the scientific, positivistic tradition whose only significant literary expression was naturalism. No doubt writers like H. G. Wells, who embraced a rational, progressive, scientific outlook, read Frazer in substantially this manner. But if this were the only basis for his appeal, *The Golden Bough* would never have become the central force that it has in a modern literature that explores the imaginative reaches of irrationalism, traditionalism, and supernaturalism. The appeal of his style has already been mentioned and will be treated more fully in a subsequent chapter. But it is doubtful whether even this would have sufficed to make of the book a mine from which, to use Keats's metaphor, writers could load their every rift with ore. Something more was required.

This something consisted of two main elements: one was the subject-matter or content of *The Golden Bough* itself, and the other, its singular appropriateness to prevailing literary tastes. Without the latter, the former might not have exercised the widespread literary and general cultural fascination that it did.[34]

---

[34] The relation of the interest in myth and general literary taste is, of course, further complicated when we consider the European scene as a whole. From Goethe's initial recognition that myths must be created to replace lost or vitiated religious symbols, through Schopenhauer's stress on

Though the nineteenth century in England had a strong Utilitarian, progressive, and social orientation, this was by no means the entire story. It also had pronounced, though perhaps less emphatic, spiritual, introspective or individualistic, and antiquarian characteristics. Expressions of these last run through such movements as the popular inclination toward hero worship, the pre-Raphaelite movement and its sympathizers, and the aestheticism of the end of the century. All these have two principal interests in common—the mythology of the past and empirical facts or observations, mainly of nature.

The general Victorian taste for hero worship had a number of reinforcing agents,[35] but one of the most important was the age's diversified conviction of the need for a leader. From Wordsworth's *Character of the Happy Warrior*, through Browning's *The Lost Leader*, Carlyle's historical quarryings, Mill's Bentham-Coleridge disjunction, and on to Wilde's artist, the search persisted, even though the figure's lineaments were continually changing. But not all the search occurred directly or was focussed on contemporary social and historical occasions. If the immediate scene could neither provide nor sustain leaders of a truly heroic stature, literature was not similarly restricted. To an audience informed by a classical education and shaped by at least a nominal acquaintance with Continental culture, ancient mythology and

the impossibility of apprehending the absolute by rational means, Wagner's heroic struggles to determine the aesthetic viability of myths from past cultures, Stefan George's quite deliberate effort to make his life as well as his works assume a mythic shape, and on to Gauguin's emancipatory primitivism, the artistic mind was seriously engaged by mythology, whether the prevailing literary mod was romanticism, realism, or symbolism. What helped make *The Golden Bough* germane to most of these diverse moods was its possession of several strata of material—classical myths, medieval legends, primitive tribal lore, and great ancient religions—each of which might reasonably appeal to a particular taste or interest. Thus in the final analysis it is perhaps impossible to assign a priority of influence to either Frazer's content or the prevailing literary preferences.

[35] Among those mentioned by Houghton, p. 310, are the renewed interest in the mythology of Homer and the medieval ballad, the physical presence of combatants from the Napoleonic wars, and the general esteem for Byron and Scott. Scott is particularly relevant to the establishment of a climate receptive to Frazer, for in such works as *The Lay of the Last Minstrel* and *Marmion* he sought to recall and illuminate past behavior and mores by reference to things combining historical and anthropological significance.

medieval legend—the Trojan War and King Arthur—afforded inexhaustible and profoundly moving opportunities for contemplating or vicariously playing the noble, tragic, and even godlike hero.

In Tennyson's *Ulysses*, *Morte d'Arthur*, and *Idylls of the King*, the devout could read legends designedly adumbrative of their Christian faith and its embattled circumstances. A more pantheistic, self-exalting, and pragmatic use of mythical images from across the Atlantic anticipated this trend when Whitman declared:

> Magnifying and applying come I,
> Outbidding at the start the old cautious hucksters,
> Taking myself the exact dimensions of Jehovah,
> Lithographing Kronos, Zeus his son, and Hercules his
>   grandson,
> Buying drafts of Osiris, Isis, Belus, Brahma, Buddha,
> In my portfolio placing Manito loose, Allah on a leaf,
>   the crucifix engraved,
> With Odin and the hideous-faced Mexitli and every idol
>   and image,
> Taking them all for what they are worth and not a
>   cent more.[36]

Those who stood on a sharper pinnacle of doubt, on the other hand, could find in Arnold's *Sohrab and Rustum* and *Balder Dead* mythical beings capable of preserving cultural and moral coherence by acting as surrogates for the deity whose literal existence could no longer be entertained. For the one, mythology functioned as literary mimesis, for the other as an evolving form of the religious imagination. But in both cases it was held to be an important repository of spiritual values.

The age's interest in the hero was supported not only by its need for leaders but also by its growing passion for what might

---

[36] Walt Whitman, *Leaves of Grass* (New York: Modern Library, n.d.), p. 62. This collection follows the 1891-1892 edition, but this particular passage was substantially present as early as the edition of 1855. In the later edition one line was omitted, "Buddha" replaced "Adonai," and some minor changes in diction and punctuation were made.

be called natural revelation. Diverse pressures, including the new ideas on evolution, were turning men's attention from a transcendent to an immanent deity and as a result there was an intensified concern with nature as a sympathetic object and with art as a religious form. William Morris suggested how the former develops into the Frazerian emphasis on the magical cycle of nature when he created the following narrative emblem of *The Earthly Paradise*:

> Folk say, a wizard to a northern king
> At Christmas-tide such wondrous things did show,
> That through one window men beheld the spring,
> And through another saw the summer glow,
> And through a third the fruited vines a-row,
> While still, unheard, but in its wonted say,
> Piped the drear wind of that December day.[37]

Perhaps the most influential figure in this general development, however, was John Ruskin, who combined an interest in both modes that materially affected the outlook of the later nineteenth century. Rossetti, Holman Hunt, Pater, and others of the 90s learned from him how to intensify visual minutiae so as to yield a contemplative perception of their fundamental nature or essence. "Good art," he once declared, "always consists of two things: First, the observation of fact; secondly, the manifesting of human design and authority in the way that fact is told."[38] Like Huxley, surprisingly enough, Ruskin sought to penetrate to objects' informing pattern or archetype. And it is this same habit of mind that Frazer was to exhibit at the end of the century in *The Golden Bough* when he sought to reveal the quintessential

[37] William Morris, *Collected Works* (London: Longmans, Green, 1910-1915), III, 2. This one instance will have to serve as representative of the deep Victorian interest in the imaginative interrelationships possible between myth and nature. Even the most casual perusal of Douglas Bush's compendious *Mythology and the Romantic Tradition* (Cambridge, Mass.: Harvard University Press, 1937) reveals the richness and provocativeness of the subject as well as the need for a detailed exploration of it. A useful step in this direction is James Kissane's "Victorian Mythology," *Victorian Studies*, VI (September 1962), 5-28.

[38] *The Works of John Ruskin*, eds. E. T. Cook & Alexander Wedderburn (London: George Allen, 1903), XVI, 269-270.

character of both natural scenes and human behavior. Frazer possessed great skill in investing physical description with the complex resonances of almost Sophoclean reflections, and a narrative ingenuity in maintaining pace while summarizing prosaic material. Modulating both was his subtle retention of Biblical rhythms and phrasing. In all these respects so closely did his talent resemble that of Ruskin that we can scarcely fail to sense the older man's influence.

The intensified concern with the factual, the concrete, and the local—the concern with exact detail—which Ruskin spearheaded, became a device for disciplining the artistic imagination whether of the painter or the writer. That it should have been exaggerated into ornateness was but the excess that defined its true function. To Tennyson, Constable, Ruskin, Turner, and the pre-Raphaelites the natural world assumed an unparalleled beauty. It did so precisely because its specific forms were intuitively felt to be fleeting and only through art could they be either preserved or honored. And if, as many thought, the microscopic examination of the natural world was a Christian act, then its rendering in an aesthetic form must similarly be a kind of religious worship. Thus, it is perhaps in an ultimate sense no accident that *The Golden Bough* should carry as its frontispiece Turner's evocative picture of the same title. Intuitively Frazer thereby proclaimed his role as the century's culmination of one of its most important traditions, that of the religious, symbolic nature of art. And if in his contributions to the tradition he appears closer in temper to Matthew Arnold than Ruskin, that is as much an index of his decade as of his personal inclinations.

What is important to notice is the continuity that obtains. Frazer, as much as either Ruskin or Arnold, labored to instruct and morally to persuade his audience through the impact of his art. As Turner's painting suggests, the concrete details of visual art were frequently adapted to a narrative pattern which would attract an age devoted to stories and instruction. In this regard, *The Golden Bough* grew directly out of the same tradition as did works by Tennyson, Arnold, Swinburne, Morris, and the Rossettis. All fused a basically narrative pattern with a strongly visual and pictorial use of image. Carried to the peak of intensity, this would ultimately have yielded something very like Symbolism even if Continental influences had not given it the particular dimensions and character that they did.

To invoke, as has been done, the names of Ruskin, Arnold, and Tennyson suggests perhaps that Frazer's mythological lore and pellucid style primarily support the didactic, ideal role of Victorian hero worship. The dying god and divine king of *The Golden Bough* would have strengthened the courage and resolution of many Victorians faced with the commercial savagery and intellectual trials of their own time. But it would be a mistake to see that as the book's only function. It also catered to the age's need to escape from the spectacle of ignorant, deluded masses mired in economic and moral squalor, the bourgeois vulgarized by their plutocratic exploitation of others, and an industrial empire whose ugliness was in direct ratio to its power. The surcease from the constricting limitations of the present found by so many in Kingsley's *The Heroes*, Tennyson's *Idylls of the King*, and Morris' *Life and Death of Jason* established an attitude that Frazer in turn could not help but foster. What *The Queen of the Air* was to the sensitive temperament in 1869, *The Golden Bough* was to those of even more delicate refinement in 1890. Each provided materials and a perspective by which artists might aesthetically or fictively transform and so transcend their immediate environment.

At first glance there appears to be a world of difference between Ruskin's airily bright, inspiring Athena and Frazer's bloody rites. The refined scrupulosity of men like Pater, Wilde, Swinburne, Dowson, and Johnson would seem more at home with the civilized figure of Ruskin than with *The Golden Bough's* barbaric gods and worshippers. What, however, gave the aesthetes and their immediate ancestors an affinity with Frazerian myth and ritual was a certain similarity in key ideas. Pater, the intellectual leader of the movement, believed that whatever the human mind had once believed must always retain some intrinsic value and significance.[39] Frazer, more firmly rationalistic

---

[39] G. C. Monsman's *Pater's Portraits* (Baltimore: The Johns Hopkins Press, 1967), points up quite clearly Pater's involvement with myth and his adumbration of Frazer.

in outlook, did not go quite so far. Still, he did emphasize the importance of searching the past for the origins of institutions and movements so that their true worth and meaning could be grasped. The Rhymers' Club eagerly seized on Pater's view as a warrant for pursuing interests in spiritualism, esoteric ritualism, cultism of mystical sorts, and the magic of ancient religious faiths. Frazer collaborated by making available a great deal of this material in an entrancing style, even though he was unsympathetic to the contemporary truth of any of it. Similarly, there is a close resemblance between Frazer's stress on the peasantry's retention of ancient religious beliefs and customs and Pater's emphasis on the folk religion of Numa that subsisted beneath and prior to the official forms. And when we look carefully at *Marius the Epicurean* and *The Golden Bough*, it is clear that both deliberately sought to move their readers to accept a cultured agnosticism as the only appropriate attitude for their age. Perhaps, however, the closest affinity between Frazer and the aesthetic strain in nineteenth-century thought is found in *The Golden Bough*'s circumspect and dispassionate catering to the fascination with those interrelations of pain, love, and death that polite society had for so long tabooed.

Representative here is Swinburne, whose ancient world stressed the physical and emotional emancipation of man. In doing so, he created an ideal made up of nakedness and happiness in equal measure. Yet he also celebrated creatures of uninhibited ruthlessness accepting pain and suffering, creatures who were grounded in the fertility rhythms of the natural world. Thus, in *Atalanta in Calydon* his metrical virtuosity may conceal but it cannot obliterate his Frazerian interest in the sexual roots of religious ceremonies:

> And Pan by noon and Bacchus by night,
> Fleeter of foot than the fleet-foot kid,
> Follows with dancing and fills with delight
> The Maenad and the Bassarid.[40]

[40] A. C. Swinburne, *Complete Works*, eds. E. Gosse & T. J. Wise (London: W. Heinemann, 1925-1927), VII, 272.

Nor can we avoid seeing how *The Triumph of Time* helped prepare the age for *The Golden Bough*'s great mother goddesses and
their ambivalent relationship to their worshippers:

> Fair mother, fed with the lives of men,
> Thou art subtle and cruel of heart, men say.
> Thou hast taken, and shalt not render again;
> Thou art full of thy dead, and cold as they.
> But death is the worst that comes of thee;
> Thou art fed with our dead, O mother, O sea,
> But when hast thou fed on our hearts? or when,
> Having given us love, hast thou taken away?
>
> O tender-hearted, O perfect lover,
> Thy lips are bitter, and sweet thine heart.
> The hopes that hurt and the dreams that hover,
> Shall they not vanish away and apart?
> But thou, thou art sure, thou art older than earth;
> Thou art strong for death and fruitful of birth;
> Thy depths conceal and thy gulfs discover;
> From the first thou wert; in the end thou art.[41]

In the attention they pay to sado-masochistic erotic pleasures
these and other Swinburne works look forward to Pater's *Denys
l'Auxerrois* and *Apollo in Picardy* and then on to Dowson's
Cynara, Johnson's *Dark Angel*, and Wilde's *Picture of Dorian
Gray*.

Admittedly, not all the works of these authors were directed
to myths and legends of the past. Insofar, however, as they
aspired to a timeless realm beyond the historical process, they
were bound to feed their longing for release from the present by
at least reading tales of incredible worlds and experiences. As the
impress of French literature—of Gautier, Baudelaire, Verlaine,
and Huysmans—grew, the search for *frissons* of evil intensified
and became more bizarre. At the same time the passion for myths
became less classical and more primitive. For the rise of comparative religion and its anthropology helped delineate the sub-

[41] Swinburne, I, 178.

stratum of savagery inhering in myths of all ages. Consequently scholars like Tylor, Robertson Smith, Lang, and Frazer quickly assumed the role of popular guides to shocking behavior subtly intensified by their religious context. Representative here is a poem such as Tennyson's *Dawn*, which appeared after *The Golden Bough*. It opens with a Frazerian juxtaposition of ancient Mediterranean worship and contemporary savagery:

> Red of the Dawn!
> Screams of a babe in the red-hot palms of a Moloch of Tyre,
> Man with his brotherless dinner on man in the tropical wood,
> Priests in the name of the Lord passing souls through
>   fire to the fire,
> Head-hunters and boats of Dahomey that float upon human
>   blood![42]

Such tales as that told by Frazer of Mexican rituals in which the victim's living heart was torn from his or her body amid unparalleled pomp and pageantry gave aesthetes both the glimpse of evil and terror they felt necessary and the panorama of ceremonious ritual they relished.

What began as an escape from the physical and cultural unbearableness of the age became a committed encounter with hieratic reality for successors like Yeats and a full-scale confrontation with evil for those like Conrad and Eliot. Myths broadened their significance from that of a predominantly ornamentative beauty to a dynamic illumination of the wellsprings of the human imagination. In this historical development, no work provided a broader basis or a more suggestive set of metaphors and images for this transition than did *The Golden Bough*. As has been intimated, it did so for two main reasons. For one thing, it expanded the mythological interests of the age. In addition, it exemplified the other recurring emphasis of the period, the passion for the resonant concreteness of the observed object.

Much of nineteenth-century English art and literature was an

[42] Alfred Lord Tennyson, *Complete Works*, ed. William J. Rolfe (Boston: Dana Estes, 1898), xii, 166. Tennyson was read to from Frazer's work while having his portrait painted by Watts in 1891. See R. Angus Downie, *James George Frazer: Portrait of a Scholar* (London: Macmillan, 1940), p. 20.

attempt to compensate for the ugliness of the early industrial world and so was grounded in a historical symbolism that forged aesthetic myths of varying power. Nevertheless, the lesson of concreteness and accuracy of detail, taught in different ways by Carlyle, Darwin, and Ruskin, was also easily adaptable to the temper of realism. As a result, escape from social reality easily modulated into stern acceptance and then into formal transcendence in which content ceased to be of prime importance. But if both symbolism and realism were rooted in the concrete, it was because they represented two different modes of celebrating an organic set of human experiences. And it was just this overwhelming need to render those human, fleeting assemblages of reality which time and history were rapidly bearing into the darkness that led in the twentieth century to such diverse movements as imagism, naturalism, regionalism, modernism, and experimentalism in all their varieties and hues. To render the detail, to make the part do duty for the whole, to deny the narrative pattern with its endorsement of unidirectional time by dislocation of temporal sequences, to seek composite versions of selfhood in the fragments of the past—in a word, to live without the literal hope of immortality was the task confronting twentieth-century literature. And in suggesting solutions and viable means, *The Golden Bough* was as fruitful as it was relentless in conveying the nature and depth of the problem.

CHAPTER II

The Controlling Ideas of
The Golden Bough

[I]

As was suggested at the beginning of the previous chapter, an understanding of *The Golden Bough* involves both its cultural milieu and its intellectual content. Doubtless virtually everyone interested in literature has some conception of what *The Golden Bough* is about, of its subject and its central thesis. But since Frazer pursued his themes into a labyrinth of detail and related issues, the entire pattern proves to be rather more complex than would appear at first sight. Yet to appreciate the uses made of *The Golden Bough* by modern writers it is just this total pattern that must be carried in mind. This remains true even though most authors have perused the book casually or piecemeal instead of studying it systematically. Thus the material summarized here should not be equated with the extent of most writers' knowledge of *The Golden Bough*. Some, such as Robert Graves, have a great and detailed familiarity with all volumes. Others, and these are the majority, have a firsthand knowledge of certain volumes or parts, augmented by a general acquaintance with the remainder that is perhaps less, and certainly no more, specific than that sketched in this chapter.

The following outline of Frazer's basic ideas and controlling concepts is based on the third edition of twelve volumes published between 1907 and 1915. As the last edition (the one in 1922 was merely an abridgment) and the fullest, it naturally takes scholarly priority over the two-volume edition of 1890 and the three-volume version of 1900. And the same is true in the case of the book's use by creative artists. Though Frazer changed his position on certain issues in the course of the three editions, none of these shifts materially affects the question of literary impact and its assessment. Where an author, such as Yeats, draws on another edition, the material he is attracted to is usually either one of the large general views which Frazer held unchanged throughout his career or else some of the narrative and descriptive illustrations that make up so much of *The Golden Bough* of whatever edition. In short, the difference between the editions is, for students of literature at any rate, a matter more of expansion than of radical revision. Consequently the one that is most inclusive offers the best opportunity of grasping the full dimensions of *The Golden Bough*'s literary impact. At the same time the stages by which that impact was made need to be borne in mind. To that end chapter three takes up the dissemination of *The Golden Bough*'s views as they were applauded, interrogated, defended, and refuted in reviews, books, and articles.

A convenient starting point for a sketch of *The Golden Bough*'s controlling ideas is Frazer's own statement concerning the book's organization: "The present volumes, forming the first part of the whole, contain a preliminary inquiry into the principles of Magic and the evolution of the Sacred Kingship in general. They will be followed shortly by a volume which discusses the principles of Taboo in their special application to sacred or priestly kings. The remainder of the work will be mainly devoted to the myth and ritual of the Dying God."[1] The first part of *The Golden Bough*, then, is entitled "The Magic Art and the Evolution of Kings," and as we come to see, the two topics are closely interrelated. Opening this section and defining its central problem is the richly detailed and evocatively phrased account of Nemi. Its "strange rule of the priesthood or sacred kingship," Frazer says, was one of the two things he sought to explain "when I originally conceived the idea of the work," the other being "the legend of the *Golden Bough* . . . which the voice of antiquity associated with the priesthood."[2] The ritual at Nemi is prototypical of the priest-king in both its savagery and mystery:

In the sacred grove there grew a certain tree round which at any time of the day, and probably far into the night, a grim figure might be seen to prowl. In his hand he carried a drawn

[1] *GB*, I, viii.   [2] *GB*, I, vii.

sword, and he kept peering warily about him as if at every instant he expected to be set upon by an enemy. He was a priest and a murderer; and the man for whom he looked was sooner or later to murder him and to hold the priesthood in his stead. Such was the role of the sanctuary. A candidate for the priesthood could only succeed to office by slaying the priest, and having slain him, he retained office till he was himself slain by a stronger or a craftier.[3]

This figure who guards the sanctuary of the goddess Diana at Nemi illustrates on a limited plane and in a sample form the nature of early kingship. On what today we might term the secular, sociopolitical level, he is a king, for he is the sole human ruler over the sacred grove reserved for Diana. The character and limited size of his kingdom indicate further that he is what Frazer calls a departmental king of nature, that is, someone who is supposed to rule over a particular element or aspect of nature.[4] His reign is not confined primarily to controlling his own subjects and framing domestic policies; instead, his central concern is, as in most small kingdoms, with protecting his realm against aggression. In short, he is both legal and military head of a region, both king and warrior. This, however, does not exhaust his functions. For on the sacred or religious level, he is also the priest who attends to the affairs of the goddess and stands as an intermediary between her and her worshippers in order to command for her the proper reverence and respect.

The King of the Wood, as Diana's guardian is called, is, then, a priest-king, though, to be sure, on a microcosmic scale. This joining of secular royalty and the priesthood in one individual is, according to Frazer, who provides numerous examples such as the Roman King of the Sacred Rites, "a common feature of societies at all stages from barbarism to civilisation."[5] The two chief characteristics of such kings are their divinity and their magical powers, which are different ways of reaching the idea of a man-god.[6] With regard to the former, Frazer remarks: "Kings were revered, in many cases not merely as priests, that is, as intercessors between man and god, but as themselves gods, able to be-

[3] *GB*, I, 8-9.　　[4] *GB*, II, 1-6.　　[5] *GB*, II, 1.　　[6] *GB*, I, 51.

stow upon their subjects and worshippers those blessings which are commonly supposed to be beyond the reach of mortals, and are sought, if at all, only by prayer and sacrifice offered to super-human and invisible beings."[7] The magical powers possessed by the king, on the other hand, derive in many cases from the fact that his office evolved out of that of the magician, particularly the rain-maker.[8] Frazer, however, does not intend this to be con-strued as a universal development nor a complete explanation.[9] Thus, a complementary interpretation is that since the gods were regarded as magicians, it would follow then that divine kings, their human counterparts, also would possess magical powers.[10] Such reliance on alternative or dual hypotheses is a typical Fra-zerian pattern and characteristic of his empirical, tentative, and thoroughly candid approach to the difficulties of erecting ade-quate theories.

Because of this intimate relation between the offices of king and magician, it is imperative to grasp the principles and scope of magic if the evolution of kingship is to be understood. Magic, according to Frazer, can be subdivided into two related classes he dubs Homeopathic and Contagious. The former is that kind in which the magician imitates the effect he wishes to produce. The latter operates by the magician's affecting an object or ob-jects once in contact with the thing or person he wishes to influ-ence. The one operates by similarity, the other by contiguity. The commonest form of the homeopathic type is that which uses magical images of the person or thing to be affected. Such images have been used to destroy persons, to increase cattle or game, to ward off demons, to stimulate conception and facilitate child-birth, as well as to win love and to preserve or repair harmony between husbands and wives.[11] In contagious magic the object replacing the image as the magical medium is usually some severed portion of the individual's body or some copy of itself made by a part of the body. Thus, spells can be applied to hair, nails, teeth, blood, and even to a man's clothes or the impressions left by his body in sand or earth, especially footprints.[12]

Both forms are thought by the primitive mind to be capable of

---

[7] *GB*, I, 50-51. [8] *GB*, I, 342. [9] *GB*, I, 332-334.
[10] *GB*, I, 240-242. [11] *GB*, I, 55-78. [12] *GB*, I, 175-207.

41

functioning in the natural as well as the human worlds.[13] Consequently, there is as much emphasis on magic's controlling the weather—for instance, on its directing the rain, the sun, and the wind so that vegetation may flourish and provide food for the community—as there is on its being used to cast spells on individuals. Indeed, these functions reflect Frazer's distinction between public and private magic, between sorcery employed for the benefit of an entire community and that directed at aiding or injuring an individual. Where the former is practiced, the magician becomes a public functionary endowed with a role of great importance in the community. As a class, they assume in Frazer's eyes a major political as well as religious significance for the evolution of society: "when the welfare of the tribe is supposed to depend on the performance of these magical rites, the magician rises to a position of much influence and repute, and may readily acquire the rank and authority of a chief or king."[14] Since the most skilled magicians are likely to be substantially deliberate in their deceptions and at the same time to acquire the greatest eminence and power, at this point in the evolution of society the major share of human destiny "tends to fall into the hands of men of the keenest intelligence and the most unscrupulous character."[15]

Though deploring this apparent rewarding of immorality, Frazer certainly does not regard it as a cultural disaster. One result he sees is the shift of political power from an oligarchy of tribal elders to a monarchy, a shift he regards as historically imperative if man is to move out of his earliest savagery. In this state, man is, for Frazer, the most enslaved of creatures, a pitiable and helpless servant and prey of the past as objectified in the ceaseless demands of custom and tradition. But when one-man rule occurs, the consequence is in most cases an expansion of tribal power at the expense of neighbors. These, in turn, provide wealth and slaves and so create a leisure class able to devote themselves to the acquisition of knowledge. Naturally enough Frazer regards this as the greatest force for improvement of the human condition through social, industrial, and intellectual progress. Historically, it is not at all fortuitous that every great early civilized ad-

[13] *GB*, I, 52-54.   [14] *GB*, I, 215.   [15] *GB*, I, 216.

vance, whether in Babylonia, Greece, Egypt, or Peru, occurred under despotic tyrants who ruled as both kings and gods. Such are the benefits stemming from the original use of magic in public ceremonies.[16]

Though warning that the magician never takes an intellectual view of his subject but always regards it as a practical art, Frazer nevertheless aligns magic with science in basic outlook. Both view the world as rigid and invariable and founded on impersonal laws the knowledge of which permits us to gratify our wishes in any respect.[17] Religion, on the other hand, is opposed in principle to both. It regards the world as elastic or variable, capable of being altered by the superhuman personal powers whose creation it is.[18] While the contrasting perspectives of magic and religion ultimately resulted in deep-seated hostility between priest and magician, this did not occur, according to Frazer, until comparatively late in human history. In the earlier period, magic and religion were partly confused and were employed simultaneously, so that the functions of priest and wizard were often fulfilled by the same individual. Only in the very earliest stage of human development did magic exist by itself. It did so, Frazer suggests, because it constitutes the simplest possible exercise of mental powers, namely, the confused and mistaken association of ideas. When its practical inadequacy as a means of coercing nature was discovered, then the general cultural shift from magic to religion occurred, marked perhaps by the belief that the gods are magicians.

Yet despite the differences in principle, magic and religion have frequently been confused with one another and are usually closely interrelated. Thus, according to Frazer, primitive man performed religious and magical rites simultaneously in an endeavor to gain his objectives. The same intermingling of ceremonies also persists into higher cultures, such as those of ancient India and Egypt. A further revelation of its tenacity is afforded by modern Europeans, particularly the peasants and lower classes, who continue to mingle religion and magic. Each group is, in its own way, representative of those ignorant classes that

[16] *GB*, I, 216-219.   [17] *GB*, I, 220-221.   [18] *GB*, I, 224.

Frazer finds making up the bulk of mankind at all times and in which the belief in magic is all but universal.[19]

As a result of his consideration of primitive magic, Frazer suggests a further similarity and contrast in the divine king and the magician. Since the latter develops into the former, and since he possesses his magical powers in common with the gods, it follows that he too becomes a divine creature.[20] Yet both the magician and the king are also men, living human beings, so that in effect we are confronted by two types of man-god. Frazer calls them the religious and the magical, and they, of course, in some sense parallel the king and the magician both in their differences and in the fact that they can exist conjointly in a single individual. The religious and magical man-gods are characterized as follows:

> In the former, a being of an order different from and superior to man is supposed to become incarnate, for a longer or a shorter time, in a human body, manifesting his superhuman power and knowledge by miracles wrought and prophecies uttered through the medium of the fleshly tabernacle in which he has deigned to take up his abode. . . . On the other hand, a man-god of the magical sort is nothing but a man who possesses in an unusually high degree powers which most of his fellows arrogate to themselves on a smaller scale; for in rude society there is hardly a person who does not dabble in magic. Thus, whereas a man-god of the former or inspired type derives his divinity from a deity who has stooped to hide his heavenly radiance behind a dull mask of earthly mould, a man-god of the latter type draws his extraordinary power from a certain physical sympathy with nature. He is not merely the receptacle of a divine spirit. His whole being, body and soul, is so delicately attuned to the harmony of the world that a touch of his hand or a turn of his head may send a thrill vibrating through the universal framework of things; and conversely his divine organism is acutely sensitive to such slight changes of environment as would leave ordinary mortals wholly unaffected.[21]

[19] *GB*, I, 228-230, 231-233, 235-236.
[20] *GB*, I, 375.   [21] *GB*, I, 244-245.

In short, the relation of the religious form to the world is micro-cosmic, while that of the magical figure is roughly pantheistic. The direction of the former is centripetal, that of the latter centrifugal; between them, they constitute the poles between which all possible views of man's relation to the world are ranged.

This notion of incarnation, for that is what is at the heart of both the divine king and the sacred magician, is of great antiquity. According to Frazer, it "belongs essentially to that earlier period of religious history in which gods and men are still viewed as beings of much the same order, and before they are divided by the impassable gulf which, to later thought, opens out between them."[22] Originally incarnation was treated both as a temporary and as a permanent state. Frazer summarizes the nature of both in the following fashion: "In the former case, the incarnation—commonly known as inspiration or possession—reveals itself in supernatural knowledge rather than in supernatural power. In other words, its usual manifestations are divination and prophecy rather than miracles. On the other hand, when the incarnation is not merely temporary, when the divine spirit has permanently taken up its abode in a human body, the god-man is usually expected to vindicate his character by working miracles."[23] A connection between the two is to be found in the fact that occasionally the temporarily inspired person is granted divine power in addition to his insight.[24] In such cases, and so long as the state of incarnation lasts, he is regarded as the protector of his community or tribe. Consequently, he bears some relation to the temporary king, a figure about whom more will be said later.

[II]

The second part of *The Golden Bough* is entitled "Taboo and the Perils of the Soul," but "it does not profess to handle the subject as a whole, to pursue it into all its ramifications, to trace the manifold influences which systems of this sort have exerted in moulding the multitudinous forms of human society."[25] Instead, it confines its attention to those principles and illustrations of taboo

[22] *GB*, I, 374-375. [23] *GB*, I, 376. [24] *GB*, I, 385-386.
[25] *GB*, III, vi.

which either refer directly to or else illuminate the sacred figures of the king and the priest. In turning to this topic, Frazer is not so much commencing afresh on a different subject as elaborating a particular aspect of the one already considered. For him, taboo is essentially a special aspect of the field of magic itself. He relates it to the whole in this way: "The system of sympathetic magic is not merely composed of positive precepts; it comprises a very large number of negative precepts, that is, prohibitions. It tells you not merely what to do, but also what to leave undone. The positive precepts are charms: the negative precepts are taboos."[26] From this it follows that "the aim of positive magic or sorcery is to produce a desired event; the aim of negative magic or taboo is to avoid an undesirable one."[27] In neither case is there any logical or factual relation between the event and the ritual observance. Logically, breaking a taboo would weaken the preventive spell. Practically, it visited on the violater psychological reactions so powerful as to manifest themselves in physical illness and even death unless purged through confession or other purification ceremonies. For Frazer, all this is the result of a fallacious association of ideas and thus is simply imaginary. Yet he is far from regarding either magic or taboo as socially and culturally useless. Thus, he suggests that much of modern morality and custom may profitably be studied as forms of taboo survival.

It is through the human concern for survival that the volume's reference to the perils of the soul becomes important. According to Frazer, primitive peoples think of the soul as a little man concealed inside the human body who provides it with the ability to live and move. This same little creature is also used to account for death as well as life, for "as the activity of an animal or man is explained by the presence of the soul, so the repose of sleep or death is explained by its absence; sleep or trance being the temporary, death being the permanent absence of the soul."[28] As a result, the avoidance of death is bound up with the location of the soul. Consequently, the survival instinct concentrates on preventing the soul from escaping out of the body and, if it does elude its restraints, on making sure that it will come back and reenter the body. The various and often intricate steps to this

[26] *GB*, I, 111.   [27] *GB*, I, 112.   [28] *GB*, III, 26.

end constitute specific taboos. These are "nothing but rules intended to ensure either the continued presence or the return of the soul. In short, they are life-preservers or life-guards."[29]

Since society tries to guard against its own disintegration, taboos of various sorts are observed by every member of the community. *The Golden Bough* organizes a representative selection of these under four headings—acts, persons, things, and words—and devotes a chapter to each. Preeminent among tabooed acts is that of contact with strangers, who without exception are thought to be practitioners of the more sinister forms of magic and witchcraft. Since complete abstention from relations with other peoples is impracticable, certain purificatory ceremonies are employed to disenchant strangers or at least to counteract and nullify their magical powers. This same interest in avoiding evil and ultimately death accounts for the regulations concerning the king's eating and drinking, exposing his face, and leaving his personal quarters.[30]

Tabooed acts are either banned or else carefully regulated because of the misfortune they may inflict on those who perform them. In the case of tabooed persons, however, it is the individuals themselves who are held to be dangerous. Hence they are set apart from the community as a whole in different ways and for varying lengths of time. Among those who are so marked off from the normal person are chiefs and kings, mourners for the dead, warriors preparing for battle, persons guilty of murder or accidental manslaughter, hunters and fishermen preparatory to and during their work, and women giving birth.[31] The objects that are tabooed combine the attitude toward acts and that toward persons. Some are thought to be dangerous in their own right; others are banned or restricted because they may serve as media for the magical transmission of evils, illnesses, and even death itself.[32] Instances of the former are sharp weapons, blood, certain foods, and knots or rings. Potential media for misfortune include everything of a personal nature connected with the individual

[29] *GB*, III, 27.
[30] *GB*, III, 102-105, 107-109, 116, 120-126.
[31] *GB*, III, 131-136, 138-155, 157-160, 165-188, 190-223.
[32] *GB*, III, 237-251, 258-283, 287-317.

and especially parts of his body such as hair. Should such things fall into the hands of an enemy or evil sorcerer, they could be used to inflict harm, including death, on their original possessor.

This series of taboos surrounding tangible things is matched by the prohibitions imposed on language and speech. These run primarily to the avoidance of mentioning personal names, for these are thought to be as much a part of an individual as any portion of his body. A similar injunction forbids reference to the names of familiar relations, presumably for much the same reason. The names of the dead are tabooed because of the fear that mentioning them will summon their ghosts and souls.[33] Nor are the names of gods and spirits to be spoken since "the mere utterance of them may work wonders and disturb the course of nature."[34] Similarly, the names of the human representatives of the gods, that is, of kings and other sacred persons, are also tabooed.[35] The general explanation of these linguistic customs is implied in Frazer's remark that "when the name is held to be a vital part of the person, it is natural to suppose that the mightier the person the more potent must be his name."[36] But this potency can attain a degree that renders its vehicle exceedingly dangerous. Naturally, therefore, means are taken to prevent it from being either dissipated or needlessly inflicted on innocent persons.[37] Thus taboos are literally lifeguards as well as guarantees for the continued existence of the soul in the body. As such they testify in their number and the strictness of their observance to the massive part played in primitive life by fear, an emotion in which Frazer locates the psychological source of religion.[38] In *The Golden Bough* as well as in later works like *The Belief in Immortality* and *The Fear of the Dead in Primitive Religion*, he suggests that fear felt for the spirits of the dead is "one of the most powerful factors, perhaps, indeed, the most powerful of all in shaping the course of religious evolution at every stage of social development from the lowest to the highest."[39]

As this summary has suggested, taboo does not confine its attention solely to those occurrences patently relevant to the domi-

---

[33] *GB*, III, 318-320, 335-347, 353-355.
[34] *GB*, III, 384.   [35] *GB*, III, 374-383.   [36] *GB*, III, 384.
[37] *GB*, X, 6-7.   [38] *GB*, IX, 93.   [39] *GB*, VIII, 36-37.

nant foci of human existence, namely, life and death. Many, and indeed we might almost say most, of the forms of behavior with which it concerns itself are simple, ordinary, and commonplace in character. After presenting numerous instances of specific taboos, Frazer observes that "in primitive society the rules of ceremonial purity observed by divine kings, chiefs, and priests agree in many respects with the rules observed by homicides, mourners, women in childbed, girls at puberty, hunters and fishermen, and so on" and suggests that to the primitive mind "the common feature of all these persons is that they are dangerous and in danger."[40] No distinction is drawn here between what is holy or pure and what is unclean and polluted. Instead there is another distinction at work, that between those things which possess an overwhelming power either to attract or to repulse and those which are purely ordinary in the reactions they provoke.[41] The former is the sacred and the latter the profane. Thus, all the tabooed persons mentioned are in this sense sacred. That is, they are intimately related to and replete with the power underlying all life, a state that in excessive measure renders them dangerous and awesome to the rest of the world.

Among these persons, the most important is the priest-king. His life is "protected by a system of precautions or safeguards still more numerous and minute than those which in primitive society every man adopts for the safety of his own soul."[42] Their general effect is to isolate the king and so to limit his accessibility, particularly for strangers. The taboos which regulate the life of the priest-king are imposed upon him by his people rather than demanded by him out of an obsessive regard for his own welfare. The minute rules of taboo that regulate his life aim at preserving the established order of nature and avoiding the de-

[40] *GB*, III, 224.

[41] Frazer himself does not make or so name this distinction, but it is implicit in what he says. For explicit elaborations of it, see R. MacCallum, *Imitation and Design* (Toronto: University of Toronto Press, 1953), p. 99; G. Van Der Leeuw, *Religion in Essence and Manifestation*, tr. J. E. Turner (London: Allen & Unwin, 1938), pp. 44-49; E. O. James, *The Beginnings of Religion* (London: Hutchinson's University Library, n.d.), pp. 32-38, 43; R. R. Marett, *Psychology and Folk-lore* (London: Methuen, 1920), pp. 161-162.

[42] *GB*, III, 101.

struction of the world, which is thought to eventuate from the natural death of the king.[43] To many primitive peoples, we must remember, the priest-king is regarded as an incarnation of various divine beings, that is, he constitutes the connecting link between men and the gods. From the latter stems all power and potency wielded by men; hence, it is essential that the link be preserved unbroken. Since the king is both man and god, he of all men is most intimately in contact with the power of life. As a result, his life is considered to be sympathetically bound up with the prosperity and welfare of the country as a whole.[44] Thus, in a sense he becomes the human form of the nation or society. By employing his magical and divine powers to provide favorable weather, both sun and rain, and good crops, he himself flourishes and becomes greatly renowned, just as the country itself becomes prosperous. By the same token, his responsibility also involves him in punishment—beatings, banishment, and even death—if drought and pestilence should spoil the crops upon which the people depend for survival.[45] The taboos to which he must conform are calculated to preserve the king's powers and hence the fruitfulness of the land and the lives of its inhabitants.

[III]

Yet taboos, no matter how strong and elaborate, are ultimately incapable of exorcising the fact of human mortality. Even semi-divine priest-kings must face death. The way in which they do so is considered in some detail in the fourth volume of *The Golden Bough*, entitled "The Dying God." The central fact Frazer attempts to explain is the custom of killing the sacred king either when his strength appears to be failing him or at the conclusion of a reign of preordained length.[46] Essentially his answer is that "the motive for slaying a man-god is a fear lest with the enfeeblement of his body in sickness or old age his sacred spirit should suffer a corresponding decay, which might imperil the general course of nature and with it the existence of his worshippers, who believe the cosmic energies to be mysteriously knit up with those of their human divinity."[47] The aim of the king's taboos is to pre-

---

[43] *GB*, III, 2, 7.   [44] *GB*, IV, 21, 165; V, 183.   [45] *GB*, I, 353.
[46] *GB*, IV, 14-46, 47-58.   [47] *GB*, IV, V.

serve his vigor and the health of the world as a whole. But when at length this becomes impossible due to man's inevitable physical decline, the tribal attitude undergoes an apparent reversal and the people prepare for the king's ritualistic death.

In reality, the act of slaying the king constitutes the final taboo imposed on him. Hence his worshippers are not actually reversing their attitude or disavowing him when they put him to death. Indeed, this custom "springs directly from their profound veneration for him and from their anxiety to preserve him, or rather the divine spirit by which he is animated, in the most perfect state of efficiency."[48] An index both of their concern for his perfection and of the primitive interweaving or identifying of physical and spiritual states appears in the insistence that the king be utterly devoid of any bodily defect or blemish.[49] He is their guardian and guarantee against death, disease, and desolation. Consequently they believe that "the only way of averting these calamities is to put the king to death while he is still hale and hearty, in order that the divine spirit which he has inherited from his predecessors may be transmitted in turn by him to his successor while it is still in full vigour and has not yet been impaired by the weakness of disease and old age."[50] Such a preference for violent rather than natural death derives in part too from the conviction that under such circumstances there is a far better chance of catching the soul, on which the successor's vigor depends, as it leaves the body. Natural death is interpreted as either the soul's refusal to return to the body or its being forestalled in its efforts by some magical or demonic wiles.[51] From the foregoing, it is clear that the important aspect of the sacred kingship is the office or function rather than the individual. The essential factor is that the continuity of power be maintained unimpaired. In the face of this necessity the lives of the actual officeholders must be sacrificed.

Such a custom of regicide, particularly if it is observed annually as in early Babylonia or even octennially as in Greece, raises the question of the supply of kings.[52] Granted, as Frazer suggests, ancient peoples were more willing to sacrifice their lives

[48] *GB*, IV, 27.　　[49] *GB*, IV, 38.　　[50] *GB*, IV, 27.　　[51] *GB*, IV, 10.
[52] *GB*, IV, 113-117, 58, *passim*.

than is modern Western man. Nevertheless the practice could hardly fail to have a dampening effect on those who were in the direct line of descent from the ruling monarch. As a result, the custom of regicide gradually underwent modification by the introduction of temporary kings who took the place of the actual monarchs for a short time. Kings whose reign was limited by law and custom abdicated in favor of a temporary substitute when their terms were about to conclude. The substitute then enjoyed most of the royal prerogatives, especially those of a divine or magical order such as making the crops grow, during his tenure of office. At its conclusion, however, he was put to death and the real king once more assumed his throne.[53]

In its original form, this modification was acceptable only if the substitute possessed the same attributes of divinity as the king himself. And, as Frazer remarks, "no one could so well represent the king in his divine character as his son, who might be supposed to share the divine afflatus of his father. No one, therefore, could so appropriately die for the king and through him, for the whole people, as the king's son."[54] Such sacrifices were variously explained as tributes paid to the gods, as substitutes for the death of the father whose life was in this way renewed, and as an act necessary to forestalling the son's endangering the life of the father through absorbing or taking over his life form or spiritual energy.[55] At a later time, however, the sacrificing of an innocent person became antipathetic to society. Instead, a condemned criminal replaced the king's son or other innocent persons as the temporary king whose reign was a dramatic enactment of the ritual of the dying god.[56]

While substitution played an important part in the social evolution of the sacred king, transformation occupied an equally vital function in the development of his ritual. As we have seen, in all probability the earliest custom was that of putting the king to death either when he showed signs of physical impairment, especially in regard to sexual potency, or at the conclusion of a predetermined period. A modification of this is detectable in the habit of simple combat practiced by the King of the Wood

[53] *GB*, IV, 142-147, 155-156, 148, *passim*.
[54] *GB*, IV, 160.   [55] *GB*, IV, 188.   [56] *GB*, IV, 115.

at Nemi. It still constitutes a check on his physical condition, but it also affords him a kind of temporary reprieve not originally available. The logical successor to this custom was what might be called semi-mock sacrifices, in which the victim was wounded but not killed. And from this to various forms of wholly miming the sacrifice is but a step. These last range from the performance of mock human sacrifices in effigy to mimetic rituals such as that of beheading the king, in which three or four hats set one above the other are struck off the performer's head by a wooden sword. With the advent of symbol and personification in the rites, the miming becomes less directly realistic and imitative. Thus, the spring customs of the European peasantry include several ceremonies that involve the simulated death of a divine being. Among these are those known as burying the Carnival, the carrying out of Death, and sowing the Old Woman, which constitute a fusion of scapegoat and dying-god rituals aimed at dispelling the evil and moribund so that the vitality of life may continue unhampered.[57]

In "Adonis, Attis, Osiris" and "Spirits of the Corn and of the Wild," the fifth and sixth volumes of *The Golden Bough*, the figure of the dying and reviving god is examined in much greater detail. The fifth devotes itself to the dying gods that occur in ancient Oriental religions. Of these, the most important, as the title indicates, are the Syrian Adonis, the Phrygian Attis, and the Egyptian Osiris. The sixth volume moves the survey westward into the religion of ancient Greece, where Dionysus and Demeter and her daughter Persephone become key figures. And "Balder the Beautiful," the concluding part of *The Golden Bough*, takes us from the East and the Mediterranean to the North and the Baltic where we find the Norse dying and reviving god.

Despite individual variations among them, these figures have a substantial similarity in both the myths and the rituals attached to their names. An individual in the full bloom of life is beloved either by another person or by the gods themselves. But when hero or heroine and beloved are most happy and their lives seem to have flowered into fulfillment, then the antagonistic forces of evil and death attack and kill the hero-god. These forces may ap-

[57] *GB*, IV, 205-265.

pear in the form of wild animals, such as the boar that fatally wounds Adonis; or of chthonic daemons, like Pluto, the lord of the dead, who carries off Persephone; or of treacherous human beings, such as Osiris' brother, Set (also known as Typhon), who first imprisons the culture-hero in a coffin and later dismembers his body; or of well-meaning but misled dupes, like Hoder, the blind brother of Balder, whom the deceitful and malevolent Loki persuades to throw the magical branch of mistletoe at Balder. Consequently, death may come to the god as an accidental but physically severe wound (Adonis); as a physically trivial but magically fatal blow (Balder); as deliberate emasculation (Attis); as rape and sexual violation (Persephone); or as dismemberment (Osiris and Dionysus). After his death, the god passes to the land of the dead, which is usually underground. Then he is either rescued and resurrected into the land of the living by his beloved, as Osiris is by Isis and Tammuz by Ishtar, the Babylonian version of Adonis; or else an agreement is made that he will spend half his time in each of the two realms, as in the cases of Persephone and Adonis; or he is literally reborn, as some accounts have it concerning Dionysus. In any event, the god by his revival and resurrection demonstrates the omnipotence of that divine power of life it is his role to manifest. Thus, it is eminently appropriate that the volume which brings the discussion of the dying and reviving god to a conclusion should end with a note on the crucifixion of Christ.

Frazer's general explanation of the dying and reviving god derives from his detailed examination of the rites and customs with which the god's worshippers surrounded their deity. The death, departure, resurrection, and return of the god was celebrated annually with ritual observances by his worshippers. These observances took the form of sacred dramas, often extending over several days, in which the ordained suffering, eclipse, and revival of the god was presented mimetically either by images or by human actors.[58] With the announcement of the death of the god, the worshippers mourned his loss with tears and lamentation. They beat their breasts and slashed their bodies with knives or sharp instruments so that they might make blood-offerings. Among the

[58] *GB*, vi, 85.

mourners, the feminine was dominant. In the case of Adonis, the chief sorrowers were women; in that of Attis, the god's priests were self-emasculated eunuchs; in the case of Osiris, his priests imitated Isis' unhappy search for the remains of her lost love. It was customary for the priests and worshippers of Adonis and Osiris to shave their heads both as a sign of their sorrow and as a sacrifice of the seat of their strength to the attempted resurrection of the god. More barbaric was the sacrifice of Attis' followers, for they severed their genitals that the great mother goddess, Cybele, might be impregnated by their life-giving energy and so transmit it to the world.[59]

When the ritual mourning was concluded, images of the god, clad to imitate corpses, were buried. The figure of Adonis was usually given a watery grave by being thrown into the sea or a spring, while Attis and Osiris were customarily laid in underground sepulchers. Attis and Adonis were thought to come to life again the day following their burial, and to return to the world and their worshippers. The emotions prompted by this ritual resurrection are perhaps best suggested in Frazer's description of Attis' ceremony: "When night had fallen, the sorrow of the worshippers was turned to joy. For suddenly a light shone in the darkness: the tomb was opened: the god had risen from the dead; and as the priest touched the lips of the weeping mourners with balm, he softly whispered in their ears the glad tidings of salvation. The resurrection of the god was hailed by his disciples as a promise that they too would issue triumphant from the corruption of the grave."[60] The day after the god's revival was devoted to public celebration of the event, a festival of joy, as it was known in the rites of Attis. The connection with the species of festival known as saturnalia is suggested by the fact that "a universal licence prevailed. Every man might say and do what he pleased. People went about the streets in disguise. No dignity was too high or too sacred for the humblest citizen to assume with impunity."[61] In a sense, the Hilaria was an inversion of the Saturnalia. Though they both temporarily reversed the structure and behavior of society, the former celebrated the res-

[59] *GB*, v, 224-226, 268-271; vi, 85-86.
[60] *GB*, v, 272.   [61] *GB*, v, 273.

urrection of the god, and the latter culminated in the real or mimetic death of the mock or temporary king, who was the human incarnation of the dying god at the moment of his death.

Frazer's explanation of these festivals and rites draws on the fact of their annual recurrence, their rhythmic pattern of birth, marriage, reproduction, death, and rebirth, and their connection with and use of certain kinds of vegetation. In the world of nature, the recurrence of these rites is matched by that of the seasons, while their rhythmic rise and fall parallels the lot of all living things. For Frazer, the myth and ritual of the dying god is not only analogous to but derivative from these natural phenomena. The matrix in which the notion of the dying and reviving god centers is the following:

> The spectacle of the great changes which annually pass over the face of the earth has powerfully impressed the minds of men in all ages, and stirred them to meditate on the causes of transformations so vast and wonderful. Their curiosity has not been purely disinterested; for even the savage cannot fail to perceive how intimately his own life is bound up with the life of nature, and how the same processes which freeze the stream and strip the earth of vegetation menace him with extinction. ... They now pictured to themselves the growth and decay of vegetation, the birth and death of living creatures, as effects of the waxing or waning strength of divine beings, of gods and goddesses, who were born and died, who married and begot children, on the pattern of human life.

> Thus the old magical theory of the seasons was displaced, or rather supplemented, by a religious theory. For although men now attributed the annual cycle of change primarily to corresponding changes in their deities, they still thought that by performing certain magical rites they could aid the god, who was the principle of life, in his struggle with the opposing principle of death. They imagined that they would recruit his failing energies and even raise him from the dead. The ceremonies which they observed for this purpose were in substance a dramatic representation of the natural processes which they wished to facilitate.[62]

[62] *GB*, v, 3-4.

Since changes in vegetation are easily apparent and recur on the yearly cycle rather than over a longer span, the dying and reviving god was primarily a vegetative deity. Yet, as Frazer observed, "the two sides of life, the vegetable and the animal, were not dissociated in the minds of those who observed the ceremonies. Indeed they commonly believed that the tie between the animal and the vegetable world was even closer than it really is; hence they often combined the dramatic representation of reviving plants with a real or dramatic union of the sexes for the purpose of furthering at the same time and by the same act the multiplication of fruits, of animals, and of men. To them the principle of life and fertility, whether animal or vegetable, was one and indivisible."[63] Hence, Adonis, Attis, and Osiris were regarded not only as man-gods possessing individual characteristics and personal attributes; they were also associated with specific animals and kinds of vegetation. Thus, all three were linked with the pig or wild boar which at first was identified with the god himself. Later, the wild boar was regarded as an embodiment of the god's enemy. This view was influenced by the havoc such animals wrought on crops, by the fact that the gods were vegetative deities, and by their gradual replacement of theriomorphic by anthropomorphic characteristics. In later cultural stages the original animal and vegetable forms of the deities were wholly anthropomorphized. Then myths were evolved to explain the close connection between the god of human appearance and certain animals and plants. These myths tended to explain the reverence for and the exceptional sacrifice of, say, a sacred animal in terms of past assistance and harm brought the god by the animal.[64]

Also associated with the pig was Demeter, the mother and duplicate of the corn-goddess, Persephone, while both Osiris and Dionysus were identified with the bull or ox.[65] The latter's dual identification with the bull and the goat provides the closest connection between the animal and vegetative aspects of the dying and reviving god. As the bull, Dionysus is linked to the corn-god who is worshipped by agricultural peoples. And as the goat he

[63] *GB*, v, 5.
[64] *GB*, VII, 22-23; VIII, 22, 25, 33, 29-32.
[65] *GB*, VIII, 3, 16, 34.

is related to the tree-spirit who is man's divinity during his pastoral stage of existence.[66] The nomadic and pastoral deities antedate the agricultural gods, but they easily melt into them, as *The Golden Bough* demonstrates at length. Consequently Adonis, Attis, Osiris, and Dionysus are tree-spirits as well as cereal deities. Adonis is linked with the myrrh-tree, the anemone, and the red rose; Attis with the almond and pine tree and violets; Osiris variously with the pine, sycamore, tamarisk, and acacia trees, grapes, and ivy; and Dionysus with fruits, especially apple and fig trees, grapes, and pomegranates.[67] In all these cases, the animal as well as the vegetable, the object is not simply the representative or emblem of the god; it is the god's incarnation in animal or vegetable form. As a result, all of these manifestations are equally divine in the eyes of their worshippers: the term "Adonis," for instance, in a certain sense subsumes both a particular divine man and a certain tree and flower.

From the foregoing, we are in a better position to grasp the scope of those sacred dramas which commemorate and celebrate the myth of the dying and reviving god. Since Adonis and the rest constitute multiple forms of divinity, their death is of momentous significance. Not merely the loss and confusion attendant upon the death of a leader but the actual disintegration of the world and the return of chaos is the issue at stake. The dying and reviving god is the core of human existence and the linchpin of the universe. If he fails to survive, man and his world are doomed to extinction. Thus, the god becomes the supreme embodiment of those lifeguards and guarantees against mortality which surround the sacred king. It is clear therefore why the ritual celebration of the god's death and resurrection should be magical in intent as well as dramatic in form. In many such rites even the myths recited were designed to function as narrative spells producing events similar to the ones described in the myths.[68]

We have already noted how the ritual slaying of the king is, in effect, his final taboo, the last custom to which he must conform.

[66] *GB*, v, 232-233; VIII, 1-4, 36-37.
[67] *GB*, v, 226-227, 263, 267, 277; VI, 108-112; VII, 2-4, 14.
[68] *GB*, VII, 1, 106.

In similar fashion, the enactment and celebration of the god's death is the ultimate taboo imposed on his worshippers. This parallel between the sacred king and the dying god is central to the general relationship of myth and ritual and also to the unity of *The Golden Bough*. The similarity in the deaths of the two figures is not coincidence but the result of their being closely interrelated, as Frazer makes quite explicit on a number of occasions. At one point, he succinctly summarizes the conclusion to which his evidence has led him:

> The Semitic Adonis and the Phrygian Attis were at one time personated in the flesh by kings, princes, or priests who played the part of the god for a time and then either died a violent death in the divine character or had to redeem their life in one way or another, whether by performing a make-believe sacrifice at some expense of pain and danger to themselves, or by delegating the duty to a substitute. Further we conjectured that in Egypt the part of Osiris may have been played by the king himself.[69]

In other words, the sacred king is the actual, living counterpart of the dying god. On the level of ritual and mankind, the central figure is the former; on that of myth and divinity, the latter. The king, however, is not simply acting a role in the sense in which we understand the phrase today. The drama in which he is participating is not merely entertainment but is fundamentally religious and sacred. The king and through him his people or nation hope to achieve something for themselves by their dramatic representation of the life and death of the god. Thus, the rites they enact are not only commemorative but also imitative. What the king and his followers seek to bring about by this performance is made clear from the great Egyptian festival known as the Sed. According to Frazer, "the intention of the festival seems to have been to procure for the king a new lease of life, a renovation of his divine energies, a rejuvenescence."[70] As a result, "apparently the essence of the rites consisted in identifying the king with Osiris; for just as Osiris had died and risen again from the dead, so the king might be thought to die and live again with the god

[69] *GB*, vi, 151.   [70] *GB*, vi, 153.

whom he personated. The ceremony would thus be for the king a death as well as a rebirth."[71] When we remember that the king was actually the human form of the nation or tribe, we see that the myth and ritual of the dying and reviving god embodies the regeneration of both society and the individual.

On the most literal level, the very possibility of regeneration implies that the present state of existence has fallen off from its original strength and purity. A particularly powerful exemplification of this view appears in *The Golden Bough*, and more fully in *The Belief in Immortality*. This is the primitive conviction that man was originally immortal and that death was irrevocably visited upon him only through sorcery, demons, or accident.[72] There is, of course, a vast difference between the Christian idea of the redemption of a fallen world and the primitive notion of employing religio-magical rites in order to restore the human symbol of life, the divine king and man-god, to its full power. Yet, as Frazer suggests, the two views are related.[73] In both cases, the degeneration of the original state of life is equated with the presence of evils produced by demons. Thus, to restore life to its first vigor one must expel from the community all evils, afflictions, and sorrows together with those demons, ghosts, witches, and spirits of the dead which give rise to them. From individual attempts to remove personal woes there gradually developed communal endeavors to eradicate the afflictions of an entire people or nation. As Frazer says, "the public attempts to expel the accumulated ills of a whole community may be divided into two classes, according as the expelled evils are immaterial and invisible or are embodied in a material vehicle or scapegoat."[74] Among the vehicles used were trees, stones, animals, effigies, men, and even children. In striking contrast to the sacred king, the human scapegoat was selected on the basis of ugliness or physical defect.[75] From the individual expulsion to those by means of scapegoat, we see a development which renders the ritual both with greater formality

---

[71] *GB*, VI, 153.

[72] *GB*, IX, 302-304; *The Belief in Immortality* (London: Macmillan, 1913), I, 31-58.

[73] *GB*, IX, V, 72-73, 109, *passim*, 70.   [74] *GB*, IX, 109.

[75] *GB*, IX, 195, 255; for an exception to this rule, see IX, 277.

and with increased concreteness. It is to the charting of this belief and practice that Frazer devoted "The Scapegoat," the ninth
volume of *The Golden Bough*.

Just as the expulsion rites shifted from individual to communal
and from invisible to material objects, so they gradually moved
from occasional to periodic performances.[76] In part, this is a concomitant of their being celebrated communally. A community's
need for certain efficacious ritual practices must be ordained by
custom and consecrated by antiquity if even the most rudimentary order is to be preserved. When the evils afflicting a society
are dispelled periodically, "the interval between the celebrations
of the ceremony is commonly a year, and the time of the year
when the ceremony takes place usually coincides with some well-
marked change of season, such as the beginning or end of winter
in the arctic and temperate zones, and the beginning or end of
the rainy season in the tropics."[77] Since the myth of the dying and
reviving god was also customarily enacted at such crucial times,
especially at sowing or harvest times, in the spring and autumn,
we are not surprised to learn that the divine man or his animal
surrogate often served as a scapegoat.[78] In addition to the reason
adduced from the temporal proximity of these rites, Frazer also
suggests that the use of the dying god as scapegoat stems from
the fusion of two customs originally unrelated:

> On the one hand we have seen that it has been customary to
> kill the human or animal god in order to save his divine life
> from being weakened by the inroads of age. On the other hand
> we have seen that it has been customary to have a general ex-
> pulsion of evils and sins once a year. Now, if it occurred to peo-
> ple to combine these two customs, the result would be the em-
> ployment of the dying god as a scapegoat. He was killed, not
> originally to take away sin, but to save the divine life from the
> degeneracy of old age; but, since he had to be killed at any
> rate, people may have thought that they might as well seize the
> opportunity to lay upon him the burden of their suffering and
> sins, in order that he might bear it away with him to the un-
> known world beyond the grave.[79]

[76] *GB*, IX, 123.   [77] *GB*, IX, 224.   [78] *GB*, IX, 226.   [79] *GB*, IX, 227.

The rites of expulsion included beating the scapegoat, particularly on the genitals, dancing by priests and worshippers in general, and masquerades and processions accompanied by a great deal of noise-making.[80] The aim of all these rites was "both to stimulate the growth of vegetation in spring and to expel the demoniac or other evil influences which were thought to have accumulated during the preceding winter or year."[81] At a later point in history such ceremonies designed both to purify and to fertilize were inclined to place greater emphasis on the first goal so that the second was ultimately forgotten.[82] Almost invariably, these public and periodic expulsion ceremonies were "preceded or followed by a period of general license, during which the ordinary restraints of society are thrown aside, and all offences, short of the gravest, are allowed to pass unpunished."[83]

The best-known of these festivals and the one that has supplied the generic name for the whole group is the Roman Saturnalia. The chief characteristics of the festival are its devotion to the extravagant pursuit of pleasures and merriment of all kinds, its inversion of society and abolition of the distinction between master and slave, and its election of a mock king who ruled over the festival and then was killed as the human representative of the god.[84] The first of these practices introduces the notion of mating and birth, the theme of fertility and regeneration in general. The second provides a secular and human analogue to the abolition of the distinction between deity and worshipper; it emphasizes the theme of communion and identification. The third is the logical development of the preceding feature, for through the ideas of death and sacrifice it elaborates the theme of incarnation. The ritual's composite figure, who as the dying god is concerned with the regeneration of life and as the scapegoat with the purgation of evil, suffers death in a variety of ways. These include stoning, being hurled into the sea from a cliff, being burned on a pyre, crucifixion, suicide by cutting his own throat, and hanging.[85] Yet in all these, what is established is not his mortality but his divin-

---

[80] *GB*, IX, 229, 231-241, 242-251, 256.
[81] *GB*, IX, 251.   [82] *GB*, IX, 259.   [83] *GB*, IX, 225.
[84] *GB*, IX, 306-311.
[85] *GB*, IX, 253-254, 255, 257, 309, 311, 408.

ity. That is to say, incarnation conquers death and thereby introduces the resurrection which, in turn, promulgates regeneration. Thus, the cyclic form of existence completes itself and is capable of self-perpetuation on all its levels, seasonal, vegetative, human, mythic, and religious.

[IV]

The three key observances which enable existence to maintain its cyclic character are those of purgation, purification, and regeneration. At the core of these are the natural forces of fire, water, and sexual intercourse. The symbolic and magical power of fire is discussed at great length in "Balder the Beautiful," the concluding section of *The Golden Bough*. The custom of lighting bonfires over which people jumped, around which cattle and other domestic animals were driven, and in which effigies and, originally, living persons were burned was, as Frazer indicates, widespread, being observed throughout Europe, Asia, and parts of Africa. The fires were lit, however, only on certain days, such as Easter and May Day in the spring, St. John's Day in midsummer, All Hallow's Eve in the autumn, and Christmas Day and Twelfth Day Eve in the winter.[86] In addition to these more or less calendrically fixed celebrations, the fire rites were frequently performed at times of particularly calamitous distress for the community. As such, they were called "need-fires," and it is from them, Frazer suggests, that all other fire-festivals derived.[87]

Frazer's explanation of these fire-festivals attempts to reconcile the two major theories already advanced by other scholars. One of these holds that the festivals are magical ceremonies designed to guarantee a proper supply of sunshine for all forms of life by imitating with fires the celestial light and heat of the sun. The other holds that these fires are purificatory or purgative and aim essentially at burning and thereby removing all those forces which threaten animal, vegetable, and human growth. Frazer's reconciliation suggests that the purgative properties of the fires were perhaps derived directly from those of sunshine, so that the festivals had both a positive and a negative function. They were

[86] *GB*, x, 106-107.   [87] *GB*, x, 269.

designed both to encourage growth and to eliminate all hindrances to that growth.[88]

Since fire appears to be the chief purgative force, it is not surprising to find water constituting the major purificatory and initiatory element. The close connection between being freed from an old state of sin and evil and being introduced to a new state of purity and innocence is attested to by the fact that "the midsummer festival comprises rites concerned with water as well as with fire."[89] As part of this celebration, people bathed in the sea, rivers, or springs, and poured water over each other in the belief that their sins would be washed away.[90] At this time of year, water was also reputed to acquire certain marvelous and beneficial properties, such as the power of prophecy, of healing all diseases, and of preventing disasters and misfortunes in the future.[91] Thus, from both the rites themselves and their purposes it is apparent that water here is a baptismal agent. In the water rite and its properties, we find the twofold significance of baptism, that is, the convert's repentant attitude toward his past sins and his new attitude of faith in the deity. The actual rite connects with the former, while its powers are analogous to the latter. The similarities between these primitive rites and the sophisticated religious notion of baptism is further borne out by the fact that the day on which the midsummer festivals of fire and water were traditionally held ultimately came to be considered as belonging to St. John the Baptist.[92]

These crude peasant observances of baptismal initiation or rebirth are matched in the myth and ritual of the dying god by the mystery ceremonies connected with Attis which "aimed at bringing the worshipper, and especially the novice, into closer communication with his god."[93] In the course of these ceremonies, the initiate was baptismally drenched in the blood of a bull, after which he was regarded "as one who had been born again to eternal life."[94] Significantly enough, "for some time afterwards the fiction of a new birth was kept up by dieting him on milk like a new-born babe."[95] That is to say, although the purification of

---

[88] *GB*, x, 329, 330. [89] *GB*, x, 216. [90] *GB*, v, 246; x, 216-219.
[91] *GB*, v, 247-248. [92] *GB*, v, 249. [93] *GB*, v, 274.
[94] *GB*, v, 274. [95] *GB*, v, 275.

baptism issues in regeneration, it is at first passive in character. The god and the worshippers have been reborn and so regenerated, but they are not yet capable of exercising their own creative and fructifying powers in the regeneration of others. Yet if the continuity of life is to be preserved and chaos averted, the reviving god and his human counterpart, the sacred king, must attain the active power of maturity, the ability to contribute to the continuity of life. On the most literal, immediate, and fundamental level this is the physical capacity to propagate one's own species.

Consequently, the final rite in the revival of the god is that of Sacred Marriage. It is essential that he demonstrate his restoration to the full vigor of manhood. Also he must provide a successor to the sacred king in order that the connection between divinity and humanity remain unbroken. Thus, it was customary for the queen or some other woman to be regarded as the consort and exclusive sexual property of the god. The various phases of the rite are graphically illustrated in a series of Egyptian wall paintings. According to Frazer's summary of them, "the nativity is depicted in about fifteen scenes, which may be grouped in three acts: first, the carnal union of the god with the queen; second, the birth; and third, the recognition of the infant by the gods."[96] In the case of the queen, the god becomes incarnate in her husband, the king; that is, the king and queen dramatically enact the myth of the divine union. Those women other than the queen who inhabited the temple of the god and were regarded as married to him were simultaneously prostitutes and sacred persons.[97] As the wives of the god, they shared his holy character, but since their spouse was capable of incarnating himself in any male form, they distributed their favors indiscriminately.

As Frazer suggests, this custom was not an orgiastic expression of lust but rather a solemn religious duty. In some cases it was an obligation imposed on all women before marriage. In others it was not confined to maidens, but both widows and married women who had tired of their husbands could assume the role. The explanation of this rite is both functional and historical. From the

---

[96] *GB*, II, 131.   [97] *GB*, V, 40-41.

functional standpoint this human mating in the god's sanctuary aimed to imitate the divine union of the god and goddess so that the fertility of living things might be assured and encouraged. From a historical point of view the custom is best understood, Frazer thinks, as deriving from an original state in which sexual rights were communal. The two views taken together explain why after marriage became a recognized social institution, for most women the custom was modified to the sacrifice of symbolic substitutes such as hair and obscene emblems, while at the same time it was continued by a certain number of women. In this way, the demands both of new modes of social adaption and of traditional religious customs of guaranteeing the communal welfare could be met.[98]

Frazer's explanation of their behavior once again reminds us that ritual is essentially mimetic in character and that the myth of the dying and reviving god has animal and vegetable as well as human connotations. He observes that "in their licentious intercourse at the temples the women, whether maidens or matrons or professional harlots, imitated the licentious conduct of a great goddess of fertility for the purpose of ensuring the fruitfulness of fields and trees, of man and beast; and in discharging this sacred and important function the women probably were supposed . . . to be actually possessed by the goddess."[99] Thus, the queen and the prostitute emphasize complementary aspects of the same rite of Sacred Marriage; for in the union of the former it is the man who becomes the incarnation of the deity, while in the union of the latter it is the woman who is so honored. Taken together, they constitute the complete form of the observance, that is, the celebration of the Sacred Marriage simultaneously on its mythic and divine level and on its human and ritualistic level.

The foregoing pages have summarized a number of specific issues articulated in *The Golden Bough*. As has already been intimated, Frazer, being neither philosopher nor theorist, is not preeminently interested in precise formulations of large general positions or ideas. At the same time he does evolve certain overriding conclusions from the mass of detailed evidence considered. And in concluding this survey of *The Golden Bough*'s con-

[98] *GB*, v, 36, 39, 40-41, 63.   [99] *GB*, v, 71.

trolling concepts we can perhaps do no better than to state flatly and cursorily what Frazer's basic convictions, both implied and stated, seem to be.

First, the evolutionary view appears with his notion that man develops socially and psychologically through three stages. While early man moves historically from a society founded on the hunt through a pastoral order to an agricultural state, he also progresses from a psychological state controlled by magic to one under the sway of religion, and finally to a scientific view of life. Second, ignoring or perhaps simply unaware of the discrepancies involved, Frazer goes on to suggest, following Mannhardt and in contradistinction to Max Müller, that primitive deities were primarily vegetative spirits rather than solar gods.

The third point implicitly stressed by Frazer is that Christianity derives from these primitive fertility or vegetative cults in which the dying and reviving god is central. Further, the myths surrounding these and related deities, though sometimes etiological and even euhemeristic, are more often dramatic or narrative records of rites performed. As such, they reveal traces of earlier social customs, such as the killing of the sacred king-god. Finally, since most of these fertility cults originated in the Orient or Asia Minor, Frazer suggests that their entrance into the European West weakened the Roman empire, which in his eyes put its trust in the state as the supreme good, and so led to the disaster of the Dark Ages, from which the rationalism of the eighteenth and nineteenth centuries are only now leading us. The sanguinity of this last view is tempered by the long vista of human life stretching from prehistory to the present, for in it Frazer has seen a recurrent pattern of expectations unrealized and disasters enacted. And it is precisely this dual perspective of intelligence and hopelessness, of rational dreams and tragic awareness mirrored in a style of ironic nobility that made *The Golden Bough* the enchanted glass of twentieth-century writers. In it they might see both their own dilemmas reflected and the future of their world presaged with all the tantalizing ambivalence of life itself.

CHAPTER III

The Intellectual
Influence of
The Golden Bough

[I]

One critic has assigned *The Golden Bough* to the class of unclassifiable books, a genre which includes such diverse works as *The Anatomy of Melancholy, Don Juan, Sartor Resartus, Moby Dick,* and *Finnegans Wake.*[1] While he sees Sir James Frazer's crowning achievement as an anomaly, more importantly he relates it to a predominantly literary ambience. A similar view of *The Golden Bough* has also been taken by one of the most eminent anthropologists of the twentieth century. A. L. Kroeber places Frazer in historical perspective by aligning him with literary and other fields outside anthropology.[2] Even in his own day some reviewers found *The Golden Bough* characterized by poetic and allegorical interpretations and commendable for its exquisite style rather than for scientific accuracy and coherence. Indeed, from the first *The Golden Bough* attracted a great many readers who were not primarily specialists in anthropology but who nevertheless found its material stimulating and its presentation attractive.

Some of Frazer's appeal was rooted deep in the prevailing concerns of nineteenth-century cultural life, as chapter one suggested. Some also derived from the distinctive verbal texture and structure of *The Golden Bough,* as chapter four will show. These and related qualities made Frazer peculiarly relevant to the evolution of a radically new sensibility that nevertheless sought to

[1] Harry Levin, *James Joyce* (New York: New Directions, 1941), p. 165.
[2] A. L. Kroeber, *The Nature of Culture* (Chicago: University of Chicago Press, 1952), p. 145; cf. his "Critical Summary and Commentary" in *Method and Perspective in Anthropology,* ed. R. F. Spencer (Minneapolis: University of Minnesota Press, 1954), p. 277.

preserve and deepen its relations to the past. *The Golden Bough* is certainly the culmination of the classical anthropological tradition, and its conceptual strategies are informed by the key concepts of the age. Here, however, the main concern is to establish the extent to which Frazer's ideas and influence were diffused throughout the humanities and social sciences. The purpose is to suggest that no matter what the ground of the artist's primary interests he could scarcely indulge them without coming into contact with Frazer's ideas and finding him to be one of the age's seminal minds.

Essentially there are three distinct but related ways in which writers absorb *The Golden Bough*: through the text itself, through reviews of it in specialist and general periodicals, and through the works of other scholars both in anthropology and other disciplines. Since the chapters on individual authors deal with the first of these, the bulk of attention here is concentrated on the other two modes, especially the latter. Beginning with Frazer's own field of anthropology, the impact of *The Golden Bough* is traced through representative works in comparative religion, classics, archaeology, psychology, sociology, philosophy, and history, in the hope that we may gain a sharper sense of both the range and diversity of Frazer's influence.

The recondite and strange data of anthropology, folklore, comparative religion, and the classics found in *The Golden Bough* are engrossing in their own right. Nevertheless, Frazer's volume would probably not have had so great an influence on literature had it not appeared at a remarkably propitious moment. In the first place it marked the culmination, in subject and method, of a long line of development extending back to the eighteenth century. Frazer's concern with the nature and interrelations of religion, myth, cult, and ritual was shared in divers ways by such men as Hume, Herder, Heyne, Creuzer, Spencer, Mannhardt, Tylor, and Robertson Smith.[3] Similarly, the comparative method,

---

[3] For extended accounts of this development, see Marvin Harris, *The Rise of Anthropological Theory* (New York: Thomas Y. Crowell Co., 1968), especially Chs. 2-11; W.K.C. Guthrie, *The Greeks and Their Gods* (London: Methuen, 1950), Ch. 1; W. Schmidt, *The Origin and Growth of Religion*, tr. H. J. Rose (London: Methuen 1931); Jane Harrison, "The Influence of Darwinism on the Study of Religions," in *Darwin and Modern*

to which he adhered throughout his lifetime, was the product of many hands, most notably Lafitau, Montesquieu, de Brosses, Pitt-Rivers, Maine, Darwin, and Tylor.[4] Thus, *The Golden Bough*, apart from its own intrinsic merits, represented the flowering of a school of anthropology rather than the founding of a new movement. The evolutionary school originated as early as the 1860s and achieved its greatest influence around 1910 when the third edition of Frazer's classic was coming off the presses.[5] By appearing in its most complete form when it did, *The Golden Bough* gained a ready-made audience predisposed towards its subject, method, and attitude. It also escaped being overwhelmed by the views of Franz Boas, which were destined to dominate virtually the entire field of anthropology in one way or another and which exerted their full effects from 1925 to almost the present.

The second historical aspect conditioning the popularity of *The Golden Bough* was the period's climate of opinion. Numer-

---

Science, ed. A. C. Seward (Cambridge: Cambridge University Press, 1909), pp. 494-511; Richard Chase, *Quest for Myth* (Baton Rouge: Louisiana State University Press, 1946); Reverend Louis Bouyer, *Rite and Man*, tr. M. J. Costelloe, S. J. (Notre Dame: Notre Dame University Press, 1963), Ch. 2; T. K. Penniman, *A Hundred Years of Anthropology*, 3rd ed. (London: Duckworth, 1965); R. H. Lowie, *The History of Ethnological Theory* (New York: Rinehart, 1937); H. R. Hays, *From Ape to Angel* (New York: Knopf, 1958); A. Kardiner & E. Preble, *They Studied Man* (New York: World, 1961), Part I; Clyde Kluckhohn, *Anthropology and the Classics* (Providence: Brown University Press, 1961), Ch. 1; B. Malinowski, *A Scientific Theory of Culture* (Chapel Hill: University of North Carolina Press, 1944), Ch. 3 and "Sir James George Frazer: A Biographical Appreciation," pp. 179-195.

[4] On the growth and nature of the comparative method, see E. H. Ackerknecht, "On the Comparative Method in Anthropology," in *Method and Perspective in Anthropology*, pp. 117-125; John A. Irving, "The Comparative Method and the Nature of Human Nature," *Philosophy and Phenomenological Research*, IX (March 1949), 545-556; Arnold van Gennep, *Les Rites de Passage* (Paris: E. Nourry, 1909), pp. 6-9, and *Religions, Moeurs et Legendes* (Troisième Serie) (Paris: Société du Mercure de France, 1911), pp. 9-15; Melville Herskovits, "Some Problems of Method in Ethnography," in *Method and Perspective in Anthropology*, pp. 18-19; Kroeber, "Critical Summary and Commentary," pp. 273-281. For Frazer's own comments on the comparative method, see *The Gorgon's Head* (London: Macmillan, 1927), pp. 281-284.

[5] Kroeber, *The Nature of Culture*, p. 147.

ous concepts and issues of current interest were also ingrained in the very fabric of the book. Indeed, part of the reason for Frazer's tremendous influence on modern literature is that his work constitutes a fertile matrix and mirror of ideas, observations, beliefs, and images central to the age. Both in *The Golden Bough* and the age the movements of these ideas were charted by a compass whose cardinal points were the concepts of rationality, fertility, irrationality, and sterility. The major topics explored were sex, superstition, and survival (an alliterative if not particularly novel triad).

From the turn of the century through the post-World War I era and into the 20s the concern with man's sexual impulses and their relation to the rest of his life was articulated with increasing intensity. And though it was Freud, Jung, and the other psychoanalysts who spearheaded this trend, Frazer too was intrigued by the way in which "the sexual instinct has moulded the religious consciousness of our race."[6] Consequently he devoted much space to charting the phallic character of primitive cults. Whether he would admit it or not, Frazer's detached chronicling of these was the anthropological equivalent of Freud's exploration of modern man's sexual impulses, and by this chronicling he helped open an area for research that was to be more assiduously explored from various points of view by such scholars as Westermarck, Crawley, Hartland, Malinowski, and Briffault.

Although Frazer gave scant credence to theories of the unconscious and steadfastly refused to read Freud, he too contributed to the twentieth century's mapping of the levels and modes of human consciousness. *The Golden Bough* is crowded with illustrations that are dramatic analyses of prophetic foresight, shamanistic trances, mass psychology, and the denial of commonsense categories of thought. Like *Being and Nothingness*, it merges psychology and the concrete scene of fiction, but in an infinitely more readable form. To Frazer, these habits of thought revealed the functional, pragmatic, and superstitious character of institutions as diverse as religion, government, private property, and marriage. To many of his readers, this view intensified their own

[6] *GB*, vii, viii.

convictions of the base ulterior purposes and deleterious effects of human institutions and so deepened their own scepticism and disillusionment.

From his investigation of the origins and growth of human society and consciousness, Frazer derived key concepts which reveal his affinities with those other seminal minds of the age, Marx and Darwin. It is true that he never really grasped the economic dimensions of primitive society in anything like their full complexity. Still he was able to seize on one salient fact about human institutions. Implicitly in *The Golden Bough* and more openly in *Psyche's Task*, he shows that man's motives and arguments for his actions are quite other than what he asserts. Like Marx, Frazer analyzes the functional character of institutions as the product of pragmatic and superstitious forces. And though the differences between the two men are considerable, yet it is possible from our present vantage point to see broad similarities in their impacts on their time. Each showed his readers by a massive accumulation of evidence precisely how much of what had hitherto been thought about mankind and his history could no longer be credited. And more. Each found the explanation of this mistake in a complex of superstition, self-aggrandizement, and historical necessity.

Important as these notions were in their several ways to Freud, Marx, and Frazer, the really crucial issue was the struggle for survival propounded in the Victorian age and enacted with unparalleled opulence and variety in the twentieth century. While Darwin, Freud, and Marx were framing the issue in biological, psychological, and socio-economic terms, Frazer was developing his own dialectic of myth and reality. For his primitive subjects the struggle for survival is twofold. On the one hand, there is the loosely Darwinian and Marxian aspect. This is provided by attacks from rival tribes or nations together with the attrition caused by drought and starvation. Coupled with these are rulers who repress by economic demands, social traditions, and religious appeals. On the other hand, what might be called the Freudian dimension represented by psychological projections such as myths and deities also figures prominently in the struggle. Frazer's ancient peoples seek to endure by invoking myths of divine assistance and rites in which perfect performance assures divine conquest over enemies and hence human survival. In effect, Frazer mediates between the external and internal worlds of Marx or Darwin and Freud, as he himself reveals when he remarks that "to the preservation of the species the reproductive faculties are no less essential than the nutritive."[7] And in so doing, he shows that the individual and the land are the twin foci of man's endless battle for existence, themes which have been as inexhaustible for modern literature as they have been imperative for modern life.

The net result of concentration upon the concepts of sex, superstition, and survival, by both *The Golden Bough* and the age itself, was to suggest that the primitive savage was still deeply ingrained in modern man and posed a serious threat to civilization itself. In view of this revelation of the irrational character of much of human life, there was, it was felt, an imperative need for an overhauling of man's views concerning culture, society, and the individual. Yet at the same time that Frazer was apparently documenting these convictions, he was also proving himself one of the foremost contributors to his generation's newly awakened sense of the continuity and intelligibility of human life in the face of anarchy, chaos, and disorder. In organizing his abundant anthropological material under the controlling concept of the dying and reviving vegetative and fertility deity, Frazer exhibited both the rational powers of man, which his researches had seemed to deny, and the religious character of man's salvation, which his personal inclinations had led him to question. By implication, then, *The Golden Bough* challenges its readers—particularly the creative artist—to produce a similarly ordered vision out of the disparate facts and antagonistic strains of his own experience.

In relation to its age, then—an age of which we are still a part —*The Golden Bough* embraces two pairs of antithetical concepts. It presents not only the irrational and unstable character of human life and affairs but also its order and stability. On vegetative, sexual, psychological, social, and cultural levels alike, it sees fertility and sterility as succeeding one another in a systolic

[7] *GB*, VII, viii.

and diastolic universal rhythm. In effect, it was in *The Golden Bough* more than any other single work that the twentieth century might read the significance of its emergence from Victorian prudery concerning sexual drives; of its traumatic experiences inspired by the Boer War, and Irish civil conflict, and World War I; of the economic character of its existence emphasized by the Russian revolution, the British General Strike, and the world depression of the 1930s; of the codifying of irrational impulses into a philosophical position, whether that of Nietzsche, Bergson, Kierkegaard, the dadaist, or the existentialist; and of its religious and cultural problems created by the Higher Criticism, the comparative method, and the science of Huxley as well as of Einstein.

[II]

How *The Golden Bough* came to occupy so central a position in the thinking of the modern world is an inordinately complex matter. For present purposes, however, it must suffice if some general indications can be given as to how it came to influence literature so pervasively and profoundly. No effort will be made at this point to describe precisely the way by which any individual author came to be influenced by it. Instead, the possible ways will be surveyed with a view to suggesting that an acquaintance with Frazer's study demanded neither a penchant for the curiosities of antiquarian lore, a passion for primitive savages, nor even a gentlemanly grounding in the classics, though, to be sure, their possession would increase the probability of that acquaintance.

Obviously the most direct form of influence was that which resulted from authors actually reading *The Golden Bough*. Included in those so influenced are William Butler Yeats, T. S. Eliot, D. H. Lawrence, Edith Sitwell, Naomi Mitchison, Robert Graves, Richard Aldington, Archibald MacLeish, John Peale Bishop, Ezra Pound, and Caroline Gordon, to mention but a few of the more obvious names. Consequently, their works not only reflect the general contentions of *The Golden Bough* but also allude to specific and individual points, as subsequent chapters will demonstrate. And yet even before the artist actually picked up Frazer's book, he could easily have had some idea of its basic concepts. From approximately the 1850s to the end of the century or a little later, periodical reviews became an increasingly central means of disseminating new information and ideas. Their generally high level of fairness and acumen assured the reading public of quick access in a responsible manner to the most alert and influential minds of the age. Starting in 1890, throughout Frazer's career reviews, summaries, and critiques of his work occupied extended space in numerous periodicals. Among these journals were many directed to the nonspecialist concerned with matters of general and current interest. Both in England and America such publications as *The Athenaeum, The Dial, The Nation, The Edinburgh Review, The Quarterly Review, The Hibbert Journal, The Living Age, The North American Review*, and *The Virginia Quarterly*, all thought appraisals of *The Golden Bough* and Frazer's other works would be welcomed by their readers. Perhaps the most striking demonstration of the widespread attention given his work is provided by the *Friday Literary Review*, a weekly supplement of the *Chicago Evening Post*. It printed an essay on *The Golden Bough* about the same time that Ezra Pound was urging equally new and startling matter on Harriet Monroe and *Poetry* magazine.[8] In virtually all these cases the reviewer presented in some detail the gist of Frazer's overriding theme before advancing his own criticisms and opinions. As a result, from them an interested author could easily derive a working notion of Frazer's central contentions.

Frazer's ideas became even more accessible as a result of the attitudes engendered by his work. While, as we shall see, there was immense sympathy for and praise of *The Golden Bough* and his related studies, there was also a sharply critical strain running through the scholarly and lay reactions from the very outset. As the development of Freud's influence shows, suspicion and hostility are frequently powerful factors in spreading new or disturbing ideas. Thus, when reviewers and others criticized Frazer, they were also piquing the curiosity and interest of intellectuals and artists who were critical of modern society and groping toward new bases of human conduct. Indeed, many of these re-

[8] See Irving Howe, *Sherwood Anderson* (New York: William Sloane Associates, 1951), pp. 57-58.

views anticipated the major objections against Frazer raised by later anthropological specialists. For instance, in *The Edinburgh Review* for October, 1890, the reviewer comments, "it does not seem to us probable, or even possible, that the utmost ingenuity and learning can hope to succeed in unravelling an ancient interdict of this trivial kind [concerning the priest of Nemi] by stringing together a few conceptions that are so general and natural as to be applicable to almost any special case."[9] He insists that much of Frazer's material could as well fit into a totally different pattern elaborated by someone else[10] and concludes that the general theory, though interesting and containing a number of new facts, does not substantially enlarge "our horizon beyond the solid landmarks already set up by the leading pioneers in this field of exploration."[11]

On specific points, he objects that primitive peoples are neither so coherent nor so orderly as Frazer makes them appear,[12] that they will readily plead custom as the explanation for anything and everything,[13] and that mythology is an unsafe guide to a clear understanding of the real origins of religion since it stems largely from a desire to veil and obscure those real origins.[14] On a more general level, his dislike for the circuitousness and digressive nature of Frazer's treatment anticipated the contemporary anthropologist's emphasis on incisive statements and limited topics.[15] Similarly, the remark that "throughout his book, he leans too much toward the poetic and allegorical interpretation of customs and manners that derive easily enough from the incidents and circumstances of everyday life"[16] suggests the more recent emphasis on contextual explanations and pragmatic factors.

Nor are these strictures isolated instances advanced by a single dissenter. In 1891, another reviewer suggested that Frazer could go further in interpreting the myth of the harvest maiden as a

---

[9] *The Edinburgh Review*, CLXXII (1890), 547.
[10] *The Edinburgh Review*, CLXXII (1890), 570.
[11] *The Edinburgh Review*, CLXXII (1890), 572.
[12] *The Edinburgh Review*, CLXXII (1890), 548-549.
[13] *The Edinburgh Review*, CLXXII (1890), 546.
[14] *The Edinburgh Review*, CLXXII (1890), 574.
[15] *The Edinburgh Review*, CLXXII (1890), 541.
[16] *The Edinburgh Review*, CLXXII (1890), 543.

representation of the hopes and fears of the agriculturist.[17] The same writer found Frazer's arguments concerning totemism unconvincing, the evidence for the theory concerning the golden bough itself much more doubtful than the rest of the interpretation, and the proof for the theory of the external soul inadequate. He also doubted that the death of the priest was a sacrifice analogous to that of a scapegoat.[18] Several years later *The Golden Bough* was spoken of as being much more important for the "wealth of illustration and its exquisite style" than "for originality of idea."[19] William Robertson Smith's *Religion of the Semites* is characterized as a more vital contribution to the study of religion, while E. B. Tylor is regarded as *the* great anthropologist and everyone else as working within and merely modifying his essential framework.[20]

In 1901 the author of a review of the second edition of *The Golden Bough* thought the rite at Nemi needed more consideration on the purely classical evidence and suspected that weak links exist which might upset Frazer's consideration of it as a complete whole.[21] Nor do the parallels between the rites at Nemi and modern European fire customs really work out; it is unwise to connect customs containing unlike elements without showing by careful inquiry how and from whence the unlike features appear.[22] By the same token, the extensive research into water and fire worship, which is so central to the work as a whole, would be greatly simplified by treating it on the basis of ethnology rather than of geography. Then, too, Frazer's views on Druidic cults, the worship of the mistletoe, and related rites are largely vitiated by his attempt to prove them part of one homogeneous pattern of belief. *The Edinburgh Review* of the same year objected to Frazer's use of *a priori* arguments. It pointed out that there is a fatal discrepancy between his science and his metaphysics, which postulates the ultimate replacement

[17] *The Quarterly Review*, CLXXII (1891), 195.
[18] *The Quarterly Review*, CLXXII (1891), 196, 201, 202-203, 204.
[19] *The Edinburgh Review*, CLXXX (1898), 312.
[20] *The Edinburgh Review*, CLXXX (1898), 311.
[21] *The Athenaeum*, CXIV (1901), 236.
[22] *The Athenaeum*, CXIV (1901), 237.

of science by a more perfect hypothesis.[23] It also said that Frazer had not made clear how there originated the idea that a god might become incarnate in a man and that more evidence was needed to prove that the king who is slain is also a god and that the king who is a god is also slain.[24]

Similarly, L. R. Farnell, the learned Oxford classical scholar, wrote that there was little support for Frazer's view that the ceremonious slaying of the king is part of the monarchical system of the old Latin race.[25] To him, the weakest part of the study was the attempt to show that the priest of Nemi enacts a sacred marriage with Diana of the Grove.[26] Farnell also says that part of the case for the matrilineal hypothesis as applied to Greece has been omitted and that some of the arguments which are admitted are irrelevant. More important, however, is his detailed insistence that Frazer's classification of magical processes as homeopathic and contagious is inadequate.[27] This was to become one of the most common charges levelled against the author of *The Golden Bough* by succeeding generations of anthropologists, psychologists, and philosophers of religion. As a capstone to these early criticisms of Frazer, there is none more significant for the future development of anthropology than Farnell's concluding comment in this review of 1906:

> we know Dr. Frazer as an anthropologist of great knowledge and wide range. But in his handling of the Mediterranean religions, whether he is concerned with legend or with cult, his judgments lack authority and the impress of special insight or adequate study. And the failure of this part of the treatise on early kingship suggests the question which some anthropologists are now putting to themselves, whether the time has not come to study more deeply special ethnic areas, rather than to make continual free excursions round the globe.[28]

[23] *The Edinburgh Review*, CXCIV (1901), 348.
[24] *The Edinburgh Review*, CXCIV (1901), 353-355.
[25] *The Hibbert Journal*, IV (1906), 932.
[26] *The Hibbert Journal*, IV (1906), 931.
[27] *The Hibbert Journal*, IV (1906), 929.
[28] *The Hibbert Journal*, IV (1906), 932.

The above remarks show clearly that in neither anthropological nor lay circles was Frazer's work ever accepted wholly and without reservations or criticisms.[29] From this, it would appear that if these same earlier critics also praised and agreed with a number of Frazer's findings, they did so not so much out of ignorance of the scientific method as out of a sense of the wider import of Frazer's writings, extending beyond anthropology itself. The scientific approach to anthropology at the turn of the century was doubtless rudimentary and unsophisticated by contemporary standards. Yet in significant measure this was due to a wider range of interests which refused to countenance isolated specialization and the piecemeal approach to fundamental problems. This attitude permitted Frazer to write essays and poetry after the fashion of Addison and Lamb and to discuss physics with Clerk Maxwell, Jane Harrison to take up the study and translation of Russian literature including seventeenth-century texts, and Gilbert Murray to devote much time and energy to the League of Nations and other liberal political causes. And it is reflected in the praise accorded *The Golden Bough* by the reviewers already alluded to.

Amid the numerous points of agreement on specific details, many of which have been outmoded by subsequent studies, several general features are continually reiterated. Thus, in 1890, a reviewer of *The Golden Bough* and a reviewer of Jane Harrison's

[29] Other evidence to support this view can be found in: L. Marillier, "M. Frazer et La Diane de Nemi," *Revue de l'Histoire des Religions*, xxv (1892), 71-99; A. Lang, "'The Golden Bough,'" *Fortnightly Review*, lxxv (1901), 235-248; A. Lang, "Mr. Frazer's Theory of the Crucifixion," *Fortnightly Review*, lxxv (1901), 650-662; E. S. Hartland, "'The Golden Bough,'" *Man*, O.S. 1 (1901), 57-60; G. d'Alviella, "Le Rameau d'Or," *Revue de l'Histoire des Religions*, xlviii (1903), 68-71; A. van Gennep, "'Adonis, Attis, Osiris,'" *Revue de l'Histoire des Religions*, liv (1906), 436-440; R. Dussaud, "'Adonis, Attis, Osiris,'" *Revue de l'Histoire des Religions*, lv (1907), 113-115; R. Dussaud, "'Adonis, Attis, Osiris,'" *Revue de l'Histoire des Religions*, lviii (1908), 262-264; P. W. Schmidt, "'The Golden Bough,'" *Anthropos*, vii (1912), 259-261; R. Hertz, "'The Golden Bough,'" *Revue de l'Histoire des Religions*, lxvi (1912), 385-397; E. S. Hartland, "'Spirits of the Corn and of the Wild,'" *Man*, xiii (1913), 25-28, "'The Scapegoat,'" *Man*, xiv (1914), 86-88, "'Adonis, Attis, Osiris,'" *Man*, xiv (1914), 186-188.

archaeological commentary on *Mythology and Monuments of Ancient Athens* agreed as to the soundness of their etiological method of explaining myths.[30] That is, myths were regarded as invented explanations of rituals and religious ceremonies; hence —logically, if not chronologically—ritual precedes myth.[31] A second point impressively documented by *The Golden Bough* in the eyes of the early reviewers was that the primitive Aryan, as he is called by Frazer, is still alive today and that many of the savages' conceptions, including those concerning the supernatural, persist in numerous popular customs.[32]

The third point to impress the reviewers was the widespread influence of Darwin's views on evolution. According to *The Edinburgh Review*, "nowhere has the doctrine of evolutionary development produced a more remarkable change than in the point of view from which recent writers have approached the study of primitive ritual and beliefs."[33] This centrality of evolution to Frazer's thought was a point strongly emphasized by acquaintances such as H. J. Fleure and J. H. Hutton, H. N. Brailsford, and Bronislaw Malinowski.[34] They suggested that Frazer's conscious aim for his work as a whole was to build up a vast picture of the gradual development of the human mind and to draw a parallel between physical and mental evolution.

A final point of broad nature was made by nearly all Frazer's reviewers. They were all struck by the profound influence which such investigations of "the origin of human ideas and institutions, their causes and their tendencies, their genealogy and interconnexion" have had on "contemporary habits of thought."[35] But even beyond the immediate influence, it was repeatedly predicted that *The Golden Bough* would be of lasting service to the history of human thought.[36] Nor would it be limited to the pas-

---

[30] *The Nation*, LI (1890), 295; *The Quarterly Review*, CLXXI (1890), 127.

[31] *The Quarterly Review*, CLXXII (1891), 206.

[32] *The Nation*, LI (1890), 295; *The Athenaeum*, XCVI (1890), 156; H. N. Brailsford, *The New Statesman and Nation*, XXI (1941), 501; cf. *GB*, I, xii.

[33] *The Edinburgh Review*, CLXXII (1890), 538-539.

[34] *Nature*, CXLVII (1941), 635-636; *The New Statesman and Nation*, XXI (1941), 502; B. Malinowski, *A Scientific Theory of Culture* (Chapel Hill: University of North Carolina Press, 1944), pp. 187-188.

[35] *The Edinburgh Review*, CLXXII (1890), 538.

[36] *The Athenaeum*, CXIV (1901), 237.

sive role of a mere historical record. It was "bound to influence not only anthropological, but also philosophical thought for a considerable period,"[37] for it was "in this department of knowledge the greatest work produced in this generation."[38] Frazer stands with Marx and Freud, just behind Darwin as an influence on the thinking of the modern world. His greatest achievement was "to have resolutely collected and classified a vast mass of apparently heterogeneous material, not in order to support the pretensions of some one abstract explanation, some 'key to all mythologies,' but rather so as to transmit a concrete impression of an epoch of the human mind."[39] *The Golden Bough* is pregnant with suggestion for those who are prepared to ponder it well.[40] Frazer's amassing of empirical evidence was initially accumulative rather than constructive, but "in its whole result it is creative work of the superbest magnitude. That man's visions afford the leading clue to his cultural evolution could only be demonstrated massively, and he has done it."[41]

[III]

As the foregoing comments suggest, *The Golden Bough* constitutes a fertile matrix of ideas, observations, beliefs, and images on which not only the scientific anthropologists but also the scholars and creative minds of all fields of interest can draw. Like Freud's theories, however, it also had a diffused influence which operated virtually independently of the texts themselves. People doubtless learned of Frazer as they did of Freud, by word of mouth in casual conversations and impassioned artistic debates, but they also found him in reading scholars and popularizers influenced by him. What is most significant in this connection is the extent of that influence. Following its first edition, Frazer's ideas made themselves felt in nearly every area of the humanities and social sciences, including literary history and criticism. And it is to this extremely subtle, complex, and allusive kind of influence that the remainder of the chapter devotes itself.

---

[37] *The Athenaeum*, CXIV (1901), 236.
[38] *The Edinburgh Review*, CXCIV (1901), 362.
[39] *The Athenaeum*, CXXVII (1914), 6.
[40] *The Quarterly Review*, CCLXVII (1936), 28.
[41] *Nature*, CXLVII (1941), 635.

No attempt, of course, is made to trace in detail the whole panorama of Frazer's influence, for that is the subject for a study in itself. Yet even a broad superficial sketch will suffice to demonstrate that had an author of the 1900s or later no original interest in anthropology, he could scarcely have avoided its concepts which had been carried over to other fields. This acquaintance might in turn have drawn him to *The Golden Bough* itself. In any case Yeats, Eliot, Lawrence, and the rest were not dallying with wholly recondite lore or insignificant topics.

The writer as a human being naturally shares in the problems and hopes of mankind at large and possesses some measure of curiosity which culminates in the idle acquisition of information whether through direct experience or books. This alone would suffice to send many authors to books, including *The Golden Bough* and Frazer-influenced studies. This tendency, however, was intensified during the twentieth century, particularly its first quarter, for to many the age produced a sense of crisis. The staid, ordered calm and serenity of the Victorian and Edwardian eras seemed to be in the process of giving way to the chaos of World War I, revolutionary anarchy, and the wild gaiety of disillusionment. Consequently the search for explanations of the human situation was intensified, even as was the attempt to provide such explanations. For those who saw the answer to man's fate in the individual there were the new and startling revelations of psychoanalysis; for those who thought that the explanation was to be found in society there were political science and sociology; and for those who found meaning only in God there was religion. In each case the fundamental questions being asked were no different than they had ever been: what is man really like? what is the basis of society and what is its relation to the individual? what is God's nature and in what relation does man stand to Him? But new and often conflicting answers were being given to all these questions. And nowhere was twentieth-century man's dilemma revealed more dramatically than in history and ethics. Answers to the questions "what has happened?" and "how should man behave?" were essential if humanity were to endure.

The most striking feature of this situation is the fact that Frazer's influence was present in all the above fields as well as in anthropology and the classics, where he played a direct part. Even the most cursory glance at the writings of such men as Bergson, Toynbee, Spengler, Wells, Pareto, Durkheim, Westermarck, Wundt, Freud, Jung, and Sorokin, to mention but a few, reveals that they deal with topics, employ concepts, and frequently formulate solutions first developed by Frazer. It is, however, unlikely that *The Golden Bough* would have pervaded other disciplines had it not exerted a powerful influence on anthropology first. Indeed, to discuss all those early anthropologists and folklorists who, in Malinowski's phrase, "take their cues and orientations from Frazer—whether they agree or disagree with him"[42] would be to prepare a virtually complete bibliography of the field.

Some idea of the extent of Frazer's influence can be gained, however, from the fact that he was the driving inspiration and epistolary guide of the ethnographic field-work performed by such major figures as W.H.R. Rivers, C. G. Seligman, C. S. Myers, A. W. Howitt, the Reverend Fison, Sir Baldwin Spencer, and F. J. Gillen, as well as a host of lesser men. He himself had never been on a field trip and indeed was the leader of the armchair or, as Andrew Lang christened it, Covent Garden school of anthropology. All the more does his correspondence, full of queries and shrewd suggestions, testify to the respect with which he was regarded by his colleagues. Similarly, the studies of A. E. Crawley, E. S. Hartland, and Andrew Lang all reflect in varying degrees the opinions and basic attitudes of *The Golden Bough*. Thus, Crawley dedicates *The Mystic Rose* to Frazer "in gratitude and admiration" and calls *The Golden Bough* a "monumental work," declaring that it, "like Professor Tylor's *Primitive Culture*, marks an epoch in the study of man."[43] Even more significant than this praise is the assertion that his own study of the origin of marriage begins from Frazer's point about the primitive sense of the danger involved in the sexual act. And his own thesis is bolstered throughout by evidence and ideas drawn from *The Golden Bough*.[44] As early as 1894 E. S. Hartland in *The Legend of*

[42] Malinowski, p. 183.
[43] A. E. Crawley, *The Mystic Rose*, 4th ed. (London: Watts & Co., 1932), p. xiii. This preface is the same as that in the 1st edition of 1902.
[44] Crawley, pp. xiv, 9, 10, 15, 57, 93, 106, 120, 166, 175-176, 224, *passim*.

Perseus was acknowledging Frazer to be a distinguished anthropologist and his discussion of Attis to be acute and exhaustive at the same time that he was finding in *The Golden Bough* numerous illustrations of his own points.[45] And in both *Primitive Paternity* and *Ritual and Belief* he continued to use Frazer's interpretations and evidence while emphasizing aspects he felt had been overlooked.[46] But perhaps the most important single testimonial to Frazer's anthropological influence is that of his elder and friend, William Robertson Smith, to whom he dedicated *The Golden Bough*. In the preface to the first edition of his own epoch-making study, *The Religion of the Semites*, Smith comments on the great aid he had received from Frazer. And he goes on to remark that "I have sometimes referred to him by name, in the course of the book, but these references convey but an imperfect idea of my obligations to his learning and intimate familiarity with primitive habits of thought."[47]

Yet Frazer's influence was not restricted to his elders and contemporaries in anthropology.[48] For instance, the two collections

[45] E. S. Hartland, *The Legend of Perseus*, 3 vols. (London: D. Nutt, 1894-1896), I, 203; II, 30, 39, 44, 239n.

[46] E. S. Hartland, *Primitive Paternity*, 2 vols. (London: D. Nutt, 1909-1919), I, 89, 91, 97, 99, 100, 102; II, 127, 179n, 222; *Ritual and Belief* (London: Williams & Norgate, 1914), pp. xi, 64n, 68, 73, 143, 163, 167, *passim*.

[47] William Robertson Smith, *The Religion of the Semites*, ed. S. A. Cook, 3rd ed. (London: A. & C. Black, 1927), p. xvii. The intellectual relationship between Smith and Frazer was essentially reciprocal. See *GB*, I, xiv and *The Gorgon's Head* (London: Macmillan, 1927), pp. 278-290.

[48] Frazer's impact pervades and subtly molds rather than dictates the character of such studies as R. R. Marett's *Sacraments of Simple Folk* (Oxford: Clarendon Press, 1933), *Faith, Hope, and Charity in Primitive Religion* (New York: Macmillan Company, 1932), and *Head, Heart, and Hands in Primitive Evolution* (London: Hutchinson, 1935). This is also true of Bronislaw Malinowski's *Myth in Primitive Psychology* (New York: W. W. Norton & Co., 1926), *Argonauts of the Western Pacific* (London: G. Routledge & Sons, Ltd., 1932; New York: E. P. Dutton & Co., 1932), which contains a Preface by Frazer, *Sex and Repression in Savage Society* (London: K. Paul, Trench, Trubner & Co., Ltd., 1927; New York: Harcourt, Brace & Co., Inc., 1927), *The Father in Primitive Psychology* (London: K. Paul, Trench, Trubner & Co., Ltd., 1927), and the posthumous *Sex, Custom and Myth* (New York: Harcourt, Brace & World, 1962). Similarly, anthropological studies such as E. A. Westermarck's *Ritual and Belief in Morocco* (London: Macmillan and Co., Ltd., 1926) and E. O. James's *The Origins of Sacrifice* (London: J. Murray, 1937) were shaped by Frazer's

of essays edited by S. H. Hooke under the titles of *Myth and Ritual* and *The Labyrinth*, while exploring in considerable detail Babylonian, Assyrian, and Egyptian beliefs, rites, and customs, work in terms of patterns and concepts adumbrated in *The Golden Bough*. More recently, in a similar collection entitled *Myth, Ritual and Kingship* two contributors—G. Widengren and S.G.F. Brangdon—in assessing the British myth and ritual school started by Hooke, agree that "the influence of Frazer . . . is conspicuous everywhere" and that the movement is clearly "an intelligible derivation from the work of Frazer and the new estimate of the function of ritual and myth."[49] In addition, Brangdon ob-

---

views. The same is true of works more pointedly concerned with the study of religion, comparative or otherwise, such as G. B. Gray's *Sacrifice in the Old Testament* (Oxford: The Clarendon Press, 1925), W.O.E. Oesterley's *The Sacred Dance* (Cambridge: The University Press, 1923), and E. O. James's numerous works including *Christian Myth and Ritual* (London: J. Murray, 1933).

The above evidence should not, however, be taken to mean that Frazer was accepted uncritically as the final authority on all matters religious and anthropological. Early reviews have already been cited to suggest that such was very far from the case. In addition, there were a significant number of scholars, both professional and amateur, who criticized many of Frazer's views and interpretations with considerable vigor. Such criticism, of course, testifies in a particularly pointed way to the importance of the opinions espoused by *The Golden Bough*. The very amount of space devoted to their refutation indicates the measure of their persuasiveness for the scholarly and general intellectual audience of the early years of the twentieth century. Representative instances of such critical appraisals, which nevertheless stress Frazer's vital contributions to anthropology and comparative religion, are J. M. Robertson, *Pagan Christs* (London: Watts and Co., 1903), pp. xiv, 12, 13-14, 18, 19, 25, 114, 136-140, 320-321; Grant Allen, *The Evolution of the Idea of God* (London: Grant Richards, 1904), pp. v, 56, 59, 91, 138, 174, 228, 239, 246, 272-300, 312, 315, 336-346, 349-355; Irving King, *The Development of Religion* (New York: Macmillan, 1910), pp. 147, 151, 165-168, 189, 227, 228, 241, 243-246; E. Washburn Hopkins, *Origin and Evolution of Religion* (New Haven: Yale University Press, 1923), pp. 4, 5, 116-117, 120, 170; William Ridgeway, *The Dramas and Dramatic Dances of Non-European Races* (Cambridge: Cambridge University Press, 1915), pp. 13, 19, 22, 31, 35, 53, 57, 62, 86, 89, 119, 336, 340, 346, 385.

[49] G. Widengren, "Early Hebrew Myths and Their Interpretation," in *Myth, Ritual and Kingship*, ed. S. H. Hooke (Oxford: Oxford University Press, 1958), p. 152; S.G.F. Brangdon, "The Myth and Ritual Position Critically Considered," in *Myth, Ritual and Kingship*, p. 263. A similar view has been taken by the great Scandinavian religious scholar Sigmund Mowinckel in his *He That Cometh*, tr. G. W. Anderson (Oxford: Black-

serves of Frazer that "by reason of his prodigious labours in assembling material and in advancing certain hypotheses in the interpretation of it his name still remains, despite criticism and changing modes of thought, the most significant in this field of study."[50] Coming as it did in 1958, this assessment is revealing testimony of the continuing influence exercised by Frazer in his chief field of study.

Though undoubtedly most thoroughly known in England, *The Golden Bough* was far too central to the anthropology of the time not to be drawn on by scholars of other countries also. Some evidence of this is afforded by the frequency with which it and other of Frazer's works were translated into foreign languages. The second edition appeared in French in 1903-1911, while the third edition was translated in its entirety by 1931. The abridged edition was even more widely circulated, appearing in Swedish, Italian, and German during the 1920s.

In Germany, Frazer's influence was often of a rather negative kind, the German scholars arguing against his seemingly naive and simple theoretical framework. Yet despite this a number of individual and original thinkers were able to sift Frazer's work and to use it as a starting point for their own explorations. One of the earliest of these was K. T. Preuss in a series of articles in *Globus* for 1904-1905 and *Aus Natur und Geisteswelt* for 1914. Somewhat later and of rather more importance was Father William Schmidt, whose mammoth *Der Ursprung der Gottesidee* (1926-1935) is one of the few studies to rival Frazer in scope, though devoted to supporting rather than undermining Christianity's claims to supernatural sanctions and spiritual primacy. Another scholar of encyclopedic range is Richard Thurnwald, who developed out of Frazer's approach a position similar to that of Malinowski. More concerned with religion as an institution possessing contemporary significance are H. Frick's *Ideogramm*,

---

well, 1956) where he suggests that the English and American interest in the oriental concept of kingship derives from older ethnological and religious works and Frazer's books in particular (p. 23). *The Golden Bough*, he declares, p. 31, n. 8, "will always retain its worth, even if theories and interpretations change." He too thinks that the myth and ritual school has added to earlier investigations by "the combination of them with the views of Frazer and his school on primitive life and anthropology" (pp. 26-27).

[50] Brangdon, p. 262.

Mythologie und das Wort (1931) and Gerardus Van Der Leeuw's *Phänomenologie Der Religion* (1933).

In France the glancing mention of Frazer in Count Goblet d'Alviella's *L'Idée de Dieu* reveals both that his name was beginning to be known and that his influence was not yet widespread. The growth of Frazer's influence is dramatically underlined by comparing this study of d'Alviella's which appeared in 1892, with his *Croyances, Rites, Institutions* of 1911. An even more avowed advocate of *The Golden Bough*'s approach was Salomon Reinach whose numerous articles were collected under the title *Cultes, Mythes et Religions*. In dealing with problems in anthropology, comparative religion, and the classics, he drew not only on *The Golden Bough* for evidence and explanations but also on Frazer's other anthropological and classical studies.[51] Throughout he regarded himself as a popularizer of anthropological explanations and particularly of those espoused by the English school, whose most characteristic representative was *The Golden Bough*. A more scholarly attitude but one no less admiring of the achievements of English anthropologists including Frazer is found in the numerous books of Arnold van Gennep. Of these perhaps the most important is *Les Rites de Passage* which was to influence Jane Harrison and F. M. Cornford as well as more recent literary critics. In it, though he distinguishes between his "dynamist" approach to rites and that of Mannhardt and Frazer, nevertheless, he either accepts Frazer's views or draws on them for supporting examples far more often than he criticizes them.[52]

Perhaps the most closely knit and influential group in French anthropological and sociological circles was that headed by Emil Durkheim. As Kroeber remarks, Durkheim was "like most of his countrymen, more interested in sharp principles than in variety of comparative data."[53] It was, nevertheless, to a great extent Fra-

---

[51] See Salomon Reinach, *Cultes, Mythes et Religions*, 2nd ed., 4 vols. (Paris: Leroux, 1908-1923), I, vi, 10, 16, 51, 52, 60, 68, 180, 332-338; II, 88n, 89, 101, 102; IV, 24, 131 ff., *passim*.

[52] A. van Gennep, *Les Rites de Passage*, pp. 6-9, 22, 24, 28, 36-37, 49, 51, 91, 96, 100, 116, 126, 131, 161, *passim*. See also *Religions, Moeurs et Legendes*, pp. 13, 127, 146-147; *L'État actuel du Problème totémique* (Paris: Leroux, 1920), pp. 253, 266, 293, 319-320.

[53] Kroeber, p. 146.

zer's material as well as that of Spencer and Gillen from which he elaborated his "laws." This influence of *The Golden Bough* emerges most clearly in Durkheim's last book, *Les Formes Elémentaires de la Vie Religieuse*. There he, like Frazer, shows, for example, that the concrete forms of religion change but its essence remains, and that it was religion that molded heterogeneous individuals into a unified social system.[54]

[IV]

With its prominent position in anthropology firmly established, *The Golden Bough* began almost immediately to make its influence felt in classical studies. Probably the first to make extensive use of Frazer's ideas was Grant Allen, who in 1892 published a translation and edition of Catullus' long poem on Attis. Included in the edition were three essays, of which one dealt with the myth of Attis and one with the origin of tree-worship. In them he drew heavily on *The Golden Bough*, which he calls "a profound and epoch-making work" and a "learned and conclusive treatise" that cannot be ignored.[55] Allen's ideas are of less importance than is the swiftness with which he absorbed and applied the perspectives afforded classical literature by *The Golden Bough*. When

[54] See P. A. Sorokin, *Contemporary Sociological Theories* (New York: Harper, 1928), p. 474n, and *Social and Cultural Dynamics*, 4 vols. (New York: American Book Co., 1937-1941), IV, 357. Other works carrying on Durkheim's program and emphasis that received much impetus from Frazer were H. Hubert's and M. Mauss's *Mélanges d'Histoire des Religions* (Paris: F. Alcan, 1909), Arnold van Gennep's *Les Rites de Passage* (Paris: E. Nourry, 1909), and *L'Etat actuel du Problème totemique*, and perhaps best known of all to the average reader, Lucien Lévy-Bruhl's *Les Fonctions mentales dans les Sociétés inférieures* (Paris: Presses Universitaires de France, 1951), *La Mentalité primitive* (Oxford: Clarendon Press, 1931), and *L'Ame primitive* (Paris: F. Alcan, 1927 [2 ed.]). Studies more specifically devoted to comparative religion that drew on *The Golden Bough* and Frazer's other works were van Gennep's *La Formation des Legendes* (Paris: E. Flammarion, 1910) and *Religions, Moeurs et Legendes* (Paris: Société du Mercure de France, 1908-1914).

[55] Grant Allen, tr. & ed., *The Attis of Catullus* (London: D. Nutt, 1892), pp. 20, xi. His close familiarity with *The Golden Bough* is made clear by the frequent quotations from it and by his using of its information about such subjects as the myth of Attis, tree worship, the supply of primitive kings, the use of the king's son as a victim, food offerings to ghosts, and the hiding of the corn-spirit in the last sheaf of the crop. See pp. 20-28, 36, 49-51, 52-54, 60, 64, 65, 96, 104-108, 80, 117, 83-87, 113-114.

we remember that Frazer's first edition appeared only in 1890, the significance of Allen's use of it increases considerably.

Though Allen was perhaps the first to bring *The Golden Bough* to bear on the interpretation of the classics, he was considerably less important later than the four major figures in what came to be called the Cambridge School of Anthropology. Only one of these, Frazer himself, could really be termed an anthropologist. The others, Jane Harrison, Gilbert Murray, and F. M. Cornford, were classical scholars. As a result of *The Golden Bough*, however, they became interested in more than a purely philological approach to Greek literature and thought. The essence of their interest is indicated by Jane Harrison in the preface to her *Prolegomena to the Study of Greek Religion*. There she urges that ritual be studied for an understanding of the religion upon which the classics are founded but only as a means to a further end: "literature is really my goal. I have tried to understand primitive rites, not from love of their archaism, nor yet wholly from a single-minded devotion to science, but with the definite hope that I might come to a better understanding of some forms of Greek poetry."[56]

Similarly, Gilbert Murray drew on *The Golden Bough* for facts and the ritual emphasis in *The Rise of the Greek Epic* and *The Classical Tradition in Poetry* as well as in his individual studies of Euripides, Aristophanes, and Aeschylus. Because they were written for more popular audiences, these studies helped immeasurably in disseminating the ideas on myth and ritual of Frazer and the Cambridge School. The clearest example of how he wedded anthropological interests to classical studies is his contribution to Jane Harrison's *Themis*, which bears the revealing title "An Excursus on the Ritual Forms Preserved in Greek Tragedy." In it he develops in detail Frazer's point about the intimate connection of rites with myths or stories. And about the same time, F. M. Cornford, the youngest of the group, was arguing in his *Thucydides Mythistoricus* that the most prosaic and rational

---

[56] Jane Harrison, *Prolegomena to the Study of Greek Religion* (Cambridge: Cambridge University Press, 1903), p. vii; cf. her *Themis* (Cambridge: Cambridge University Press, 1912), pp. xx-xxi. See also Gilbert Murray, *A History of Ancient Greek Literature* (London: Heinemann, 1897), pp. xiv-xv.

of Greek historians ordered his narratives in accord with the dramatic form of tragedy. The extent of his indebtedness to Frazer's orientation is seen, for example, in his insistence that the story of Miltiades' disgrace is really a temptation myth and that this can be understood only by the study of mythical types.[57] An even more important illustration of *The Golden Bough*'s impact was his full-length examination of myth and ritual in literature, *The Origin of Attic Comedy*. To carry over this approach from the classics to modern languages was but a step once the initial use of ritual had been established. And in 1914 Murray took this step when he delivered the British Academy's annual Shakespeare lecture on *Hamlet and Orestes, a Study in Traditional Types*. Where readers had hitherto considered Greek ritual and religion through its literature, they were now being taught, at least by implication, to read all literature as ritual forms.[58]

Miss Harrison, Murray, and Cornford provided the impetus that introduced Frazer and *The Golden Bough* into classical circles. Once they had done so they were quickly joined by other scholars who were either attracted by the potentialities of their

[57] F. M. Cornford, *Thucydides Mythistoricus* (London: Edward Arnold, 1907), p. 164.

[58] This group may have affected the nature of modern literature and criticism in other ways as well. It is significant that I. A. Richards in *The Meaning of Meaning*, 10th ed. (London: Kegan Paul, 1956), pp. 26, 31-32, should refer approvingly to Cornford's remarks on language and that following the publication of Richards' *Mencius on the Mind* (1932), which is subtitled "Experiments in Multiple Definition," Cornford should begin his series of translations of Plato, which attempted to supply the exact shade of the philosopher's meaning through commentaries integrated into the text. In turn, Richards devoted a chapter in his study of *Coleridge on Imagination* (1934) to "The Boundaries of the Mythical."

Similarly, Miss Harrison's strong attraction to the plastic arts may have contributed to a growing interest in their interaction with literature. Her earliest works were *Introductory Studies in Greek Art* (1885) and *Greek Vase Paintings* (1894), fused her twin interests in both its title and content. In the *Prolegomena* and *Themis* she continually interprets religious rites and literary passages in the light of a series of statues and paintings. Her approach is almost invariably visual, concentrating on the actual physical image as a means of focussing both her thoughts and emotions. Such a method possesses obviously suggestive analogies both to the point of view of imagism, especially its classically oriented members like H. D., and to the sophisticated iconographical techniques of such scholars as Erwin Panofsky and G. R. Kernodle.

approach or else unable to ignore its facts and general relevance. The most important of those in the former category was A. B. Cook, also a Cambridge man, whose *Zeus, A Study in Ancient Religion* consists of several cumbersome but fascinating volumes which completely exhaust their subject. Equally learned but less sympathetic to the looseness with which Miss Harrison and Murray were inclined to approach their material was the Oxford scholar L. R. Farnell. In his *magnum opus, The Cults of the Greek States*, he pays handsome tribute to the new interest and fruitful research in Greek myth and ritual Cambridge has generated. He acknowledges the valuable assistance he received from the work of Robertson Smith, Frazer, and Andrew Lang. At the same time he points out that his own work has a different aim from theirs, namely, "to disentangle myth from religion, only dealing with the former so far as it seems to illustrate or reveal the latter."[59] Both here and in his other works, such as *The Evolution of Religion, Greek Hero Cults and Ideas of Immortality*, he draws on Frazer's store of facts for evidence and illustration while avoiding the more speculative hypotheses advanced by Murray and Miss Harrison.

Though the anthropological approach to classical studies has been severely challenged in recent years, as the works of Pickard-Cambridge and W.K.C. Guthrie suggest, it has still continued to produce lively and provocative studies. Thus, George Thomson, though writing from an avowedly Marxian standpoint in his *Aeschylus and Athens*, admits that the Cambridge School's writings provided him with much that was central to his method and thesis. Rhys Carpenter, writing of an even more remote period in his *Folk Tale, Fiction, and Saga in the Homeric Epics*, quotes and otherwise draws on *The Golden Bough* for his analysis of the cult of the sleeping bear. An even more thoroughgoing use of the anthropological approach has recently been provided by E. R. Dodds in *The Greeks and the Irrational*. In his preface he gives what is probably the most succinct and lucid, yet modest, answer to those who would object to this approach either in the classics or in modern literatures. He declares: "Tylor's ani-

[59] L. R. Farnell, *The Cults of the Greek States*, 6 vols. (Oxford: Clarendon Press, 1896-1909), I, viii; see also vii, ix.

mism, Mannhardt's vegetation-magic, Frazer's year-spirits, Codrington's mana, have all helped in their day to illuminate dark places in the ancient record. They have also encouraged many rash guesses. But time and the critics can be trusted to deal with the guesses; the illumination remains."[60]

This last sentence applies admirably to the most thoroughly literary of these anthropologically orientated classical studies, Robert W. Cruttwell's *Virgil's Mind at Work*. Subtitled "An Analysis of the Symbol of the 'Aeneid,' " it draws heavily on *The Golden Bough* and Frazer's classical editions for justification and illumination of its extraordinarily close reading of Virgil's text. Antedating Cruttwell and proving an influential ground-breaker for his work was W. F. Jackson Knight, the brother of the well-known Shakesperian critic G. Wilson Knight. In three books, *Vergil's Troy*, *Cumaean Gates*, and *Roman Vergil*, which appeared between 1932 and 1944, he explored various aspects of Vergil's art and thought. The most noteworthy of these for our purposes was the ritual pattern of initiation in the *Aeneid*, especially in Book VI, which Knight worked out with the aid of substantial familiarity with anthropological researches, particularly those of *The Golden Bough*. The persistence of this Frazer-generated approach, with its emphasis on the aesthetic relevance of myth and ritual, is demonstrated by Jack Lindsay's recent study *The Clashing Rocks*, which examines early Greek religion and culture in an effort to arrive at "a coherent theory of the nature and origin of Tragedy and Comedy, their relation to the struggles of both the dark ages and the posthomeric world."[61] He testifies to his conscious reliance on the work of the Cambridge School as well as to his awareness of the strictures levelled at its views when he remarks:

> My mind has been playing round these problems ever since I read Jane Harrison some fortyfive years ago. . . . I have called my positions new and challenging, and I think that is correct. At the same time I feel, humbly enough, that my book belongs

[60] E. R. Dodds, *The Greeks and the Irrational* (Berkeley: University of California Press, 1951), p. viii.

[61] Jack Lindsay, *The Clashing Rocks* (London: Chapman & Hall, 1965), p. 3.

to the line of English works in cultural anthropology that was largely founded by Jane Harrison and extended by thinkers like Cornford, Cook, and others. This great school is rather out of fashion today in England; and I am therefore all the happier in making a gesture of piety towards it.[62]

While archaeology deserves a large share of the credit for the nineteenth and twentieth centuries' increased understanding of the classics, it is nevertheless somewhat surprising to find it also showing Frazer's influence. Thus, one of his suggestions is worked out in detail and demonstrated conclusively by D. Randall-MacIver in *Italy Before the Romans*, a work that D. H. Lawrence, for one, was to peruse with care. Similarly, R.A.S. Macalister, a celebrated authority on archaeology, particularly that of Ireland, acknowledges his debt to Frazer and A. B. Cook in *Tara: A Pagan Sanctuary of Ancient Ireland*, a work that helps illuminate *Finnegans Wake*. A semipopular work further demonstrates Frazer's influence in this field. W. H. Matthews, a folklore enthusiast and amateur archaeologist, draws on *The Golden Bough* in *Mazes and Labyrinths*, a study of the labyrinth from earliest times down to recent examples such as Hampton Court. Still more recently, G. R. Levy has brought together anthropology and archaeology in an effort to illuminate prehistory generally and the Bronze Age and the origins of the epic in particular.

[V]

Impressive though it is, Frazer's influence on anthropology and classics is hardly surprising. The full measure of its seminal role is appreciated only when the degree to which it extends outside its own special domain is seen. Particularly receptive to the material and insights of *The Golden Bough* were psychology and sociology together with their offshoots, psychoanalysis and social psychology. In Germany, Wilhelm Wundt, one of the first to develop experimental psychology, also grasped the significance of anthropology for psychology. He explored their relationships at some length in his *Völkerpsychologie* and also in *Elemente der Völkerpsychologie*. While developing an elaborate framework

[62] Lindsay, pp. 3-4.

that was vastly more theoretic and schematic than anything in *The Golden Bough*, he also acknowledged the great merit and wealth of detail in Frazer's study, from which he drew considerable evidence for his own complex theories.[63] It also provided him with certain concepts such as the development of humanity through universal and distinct stages, the connection of totemism and animism, the essentially theistic character of religion, and the intimate connections between myth and ritual.

A work by a more controversial and celebrated figure was *Totem and Taboo*, Freud's first excursion into what might be called psychical anthropology. In it Freud followed out his own and Jung's earlier observations of the connections between neurotics and primitive peoples. Unlike Abraham's earlier *Traum und Mythus*, Freud did not draw on mid-nineteenth-century German mythologists. Instead, as he remarks in his autobiographical essay, "the chief literary sources of my studies in this field were the well-known works of J. G. Frazer ('Totemism and Exogamy' and 'The Golden Bough'), a mine of valuable facts and opinions."[64] As we would expect, Freud's theory of totemism was considerably different from the views advanced by Frazer. This, however, is due to his having added the Oedipus complex rather than to any fundamental break with his anthropological guide. For both men the totem was linked to the soul or those feelings of reverence, awe, and fear experienced by man when thinking of death and its significance.[65] In particular, Freud followed Frazer's stress on the tribal custom of individuals assuming the name of their totem.[66]

In addition, *Totem and Taboo* together with his general theo-

[63] W. Wundt, *Elements of Folk Psychology*, tr. E. L. Schaub (New York: Macmillan, 1916), pp. 38, 152, 189-90; *Völkerpsychologie* (Leipzig: W. Engelmann, 1905-1906), I, 541; II, 16, 17, 23, 32, 39, 180, 190-191, 208, 243, 245, 247, 248, 256, 264, 268, 306, 325, 329, 339, 407, 445; IV, 16, 94, 102, 116, 264n, 277, 295, 331, 333, 336, 344, 345, 357, 396, 416, 420, 499, 500, 540.

[64] Sigmund Freud, *The Problem of Lay-Analyses*, tr. J. Strachey (New York: Brentano's, 1927), p. 308.

[65] Freud, of course, denies, pp. 308-309, that Frazer's views were of any assistance, but he was deceived by the differences in terminology and so failed to see those broader concepts which link him to Frazer.

[66] H. L. Philp, *Freud and Religious Belief* (London: Isaac Pitman, 1956), p. 50.

ries provided the impetus for a number of studies which, though essentially psychoanalytic, availed themselves of mythical topics and anthropological data. Indeed, most psychoanalysts seem to prefer the ritual theory of mythology with its stress on man's elaborate concern with fertility in its various forms, a theory first popularized by Frazer.[67] Nor is this psychoanalytic interest in Frazer confined to Freudians. In 1912 Jung paralleled the Darwinian cast of Frazer's mind when he proclaimed in the subtitle that his *Wandlugen und Symbole der Libido* was "a contribution to the history of the evolution of thought." And in tracing out the unconscious origin of the hero, the nature of his sacrifice, and his rebirth he drew on Frazer's facts and central contentions as well as on many of the literary texts cited by Frazer. And in his more recent *Symbolik des Geistes* he followed *The Golden Bough*'s views on tree worship, the external soul, and the connection between Old Testament and certain primitive rites.[68]

At the same time, there was also a trend in traditional psychology toward the explanation of the origin, nature, and function of religion. One of the first to approach this topic was James H. Leuba, who as early as 1896 was writing on the subject in the *American Journal of Psychology*. His most ambitious book, *A Psychological Study of Religion*, drew not only on Frazer but also on other writers, such as Durkheim, Crawley, Hartland, and Wundt, who had been influenced by Frazer in their own right. Both here and in his smaller and more popular study, *The Psychological Origin and the Nature of Religion*, he relied on *The Golden Bough* for much of his data and basic orientation, though this did not prevent him from correcting what he regarded as Frazer's theoretical inadequacies. A few years later his *Belief in God and Immortality* was heavily dependent on Frazer's *Belief*

[67] See, e.g., R. Money-Kyrle, *Superstition and Society* (London: Hogarth Press, 1939), *The Development of the Sexual Impulses* (London: Kegan Paul, 1932), *The Meaning of Sacrifice* (London: Hogarth Press, 1930), and J. C. Flugel, *Men and their Motives* (London: Routledge, 1934). See also Roheim's *Australian Totemism* (London: Allen & Unwin, 1925), and *The Riddle of the Sphinx* (London: Hogarth Press, 1934) as well as Reik's trilogy on Biblical myths and motifs.

[68] See C. G. Jung, *Symbolik des Geistes* (Zurich: Rascher, 1948), pp. 73, 198, 216, 308.

in Immortality. In his later work *God or Man?*, which is more broadly cultural in character, he continued to refer favorably to Frazer as possessing unrivalled knowledge of uncivilized man. The same general attitude is to be found in E. S. Ames's *Psychology of Religious Experience* whose method, the author says, involves the history of religion. He, too, drew on *The Golden Bough* for evidence, illustrations, or ideas. Another work on the same general subject, but written by a doctor rather than a psychologist, is D. Forsyth's *Psychology and Religion*. Its author declares that the stimulus for the entire book is to be found in the writings of Frazer and Freud. These are but a few of the works in this field, but they suffice to indicate clearly that *The Golden Bough* was neither unknown nor unimportant in its researches.[69] It is not without significance that the psychology of religion had its real beginnings about 1900, only a few years after the first, and at almost the same time as the second, edition of Frazer's great work.

Frazer himself never really became cognizant of the social dimension implicit in his study of mythology, customs, and beliefs. His work nevertheless provided a challenge to the young and growing discipline of sociology. Attention has already been called to Frazer's influence on Durkheim and his associates, who dominated French sociology. A somewhat similar figure in England was E. A. Westermarck, whose writings included not only anthropological but also sociological and philosophical studies. Thus, for example, his *History of Human Marriage* was anthropological in approach, being specifically indebted to Frazer, and sociological in subject. He also reflected and drew explicitly on *The Golden Bough*'s interpretations and data in his later work, *Early Beliefs and their Social Influence*, a book whose title suggests its sociological interests.

The Russian-born sociologist, Pitirim Sorokin, shows similar familiarity with Frazer's work. In his survey *Contemporary Sociological Theories* he not only accepted specific ideas from Fra-

---

[69] See also J. B. Pratt, *The Religious Consciousness* (New York: Macmillan, 1920), F. C. Bartlett, *Psychology and Primitive Culture* (New York: Macmillan, 1923), I. King, *The Development of Religion* (New York: Macmillan, 1910), and W. A. Brend, *Sacrifice to Attis* (London: Heinemann, 1936).

zer but used them to refute individuals such as Ludwig Gumplo-
wicz and the geographical school. In addition, though aware of
Frazer's methodological and logical naïveté, he praised his efforts
to study the forces that shape and control social phenomena and
pointed out that field-studies have corroborated many of his assertions and theories. The same extensive reliance on Frazer for
knowledge about primitive peoples is present also in his *Social
Mobility* and *Principles of Rural-Urban Sociology*. Equally noteworthy in the latter is the use of the comparative method to establish the beliefs and mental capacities of rural and agricultural
groups. While used less emphatically and consistently, *The Gold-
en Bough* still appears as a part of Sorokin's thought in the more
recent and more speculative *Social and Cultural Dynamics*. Nor
is he alone in perceiving Frazer's relevance to the study of society. W. G. Sumner and A. G. Keller drew numerous insights
from *The Golden Bough* for their mammoth work *The Science
of Society*, and in addition recommended it as both vitally significant and highly readable.[70]

[VI]

From the practical descriptions of sociology to the more theoretical concerns of ethics and philosophy in general was but the
briefest of steps for many thinkers in the early years of this century. Because philosophy then was still closer to the humanities
than the sciences, it quickly came to show signs of acquaintance
with *The Golden Bough* and related anthropological studies.
Thus, it was to be expected that Westermarck would bring his
Frazer-oriented research into primitive beliefs and institutions
to his writing of *The Origin and the Development of the Moral
Ideas*. A quarter of a century later, when his *Ethical Relativity*

[70] P. Sorokin, *Contemporary Sociological Theories*, pp. 54, 168, 172, 412,
474n, 486, 662, 669n, 688; *Social Mobility* (New York: Harper, 1927), pp.
96, 105-106, 222, 248, 271; *Principles of Rural-Urban Sociology* (New York:
Holt, 1929), pp. 295, 395, 435-436, 439, 489, 496; *Social and Cultural Dynamics*, IV, 169n, 175, 357, 463. W. G. Sumner & A. G. Keller, *The Science
of Society* (New Haven: Yale University Press, 1927), I, xxvii, 492, 507; II,
791, 800, 802, 810, 861-862, 874, 887, 891-892, 957, 1027, 1055, 1098, 1109, 1123,
1147, 1157, 1178-1179, 1212, 1216, 1306, 1312, 1326, 1449; III, 1502, 1549, 1552,
1607, 1713, 2194. The pagination of these volumes is consecutive rather
than by volume.

appeared, it advocated the same approach and basic ideas. In both works, the influence of *The Golden Bough* can be seen from such concepts as the uniform nature of the moral consciousness, its derivation from society rather than from the individual conscience, the presence of moral valuation in all peoples regardless of degree of enlightenment, and the part played by custom in giving moral judgments the appearance of objectivity. Another philosopher similarly influenced was L. T. Hobhouse, whose *Morals in Evolution* applied the comparative method to ethical phenomena in an attempt to trace their evolving development.

The same kind of sustained interest in bringing the findings of anthropology and psychology to bear on ethics and social philosophy was exhibited by Carveth Read, who pursued the subject in several books during the first quarter of the twentieth century. Thus, in *Natural and Social Morals* (1909) he admitted that "my work is of a transitionary character, revising and illustrating the old philosophical Ethics in the light of the inductive biology, Psychology and Anthropology that have lately been established according to the methods of physical science."[71] And in declaring that one of his central working assumptions was that most religious beliefs are a natural growth of human society, he made clear that the main body of evidence for this view was drawn from *The Golden Bough* as well as Tylor's *Primitive Culture*.[72] Frazer's impress is particularly noticeable in the chapter "Religion and Morals," especially the first third, where he traces the belief in supernatural powers to a conviction of the existence of an underlying impersonal force or energy, to a belief in ghosts, and to a belief in contagious magic.[73] The influence of Frazer as well as Westermarck continued paramount in *The Origin of Man and of His Superstitions* (1920). Read explicitly acknowledges their extensive use and demonstrates it in his discussions of the three stages of primitive society, which clearly resemble those of Frazer, the useful and necessary character of superstitions, and the priority of magic over religion.[74] Nor was his familiarity with

[71] Carveth Read, *Natural and Social Morals* (London: A. & C. Black, 1909), pp. xi-xii.
[72] Read, p. 16.   [73] Read, pp. 218-219.
[74] Carveth Read, *The Origin of Man and of his Superstitions* (Cambridge:

Frazer confined to *The Golden Bough*. The second edition of *Man and His Superstitions* (1925), for instance, contains references not only to most of the volumes of *The Golden Bough* but also to *The Belief in Immortality, Totemism and Exogamy, Psyche's Task*, and Frazer's edition of Pausanias.[75]

Though ethics in general has of recent years followed G. E. Moore into linguistic considerations rather than Westermarck, Hobhouse, and Read into anthropology, two related areas—philosophy of religion and philosophy of culture—have continued to draw upon the classical anthropologists. Indeed, two of Frazer's closest followers produced works on the interrelation of ancient religion and philosophy. Gilbert Murray's *Five Stages of Greek Religion* and *Stoic Philosophy* and F. M. Cornford's *From Religion to Philosophy, Before and After Socrates*, and *Unwritten Philosophy*, all reflect what their authors had learned from *The Golden Bough*. Their concern with the developing stages of consciousness and belief, the connection between rational speculation and religious impulse, and the relation of ritual to a world view suggest the extent to which Frazer influenced their novel approach to the problems of classical thought.

Representative examples of Frazer's influence on what is more specifically the philosophy of religion are *Religion in Essence and Manifestation* by G. Van Der Leeuw and *Studies in the Philosophy of Religion* by A. A. Bowman. The former employs many concepts given currency by Frazer, such as totemism, taboo, the connection of vegetative and human fertility, the king as a figure of religious power, and the differences between priest and magician. These are wrought into a phenomenological pattern as highly speculative as it is sophisticated. The same is true of the more recent *Sacred and Profane Beauty*, which attempts to indicate the relation of art to religion from the vantage point of comparative religion and anthropology. Bowman, on the other hand, is less allusive in his treatment of Frazer, for he devotes one of the

---

Cambridge University Press, 1920), pp. v-vi, 109, but see also pp. 194, 293, 302-304.

[75] Carveth Read, *Man and His Superstitions*, 2nd ed. (Cambridge: Cambridge University Press, 1925), pp. 31, 39, 64, 65, 71, 78, 92, 95, 101, 102, 106, 115, 123-124, 132, 149, 166, 173, 186, 195, 196, 198, 207, 209, 223.

four parts of his work to "the anthropological picture of religion" and there analyzes the views of such authors as Frazer, Jane Harrison, Robertson Smith, and Durkheim for ideas and insights central to an overall philosophy of religion.[76]

A better-known philosopher who also was influenced by Frazer is Henri Bergson, whose chapters on static and dynamic religion in *Les Deux Sources de la Morale et de la Religion*, for example, are permeated by the Cambridge School's basic attitudes. And of these philosophers of culture who have seen the contemporary importance of primitive modes of life and thought the most influential is Ernst Cassirer. In the course of such works as *An Essay on Man, The Myth of the State*, and *Language and Myth* he draws on Frazer directly, though with the inevitable criticisms of his philosophical naïveté, and also indirectly through the influence of Frazer-influenced scholars like Robertson Smith, Bowman, Bergson, Durkheim, and Malinowski.[77] Similarly, James Feibleman's *Theory of Human Culture* emphasizes Frazer as a compiler of data while applying his interpretation of the scapegoat and drawing on his view of magic.

As for the other branches of philosophy, such as aesthetics, epistemology and metaphysics, they have made little direct use of *The Golden Bough* and related studies. Their level of abstractness is at odds with the peculiarly concrete and descriptive character of Frazer's writings. Nevertheless, we should not exaggerate the incompatability into a complete lack of interaction. Gilbert Ryle has suggested recently that Frazer's work was a stimulus to "the theoretical imbroglios" of twentieth-century philosophy.[78] This view is at least partly corroborated for his own philosophical position by Santayana's observation that "such investigations as those of Frazer and of Freud have shown how

[76] Indicative of the influence of Frazer and the classical evolutionists in anthropology is the fact that though this book did not appear until 1938, its anthropological material was being gathered as early as 1924. See N. Kemp Smith, ed., *Studies in the Philosophy of Religion*, by A. A. Bowman (London: Macmillan, 1938), I, xxx.

[77] See David Bidney, *Theoretical Anthropology* (New York: Columbia University Press, 1953), pp. 315-317, who also indicates tangentially how Cassirer differed from Frazer in outlook.

[78] Gilbert Ryle, *The Revolution in Philosophy* (London: Macmillan, 1956), p. 3.

rich and how mad a thing the mind is fundamentally, how pervasively it plays about animal life, and how remote its first and deepest intuitions are from any understanding of their true occasions."[79] Recently an even more striking illustration of Ryle's assertion has appeared upon the publication of Ludwig Wittgenstein's "Bemerkungen Über Frazers 'The Golden Bough.' "[80] These hitherto unpublished notes were apparently drafted at two different periods in Wittgenstein's career, the first between 1930 and 1931 and the second "not earlier than 1936 and probably after 1948."[81] That probably the most influential modern philosopher should have turned to *The Golden Bough* at such widely separated points in his career is in itself significant testimony of Frazer's capacity to engage the attention of thinkers of all persuasions and interests. Naturally, Wittgenstein was critical of Frazer, especially in his theorizing activity. At the same time, the fertility of suggestion in the specific details of *The Golden Bough* generated in Wittgenstein a series of reflections that show clearly how astute was Ryle's appraisal of Frazer's role in shaping the direction of modern philosophy. Finally, additional evidence of Frazer's possible relevance to philosophers appears in the Marxist Georg Lukacs' *Die Eigenart des Ästhetischen*, in the first volume of which, especially, he draws liberally on Frazer for evidence and illustration.[82]

[VII]

By contrast with philosophy, history was able to make substantially more use of Frazer's approach and data. Yet ironically enough, the first historian to discuss Frazer, A. W. Benn in *The History of English Rationalism*, bracketed him with his philosophical contemporaries, Bradley, McTaggart, and Moore. More significant from the standpoint of history, however, is the fact

[79] George Santayana, "A General Confession," in *The Philosophy of George Santayana*, ed. P. A. Schilp (Evanston: Northwestern University Press, 1940), p. 18.

[80] *Synthese*, XVII (1967), 233-253.

[81] *Synthese*, XVII, 234. The editorial comment is that of R. Rhees.

[82] Georg Lukacs, *Die Eigenart des Ästhetischen* (Neuwied Am Rheid: Luchterhand, 1963), Band 11, 97, 99-100, 103, 105, 111, 254, 378, 379, 401, 416, 452, 455; Band 12, 784.

that Spengler's *Decline of the West*, one of the most provocative and widely discussed books of the post-World War I era, was influenced by Frazer.[83] Though he did not refer directly to Frazer, Spengler did develop topics, such as the ritual character of Greek drama, the emphasis on primitive cultures, the development of Christianity out of pagan cults, the kinds and implications of myth, and the relation of man to nature, which are also dealt with in *The Golden Bough* and in much the same manner. A more recent historical work, fully as encyclopedic and speculative as Spengler's, that has also been influenced by Frazer and *The Golden Bough* is Arnold Toynbee's *A Study of History*. Like Frazer, Toynbee employs the comparative method, quasi-psychological concepts, and patterns of myth which provide clues to the final explanation of the phenomena of civilizations. Even more clear-cut is his use of Frazer's material in the section devoted to the relation between disintegrating civilizations and individuals. Here he discusses such figures as the creative genius as a savior, the savior with the sword, and the god incarnate in a man.

Though both Spengler and Toynbee became well known outside their own field, their works are really too large and too abstruse for many readers. A more readable introduction to Frazer's ideas in a historical context is that immensely popular book, *The Outline of History* by H. G. Wells. The pages on primitive thought reflect *The Golden Bough*'s emphasis on the part played by fear in early religion, its vegetative character, and the making of myths. And more explicitly Frazer himself is called "the leading student of the derivation of sacraments from magic sacrifices."[84] Following Wells's initial popularization of history and prehistory, a number of studies appeared, designed to introduce the common reader to the earliest sources of his culture. Among the

[83] Malinowski, *A Scientific Theory of Culture*, p. 184.
[84] H. G. Wells, *The Outline of History* (New York: Macmillan, 1921), I, 131. Other writers connected with Frazer who are drawn on are A. E. Crawley, Grant Allen, F. J. Jevons, and Andrew Lang. Similarly, both Freud's *Totem and Taboo* and Jung's *Psychology of the Unconscious*, Frazer-influenced works, are commended highly. Nor should it be overlooked that Gilbert Murray was one of those who provided advice and editorial help.

most erudite and interesting of these were Christopher Dawson's *Age of the Gods* and *Progress and Religion*. A historian of strong Roman Catholic convictions, Dawson analyzes and speculates on the relations between religion and culture. Though critical of some of the views of evolutionary anthropologists such as Frazer, he nevertheless is deeply indebted to *The Golden Bough* for many of his ideas. This is most clearly seen through his interest in the connections of primitive art and ritual, the importance of the individual for religious development, the religious significance of taboos on the priest-king, and the ritual drama as also an economic agricultural cycle. A more recent work of the same general order is Henry Bamford Parkes's *Gods and Men*, which seeks "to re-evaluate the Judaeo-Hellenic origins of our cultural heritage."[85] Especially in his first chapter he mirrors a number of the central contentions of *The Golden Bough*. Among these are the persistence of tribal attitudes in later civilizations, the inadequacy of pure rationalism and the cultural necessity of myths, the preeminence of ritual for religion, and the antiquity of killing and eating the god.

Some of these introductions were simply summaries and pastiches of work already done, as in the case of C. G. Shaw's *Trends of Civilization and Culture*.[86] Others developed hypotheses of their own which often had the merits of ingenuity if not always of plausibility. Representative here are J. H. Denison's *Emotion as the Basis of Civilization* and a series of books by Gerald Heard including *The Ascent of Humanity*, *The Social Substance of Religion*, *The Source of Civilization*, and *Is God in History?*[87] Yet in both groups, as the works mentioned indicate, *The*

[85] Henry Bamford Parkes, *Gods and Men* (London: Routledge & Kegan Paul, 1960), p. v.

[86] He leans heavily on Tylor and Frazer in his discussion of such topics as the natural and the supernatural, animism, magic, survivals of primitive belief, and the psychology of the religious consciousness despite his conviction that comparative religion "has given us cross sections of human belief instead of the linear development and historical trend." See *Trends of Civilization and Culture* (New York: American Book Co., 1932), p. 475.

[87] Others of the same highly speculative historical nature include Margaret Murray's studies such as *The God of the Witches* (London: Faber & Faber, 1931), rev. ed. 1952, and *The Divine King in England* (London: Faber & Faber, 1944); Hugh Ross Williamson's *The Arrow and the Sword*

Golden Bough was steadily drawn on both for facts and illustrations and also for general concepts useful in rearing elaborate theories.[88] The same is true in certain areas of literary history ranging from medieval and Renaissance studies to American culture, from Jessie Weston to F. O. Matthiessen and Richard Chase.[89]

[VIII]

In the light of this sketch of the humanities and social sciences, cursory though it is, it is clear that the creative artist interested in the fate of himself and his age could, like the educated layman, have avoided becoming aware of *The Golden Bough* only with great difficulty. For whether he placed his faith in the individual, society, or God, and whether he was concerned with what had been or what should be, the definition and character of each had been affected by the great anthropological pattern revealed in all its complexity and awe-inspiring strangeness by Frazer. In addition, the significance of this pattern was intensified by such diverse pressures, impinging separately and in concert, as those of Darwinism, global wars, modern science, urban industrialization, and economic depressions. An abiding interest in the myth and ritual of anthropology is as integral a part of modern literature as is its involvement with psychoanalysis and Marxism, and came about for essentially the same reasons. Thus, for literature Frazer

---

(London: Faber & Faber, 1947); and Flavia Anderson's *The Ancient Secret* (London: Gollancz, 1953).

[88] Such theories need not even be one's own but may be those of others whom in turn one has influenced, so that Frazer registers his impact on a mind and theory indirectly as well as directly. An instance of this, possibly, is Denison's transmission of Frazer's ideas to Kenneth Burke. Denison's stress on the value and cultivation of certain emotions for social construction and a successful civilization, his interest in exploring the strategies of social relations, and his use of suggestive chapter subtitles like "The Symbolism of the Kingship" and "The Drama of Representation," all would have been of great interest to Burke.

[89] See, e.g., Jessie L. Weston, *The Legend of Sir Lancelot du Lac* (London: D. Nutt, 1901), p. 72; *The Legend of Sir Perceval* (London: D. Nutt, 1906-1909), I, 330, 332, II, 251-252; H. V. Routh, *Man, God and Epic Poetry* (Cambridge: Cambridge University Press, 1927), I, 57 n. 4; C. S. Lewis, *The Allegory of Love* (Oxford: Oxford University Press, 1936), p. 120; F. O. Matthiessen, *American Renaissance* (New York: Oxford University Press, 1941), p. 73; G. Wilson Knight, *The Golden Labyrinth* (New York: Norton, 1962), p. xi.

is as fully seminal a mind as Freud or Marx. Eliot was not operating in an intellectual vacuum nor indulging in personal idiosyncrasies when he declared that *The Golden Bough* had influenced his generation profoundly. Rather he was stating a truth about man's mind, that it is, in Cornford's phrase, "like a pool in one continuous medium—the circumambient atmosphere of his place and time."[90] And in the first half of the twentieth century one of the most pervasive aspects of its atmosphere has been Frazer's suggestive exploration of what Eliot has called an "abysm of time."[91]

[90] Cornford, *Thucydides Mythistoricus*, p. viii.
[91] T. S. Eliot, "A Prediction in Regard to Three English Authors," *Vanity Fair*, XXI (1924), 29.

CHAPTER IV

The Golden Bough:
Impact
and Archetype

[I]

Significant as content and publication date are for the literary impact of *The Golden Bough*, nevertheless they leave us with an unanswered question. Why should it have been Frazer's study rather than some other work in anthropology and comparative religion that shaped modern English and American literature? Why, for instance, did not L. R. Farnell's *Cults of the Greek States* or A. B. Cook's *Zeus*, volumes equally encyclopedic and equally packed with ancient lore, acquire the same kind of status in the literary world? The content of all three is much of a piece and all were published in roughly the same decade. The explanation, then, must lie in what can be called the literary reason. Essentially, this reason has three major and interrelated aspects: the style, structure, and genre of *The Golden Bough*.

Since they stand in a diminishing order of obviousness, it is best perhaps to begin with the first. The Latinate diction, the judicious employment of periodic sentences, the eloquent peroration, the handling of sustained analogies, the apposite allusions, the leisurely development of paragraphs—all stamp *The Golden Bough* as a magnificently sustained example of the grand style and of what Sir Herbert Read has called the central tradition of English prose.[1] And though it is obviously not the dominant style of the twentieth century, it is clearly the only appropriate rhetorical mode for that study which Frazer himself called "an

[1] Sir Herbert Read, *English Prose Style* (New York: Pantheon Books, 1952), pp. 186, 191-193.

epic of humanity."[2] In describing Frazer as "a very great master of art,"[3] T. S. Eliot was concurring with Edmund Gosse's judgment that his volumes were among those whose "form is as precious as their matter."[4] And when we recall the elaborate word patterns of "The Dead" or the touching conclusion of *Finnegans Wake*, the luminous and unhurried narrative of Sir Osbert Sitwell or the bravura flourishes that heighten the travel accounts of his brother Sacheverell, it is apparent that they and *The Golden Bough* have more than a little in common. Similarly, T. S. Eliot's best prose reveals the same quality he finds in Frazer's work, a carefully adjusted combination of the tentative and the precise. Indeed, when Eliot distinguishes Frazer from Shaw and Hardy as possessing a leaner and more disillusioned sensibility whose rhythm is vibrant with the suffering of the life of the spirit, the affinities with his own work became unmistakable.

In addition, *The Golden Bough* possesses another quality that many writers in the twentieth century were to champion as a notable virtue and a cornerstone of a contemporary style. T. S. Eliot, Ezra Pound, H. D., and Ernest Hemingway—to mention only the obvious names—each in his own way stressed the importance of concreteness, of presenting the external world in all sensuous immediacy as a visual presence. They tended, by a kind of Lockean metaphor, to identify visual and intellectual clarity.

In this regard the case of Ezra Pound is particularly instructive. Building on what he had learned from Gaudier-Brzeska, Wyndham Lewis, and the other vorticists, Pound grasped the intrinsic value of the physical world in and for itself, though less as a totality than as shifting patterns of elements. This emphasis on close visual attention, while immediately derived from vorticism, also placed Pound in the Ruskinian tradition of accurate observation and intricate design.[5] And when we remember that

[2] Quoted by R. A. Downie, Frazer's private secretary, in *James George Frazer* (London: Watts & Co., 1940), p. 21.

[3] T. S. Eliot, *Vanity Fair*, XXI (1924), 29, 98.

[4] Quoted by Downie, p. 110.

[5] See Donald Davie, *Ezra Pound: Poet as Sculptor* (New York: Oxford University Press, 1964), pp. 74, 168-173; G. S. Fraser, *Vision and Rhetoric* (London: Faber & Faber, 1959), pp. 90-91.

Frazer too was a methodological descendant of Ruskin, the similarities Pound and he evince begin to appear less improbable coincidences and more integral cultural affinities. Further support for this view emerges from the convergence of their dominant habits of mind on the period of eighteenth-century Enlightenment. What Pound derived from reading Jefferson, Voltaire, and the *philosophes* and translating Fontenelle, Frazer received by editing and imitating Addison's essays, editing the letters of his favorite poet William Cowper, and providing a critical assessment of Condorcet. When to this is added Pound's admiration for such late-nineteenth-century practitioners of the scientific method as Agassiz, Fabre, and Frobenius, who both in presuppositions and approach are in the same general line of intellectual development as Frazer, it is clear why Pound would have found much to admire and emulate in *The Golden Bough*. Thus, Pound even went so far as to insist on Frazer's importance to "contemporary clear thinking" as well as to "the *art of getting meaning into words*." It is the conjunction of these two aspects in Frazer as much as his concern with folk-lore and related matters that led Pound to bestow the final accolade of declaring in his *Guide to Kulchur*: "All this Frazer-Frobenius research is Confucian."[6]

While Pound, Eliot, and the others might have felt that Frazer was too inclined to the "purple passage" and the set descriptive piece, nevertheless it is difficult to see how they could have avoided praising his images of the waste land near the Dead Sea or the gardenlike regions of Ibreez:

> Ibreez itself is embowered in the verdure of orchards, walnuts, and vines. It stands at the mouth of a deep ravine enclosed by great precipices of red rock. . . . With its cool bracing air, its mass of verdure, its magnificent stream of pure ice-cold water —so grateful in the burning heat of summer—and its wide stretch of fertile land, the valley may well have been the residence of an ancient prince or high-priest, who desired to testify by this monument his devotion and gratitude to the god. The seat of this royal or priestly potentate may have been at

[6] Ezra Pound, *Guide to Kulchur* (London: Peter Owen, 1952), p. 272.

Cybistra, the modern Eregli, now a decayed and miserable place straggling amid orchards and gardens full of luxuriant groves of walnut, poplar, willow, mulberry, and oak. The place is a paradise of birds. Here the thrush and the nightingale sing full-throated, the hoopoe waves his crested top-knot, the bright-hued woodpeckers flit from bough to bough, and the swifts dart screaming by hundreds through the air. Yet a little way off, beyond the beneficent influence of the springs and streams, all is desolation—in summer an arid waste broken by great marshes and wide patches of salt, in winter a broad sheet of stagnant water, which as it dries up with the growing heat of the sun exhales a poisonous malaria. To the west, as far as the eye can see, stretches the endless expanse of the dreary Lycaonian plain, barren, treeless, and solitary, till it fades into the blue distance, or is bounded afar off by abrupt ranges of jagged volcanic mountains, on which in sunshiny weather the shadows of the clouds rest, purple and soft as velvet.[7]

Frazer as much as the imagist or realist put precise details to an imaginative use which produced a subtle, profound, and immediate effect, and not the least of the effects produced by the waste-land and garden images was T. S. Eliot's borrowing of them for *The Waste Land*.

If Frazer's style in *The Golden Bough* was a genuine literary achievement, one to be ranked with that of Gibbon, even closer connections can be found between it and the major works of modern literature. At first sight, *The Golden Bough* appears a soberly conservative narrative in the nineteenth-century manner. Yet it possesses structural properties that might well attract artists eager for experiments in form. Frazer deliberately avoided a strictly logical and systematic arrangement of his facts and chose instead "a more artistic mould" with which "to attract readers."[8] Hence, the priest of Nemi and his rites open the book since, though not intrinsically important, they provide a simple and easily grasped image of actions and beliefs whose mystery is gradually illuminated as the more important and complex dying

---

[7] *GB*, v, 121-123.   [8] *GB*, I, viii.

gods are introduced and their functions explored. As a consequence, the form of *The Golden Bough* has been likened to that of a strict sonata.[9]

The idea of the interrelation of the arts has been handled rather gingerly by scholars ever since Lessing, with the exception of iconographic studies of literature and art. Poets, however, have been less constrained and in particular have been consistently drawn to regard myth and music as related. From Wagner through Baudelaire and Mallarmé to Rilke and Valéry, these forms have been held to epitomize the ultimate mystery of human expression—the creation of untranslatable order, harmony, and insight that conveys more than it says. More recently, such critics as Elizabeth Sewell and Claude Lévi-Strauss have argued that thinking mythically is a species of musical thought. If they are right, then the musical form of *The Golden Bough* may possess an appositeness that extends far beyond the bounds of simple analogy. Given his subject, Frazer may have been motivated in his development of literary structure by far deeper forces than conscious determination, forces that were powerfully operative in the last half of the nineteenth century and the early years of the twentieth century. While in view of the general poetic interest in this topic, it would perhaps be futile to argue for *The Golden Bough* as a direct source, we cannot help noting the parallel here to the interest in musical form shown by T. S. Eliot in the *Four Quartets*, Conrad Aiken in *The Divine Pilgrim*, James Joyce in *Finnegans Wake* (notably Book II, section iv), Thomas Mann in *Doctor Faustus*, and Edith Sitwell in *Façade* and some of the *Bucolic Comedies*. Certainly the musical pattern of Frazer's work created a climate in which these artists could elaborate their own interests.

Bearing in mind the claims of Miss Sewell and Lévi-Strauss, we cannot help but be struck at the way in which these authors and their works betray not only affinities with music but more or less central uses of myth as well. Miss Sitwell and Aiken both struggled early in their careers with the problems of making language reflect musical properties. Miss Sitwell's technical experimenta-

[9] H. N. Brailsford, "'The Golden Bough,'" *The New Statesman and Nation*, XXI (May 17, 1941), 502.

tion of *Façade* was directed primarily, as her brother has re-marked, on determining "the effect on rhythm, on speed and on colour of the use of rhymes, assonances and dissonances, placed outwardly, at different places in the line, in most elaborate patterns."[10] Aiken, on the other hand, was concerned less with how closely language could be identified with music. He was more inclined to regard music and particularly the symphonic form as a suggestive analogy by which contrapuntal effects might be attained in poetry.[11] But both launched their experiments in extending the nineteenth-century symbolist aesthetic with the aid of mythic themes, images, and metaphors.

Miss Sitwell's early poetry abounds in satyrs, centaurs, water gods, and nymphs of the caves, waters, woods, and mountains as well as references to Pan, Silenus, Midas, Apollo, Psyche, Hecate, and Thetis. While most of these seem the consequence of a classically oriented education, a few recall *The Golden Bough* and its rather special perspective on the ancient world. For instance, in "I Do Like to Be Beside the Seaside," there is a sprightly hint of a humorous use of one of Frazer's key mythic figures:

> Erotis notices that she
> Will
> Steal
> The
> Wheat-king's luggage, like Babel
> Before the League of Nations grew.[12]

The "wheat-king" hangs tantalizingly between commerce and myth. In doing so it adumbrates the comic and satiric possibilities of anthropological lore that Miss Sitwell explored more fully in *Gold Coast Customs*. In much the same way the tango rhythms of the poem mediate between grave stateliness and festive gaiety

[10] Sir Osbert Sitwell, *Laughter in the Next Room* (London: Macmillian, 1948), p. 185.

[11] The best single statement of Aiken's feelings about the musical analogies of poetry is his 1919 *Poetry* review of *The Charnel Rose*, the first of the "symphonies" he essayed. This review is reprinted as an appendix in his *Collected Poems* (New York: Oxford University Press, 1953), pp. 873-877.

[12] Dame Edith Sitwell, *Canticle of the Rose* (London: Macmillan, 1950), p. 58.

so that both myth and music conspire to reveal the serio-comic dialectic of the significant and trivial that life and human history afford.

Miss Sitwell's early work ostensibly focusses on the triviality of modern existence in order to illuminate the momentous character of human decisions and gestures. Aiken's symphonic poems strive through evocation, allusion, and implication to locate a perdurable universality of emotions and feelings which in true psychoanalytic fashion will all possess meaningful significance of great richness though dominated by "the shimmering overtones of hint and suggestion."[13] Representative here is *The Jig of Forslin* in which the interest in symphonic arrangements is related to "the idea of vicarious experience and . . . the part played by that phenomenon in the nature of civilized consciousness."[14] Forslin, musing and dreaming his way into his subconscious for compensatory fantasies, sees his initial dilemma in terms of Theseus and the Minotaur with a hint of bacchanalian rites:

> Persuasive violins
> Sang of nocturnal sins;
> And ever and again came the hoarse clash
> Of cymbals; as a voice that swore of murder.
> Which way to choose, in all this labyrinth?[15]

The rhymed trimeter lines with their alliterative interplay of *s* and *n*, the iterative emphasis, hard consonants, and assonance of the third line; and the shifting caesuras of the last three lines all conspire musically to suggest the protagonist's complex feeling (of temptation, danger, and uncertainty coupled with incipient panic) that the mythic images develop in a related but somewhat different medium. This same interaction of the musical properties of the absolute poetry Aiken aspired to at this time with the equally haunting, suggestive notes of ancient myth runs throughout all his early verse. *The House of Dust, Senlin: A Biography,* and *The Pilgrimage of Festus,* all gravitate with seem-

[13] Conrad Aiken, *Collected Poems,* p. 876.
[14] Conrad Aiken, *Selected Poems* (New York: Scribners, 1929), preface.
[15] Aiken, *Collected Poems,* p. 55.

ing inevitability toward the language of myth in the course of their aspiration to the condition of music.

This fusion of emphases stemmed not only from the inherent structural similarities claimed for them by Lévi-Strauss but also from the psychoanalytically inspired use of *The Golden Bough*. This is manifest in Aiken's stress upon man's mythic or imaginative death as the culmination of orgiastic festivals or ritual encounters with "the eternal mistress of the world" in the sacred wood of his deepest impulses.[16] When the world ultimately is unable to plumb the mystery of Senlin, he withdraws from its sight leaving as a reminder the behest to " 'look for my heart in the breaking of a bough,' " a phrase that graphically recalls Frazer's theory of the nature and function of the golden bough.[17] And in the last of the original symphonies, *The Pilgrimage of Festus*, the poet's philosophical concern with the human quest for truth and self-knowledge is couched in images quizzically yet seriously colored by primitive myths, vegetative cults, and a sense of the godhead's plurality inspired by comparative religion. Finally, in accents that suggest the evidence amassed in *The Golden Bough* and Frazer's elegiac conclusion, Festus realizes the unknowability of divinity construed as a transcendent and objective being:

> Dreams, gods, visions, demons,
> The strange dark music of the heart and brain
> To which man marches, on his road to pain,—
> All these I have sifted, I have sifted them like sands,
> I have searched in vain for the secret of them all
> And sadly I let them fall.[18]

And in doing so, he explicitly identifies the myths that shape and direct man's progress through time with a music that is at least in part ventricular and hence an authentication of Miss Sewell's view that Orpheus, the master musician, is the figure of myth itself.

Of all the modern authors who have sensed the possible rela-

[16] Aiken, *Collected Poems*, p. 215.
[17] Aiken, *Collected Poems*, p. 221.
[18] Aiken, *Collected Poems*, p. 259.

tions of myth and music none more thoroughly dramatizes the role of *The Golden Bough* in this perception than Ronald Bottrall. The title poem of his *Festivals of Fire* carefully integrates a deliberate emulation of the sonata form with the myth of Balder in order to mirror and diagnose the nature of the early twentieth century. In many ways it bears the impress of being modelled after *The Waste Land* and in none perhaps more than its reliance upon *The Golden Bough*, as the title, text, and notes in their several ways indicate.[19] By giving each of the four sections of the poem representative musical directions of the sonata, Bottrall alerts us to the likelihood of the poem's possessing the structure and the effects of a musical composition. This likelihood is fully borne out by the sub-sections, which vary in length, rhythm, and thematic development in manners that give them the closest technical parallels to the sonata. Thus, in line, verse paragraph, and section the poem achieves a musical expression of the dramatic unfolding of the Balder myth which both crystallizes and comments on the dilemmas of modern life.

The stages of the myth from birth through death to lamentation and anticipation of the future are ironically keyed to those features of contemporary existence—violence, banality, vulgarity, mechanized ugliness, and aesthetic as well as sensual self-indulgence—which constitute a cultural equivalent of an earlier age's sacrifice of its god. As a result, the poem utilizes the myth of the dying god not in order to sanction the possibilities of the resurrection metaphor but to achieve an ironic posture from which the full tragic waste endemic to human behavior can be appreciated. And in much the same fashion as *The Waste Land* does, it maintains a powerful tension between the nullity of the immediate situation and the ripening potentiality of the future. Thus, the poem closes with a vision of a godhead of power dominating a mechanical graveyard and investing it with a vigorous life. It does so, however, in language and rhythms so detached and taut that the irony of the whole seems to hang midway be-

---

[19] The title is derived from the subtitle of the last two volumes in Frazer's third edition, a fact substantiated by the notes which also suggest that these volumes are the source for many of the images and scenes in the poem. See Ronald Bottrall, *Festivals of Fire* (London: Faber & Faber, 1934), p. 5.

tween the mocking and the revelatory. The deliberateness of this and its representing of the poet's basic attitude toward his capacities for releasing the mythical and musical powers of language are both explicitly revealed at almost the exact center of the poem:

> We have built a kingdom of metaphor,
> Called Words our viziers. The core
> Of our 'becoming' is a fluent blur;
> Immured in euphony
> We have seen fit to discard
> Our cradle for a Celanese cocoon.
> With death as a competitor, Richard
> Jostled necessity, we saddle
> With cryptograms our rune.
> Saxophones dumb the lyre,
> Acquiescent in a complacent drone:
> By our sterility of invocation
> We have called down on the funeral pyre
> Fire, in its vocation
> Of destroyer and purifier.[20]

This meta-mythic and meta-musical assessment brings us, in a sense, full circle, for we are here substantially back with the haunting uncertainty as to whether myth and music really are allied and whether they offer access to realms other than those of mere physical sensibility.

Whatever the ultimate answer to these tantalizing questions, it is nevertheless true that Frazer himself thought of his book almost exclusively in pictorial terms. The priest at Nemi is said to be "in the forefront of the picture" while the background is crowded with priest-kings, scapegoats, dying gods, magicians, and fertility deities.[21] Indeed, there is a sense in which Frazer, like Yeats, writes under the stimulus of an actual painting, developing its implications in his own fashion and interpreting its significance. According to Frazer, the full beauty of Turner's paint-

[20] Ronald Bottrall, *Collected Poems* (London: Sidgwick & Jackson, 1961), p. 43.
[21] *GB*, I, viii.

ing of Nemi can be felt only when Macaulay's verse account of its ritual has been explained. Thus, the frontispiece and initial epigraph of *The Golden Bough* encompass its central theme. Small wonder he should speak of his book in terms of "sinuous outline" and "its play of alternate light and shadow,"[22] or that on its very first page he should urge his readers to form "an accurate picture" of Nemi.[23]

In his "Musée des Beaux Arts" W. H. Auden interprets the details of Brueghel's *Icarus* painting in language whose colloquial vigor and casualness verbally mimes the visual scene of the painter. Both modes function as illustrations of a general and abstract statement announced in the opening lines:

> About suffering they were never wrong,
> The Old Masters.[24]

Yeats, on the other hand, uses particular paintings as inciters of the imagination, which thereby is encouraged to work its metamorphic powers that draw images and scenes from their visual context into the poet's elaborate and distinctive symbolism. He is less concerned to analyze the form or significance of a painting than to assimilate its relevant aspects to his own mythic iconography, as the great example of his Leda poem makes clear.

While it is impossible to argue for the direct influence of *The Golden Bough* in this regard, nevertheless some striking and significant similarities in general attitude and method are detectable. A particularly good instance occurs in the last volume where Frazer draws evidence from art and literature for his theory of the golden bough's symbolic role as a preserver of life:

> There is some reason to suppose that when Orpheus in like manner descended alive to hell to rescue the soul of his dead wife Eurydice from the shades, he carried with him a willow bough to serve as a passport on his journey to and from the land of the dead; for in the great frescoes representing the nether world, with which the master hand of Polygnotus adorned the walls of a loggia at Delphi, Orpheus was depicted

[22] Quoted by Downie, p. 21.   [23] *GB*, I, I.
[24] W. H. Auden, *The Collected Poetry* (New York: Random House, 1945), p. 3.

sitting pensively under a willow, holding his lyre, now silent and useless, in his left hand, while with his right he grasped the drooping boughs of the tree. If the willow in the picture had indeed the significance which an ingenious scholar has attributed to it, the painter meant to represent the dead musician dreaming wistfully of the time when the willow had carried him safe back across the Stygian ferry to that bright world of love and music which he was now to see no more.[25]

Allowing for the extreme differences in purpose between Frazer and the poets, we can still see their affinities. He adumbrates Auden in his sketching of the pictorial scenic design while basing general contentions on its evidence. Similarly he resembles Yeats, whose penchant for symbolic identifications based on the learning of others Frazer here approximates. Doubtless the same could be said of many other authors—for instance, Ruskin—but this does not alter the fact that Frazer was actually read by many modern writers. As a result he may have indirectly contributed to their burgeoning sense of the richness poetry might achieve by affecting painting's structural massing of detail and color. Pound, Eliot, and Joyce, to mention only the early giants of modern literature, were not so unsympathetic to the manner and preoccupations of the late nineteenth century that they could not find in *The Golden Bough* suggestive treatments of both figures and landscapes.

Probably the most sustained poetic effort to use poetry and painting as complementary mirrors in which the myths and classical scenes found in *The Golden Bough* are reflected is the work of Sacheverell Sitwell. In a collection such as *Canons of Giant Art*, nearly all the poems are based on or derive their inspiration from works of art such as the paintings of Poussin, Mantegna, El Greco, and Claude, the sculpture of Praxiteles and the Farnese Hercules, or classical and Indian myths. Such a collocation of sources attests not only to the diversity of Sitwell's interests but to their underlying imaginative unity that may well have found its locus in *The Golden Bough*. In addition to these poems' pictorial detail, mythic subjects, wide scholarship, and comparative

[25] *GB*, XI, 294.

perspectives, they reveal yet another feature—one not conspicuous in the work of Yeats or Auden—that aligns them with Frazer as pupils to master. That is their mastery of narrative development and pace, which makes them virtual poetic equivalents of *The Golden Bough*'s unhurried, lambent creation of scenes and actions that echo with the memories of civilization's dreams and history. All of these Frazerian qualities are neatly exemplified in the following passage:

> This mortal [Bacchus] lifted to the gods by beauty
> With no trappings of bright armour to his naked body
> We will march by his shoulders from the tourist's eye,
> We'll move him from the vineyard to all the earth there was
>   for him,
> To islands of one meadow, where the goats upon the next hill
> Crop their cold pasture with a strait of sea between,
> And the shepherd in the cave-mouth
> Shouts through that trumpet to the alien hill in face of him
> And is answered like an oracle from lips of rock.
> The mainland with sweet hills of herbs
> Breathes thyme into the summer gales
> And blows ever sweeter while the bees stay to plunder
> Shutting its myriad honey-hearts with falling sun;
> Bent valleys like a serpent's tail wind into the hills
> And grow more sacred with the deeper rocks above them
> Till these very valleys are a mouthpiece of the gods,
> In lonely syllables of water dropping
> That speak like war-drums by their intervals
> And are tuned to direful warning;
> The gods have planted speech in all the ways of men,
> Their path through the cornfields is alive with sound,
> With running rumours through that golden host
> Who stoop, now this, now that way, for the word,
> While groves of trees, on sacred brows of hills,
> Speak in simpler words than these.[26]

[26] Sacheverell Sitwell, *Canons of Giant Art* (London: Faber & Faber, 1933), p. 39.

By linking his major study to painting, in both conception and execution, Frazer provides literature with an instructive and suggestive model for a deepened exploration of novel forms of texture and perspective. Like Yeats and Auden, he plays the pictorial and the verbal off against one another and so achieves their mutual illumination; like Pound and Wyndham Lewis, he carries the visual principle of the artist into literature; and like Lawrence and Virginia Woolf, he attends to even as he creates the emotional vibrations in the object and setting. Nor in the light of this are we surprised to find the late Professor Chew likening *The Golden Bough* to the vision seen by St. Anthony and the Frazerian images and figures to the nightmarish fantasies of Brueghel or Bosch.[27]

[II]

The musical and pictorial similarities between Frazer's study and modern poetry and fiction, though striking and suggestive, may be essentially analogies, lines of parallel development. What they indicate most sharply is the extent to which Frazer's structural techniques foreshadow those of some of the major artists of the twentieth century. Influence—if it enters at all—operates almost exclusively below the threshold of consciousness. A somewhat stronger case of influence as well as a partial explanation of the attractions of *The Golden Bough* is its nonchronological method of narration. This method results in a work whose structure is shaped by most of the devices that characterize modern literature. Consider what we may call *The Golden Bough*'s macroscopic form. Here is a work dealing with a vast subject which orders its material thematically; which juxtaposes conflicting evidence and scenes for dramatic purposes; which presents its point of view by indirect and oblique means; which sees human existence as a flow of recurring experiences; which employs repetition and restatement as both emotive and intellectual devices; which creates symbolic epitomes of human history out of apparently limited and simple actions; and which makes a unified whole out of an abundance of disparate scenes and topics by an intricate set

[27] S. C. Chew, "Nemi and the Golden Bough," *North American Review*, CCXVIII (1923), 816.

of references backward and forward in the narrative. Without in the least denying the other contributory forces, we may legitimately suggest that *The Golden Bough* is also, in a very real measure, responsible for the form and shape of modern literature.

In *The Waste Land, The Cantos, The Bridge,* and *Paterson* the thematic ordering of material, the dissolving perspectives, the panoramic sweep, the mingling of the profound and the trivial, the poignant and the bizarre are the same techniques employed in *The Golden Bough. The Bridge,* for instance, bears such a wealth of structural and thematic resemblances to Frazer's book that it seems impossible that it did not derive from it either directly or as a representative expression of the *zeitgeist* shaped by Frazer in the years following World War I.[28] The concern with myth, announced in the "Proem" and dramatically elaborated in the text and marginalia of "Powhatan's Daughter," is obvious. This is fortunate since it is beyond the scope of the present chapter to offer a detailed treatment of the Frazerian dimensions of *The Bridge.*

Nevertheless, we should note that these include not only controlling images, such as the Indian princess who closely resembles *The Golden Bough*'s corn-maiden, her dance of religious regeneration and fertility, the sacred river stained with the presence of the dying god, and "the mistletoe of dreams, a star," but also attitudes informed by Frazer's impact on the cultural attitudes of the times. For instance, in beseeching the bridge to descend to man and "of the curveship lend a myth to God," Crane renders his response to Frazer's disclosure of the empirical and material character of incarnation. The traditional religious language of descent is invoked here in order to utilize it as meta-

[28] See Frederick J. Hoffman, *The Twenties,* rev. ed. (New York: The Free Press, 1965), pp. 257-260. Certainly Crane was acquainted with Jessie Weston's Frazerian *From Ritual to Romance* at least by late 1927, an interest that might well have led him to look at the abridged edition of *The Golden Bough* which had appeared in 1922 and whose comparative brevity and accessibility would have made it the logical choice for Crane, who was engaged in earnest if intuitive efforts at self-education. On Crane's knowledge of Miss Weston, see *The Letters of Hart Crane,* ed. Brom Weber (Berkeley: University of California Press, 1965), p. 314.

phor whose efficacy is not contingent on its truth. Both the deity and the stories or *mythoi* of his existence derive from man and those of his creations that project the imagination beyond its material ground. Such is the central contention of both *The Bridge* and *The Golden Bough*. Similar structural resemblances further link the two works. Both open with a voyage motif; both are engaged in an effort to relate disparate areas of experience and feeling and belief, and to circumscribe them into a single orderly synthesis; both seek to achieve this order through more or less abrupt comparisons and juxtapositions which slight the conventional categories of temporal chronology and spatial contiguity; and both organize their work loosely in a fashion that permits them to deal with the great variety of subjects that most interest them—Crane by his sequence of fifteen lyrics which taken together form a unified poem, and Frazer by what some have felt to be a series of essays gathered into book form.

Similarly, we have but to think of Joyce or, in a quite different way, William Carlos Williams, to see the extent to which contemporary literature, like Frazer, conveys its point of view through selection of details and arrangement of scenes instead of by explicit pronouncements. Joyce's work, at least through *A Portrait of the Artist as a Young Man*, orders details emblematically in accord with a rhythm that matches Frazer's in its skillful use of late-nineteenth-century models. What Joyce derived from Frazer in this regard is primarily a conspectus of rhetorical strategies for the rendering of the ironic and elegiac. The doctrine of artistic impersonality lying behind this technique and most commonly associated with Joyce and Eliot finds its discursive analogue in Frazer's calm, impartial, scholarly detachment. With it, he could survey man's entire history and find it a record of incalculable folly while contemplating the destruction of his own theories with complete equanimity.

Such personal dispassionateness was virtually the polar opposite in temperament to the late Dr. Williams, who might well be thought one of the last persons to be touched by Frazer's style and erudition. Yet the predominantly staccato rhythms of *Paterson*, alien as they are to Frazer, must be set off against its declaration:

You also, I am sure, have read
Frazer's Golden Bough. It does you
Justice.[29]

In the process of creating a poetic style to render the realities of a phenomenological America, he shattered the convention of poetry as something undefiled by prose even as he made living speech of the most vigorous and diversified sort the cornerstone of poetic language. At the same time he intensified Frazer's habit of shifting topics and focus by making the unit of organization the line rather than the chapter. As a result the process is speeded up to the point where the illusion of transitions and conventional rhetorical development can no longer be sustained, a fact which neatly crystallizes the cultural, epistemological, and verbal changes that have occurred since *The Golden Bough* first appeared.

Even more striking is the extent of modern literature's attraction to cyclical theories of life, history, and culture. *A Vision* and *Finnegans Wake* both celebrate this concept with elaborate care and a wealth of detail. So does *The Golden Bough*, which not only links the astronomical, vegetative, and human worlds in a pattern of birth, flowering, death, and revival, but also closes where it began—with the sacred grove at Nemi. In Frazer's tracing of this pattern an integral part is played by repetition of facts and restatement of hypotheses and inferences. The effect is not simply one of calling to mind points in danger of being lost sight of, but also of bringing to the reader a sense of their profound significance, of their right to a brooding and thoughtful contemplation. And though it is undoubtedly the product of a particular and individual attitude toward the actual process of writing fiction, yet just the same sort of effect is achieved by Lawrence in the almost ritualistically repetitive passages of novels such as *The Rainbow* and *The Plumed Serpent*. Lawrence, like Joyce and Eliot, also finds man's life represented symbolically in commonplace and traditional acts. For them as well as for Frazer, har-

[29] William Carlos Williams, *Paterson* (New York: New Directions, 1951), p. 92.

vesting, love-making, bearing the sins of others, and performing the menial deeds of daily life, all reflect in different ways what is taken to be the essence of life.

Perhaps the most unequivocal instances of the ritualistic exaltation of the simplest and most fundamental acts of human survival through reliance on the patterns and behavior presented in *The Golden Bough* are to be found in the novels of Naomi Mitchison and John Cowper Powys. Miss Mitchison's *Corn King and the Spring Queen* acknowledges Frazer as one of its major sources. It also gives a cumulatively powerful rendering of the psychological states of specific primitive individuals cast in the role of fertility monarchs and deities.[30] Where Lawrence's repetitions are substantially Frazerian-inspired ritual equivalents, Miss Mitchison's are densely concrete fictive transcriptions of Frazer's more general accounts. She follows a single individual, Tarrik, and those around him through *The Golden Bough*'s characteristic divine-king pattern so that a sense of the credibility of the underlying beliefs is conveyed to the reader. This is achieved in part through repetitive allusions to reiterated actions and convictions and through heavily detailed descriptions of avowedly crucial religious rites. The effect is both to show us how pervasively these convictions permeated the common life of the tribe and also how psychologically possible it is to perceive god and man in the same physical vehicle. A representative instance occurs in this rendering of the changing seasons:

> It was always the same, year after year, as winter began to loosen and soften, and Plowing Eve got nearer. People came out of their houses more and talked more, looking at one another, men and women, with sudden discovery, and felt a growing and brightening of the senses, keener sight, smell, taste, hearing, touch, not quite a falling in love with the young, young spring, the incredibly pale and remote and maiden season, still wrapped about with snow. Children felt it as well. Fewer people died at that time of year. They watched the com-

[30] Naomi Mitchison, *The Corn King and the Spring Queen* (New York: Harcourt, Brace & Co., n.d.), p. 721.

123

ings and goings of the Corn King and the Spring Queen, looking for signs of the godhead that was ripening in both of them,
and getting into touch with it themselves.[31]

As the culmination of the emergence of the deity and the new
year, god, season, and man coalesce in a major creative effort:
"In the convention of the dance and in a solid noise of drums the
Corn opened the furrow, broke into the Spring, and started the
Year. . . . He was not himself a man seizing in ultimate necessity
on woman's flesh, but a god making plain his power."[32]

In the case of John Cowper Powys, the ritualistic quality of his
prose is attained less exclusively by concreteness and verisimilitude than by a complex style that continually strives to relate the
fictive events and feelings of the characters to abstract, even
metaphysical issues. Thus, in his *Glastonbury Romance*, a work
set in modern times but concerned to trace the primitive or ancient lineaments of human behavior as they are articulated in the
religious and Arthurian context of the town of Glastonbury, John
and Mary Crow are described as follows:

> And in the etheric atmosphere about those two, as they stood
> there, quivered the immemorial Mystery of Glastonbury.
> Christians had one name for this Power, the ancient heathen
> inhabitants of this place had another and quite different one.
> . . . It had its own *sui generis* origin in the nature of the Good-
> Evil First Cause, but it had grown to be more and more an in-
> dependent entity as the centuries rolled over it. This had
> doubtless come about by reason of the creative energies pour-
> ing into it from the various cults, which, consciously or uncon-
> sciously, sucked their life-blood from its wind-blown, gos-
> samer-light vortex. Older than Christianity, older than the
> gods of neolithic men, this many-named Mystery had been
> handed down to subsequent generations by three psychic
> channels; by the channel of popular renown, by the channel of
> inspired poetry, and by the channel of individual experience.[33]

[31] Mitchison, p. 238.   [32] Mitchison, p. 245.
[33] John Cowper Powys, *A Glastonbury Romance* (New York: Simon &
Schuster, 1932), p. 112.

This merging of a loosely mystical or spiritual metaphysic with *The Golden Bough*'s stress on the physical and empirical grounds of primitive religion and belief is also used to convey the psychological states of individual characters in such novels as *Wolf Solent*, *Porius*, and *Weymouth Sands*. Here too the rhetorical device of recurrent phrasing creates, perhaps unwittingly and not altogether successfully, a ritualistic effect calculated to intensify the solemnity and mystery of ordinary human experiences. Typical is the self-awareness of the hero of *Wolf Solent*, whose analysis of his outlook reveals its indebtedness to *The Golden Bough* both for content and for the emotions' ritualizing propensities:

> He fumbled about in his mind for some clue to his normal attitude to life—some clue-word that he could use to describe it, if any of his new friends began questioning him; and the word he hit upon at last was the word fetish-worship. That was it!
>
> It was a worship of all the separate, mysterious, living souls he approached: "souls" of grass, trees, stones, animals, birds, fish; "souls" of planetary bodies and of the bodies of men and women; the "souls," even, of all manner of inanimate little things; the "souls" of all those strange, chemical groupings that give a living identity to houses, towns, places, countrysides. . . .[34]

The repetitive aspect of ritual emphasized by Miss Mitchison, Powys, Lawrence, and, in a somewhat different manner, by Joyce is balanced both in modern literature and in *The Golden Bough* by another device that similarly integrates disparate spatial and temporal orders into a coherent unity. To circumscribe the complex nature of man's changing yet somehow permanent condition, works like *The Waste Land, Ulysses, Finnegans Wake,* and *The Anathemata* rely heavily, even as does *The Golden Bough*, on a multiple series of cross-references and allusions which continually underscore the contemporaneity of all time. While Eliot, Joyce, and David Jones were all familiar with Frazer's ideas and works, it is in the main unlikely that their patterns of allusion and

[34] John Cowper Powys, *Wolf Solent* (New York: Simon & Schuster, 1929), p. 64.

notes were deliberate efforts to emulate *The Golden Bough*'s habit of sustained documentation. Nevertheless, these and other writers, sought, like Frazer, workable means of controlling the modern explosion of knowledge without resorting either to exhaustive encyclopedism or deliberate abandonment of historically distant or topically recherché information. Consequently they might well have been impressed with the range and mastery of knowledge Frazer's scholarship afforded him. Certainly when we think of the training and temperament of men like Eliot, Joyce, and Pound, the extent to which the scholarly method was both congenial to, as well as a desperate bid for large-scale coherent relevance by, modern literature emerges sharply.

What makes *The Golden Bough*'s techniques of cross-reference particularly attractive and instructive to writers is their capacity to keep the focus on the author's immediate concern and to lend a status to that concern by relating it to similar ones in other times and places so that it assumes a universal or perennial character. When, for instance, Frazer documents something like the custom of secluding girls at puberty with discussions of the practice in Africa, Indonesia, the Americas, and India, a social curiosity becomes a means of insight into cultural dynamics and its symbolism. Similarly, when Frazer details items connected with magic or taboo, he suggests in a very powerful manner how commonplace and even ordinarily disgusting things can be invested with the profoundest emotional significance.

A related aspect of Frazer's scholarship that is important for modern literature is what might be called its essentially primary character. Even the most casual study of *The Golden Bough*'s footnotes convinces us that Frazer not only ransacked anthropology for his data and illustrations but went directly to other disciplines when problems in his research seemed to demand it. His view seemed to be, as R. Angus Downie has suggested, that "if, in our search for the golden bough, we might get a hint from the botanists, we must not let our ignorance of botany stand in our way, but must overcome that ignorance."[35] As a result, his notes contain a surprisingly diverse range of information all brought to bear on particular issues. Obviously such problem-solving ef-

[35] Downie, p. 105.

forts do not figure in literature, but something rather analogous does, namely, the concentration of rhetorical strategies to achieve the maximum imaginative impact. The way in which these two elements—multiple forms of knowledge and power of effect—are programmatically merged in literature is perhaps best exemplified by Ezra Pound's practice. This he summed up in the remark that readers forced to learn enough Latin or Greek or Chinese or American history to grasp certain lines in his *Cantos* were still not wasting their time because they were learning something. And as a humanistic model for modern literature's effort to attain revolutionary perspectives through a scholarly, or quasi-scholarly, use of unrelated knowledge, Pound and the others could not improve on *The Golden Bough*.

A work that strikingly extends the Frazerian mode of "scholarship" is David Jones's *The Anathemata*. Subtitled "fragments of an attempted writing," this combination of prose and poetry seeks to uncover and recall Western Christendom's "blessed things that have taken on what is cursed and the profane things that somehow are redeemed."[36] Because he is aware that the modern artist cannot expect "a reasonably static culture-phase," Jones employs a welter of notes on nearly every page to elucidate those background elements not shared by his audience.[37] Thus, in an effort to share the Catholic, Welsh, and artistic forms of knowledge that make up his chief cultural heritage, his notes explicate textual allusions to the Mass, the Bible, Celtic mythology, folk-lore and geography, and works of art ranging from *The Waste Land* to the *Odyssey*. At the same time, many of these notes also invoke a staggering array of authorities—from Frazer himself through Darwin's *Formation of Vegetable Mould through the Action of Worms*, the *British Regional Geology* series, Church Fathers like St. Augustine, to the works of Christopher Dawson and W. F. Jackson Knight. These notes are not so much aimed at proving statements as at providing connections and relations between separate observations or at deepening the imaginative resonance of images and passages in the text. In short, Frazer's scholarly, historical stress on notes as evidence or

[36] David Jones, *The Anathemata* (London: Faber & Faber, 1952), p. 28.
[37] Jones, p. 15.

secondary adjuncts to the text is displaced to make the notes illuminating and essential aspects of the work of art. So viewed,
Frazer's impact in a sense rebounds on itself. *The Golden Bough*
began by shaping or at least nudging the artists' conception of
formal coherence; its structure of massed detail and corrobora-
tory notes was then adapted to its literary equivalent of allusion
and projective metaphor; from this point of view Frazer's essay in
scientific anthropology is an imaginative orchestration of themes
in which the footnotes, cross-references, and allusions serve as
variations and secondary developments.

[III]

From these stylistic and structural affinities between *The Golden
Bough* and modern literature it is clear that even if Frazer's work
had not been directly imitated, was not a consciously employed
source, it would still have exercised an influence on creative
artists because of its imagination and technique. With this point,
the last aspect of what has been called the literary reason for *The
Golden Bough*'s success comes into view. For though a sketch has
been made of how and why Frazer rather than Farnell or Cook
or Miss Harrison or Crawley or Hartland spearheaded the drive
of comparative religion into literature, there is still the question
of why *The Golden Bough* is preeminent among his works. The
answer lies in its genre or literary mode, for in essence it is less
a compendium of facts than a gigantic romance of quest couched
in the form of objective research. It is this basically archetypal
consideration that reveals *The Golden Bough*'s impact on literature to be not fortuitous but necessary and inevitable. We have
but to compare its opening pages with those of *Folklore in the
Old Testament, The Fear of the Dead in Primitive Religion,* or
Myths of the Origin of Fire to see that in it there is much more
than simply discursive writing. The latter plunge immediately
and prosaically into their subject:

> Attentive readers of the Bible can hardly fail to remark a strik-
> ing discrepancy between the two accounts of the creation of
> man recorded in the first and second chapters of Genesis.
> (FOT)

Men commonly believe that their conscious being will not end at death, but that it will be continued for an indefinite time or for ever, long after the frail corporeal envelope which lodged it for a time has mouldered in the dust. (FOD)

Of all human inventions the discovery of the method of kindling fire has probably been the most momentous and far-reaching. It must date from an extreme antiquity, since there appears to be no well-attested case of a savage tribe ignorant of the use of fire and of the mode of producing it. (MOF)[38]

With *The Golden Bough*, however, rhetorical question, alliteration, allusion, metaphor, inversion, all are enlisted to create a genuine literary experience, what the Joyce of *Finnegans Wake* might have called an "anthropoetic" experience:

Who does not know Turner's picture of the Golden Bough? The scene, suffused with the golden glow of imagination in which the divine mind of Turner steeped and transfigured even the fairest natural landscape, is a dream-like vision of the little woodland lake of Nemi—"Diana's Mirror," as it was called by the ancients. No one who has seen that calm water, lapped in a green hollow of the Alban hills, can ever forget it. The two characteristic Italian villages which slumber on its banks, and the equally Italian palace whose terraced gardens descend steeply to the lake, hardly break the stillness and even the solitariness of the scene. Diana herself might still linger by this lonely shore, still haunt these woodlands wild.

In antiquity this sylvan landscape was the scene of a strange and recurring tragedy. In order to understand it aright we must try to form in our minds an accurate picture of the place where it happened; for, as we shall see later on, a subtle link subsisted between the natural beauty of the spot and the dark crimes which under the mask of religion were often perpetrated there, crimes which after the lapse of so many ages still lend a touch of melancholy to these quiet woods and waters,

[38] *Folk-Lore in the Old Testament* (London: Macmillan, 1918), I, 3; *The Fear of the Dead* (London: Macmillan, 1933), I, 3; *Myths of the Origins of Fire* (London: Macmillan, 1930), p. 1.

like a chill breath of autumn on one of those bright September days "while not a leaf seems faded."[39]

Granted that *The Golden Bough* is more carefully, more imaginatively written than his other works (passages in *The Worship of Nature* and his edition of Pausanias may be exceptions), this does not in itself make the book a romance rather than the encyclopedic argument we have always thought it to be. One obvious connection between it and the traditional romance that most readers feel in some measure is suggested by the applicability to both of Ezra Pound's comment: "There are few people who can read more than a dozen or so of medieval romances, by Crestien or anyone else, without being over-wearied by the continual recurrence of the same or similar incidents, told in a similar manner."[40] Equally apparent and probably more significant is their joint development of themes out of a substratum of Nature myth and fertility ideals, their use of conflation and linking by means of central leit-motifs, their merging of incongruous materials, and their readiness to hint at possible meanings without spelling them out in detail.

And if we bear in mind that *The Golden Bough* is an instance of what Northrop Frye calls displacement, we can see certain additional features that both stamp it as a romance and account for its impact.[41] First, like the medieval romances, it clearly deals with a quest—in this case, a quest to discover the meaning of the ritual observed by the priest of Diana, the King of the Wood, at Nemi. This fact alone almost explains Frazer's seminal role in modern literature, for the thematic quests of Eliot for redemption, Joyce for a father, Lawrence for a Golden Age, Yeats for the buried treasure or hidden mystery, and Miss Sitwell for purification are all adumbrated in *The Golden Bough*. While Frazer announces his quest from the beginning and completes it just prior to rounding off the narrative, he does not follow the pure romance in regarding this as the major adventure led up to by a

[39] *GB*, I, 1-2.

[40] Ezra Pound, *The Spirit of Romance* (Norfolk, Conn.: New Directions, 1952), p. 82.

[41] Northrop Frye, *Anatomy of Criticism* (Princeton: University Press, 1957), pp. 136-137, 365.

series of minor incidents and forming the climax of his story. Instead he pulls the traditional formula inside out by beginning and ending with a secondary encounter while gradually working in toward the central experiences he is dealing with, which are those of crucifixion and resurrection. The resulting effects are highly instructive for modern literature.

For one thing Frazer's de-emphasizing of plot and narrative continuity parallels much modern fiction. Nowhere is this parallel more thoroughgoing than in the tendency of both to locate their climaxes, their central, crucial experiences, in incidents of discovery or revelation almost totally devoid of action. Thus, the notion of what might be called the important unimportant situation or event, which has become a stock device of the contemporary short story, is one of the organizing principles of *The Golden Bough*.

The same reversal of the romance pattern also provides another effect central to modern literature. Thematically, it consists of the gradual accrual of meaning as the reader follows a trail of hints and artistically incomplete bits of information. Just as Frazer extends *anagnorisis* throughout the book so do *The Sound and the Fury*, *Absalom, Absalom!*, the major novels of Henry James, and the "Alexandria Quartet." Structurally, the reversal provides the idea of pattern by piecemeal. This is based on a dislocation of perspective which brings us too close to the scene or overwhelms us with detail so that only when we stand back and regard the whole work does the pattern emerge. Instances of this which come readily to mind are *Finnegans Wake*, *The Cantos*, and Dos Passos' *U. S. A.* Frazer achieves precisely the same thing, both thematically and structurally, when he forces us to follow him through a tangle of magicians' arts, species of taboo, and perils of the soul before coming upon one of his central topics—the death and resurrection of gods—in Volumes IV and V. But not even the *Adonis, Attis, Osiris* segments provide the whole core, for only in Volume VII, *The Scapegoat*, do we catch a glimpse of the earlier books' complementary theme, that of the crucifixion of gods and men.

We are told that the romance proper projects the ideals of the ruling social or intellectual class; that its quest has three stages (conflict, death, and discovery or resolution); that this threefold structure is repeated in many other features; that the quest involves two central characters (a protagonist and an antagonist); that the secondary characters are simplified and weak in outline; that the quest's most frequent goals are the slaying of a dragon and the acquisition of wealth in some form; and that the romance possesses a number of distinguishable types or phases.[42] Not only does *The Golden Bough* have a quest motif as a dominant feature, but it also exhibits all the characteristics just mentioned, though obviously not in the same way as they appear in *Perceval*, the *Perlesvaus*, or *Sir Gawain and the Green Knight*.

Unlike the medieval romances, *The Golden Bough* does not embody the ideals of an aristocratic, feudal society, but it does convey a clear sense of the values that dominated the post-Darwinian, rationalistic ethos of late-nineteenth-century England. Reason and truth are to Frazer what mystic love was to von Strassburg, chivalric honor to Chrétien, or Christian faith to von Eschenbach. Thus, in what stands as a proem to his tale of adventure he suggests that the comparative approach has not only intrinsic intellectual significance but also social usefulness derived from an unswerving adherence to truth. As a result, the real hero or protagonist of *The Golden Bough* proves to be the civilized mind which explores uncharted ways to uncover new facts about man's way of life, facts which may be simultaneously horrifying, engrossing, and revolutionary. In short, the hero is Frazer himself, who, like Nero Wolfe, solves the mysterious puzzles and crimes of mankind from an armchair. If this sedentary role seems to violate the notion of the quest or marvelous journey as central to the romance, we may recall that the wanderer was as frequently a book as an author. The varied and widely dispersed forms of folk tales, ballads, and romances are cases in point.[43] However pertinent to anthropology Andrew Lang's jibe about Covent Garden experts was, it is clearly irrelevant to *The Golden Bough* as a romance.

To find the answer to the sacred kingship of Italy in Southern India is in the best tradition of the Grail knights who traveled

[42] Frye, *Anatomy of Criticism*, pp. 186-202.
[43] Frye, *Anatomy of Criticism*, p. 57.

into distant lands seeking the goal of their quest. Like them, Frazer found himself almost insensibly embarked upon his wanderings. As he says, "wider and wider prospects opened out before me; and thus step by step I was lured into far-spreading fields."[44] The same basic image of the journey that is a quest provides the controlling frame of the entire book. In the first chapter the rational hero decides that "the survey of a wider field" may "contain in germ the solution of the problem."[45] And like Jason, Theseus, or Odysseus, he offers his listening companions "a voyage of discovery, in which we shall visit many strange foreign lands, with strange foreign peoples, and still stranger customs. The wind is in the shrouds: we shake out our sails to it, and leave the coast of Italy behind us for a time."[46] Eleven volumes and over a hundred chapters later, with all these predictions fulfilled, Frazer announces the end of the quest: "Our long voyage of discovery is over and our bark has drooped her weary sails in port at last."[47] This voyage metaphor affords a powerful summation of the nineteenth century's character as an age of scientific and geographic discovery. It is the imaginative extrapolation of those voyages of discovery taken by David Livingstone, Sir Austin Layard, and Sir Richard Burton as well as the more purely intellectual ones embarked on by Darwin, Huxley and Frazer. Through it the Victorian resemblance to the Elizabethan age is thrown into sharp relief.[48]

Within this frame of journey and incredible adventure both the quest and the central characters of *The Golden Bough* reveal their affinities with romance. Frazer's quest possesses the requisite three stages, though they are naturally blurred by his assumption that he was writing anthropology rather than literature. Secondary variations on this triple form are the book's three major subjects (magic and the sacred kingship, the principles of taboo, and the myth and ritual of the Dying God) and its three editions, the latter being equivalent perhaps to the romance

---

[44] *GB*, I, vii.   [45] *GB*, I, 42-43.
[46] *GB*, I, 43.   [47] *GB*, XI, 308.
[48] See J. H. Buckley, *The Victorian Temper* (Cambridge: Harvard University Press, 1951), p. 11; William Irvine, *Apes, Angels and Victorians* (New York: McGraw-Hill, 1955), p. 15.

hero's success on his third attempt. The stages themselves traditionally involve an extended conflict between the protagonist and
his antagonist, a vital confrontation in which at least one is slain,
and finally the discovery and exaltation of the hero as a dramatic
resolution to the quest. In *The Golden Bough* the conflict is
waged over human beliefs and customs. More particularly, two
antagonistic forces try to settle whether or not there is any connection among various religious beliefs or between religious customs generally and those usually thought of as wholly secular.
Frazer as the protagonist advances the cause of unaided reason
and objective scientific truth against the entrenched powers of
superstition whose key representative is the man of religious
faith. In one sense, like the Grail legend itself *The Golden Bough*
is the fruit of a crusade, though, as Robert Graves keeps reiterat-
ing, a highly discreet and covert crusade.[49] The similarity to the
romance pattern is heightened by Frazer's suggestion that his
task is to help his society rid itself of afflictions and weaknesses
emanating from a powerful and aged adversary who lives "in a
strong tower" and who will not hesitate to tempt the hero with
appeals to antiquity, expediency, and beauty.[50]

Though the conflict of reason and faith or science and religion
is perhaps endless, *The Golden Bough* imaginatively envisages
the second quest stage, that of the death of one of the combatants. In this case, the defeat is dealt to the representative of tradition and faith, whom Frazer calls superstition. And while it is
difficult to say just precisely at what point in the book this occurs,
we would probably not be far wrong in locating the instant of
fatality in the note on "The Crucifixion of Christ" appended to
the ninth volume. Showing that Christ died as the annual representative of a god whose counterparts were well known all over
Western Asia, Frazer intimates, "will reduce Jesus of Nazareth
to the level of a multitude of other victims of a barbarous superstition, and will see in him no more than a moral teacher, whom

---

[49] Robert Graves, *Occupation: Writer* (New York: Creative Age Press,
1950), pp. 42-43. On the Grail legend's connection with the historical Cru-
sades, see Helen Adolf's *Visio Pacis* (University Park: Pennsylvania State
University Press, 1960), p. 11.

[50] *GB*, 1, xxv-xxvi.

the fortunate accident of his execution invested with the crown, not merely of a martyr, but of a god."[51] Here Frazer joins forces with Nietzsche, for in his account of the death of a god he is slaying his antagonist who is god. As for the third stage, that of discovery, exaltation, and resolution, it occurs most unmistakably in the penultimate chapter of the entire study. Here Frazer finally discovers the link between the golden bough and the mistletoe which enables him to resolve his quest by finding a generic explanation for the exploits of Aeneas, Balder, and the Kings of the Wood at Nemi. And in so doing, he has, in effect, achieved his exaltation as a hero who completes his task and also guaranteed his recognition by his own as well as a later generation.

Traditionally the three-stage quest of the romance is directed to the slaying of a dragon and the finding of buried treasure. When we turn to *The Golden Bough*, we encounter enough dragons and treasure for scores of romances, but they don't seem to be exactly what we are after, if only because they exist in no direct, active relation to our hero, Sir James. A useful clue here is Northrop Frye's suggestion that the labyrinth is an image of the dragon or monster.[52] To anyone who has observed *The Golden Bough*'s technique of circling around and around its particular subjects—as, say, when the identification of the mistletoe as the elusive golden bough is reached after consideration of taboos concerning the earth and sun, the seclusion of girls at puberty, fire-festivals, magic flowers, the varied locations and nature of external souls, and the myth of Balder—it is clear that here is a labyrinth of gigantic size and complexity. Pretty clearly the myth underlying *The Golden Bough*—the myth beneath the myths, as it were—is that of Theseus and the Minotaur. The monster, then, which Frazer the rational hero seeks to slay is ignorance itself, whose archetypal form is a half-human, half-animal composite of ancient myth, modern folklore, and the ritual customs of both past and present. Thus, the monster is intellectual: the puzzle created by the impingement of irrational or inadequate explanations on the rational mind rooted in common sense.

Frazer's characteristic reaction to the monster is seen at the

[51] *GB*, IX, 422-423.
[52] Frye, *Anatomy of Criticism*, p. 190.

very outset when he remarks that "it needs no elaborate demonstration to convince us that the stories told to account for Diana's
worship at Nemi are unhistorical."[53] Coupled with this is his
determination to conquer his adversary by framing rational questions to be answered with the aid of his famed weapon, the comparative method. The result is his entry into the labyrinth in pursuit of the protean monster, an event dramatized by such
remarks as "we must try to *probe deeper* by examining the worship as well as the legend or myth of Hippolytus."[54] To guarantee
his return he pays out behind him a slender chain of hypotheses,
conjectures, and common-sense assumptions. His reward is not
only the destroying (at least to his own satisfaction) of falsehood
and superstition but the acquisition of the treasure buried deep
in labyrinth. For the scholar such as Frazer the ideal form of
wealth is knowledge ordered into a coherent form and issuing in
the wisdom of revelation, in this case, of "the long march, the
slow and toilsome ascent, of humanity from savagery to
civilisation."[55]

While much more could be said about *The Golden Bough* as
a displaced quest romance—for instance, its complex use of pity
and fear as forms of pleasure so that the appropriate romance
strains of the marvellous, a thoughtful melancholy, and a tender,
passive charm are pervasive—enough has been said to suggest
the plausibility of the identifications.[56] One final point still remains, however. Even if *The Golden Bough* is a quest romance,
how does this account for its importance to modern literature?
Obviously, important aspects in any answer would be its quest
motif, religious significance, and archetypal symbolism. But modern literature has also been marked by a profoundly ironic
temper which would seem at odds with the idealized world of
romance. This point brings us back to the style and structure of
The Golden Bough. Though doubtless the pure romance has little affinity with irony, it is also true that the romances closest to
us in time, whether of Hawthorne or of Hudson, usually possess
a considerable admixture of irony. And the same is true of *The*

[53] *GB*, I, 21.   [54] *GB*, I, 24; italics mine.
[55] *GB*, I, xxv.   [56] Frye, *Anatomy of Criticism*, p. 37.

Golden Bough. It was not for nothing that Frazer found his prose masters in Anatole France and Ernest Renan.

One of our most sensitive critics has pointed out Joyce's use of Renan's combination of irony and pity, and the same is true too of *The Golden Bough.*[57] It opens with "a dream-like vision" of Nemi in which descriptive charm expresses a tender pity for the human follies enacted there.[58] From this it immediately modulates into a compound irony based on the relation of man and god, which if not central is at least typical: "In the civil war its [Nemi's] sacred treasures went to replenish the empty coffers of Octavian, who well understood the useful art of thus securing the divine assistance, if not the divine blessing, for the furtherance of his ends. But we are not told that he treated Diana on this occasion as civilly as his divine uncle Julius Caesar once treated Capitoline Jupiter himself, borrowing three thousand pounds' weight of solid gold from the god, and scrupulously paying him back with the same weight of gilt copper."[59]

More germane to Frazer's central aim is his use of the comparative method for ironic purposes. Irony by incongruous juxtaposition undeniably reentered English literature with a heavy French accent, but we should not overlook the way in which Frazer's celebrated method frequently performed the same function on a broader range. Nor is it without significance that T. S. Eliot and Edith Sitwell, the two most assiduous students of Laforgue and Corbière, were also attentive readers of *The Golden Bough.* One version of Frazer's technique is the large-scale juxtaposition of ostensibly opposed but actually similar rites, as with the festivals of Adonis and St. John.[60] Another is that of the sober understatement of a hypothesis such as "there is no intrinsic improbability in the view that for the sake of edification the church may have converted a real heathen festival into a nominal Christian one."[61] Even more oblique yet pervasive is his use of terms and images that ironically expose similarities his opponent seeks to conceal, as when a worshipper of Artemis is said to pay tithes to

[57] Harry Levin, *James Joyce*, p. 217.   [58] *GB*, I, 1.
[59] *GB*, I, 4.   [60] *GB*, IV, 244ff.
[61] *GB*, I, 16.

the goddess or when it is noted that Cybele and Attis were worshipped on the site of the Vatican. And finally there is irony employed for comic purposes and directed at his own controlling concepts, like that of the dying and reviving god. Thus, in a passage such as the following we may discern the lineaments of Joyce's ironic handling of Christian rites in *Ulysses* and his more jocular chronicling of HCE's rise and fall: "in his long and chequered career this mythical personage has displayed a remarkable tenacity of life. For we can hardly doubt that the Saint Hippolytus of the Roman calendar, who was dragged by horses to death on the thirteenth of August, Diana's own day, is no other than the Greek hero of the same name, who after dying twice over as a heathen sinner has been happily resuscitated as a Christian saint."[62]

Like that of modern literature as a whole, Frazer's irony begins in realism with a wry recognition of human folly and broadens out into a mythic treatment of men who imitate gods, are sacrificed to the needs of society, seize and hold power through unscrupulous stratagems and a shrewd knowledge of mass psychology, and abase themselves. Thus, if we take Hardy, Huxley, Lawrence, and Joyce as typifying recent modes of irony, we can see how *The Golden Bough* encompasses their moods of fatalism, anger, nostalgia, and detachment and integrates them into an encyclopedic vision of the knowledge inherent in its society: In effect, then, *The Golden Bough* became central to twentieth-century literature because it was grounded in the essential realism of anthropological research, informed with the romance's quest of an ideal, and controlled by the irony in divine myth and human custom. Together these made it the discursive archetype and hence matrix of that literature.

[62] *GB*, I, 21.

CHAPTER V

The Literary Uses of
The Golden Bough

[I]

In the preceding chapter the structural and stylistic affinities between *The Golden Bough* and modern literature in general were
sketched. Subsequent chapters will examine in detail the ways in
which selected major writers have drawn Frazer's themes,
motifs, and details into the fabric of their verse and prose. To afford a transition between these two approaches the present chapter will endeavor to suggest the variety of uses to which *The
Golden Bough* has been put by twentieth-century writers generally. Such an examination of Frazer-inspired mythic perspectives and literary strategies reveals the inexhaustible vitality and
resourcefulness of the modern mythopoeic imagination. At the
same time it is clear that *The Golden Bough* has been and continues to be of seminal importance in the forging of twentieth-
century literature. For the more we have come to understand
that literature's historical roots as well as its significant texts the
more we see that one of its central activities is the adaption of a
wide variety of myths to the enduring aesthetic needs of men.

The closeness between Frazer's anthropology and the mythopoeic outlines of modern literature is clearly indicated by the extent to which *The Golden Bough* figures not only as a shaping
force but also as a participant in the imaginative world scene of
literature. What Conrad Aiken's fiction, such as *Blue Voyage*, for
instance, is in the former instance, the novels of Richard Aldington are in the latter. Where Aiken represents his characters as
"all like automatic performants of a queer primitive ritual,"[1] Aldington makes Frazer and his ideas points of reference for his

---

[1] Conrad Aiken, *Blue Voyage* (New York: Scribner's, 1927), p. 33.

139

characters. The one authenticates Frazer's views on the primitive past as a modern psychological determinant, the other shows them to be objective presences consciously attended to by society. This role of Frazer as fictive participant is especially important in demonstrating his involvement in the historical and prosaic as well as in the mythic and preternatural. The novels of Richard Aldington, then, afford a most instructive instance of Frazer's contribution to an accurate sense of the context of the period presented fictively. They indicate in striking fashion the extent to which Frazer dominated the minds and conversations of many areas of society in the 1920s and 1930s. To this extent they dramatize the more private recognition of Frazer's importance made by artists who, as Harold Monro did around 1918, determined to read *The Golden Bough*, *Folklore of the Old Testament*, and other works of the same order.[2] A novel like *All Men Are Enemies* (1933) does, in a measure, for anthropology what other writers were doing for psychoanalysis. It uses the language and ideas of *The Golden Bough* as part of both its setting and its point of view. In so doing it reveals a major shift in the cultural sensibility of the age, which marks it off in unmistakable fashion from its predecessor. For instance, one of the male characters observes a woman clutching her breasts as though, he thinks, "she wanted to tear them like the wild mourners for Thammuz."[3] And elsewhere certain of the characters are said to "live on these pictures, like mistletoe on a tree."[4] The allusions testify not so much to Aldington's trying to establish symbolic or archetypal levels in his novel as to his reflecting faithfully the prevailing interests and attitudes and expressions of his own world. Both the dying god and the parasitic mistletoe had, in effect, become household words as a result of the impact of *The Golden Bough*.

The prevalence of Frazer's role in the cultural life of the time is revealed throughout Aldington's other works. An earlier novel, *The Colonel's Daughter* (1931), develops the ironic view of

[2] See Joy Grant, *Harold Monro and the Poetry Bookshop* (Los Angeles: University of California Press, 1967), pp. 272-273.

[3] Richard Aldington, *All Men are Enemies* (New York: Doubleday, Doran, 1933), p. 207.

[4] Aldington, *All Men are Enemies*, p. 75.

many aspects of modern civilization first shown in *The Death of a Hero* (1929): "The wedding of Tom and Lizzie . . . might have provided entertainment and instruction to an anthropologist studying the persistence of magical practices and ceremonial costumes in civilised communities."[5] The Maypole is called "that cheery phallic emblem," and economic capital "that sacred totem which compels poor boobs to work for us."[6] And later one of the character's efforts to free himself from the bondage of religious belief is viewed sceptically as scarcely worthwhile for "he immediately fell into the much older and more nauseous bog of magic."[7] Here Aldington clearly reflects Frazer's view that magic preceded religion in the development of culture. More importantly, however, the novel accentuates the ironic attitude implicit in Frazer's comparative method and the anthropological perspective generally. Thus, magic is seen not so much as a primitive phenomenon but rather as a contemporary one whose form is naturally different. Instead of spells and incantations it is found to reside in "gadget-worship" and one character is "inextricably woven with the primitive feminine worship of trinkets."[8]

Perhaps the most unequivocal reflection of Frazer's shaping role in the imagination of the twentieth century occurs in *Very Heaven* (1937). One of the characters, Chris Heylin, is an assiduous student of anthropology, comparative religion, and prehistory, as well as psychology. The affinity between character and author is underscored by the informed specifying of Chris's textbooks: "On the mantelpiece stood some of the honoured ones: Frazer, Budge, Petrie, Breasted, Sayce, Hall, Wooley, Breuil, Moir, Elliott, Smith, Childe."[9] Like so many others of the period who had pondered *The Golden Bough* and similar works, Chris feels the need to bring his knowledge to bear on his own contemporary scene. In a letter to one of his friends he remarks: "I ought to have brought a team of psychologists and ethnologists

---

[5] Richard Aldington, *The Colonel's Daughter* (New York: Doubleday, Doran, 1931), p. 161.

[6] Aldington, *The Colonel's Daughter*, pp. 174, 177.

[7] Aldington, *The Colonel's Daughter*, p. 265.

[8] Aldington, *The Colonel's Daughter*, p. 265.

[9] Richard Aldington, *Very Heaven* (New York: Doubleday, Doran, 1937), p. 145.

with me. Without such interpreters I'm all at sea, and don't even know where to begin. I wish Rivers and Malinowski were available. I'm more and more convinced that ethnology should begin at home."[10] The irony at the follies in the modern world revealed by the anthropological perspective is here tempered by a desire also to find answers, explanations, and where necessary new formulations and solutions. Thus, he tests marriage in the light of arguments concerning Briffault's thesis that it is a wholly economic institution. He relates the exhilaration felt at cutting free from an old life to commence a new one to the stress in ancient religions placed on rebirth. In addition, he puzzles over the origins of civilization and wonders whether all myths and religions have a common psychological basis and what it might be. Perhaps most representative of his view is his feeling that anthropology can provide the illumination necessary to removing society's imperfections: "The world is filled with irrational beliefs and destructive prejudices. Now, if it can be shown that these things are not innate, but have their origins in dead religion or magic, we've taken the first step towards correcting them."[11]

Something very like this view of Chris's dominated the thinking of many creative artists in the twentieth century, especially after World War I. For many the war was the great traumatic revelation that the savage lay very close beneath the skin of civilized man. Rendered so aware, they quickly found further evidence of this in the forms and manners of society and in its controlling attitudes. Chris's feeling that recognizing the historicity of man's irrational and destructive impulses is the first step to eradicating them persisted in the culture at large. Among artists, however, it quickly became subordinate to a more sceptical and ironical temper. To them the central issues became whether Western culture as it had been known could survive and whether art would have a significant place in whatever equivalent substitute might develop. While there are countless ramifications of this particular issue, they all come to a head in the increasingly intense problem of the relation between art and science. Since science seemed to many artists to epitomize the secular, factual,

[10] Aldington, *Very Heaven*, p. 34.
[11] Aldington, *Very Heaven*, p. 91.

technological character of their civilization, they saw themselves as an embattled cultural minority bereft in substantial measure of their traditional role of moral and spiritual educators. The scientific habit of mind appeared, at this time in the century at least, to exclude the poetic and imaginative faculties from contributing knowledge of any order. Confronted by such apparent challenges to their autonomy and very right to existence, artists, critics, and those seriously concerned about the nature of aesthetic matters began, frequently unwittingly, a serious reexamination of the nature and grounds of their craft.

Casual consideration of modern literature usually results in a dimly felt conviction that its mythic ambience is bound up with quasi-religious attitudes and loosely idealistic philosophic views. Eliot's concern with primitive nature myths as a matrix for Christianity and Cassirer's stress upon mythic consciousness are often taken as constituting the central and indeed only stance myth may impart to literature. In point of fact, twentieth-century writers have found both more varied and more pragmatic uses for myth in their works than the examples of the great modernists— like Eliot, Yeats, and Joyce—alone would suggest. And in doing so, they are, from all the available evidence, largely indebted to *The Golden Bough* for the flexible and multiform perspective it generates with regard to myth and related matters. Doubtless there are other uses, but in general the preponderance of modern writers have deployed the materials of *The Golden Bough* for one or more of four chief purposes. With Frazer's aid they create works of what might be called an essentially contextual nature in addition to making diagnostic cultural analyses. They also find in *The Golden Bough* means of dramatizing and participating in psychological dynamics as well as of achieving philosophical positions of ironic and existential detachment.

By contextual works is meant those literary creations which focus on ancient myths or rituals in order to realize their role in the ordinary, daily existence of their time, to relate them to an even more remote and primitive past, or to find in them metaphors whose continuation into the present illumine its central dilemmas. Obviously these are representative species only; any such macroscopic descriptions clearly miss many of the discriminative nuances developed by individual works. Yet they do serve to indicate, at least for initial purposes, the dominant thrust of such works and authors.

[II]

One poet drawn to Frazer and the creation of poems of context is T. Sturge Moore, the brother of the famous Cambridge philosopher G. E. Moore. Like that of his friend Yeats, Sturge Moore's career extended from the 90s through the first quarter of the twentieth century. In so doing it paralleled that of Frazer, whose first edition of *The Golden Bough* was already being widely discussed when Moore published his *Vinedresser and Other Poems* (1899). Even more than Yeats, Moore was attracted to classical and mythological themes and situations. It is perhaps too much to say that this was wholly due to the influence of Frazer. Yet it does seem likely that this interest was reinforced and also molded by Moore's awareness of the developments in anthropology and comparative religion spearheaded by Frazer. Thus, in glancing over Moore's entire poetic corpus, we cannot help but be struck by the way in which his attention is continually drawn to classical and Biblical subjects. In dealing with them, he gives the impression by his absorption in their myths, rituals, and history, of being engaged in a poetic version of *The Golden Bough*'s comparative treatment of religions and customs.

Even more striking evidence of Frazer's influence appears in the classical deities Moore mentions most frequently and from the characteristics he attributes to them. Adonis as the god beloved and mourned by women, Hyacinth as a later version of the dying god Adonis, Marsyas as Apollo's victim, Zeus as the sky-god, Bacchus or Dionysus as a deity of both wine and agriculture whose worship has spread through all Asia, Aphrodite and Artemis as contrasting symbols of virginity and sex, Astarte as a moon-goddess and harlot figure worshipped by the Tyrians, and Demeter and Persephone as corn-goddesses, all reflect points made by *The Golden Bough*.[12] Moore as well as Frazer views

---

[12] T. Sturge Moore, *The Poems* (London: Macmillan, 1931-1933), I, 18, 240, 243; II, 57ff., 139, 165; III, 60, 61, 65, 162, 181. Cf. *GB*, VI, 23; VII, 216, 258, 263; IX, 390.

them as participating in an immense drama of love, fertility, and death which was of incalculable importance to their worshippers. Moore also resembles Frazer in that although he concentrates on classical and Mediterranean myths and rituals, he is aware of others such as the Scandinavian. Indeed, when they look north, both focus on the myth of Balder the Beautiful and particularly his death at the hands of Loki. Moore in his poem *To Loki* observes, "Thou lovely Balder by their hands didst kill" because "content thou dost abhor."[13] For the speaker, Loki is "passionless desire" and "divine mobility" which he asks to "Enter our life once more,—force us to live!"[14] In other words, he thinks of the half-divine Loki as still present in the world, ranging over its surface not only as "Mischievous Lob, or lanthorn Jack" but also as a gipsy.[15] This unmistakably echoes Frazer's contention that much of contemporary folklore and superstitious custom possesses an intimate connection with the great myths and beliefs of the past. At the same time, Moore betrays his sense of the diminution of modern life and of its need for revivification. In particular, he finds that it is in man's heart where "fade the once bright myths of heaven and hell!"[16] His nostalgia for ancient myths identifies Moore's perpetuation of much late-nineteenth-century poetry, where the concern was more with the mythological than with the mythopoeic and where myth was essentially the product of higher civilizations and thus a kind of iconographic cultural shorthand which could be used to communicate and create anew the splendors, beauty, and moral power of the past. It is in this spirit that many of his poems take up not so much the recreating as the contemplative retelling of myths like those of Zeus and Semele, Danae, Leda, Orpheus and Eurydice, and Omphale and Herakles.

Yet Moore was considerably more than a belated nineteenth-century poetic mythographer. His work strongly testifies to the subtle yet emphatic effect *The Golden Bough* had on the deployment of myth in poetry. Though much of it is ostensibly traditional in mythic attitude, it is nevertheless clearly post-Frazerian in concentration. There is a greater stress on ancient myths' in-

---

[13] Moore, I, 21.   [14] Moore, I, 20.
[15] Moore, I, 21.   [16] Moore, I, 94.

volvement with fertility themes, with their reflecting and growing out of a sustained body of primitive customs, and with their
being preeminently the means of apprehending the past as real
and alive in all its strangeness and otherness. Thus, in his loosely
allegorical treatment of Danaë he shows "the painted goddess,
its lewd sigh,/ Soused by the hiccuping roysterers, drip with
wine."[17] And in one of his Biblical poems, "Jonathan," he associates the protagonist's cry with pagan fertility rituals:

> loud as heathen maids,
> To hail that star they worship, shuddering cry,
> Because they deem it virile and a god
> Prompt to take umbrage at their virgin state.[18]

Such comparisons function in the same way as Frazer's larger
and more sustained parallels between the so-called higher religions and primitive rites. And also like *The Golden Bough*,
Moore's poetry frequently sets the myths and rituals of great ancient civilizations in a context of primitive custom. Thus, the
poems embody in their dramatic fabric such beliefs as that of the
dead's exacting rites from witches, the soul's being like a butterfly and escaping from the body through the mouth and thereafter
being capable of helping or harming living persons, the need for
injunctions against naming the dead or men in battle, and the
necessity of having a wizard for any attempts to raise the dead.[19]
Moore expresses the view of the ancient world Gilbert Murray
described near the end of the nineteenth century. The serene
classical Hellene and the aesthetic fleshly pagan no longer persist
in their original clarity. Ancient man and his world are seen anthropologically as close kin of contemporary savage tribesmen.
Moore continued to believe in and celebrate both of these earlier
nineteenth-century views, but at the same time he was receptive
to the insights afforded by Frazer. The result is a poetic rendering of the transitional state occupied by classical studies as anthropology of a Frazerian cast came to impinge upon them.

Even more germane to the temper of the age is *The Golden*

---

[17] Moore, I, 218.   [18] Moore, II, 170.
[19] Moore, I, 38, 40-41, 42, 176.

Bough's shaping power in the imaginative secularization of religious experience. Here, too, Moore affords an instructive gloss on the modern sensibility's struggles of reconstruction and accommodation. His long dramatic narrative "Judas" takes up the story on the night of the Last Supper and follows it through to Judas' suicide. In it Moore draws explicitly on *The Golden Bough*'s discussion of the parallels between Christ's crucifixion and certain Jewish rituals. A glossary appended to the poem has two entries of considerable interest. The first deals with Barabbas: "Means 'Son of the Father,' the title of Marduc (Mordecai) who is crowned to represent the power of renewed increase in the vegetable and animal kingdoms, in his father's stead, when Ariman (Haman), the previous Son of the Father, dies in his stead. The king of the country was originally slain every year, but in time one of his sons was substituted, and still later any criminal received the title and ruled for a brief symbol of the year, to die in his turn at the next year's feast."[20] The stress on vegetative fertility, the king's annual sacrifice, and the gradual process of sacrificial substitution, all suggest the closeness of Moore's acquaintance with *The Golden Bough*, which elaborates each of these points with a wealth of illustration. Any lingering doubt as to Frazer's impact on Moore is removed by the second glossary passage, which deals with the festival of Purim. It reads:

> Sir James Frazer, in "The Golden Bough," suggests that possibly Jesus may have died as Haman in the celebration of the Feast of Purim. It seems certain the Book of Esther is a pious travesty of the myth of Ishtar (Esther) and substitutes a patriotic import for the original magic. The celebration of the Feast of Purim (Sacaea) was a custom brought back from the captivity in Babylonia, the native home of this cult. Sir James' suggestion enhances the poetical and religious significance of the story of the Passion. Outworn notions of substitution and redemption would thus have conspired in the tragedy out of which more spiritual forms of those ideas were to be evolved. It is possible that pious Pharisees were shocked by this pagan

[20] Moore, II, 331.

celebration, and that the Sadducees were cynically indifferent to it, and hence efforts to suppress and revive it led to much irregularity in its celebration about this period.[21]

Clearly Moore's dramatic poem is, like Graves's *King Jesus*, a mythopoeic rendering of the cultural adaptability of the dying and reviving god figure. Both works reverse the traditional emphasis on the uniqueness of the Crucifixion. They argue—as does John Peale Bishop in his essay on *The Golden Bough*—instead that its importance is actually enhanced by recognizing it as a particularly prominent historical instance of a ritual rooted in the archetypal myth of the dying god, whose proliferation throughout the world testifies to its importance and perdurability. The value of the Crucifixion as a religious symbol lies for them not in its individuality so much as in its prevalence. In turn, the contemporary importance of Jesus consists preeminently in his having been a superior man capable of accepting the awesome obligation of enacting a ritual of fatality and of shaping history into a mythic form and therefore a felt reality. Thus, both "Judas" and *King Jesus* exemplify modern literature's inclination either to replace or to redefine the concept of transcendence as a spiritual metaphor.

For Moore the poetic interest in myth was part of the human effort to apprehend the essential nature of the past. Myth is largely dedicated to discovering the truth about men and societies whose deaths in a remote time have conferred on them an aura of mystery that is a subtle compound of secular curiosity and religious awe. At the same time, Moore's style, with its languorous rhythms and deliberate archaisms, suggests that for him the world of myth and comparative religion was also an aesthetic construct in which refuge may be sought from the pressures of contemporary dilemmas. His long, mythological dramatic poems become, then, barometers of the mythopoeic imagination's efforts to resolve these dialectical tensions. Their length afforded him both the necessary scope in which fully to explore the past and his relation to it and also the luxury of prolonged withdrawal from the modern world.

[21] Moore, II, 333.

Both Aldington's novels and Moore's poetry exemplify forms of contextualization, though with significant differences. Aldington concentrates on limning in as part of the fictive texture and density of the immediate social scene the cultural *donnée* with which both fictional and real characters of the twentieth century must come to terms as part of the process of living. Moore, on the other hand, makes myth, its *figurae* and actions, generate a universe of artifice in which release from the dialectic of time is sought in a remote verbal eternity. Where Aldington aims at creating the conditions of the historical present, Moore seeks to produce an ideal context out of present desires projected on to an infinitely remote past.

[III]

Two other species of contextualization are worth noticing for the sense of mythopoeic flexibility they convey. Each provides, as it were, an instructive qualification on one of the contextual modes mentioned above, almost, we might say, by a process of cross-pollination. In the first, myth and ritual emerge as a transcription of historical reality, as a poetic equivalent to Malinowski's functionalism, which sees myth as a hard-working cultural force concerned with the fundamental business of living and its perpetuation. Representative here are such novels as Naomi Mitchison's *Corn King and the Spring Queen* and William Golding's *Inheritors*. A number of poems by Robert Graves and Richard Aldington are of the same order, while in a more vatic or hierophantic vein so are those of H. D. and Kathleen Raine. In contrast to the focus of this mode on the past, the second species of contextualization utilizes Frazer's anthropological vision of the primitive past to crystallize the enduring dilemmas of the cultural present. Caroline Gordon uses this strategy in her novel *The Garden of Adonis*, which shows ancient ritual patterns working themselves out in the twentieth-century American South. The same is true of the short stories and novels of William Faulkner, most notably in "Dry September," "Red Leaves," *Light in August*, and *Absalom, Absalom!* What both of these modes make clear is that not all artists have been primarily concerned with effecting radical alterations or accommodations of the dying god or other mythic emblems so that Frazer's images subserve their own dominant metaphors. Some writers, of course, have utilized both modes. Thus, Jocelyn Brooke uses the transcriptive mode in his poem "The Scapegoat," which uses the first person to present both ancient ritual details and also the victim's calm acceptance that is, nevertheless, shot through with subdued regret. On the other hand, in his novel of the same title the archetypal ritual sacrifice of the scapegoat is transposed to the modern world and deflected from a solemn communal observance to a personal, familial situation reverberant with overtones of abnormal psychology.

One poet who responds to *The Golden Bough* not with efforts at imaginative displacement or extrapolation but with narrative mirroring is F. L. Lucas. His *From Many Times and Lands*, subtitled Poems of Legend and History, exemplifies the transcriptive mode. A poem entitled "The First Yule" tells a story of a tribal king who annually halts the dying sun's midwinter decline by ostensibly magical means, who ultimately loses his powers with old age and in consequence is ritually slain by his people, and who is supplanted by his son who restores the sun to health and tribal life to a fertile state. Any doubt as to the poem's indebtedness to *The Golden Bough* is removed by a footnote referring explicitly to specific pages in four different volumes of the third edition. The central concern of the poem is not to exploit the metaphoric potential of the king whose life is bound up with the fertility of his tribe and its land. Rather it is to render as vividly and simply as possible a past reality that conditions, however allusively and tangentially, our life today. The emphasis, therefore, is on scene and action rather than character and symbol. Narrative pace and simplicity of image allow Lucas to make of Frazer's material a vignette from prehistory whose reality and remoteness carry considerable emotional reverberation.

In this regard this sort of poem comes closest, perhaps, to finding an imaginative equivalent for the prose of *The Golden Bough* and the function it sought to fulfill. Like Frazer, Lucas is concerned to render the scene with maximum fidelity and to keep his interpretations of its significance to a minimum. Only in the opening and closing stanzas does he produce his version of Frazer's speculative and reflective comments. Thus, the poem begins:

> Askest why, stranger,
> We stamp, we sing,
> And black round the cavern
> Our shadows spring?
> Because we are mighty,
> Who once were nought,
> By the wisdom that Ung,
> Our grandsire, wrought.[22]

Here Frazer's theory that human progress depends on the actions and intelligence of outstanding individuals who learn more quickly than most how to bend both nature and man to their desires is given poetic form, just as the bulk of the poem derives from Frazer's scenic images and ritual actions.

More reflective in tone is the final stanza, which suggests how central and yet how tragic ritual is to man's perpetuation:

> *My* turn, ere many
> A moon be run,
> To rule the Rain
> And bind the Sun.
> I too shall be mighty,
> Who once was nought,
> By the wisdom that Ung
> My grandsire wrought.
> On with the dance!
> Tread hard the floor!
> Who knows if we meet
> Next Yule once more?[23]

The speaker of the poem is the grandson of Ung and hence the successor to his own father, the present king and wizard, whose knowledge provides the religio-magical assurance of the persistence of the sun, spring, warmth, and fertility. Implicit in the material from Frazer, in the subject itself, is the fact that tribal survival and cultural advance involve not merely an easy sense of achieved progress but an equally strong awareness of the grim

---

[22] F. L. Lucas, *From Many Times and Lands* (London: Bodley Head, 1953), p. 20.
[23] Lucas, p. 25.

sacrifices they entail. Such a poem, then, functions as a mirror or window on the anthropological scene depicted by *The Golden Bough*. The resonance it generates is that of Frazer's mythopoeic imagination rather than that of the poet, so that the reader is brought to a state of reflective contemplation on the dimmest and most remote realities of human history.

Allied to this use of Frazer to convey a sense of intensified historical reality is one which uses what might be called Frazerian geography to sound the mingled notes of love and loss that appear so recurrently in *The Golden Bough*. For instance, Richard Aldington in a poem like "The Crystal World" summons up the focal scene from Frazer to add a note of mute, static plangency to his dominant concern:

> The Roman fountains—would she not love them?
> Blue Nemi in its cup of hills, the wine
> And olives.[24]

Essentially the same strategy is used by Ezra Pound in *The Cantos*, though with something more nearly approaching a leitmotif effect. Thus in the first of the *Pisan Cantos* he suddenly interrupts his ruminative contemplation of life, history, and prison to observe: "at Nemi waited on the slope above the lake sunken in the/ pocket of hills."[25] That this is a memory of *The Golden Bough* given aesthetic form and imaginative poignancy is born out later in Canto LXXVII. There he notes:

[24] Richard Aldington, *Complete Poems* (London: Allen Wingate, 1947), p. 348.

[25] Ezra Pound, *The Cantos* (New York: New Directions, 1964), p. 465. Subsequent references are indicated in the text. At this point it might be worth observing that although Pound does make sustained and intricate use of myth, as more recent critics have indicated, nevertheless it seems extremely unlikely that *The Golden Bough* figures as a major factor—compared to numerous other shaping forces—in his views and uses of myth and primitive custom. His concern with vegetative fertility and its deification, with victimization and sacrifice, with the comparative mode of knowledge, and with imaginative structures of contrast and counterpoint, all doubtless owe something to Frazer—but not so much as to other people. In any case, given the present state of our knowledge of the *Cantos* and given the greater likelihood of more immediate sources of image and idea, it is virtually impossible to trace sources for particular passages with any real confidence.

With drawn sword as at Nemi
day comes after day.[26]

Pound sees living and the daily cycle as individual combat set against a backdrop of human history and legend; nothing could more aptly convey that sense than Frazer's opening scene and drama.

Probably the clearest instance of such geographic allusion occurs in George Barker's 1966 volume entitled *Dreams of a Summer Night*, which includes "II Poems Written Near Lake Nemi." Clearly Barker is deliberately invoking the opening scene in the first volume of *The Golden Bough*. Place-names like Ariccia, the Alban Hills, and Nemorense; images like the golden bough, the goddess of love and fertility, the moon; and epithets for the lake such as "handmirror of Diana"—all attest to the poet's determined and allusive use of that scene from Frazer which sets both the stage and the tone for his encyclopedic romance of human customs and aspirations.[27] At the same time, the poems also develop detailed natural descriptions of the region, which serve to make of them, on one level, instances of twentieth-century topographical verse. This duality of focus—the topographical and the anthropological—generates a subtle and sustained correlation between the physical world of Lake Nemi and the verbal realm of *The Golden Bough*. The former, made up of the "lovely valley," with its mimosa, doves, lake, and moon, exists not only as a geographical place but also as an imaginative scene. Barker's vision, then, is both of Lake Nemi and also of Frazer's account of it. The physical reality of the region is infused with the anthropological meaning of the ancient ritual of love and sacred marriage and its involvement with sacrifice, suffering, and death. In this way, the topographical character of the poems modulates into a meditative mode that contemplates both the value and the transitoriness of "the love that nurses its own kind."[28] The physical scene calls to mind Frazer's interpretation of its ancient his-

[26] Pound, p. 496.

[27] *GB*, I, 1-3, 6-8, 10, 12.

[28] George Barker, *Dreams of a Summer Night* (London: Faber & Faber, 1966), p. 40.

tory at the same time that the interpretation structures the perceptions of the scene and the poet's responses to it.

These, however, are basically but one response to the strangeness of man's original belief and behavior. Another response is considerably less solemn, more impressed by the bizarre and mundane sources of mankind's myths and religious impulses. Some striking instances of a playfully ironic recognition of what Kenneth Burke has called the comic quality of *The Golden Bough* appear in the work of Rupert Brooke and Robert Graves. Thus, one of the poems in Graves' *Fairies and Fusiliers* volume is entitled "Dead Cow Farm." It employs a parody of the Egyptian creation myth of Hathor, the cow goddess, in order to define the nature and future of trench combat. In doing so, Graves both alludes with irony to one of the goddesses mentioned by Frazer and also sardonically utilizes his favorite technique of connecting pagan myths with Christian beliefs. Similarly, Brooke affects a mock solemnity in his "On the Death of Smet-Smet, The Hippopotamus-Goddess." Ironic distance is achieved by the dramatic device of treating the poem as an ancient Egyptian tribal song antiphonally presented by the temple priests and the people. In characterizing her as "wrinkled and huge and hideous . . . , lustful and lewd," Brooke neatly catches the effect of Frazer's linking of the great orgiastic fertility goddesses of eastern civilizations with the license afforded more contemporary African queens and consorts.[29] The same kind of quizzical light-heartedness about ancient customs and primitive responses appears also in Graves's "Love and Black Magic," "The Bough of Nonsense," and "The Snake and the Bull." The same general sort of playfulness and ironic mythic perspective appears also in some of Norman Douglas' narratives. For instance, one of the central male figures of *In the Beginning* is a Phoenician Adonis mentioned by Frazer. His daughter's use of her guards as lovers and the general air of lechery and profligacy surrounding her suggest that she is modelled on a combination of Frazer's accounts of Astarte and Semiramis. The final Frazerian irony is that she acquires what

[29] Rupert Brooke, *Collected Poems* (New York: Dodd, Mead & Co., 1961), p. 31.

Douglas calls the disease of goodness and so becomes a religious and moral fanatic. A more recent version of *The Golden Bough*'s rhythms of fertility and death, adapted this time to contemporary British life, is Alan Sillitoe's novel *Saturday Night and Sunday Morning*. Frazer, whom Sillitoe keeps in his library, merges with Robert Graves's influence to shape the Nottingham life of Arthur Seaton, the hero, to *The Golden Bough*'s pattern of saturnalia and rebirth.[30]

The last mode of contextualization to be considered also reflects *The Golden Bough*'s deployment of scenic mythopoeia. It appears most representatively in the contemporary poet Robin Skelton. In 1960 he published "The God," first written in 1956, which is based on the chapter in *The Golden Bough* dealing with sundry forms of animal worship and its connection with totemism and taboo. Like Lucas, Skelton strives to render the scene in all its anthropological immediacy as a kind of genetic cultural vision. But unlike Lucas, he is more concerned to shape his verse in the prevailing contemporary idiom while still preserving narrative clarity. He also is prepared to make more sustained, if implicit, efforts to develop the theme's relevance to the human condition and particularly to the idea of man as a creature of the present.

Central to Frazer's treatment of the primitive worship of the bear, as in the cases of the American Indians and the ancient Ainos, is the puzzling fact of the ambiguity surrounding their feelings about the animal. On the one hand, for the greater part of the year it is regarded with profound veneration, and firmly grounded taboos against slaying it are scrupulously observed. On the other hand, at a particular moment in the year, solemn religious obligation to slay the bear is enjoined as part of a ceremonial ritual of sacrifice and propitiation. It is just this ambiguity that Skelton emphasizes when he begins:

> Feed the beast
> that you weep for, having killed.

[30] See Hugh B. Staples, " 'Saturday Night and Sunday Morning': Alan Sillitoe and the White Goddess," *Modern Fiction Studies*, x (1964), 171-181. An American parallel, to a degree, is William J. Gaddis' *The Recognitions*.

Garland the great bear
of the wood and hill.
Make him enter each house
with blessing snarl.[31]

The contradictions inherent in the tribal behavior are even more
pointed when the bear is described as "the body bayed and
torn,/ worshipped and fattened."[32] And at the approximate middle of the poem the polarization of worship and sacrificial sacrament is made explicit:

he was the hunting god
the body's rage
could recognize
and worship in his cage,
and weep and feast upon.[33]

In this way Skelton engenders a greater sense of the problematic and of its impingement upon the present. For one thing,
Skelton, like Robinson Jeffers, utilizes the irony resident in man's
killing those creatures—the gods—whom he has created in order
to save him. For Jeffers, the principal irony revolves around the
inevitability and indeed the desirability of suffering. For Skelton,
it consists by implication of man's having created for himself
a ritual analogue of vegetative time, a cycle of recurrence that
perpetuates the mystery without providing the meaning:

The seasons turn
stiffly upon
the dying and the born,
looking for him they killed
to come again

in the same shape
from the bestial Spring.[34]

The slain god is seen throughout the poem as moving by way of
his ghost or spirit into the land of ancestors, called "the fathers."

[31] Robin Skelton, *Begging the Dialect* (London: Oxford University Press,
1960), p. 28.

[32] Skelton, p. 28.   [33] Skelton, p. 29.   [34] Skelton, p. 29.

This end, however, is as much a riddle as the genesis of man, with which, in a strange way derived from the researches of Frazer and Jane Harrison, it is identified. That is, the death of an individual is thought to entail a return to an ancestral matrix— what Harrison calls "alcheringa" time—from whence issues in turn the living creature. Skelton's poem presents this as the problematic condition confronting man. The region of the fathers is an impenetrable mystery to the living:

> The unknown
> returns no message back
> but the unknown,
>
> and the seasons turn.
> What pity have
> the gathered centuries
> across the grave
> to send no more
> than this for rage and love—[35]

Here the slain god—"clumsy, rank, matt-haired,/ with slavering jaws"[36]—ultimately stands forth as the final inhuman mystery which challenges man by posing the irreducibility of the unknown against his desire for knowledge. Thus the poem closes with the image of "the new caught god" who "awaits our knives and prayers" set over against the query 'What meaning is there?"[37] In such a question we see both the extent to which Skelton moves beyond Lucas in investing the narrative pattern of *The Golden Bough* with thematic point and also the manner in which his poem captures one of the central motifs of modern literature. Compassionately yet quizzically he views against a primeval background the irony of man's passionate desire for fertility and the lengths to which his search for its emblems and signs takes him.

[IV]

For a more sustained effort to bring myth to bear on the agonies of contemporary life while utilizing the form of the long poem and the mythological drama, we turn to Robinson Jeffers.

---

[35] Skelton, p. 30.   [36] Skelton, p. 30.   [37] Skelton, p. 30.

Moore's poetic career began in 1899 and was substantially over by the time of the publication of his collected poems (1931-1932). Jeffers' first volume appeared in 1912, though it was really with the *Tamar* collection of 1924 that he achieved his characteristic manner which continued into the middle of the century. Thus, Jeffers provides an apt and instructive development of Moore's interest in the extended poetic treatment of myth. They resemble one another in their comparatist interest in the myths of a number of cultures, but they differ significantly in their motives and hence in their use of these myths. The work of Moore and Jeffers reveals how the central figure and motifs of *The Golden Bough* may be utilized for aesthetic escape and existential confrontation respectively. By calling on the resources of anthropology, and the aura of prehistory, Jeffers does not so much build a context as engage in diagnostic cultural analysis.

By his own admission, Jeffers has been concerned to explore the sources of contemporary Western civilization.[38] Since this exploration involves attending to the interaction of myth and history in particular cultures, it both resembles and derives in many respects from Frazer's interest in the genesis of society and the reconstruction of the past. Jeffers acts mythopoeically on the Hebrew-Christian, the Greek, and the Teutonic sources of our modern civilization in *Dear Judas*, *The Tower Beyond Tragedy*, and *At the Birth of an Age* respectively. The last is of particular interest to this study, for it makes extensive use of the symbol of the self-tortured god who hangs himself on a gallows for a number of nights in order to gain wisdom of all things. Earlier intimations of this thematic symbol are found in *Apology for Bad Dreams* and *The Women at Point Sur*. Prominent though it is, there are a number of other themes and figures which also attest to the impact of Frazer's work on Jeffers' poetry. Among the more obvious are the belief in a recurrent pattern of existence as developed in "The Cycle," the rite of blood-sacrifice found in "A Redeemer" and "Meditation on Saviors," the capacity to bear pain as a test of manhood suggested in "Birth-Dues," the burial ceremonies and the idea of immortality alluded to in "Ossian's

---

[38] Robinson Jeffers, *Selected Poetry* (New York: Random House, 1937), p. xviii.

Grave," "The Giant's Ring," and "In the Hill at New Grange," the warrior hero-kings of "The Broadstone" and "Iona: The Graves of Kings," the agony and revulsion implicit in the rites of resurrection touched upon in "Antrim" and "No Resurrection," the fetish worship of a stone in "Rock and Hawk," the assimilation of rain to the mourning of women for the death of the hero or god as in "Distant Rainfall," and the relation of the myths and cultures of the past to those of the present which is presented in "Thebaid," "Hellenistics," "Decaying Lambskins," and "Theory of Truth."

The pertinence of Odin, the Scandinavian deity, to *The Golden Bough*'s figure of the dying god would be apparent even without Frazer's many references to him.[39] At one point Gudrun even speaks of "the hanged God/ that my childish blood loves," while later a stage direction capitalizes the entire phrase by way of indicating Jeffers' associating of the particular Scandinavian deity to his archetypal function in Frazer's later volumes. Gudrun's hypnotic attraction to the hanged god is the achievement of self-knowledge "in the flame of reality."[40]

At least part of the knowledge acquired through the reality of suffering and pain is precisely that the hanged god is, as Moore observed of the goddess in his *Medea*, a creature of many aspects. Jeffers, however, intensifies the comparative cultural perspective by having his heroine take a more emphatically Frazerian stance:

> Ah Sigurd that I was mourning Adonis
> the mistletoe lance,
> Hoegni nail hard
> The hero's hands
> To the eagle wings, make him more than a man,
> die for me Christ,
> Thammuz to death,
> Dermot go down.
> What boar's tusk opened God's flank,

[39] *GB*, I, 241ff., 367; II, 364; IV, 13, 56-57, 160ff., 188; V, 290; VI, 220.
[40] Robinson Jeffers, *Solstice and Other Poems* (New York: Random House, 1935), pp. 76, 80.

what enemy has bound his wrists,
Nailed him on the eagle
Wave of the mountain?[41]

The effect of this, of course, is to universalize the god's death
pan-culturally. In Moore the goddess Delia appears as Orthia,
Hecate, Cynthia, Artemis, and Selene, that is, as more or less
local versions of one expression of a single culture's deity. But
in Jeffers the dying god encompasses a plurality of cultures. Like
The Golden Bough, Jeffers shows that the pattern of godhead
conceived by mankind is substantially the same.

Jeffers' regard of the hanged god as the genetic paradigm of
Western civilization becomes of the utmost importance. Eliot sees
in the multiplicity of dying gods evidence of the evolution of religious consciousness and of Christianity's uniqueness through
history's working out of the *praeparatio Christi*. Jeffers, on the
other hand, finds the hanged god to be a profoundly ironic revelation. The irony, however, is directed less at the fact of man's insistence on killing his gods—though that certainly is a powerful
motif in much of modern literature—than at the revelation of the
ultimate reality man's existence creates for himself. The Hanged
God himself articulates this revelation in response to the anguished cries of dead and dying warriors:

Pain and their endless cries.
How they cry to me: but they are I:
    let them ask themselves.
I am they, and there is nothing beside.

. . . .

                        Without pressure, without
    conditions, without pain,
Is peace; that's nothing, not-being; the pure night,
    the perfect freedom, the black crystal.
    I have chosen
Being; therefore wounds, bonds, limits and pain;
    the crowded mind and the anguished nerves,
    experience and ecstasy.

. . . .

[41] Jeffers, *Solstice*, p. 82.

> I am the nerve, I am the agony,
> I am the endurance. I torture myself
> To discover myself.[42]

Here the hanged god emerges not as a transcendent power incarnate in human form in order to save mankind but as the concentrated essence of self-aware humanity. Being, for Jeffers, is ineradicably human, living, and suffering, so that the dying god ultimately is man engaged in inflicting on himself the pain inherent in existence. Like Yeats, Jeffers construes transcendence as an imaginative act of knowledge directed at the phenomenological universe. Where the two poets differ, of course, is in the greater attention given by Jeffers to sheer physical endurance and the inflicting of violations on the human body and mind. Thus, in his mythopoeia the man-god is the embodiment of both the universal and perennial human condition and also of the particular cultural age that worships him. In his foreword to *At the Birth of An Age* he suggests that the present age suffers from self-contradiction and self-frustration "bred from the tension between its two poles, of Western blood and superimposed Oriental religion."[43] The poem as a whole works out in dramatic terms this analysis of what Jeffers calls the Christian age so that finally the hanged god of Frazer becomes the sinister emblem of cultural disintegration at the same time as his "heroic beauty of being"[44] and its power to compel worship are acknowledged. Indeed, it is the very conjunction of imaginative force and inappropriate cultural context that makes him in Jeffers' eyes such an inevitable guarantee of the fate of the civilization. For him, the dying god is what civilization does and becomes: a magnificent human creation of a divine self-crucifixion.

What Jeffers contemplates with a kind of savage pleasure George Barker recoils from with an anguished intensity reflected in a neurasthenically heightened rhetoric. Poems such as the 1937 volume *Calamiterror* and the "Vision of England '38" clinically diagnose the cultural ills of the modern world. Their social awareness, however, is sharpened by the archetypal images and rituals derived from *The Golden Bough*. Indeed, Barker's poetry

---

[42] Jeffers, *Solstice*, pp. 88-89.   [43] Jeffers, *Solstice*, p. 1.
[44] Jeffers, *Solstice*, p. 91.

generally is marked by the impact of *The Golden Bough*. In *Poems* (1935) the sun is called "gold man, king," a dead man becomes wheat and is made into flour and eaten by his son, the sexual act is related to the fertility ritual of ploughing, and the identification of tree and man established.[45] In *Lament and Triumph* (1940) England is cast as St. George's green girl raped by modern commerce and her rescue is sought by the poet through the intercession of the Cappadocian saint discussed by Frazer. Similarly, the poet explores various sacrifices including that of "hanging my hand/ My harp hand on the Haman tree," a remark that clearly alludes to Frazer's notion of Haman as a temporary king who suffers crucifixion in an anticipation of Christ's later role.[46] *Eros in Dogma* (1944) invokes the mistletoe and Balder of Frazer's last volumes to give ironic point to the wretchedness of modern wartime existence. It also universalizes the scapegoat figure in Frazerian fashion by placing it in a comparative context of Christian and primitive existence in order to conclude "everyone is our scapegoat everyone." This fact follows from modern man's separation from his past so that "liberated independent we are lost,/ The scapegoat generations."[47]

It is in *Calamiterror*, however, that Barker brings *The Golden Bough* to bear in the most sustained fashion on the diagnosis of the cultural ills of the modern world. In it the pre-war, pleasure-seeking "gay paraders of the esplanade," are unaware of the poet's horrified recognition that "the green dream in the summer tree is death."[48] Man "springing from the maternal tree" grows to maturity, but the emblems of human fertility are metamorphosed into signs of death, "a gasmask terrible green and fatal."[49] The impending holocaust presaged by *"Berliner/ Tageblatt, Daily Telegraph, L'Humanité, Isvestia,/* The air like newsboys shrieking, recounting/ Instances of hate, of insult, aggravation," is but "the ancestral voice" which speaks of man's inevitable and anguished struggle to create that issues in destruc-

---

[45] George Barker, *Poems* (London: Faber & Faber, 1935), pp. 12, 41, 49.
[46] George Barker, *Lament and Triumph* (London: Faber & Faber, 1940), p. 34.
[47] George Barker, *Eros in Dogma* (London: Faber & Faber, 1944), p. 33.
[48] George Barker, *Calamiterror* (London: Faber & Faber, 1937), pp. 9, 18.
[49] Barker, *Calamiterror*, pp. 23, 19.

tion, death, and torment.[50] Human life, just as in *The Golden Bough*, is associated with the tree as the emblem of both fertility and sterility. The tree, as the very opening of the poem makes clear, is identified with the human being; the "bloodred babe" at birth carries "maypole at thigh" as a sign of the fusion of human and vegetative fertility.[51] The same image, however, serves the opposite function when one sees "the tall tree spine supporting vertical/ The crucified to life bare body blood."[52] Dominating the entire poem is this archetypal image of the Attis-like hanged god whose life is a commitment to death and whose death is a crucifixion on the tree of life and existence. Barker sees modern man here as a form of Frazer's figures of primitive taboo consigned to be suspended between heaven and earth, unable to achieve either: "the sin man hangs in a vacuum."[53]

Of all the poems in the twentieth century to bring *The Golden Bough* to bear on cultural analysis and diagnosis there is none more famous than *The Waste Land*. Of the many emulators of it in the 1920s there is none more significant, however, than Archibald MacLeish's "The Pot of Earth," which appeared in 1925. Frazer's influence may have occurred even earlier in MacLeish's work, but it is impossible to say for certain since his early poems, like those of Edith Sitwell, are tantalizingly ambiguous with regard to the possible presence of Frazerian myths and customs. But with "The Pot of Earth" there is no question, for its epigraph is an excerpt from the opening paragraph in chapter ten of the first volume of *Adonis, Attis, Osiris*, the same part of *The Golden Bough* Eliot refers to in his Notes. MacLeish's title itself refers to the gardens of Adonis, which were shallow vessels containing flowers and cereals that functioned as fertility or resurrection charms for the dead Adonis.[54] Significantly enough, the title of the poem's first section is "the sowing of the dead corn," and it opens with the image of the ship of death which also occurs in Yeats and Lawrence:

> Silently on the sliding Nile
> The rudderless, the unoared barge

[50] Barker, *Calamiterror*, p. 39. [51] Barker, *Calamiterror*, p. 13.
[52] Barker, *Calamiterror*, p. 13. [53] Barker, *Calamiterror*, p. 16.
[54] *GB*, v, 236ff.

> Diminishing and for a while
> Followed, a fleck upon the large
> Silver, then faint, then vanished, passed
> Adonis who had once more died
> Down a slow water with the last
> Withdrawing of a fallen tide.[55]

The whole poem develops on a mythic and a modern level of action and thought, and the two are related by the figure of a woman who lives, loves, gives birth, and dies. In this context, commonplace remarks take on added significance, suggesting the permeation of the contemporary by Frazer's mythic focus:

> Shall we go
> Up through the Gorge or round by Ryan's place?
> I'll show you where the wild boar killed a man.
> I'll show you where the . . .
> Who is this that comes
> Crowned with red flowers from the sea?[56]

After her marriage, the woman's window-box, the gardens of Adonis, and her conception and gestation are all interrelated until, in a sense, they become the same thing on different levels:

> How does your garden grow, your garden
> In the shallow dish, in the dark, how does it grow?
> Tomorrow we bear the milk corn to the river,
> Tomorrow we go to the spring with the pale stalks:
> Has your garden ripened?
>
> .   .   .   .
>
> What is this thing that sprouts
> From the womb, from the living flesh, from the live body?[57]

And with her death in the spring, the woman sees it as a birth and a release:

> I have borne the summer
> Dead, the corn dead, the living
> Dead. I am delivered.[58]

---

[55] Archibald MacLeish, *Collected Poems, 1917-1952* (Boston: Houghton Mifflin, 1952), pp. 179-180.
[56] MacLeish, p. 185.   [57] MacLeish, pp. 189-190.   [58] MacLeish, p. 196.

Then the poem closes with an offer to interpret the secret of life:

> I will show you the mystery of mysteries.
> I will show you the body of the dead god bringing forth
> The corn. I will show you the reaped ear
> Sprouting.[59]

As the foregoing passages make clear, the poem draws extensively on *The Golden Bough* for such details as the violent death of Adonis wounded by the boar, the red flowers thought to result from the god's blood, the shallow dishes in which seeds germinate, grow, and die in a swift vegetative reenactment of the god's course, the committing of the plants to a watery grave, the linking of death and resurrection as vegetative, seasonal and personal, and the god's corpse bodying forth the new, living corn.[60] At the same time "The Pot of Earth" obviously leans on *The Waste Land* for structure, theme, and inspiration. Without Eliot's work MacLeish's poem would have been unthinkable, just as would have all the other "imitations." Yet this in no way diminishes the fact of MacLeish's own direct, informed acquaintance with *The Golden Bough*. Most of the mythical and anthropological details employed in the poem could not have been acquired simply by a reading of Eliot's poem or even of the notes to it. Indeed, his details are not only different in significant ways from those in *The Waste Land* but they are also more explicit and precisely traceable to Frazer's work. Where the two converge, of course, is in their finding "the mystery of mysteries" in the figure of the dying god whose imaginative presence is at the core of all cultural vitality.

Similar in this basic concentration is John Peale Bishop, a poet less widely known than MacLeish but one who reveals the impact of Frazer in more sustained fashion. With the exception of Samuel Chew's 1923 article, Bishop's *Virginia Quarterly* essay in 1936 was the first by a literary critic devoted wholly to *The Golden Bough* and its implications for the human condition.[61] Given the Christian orientation of the essay, it is understandable to find an

---

[59] MacLeish, p. 197.   [60] *GB*, v, 11-12, 224-226, 227, 236-237.
[61] John Peale Bishop, "The Golden Bough," *Virginia Quarterly Review*, XII (1936), 430-447.

earlier poem like "The Promise" also revealing the pressure of comparative religion and taking up the theme of Christ as a dying god. In a different way Bishop also follows Frazer's concern with the ritual basis of sex in poems like "And When the Net was Unwound Venus was Found Ravelled with Mars," where the dangers of the experience are suggested by a casual allusion to Adonis' fate: "what darkness let become a face: when lifted/ bristled like a boar's."[62]

Because he was a poet of carefully deliberated rather than occasional themes, his mind turned again and again to instances of crisis in the human soul. These he represents dramatically, elegiacally, and lyrically in such motifs as the collapse of civilization, birth, death, and resurrection, particularly of a god. Representative instances are "Ode," "Twelfth Night," "Wish in the Daytime," and "The Return." The personal myth Bishop sought to elaborate was in essence focussed on human culture, its rise and decline, and its mode was what Cornford called "mythistoria"; the last days of the Empire before the fall provided the social dimension. At the core of the religious aspect is the dying god, though it is not so much he himself as his memory that is important. This pattern deliberately generates an added resonance from the fact that Frazer links the fall of Rome with the increase of Oriental dying-god cults in the Empire. Central here is the realization that "the unchanging god" is the eternal constant set against the culture in all its transitoriness.[63] In this knowledge, men "await/ The god in death." Above all others, Christ is the archetype of these waiting men, for he is *the* dying and reviving god.[64] This conviction, as the *Virginia Quarterly* essay makes clear, is largely shaped by Bishop's reading of *The Golden Bough* and is evidenced most clearly in "Whom the Gods Love," "Trinity of Crime," "Resurrection," and "The Emperor also was a God." In this fashion Bishop gives an emphatically Christian inflection to the same note—the cultural centrality of the dying god—that MacLeish, Jeffers, and others have struck in a more resolutely secular and comparatist manner.

[62] John Peale Bishop, *Collected Poems* (New York: Scribner's, 1948), p. 14.
[63] Bishop, *Collected Poems*, p. 83.   [64] Bishop, *Collected Poems*, p. 84.

[V]

The authors so far considered have exemplified *The Golden Bough*'s adaptability to the mythopoeic creation of works of socio-cultural context and of probing genetic analysis. Because of the concentration on phenomenological constants such as imagery, and conceptual frames such as narrative patterns, these works are marked by a higher degree of clarity and simplicity than is commonly the case in modern literature. This, however, does not mean that either myth as a literary factor or *The Golden Bough* as a shaping force is restricted to traditional techniques or static ideas. The third chief use of mythopoeic materials to be discussed here amply demonstrates this, for it dramatizes the psychological dynamics involved in the interaction of the twentieth-century ego with the world that is both its womb and its prison-house. A recent extended illustration of this use is provided by John Wain in his long poem *Wildtrack*.

His strategy of deploying *The Golden Bough* for mythopoeic purposes is significantly more emphatic and experimental than any hitherto discussed. To some extent, it derives from the radical poetics of *The Waste Land*, *The Cantos*, and *The Bridge* though with a rather different concentration of interest. In a manner that obviously owes something to William Carlos Williams' *Paterson*, Wain includes direct prose quotations from *The Golden Bough* as part of the fabric of the poem itself. For Williams, of course, this technique is an integral part of his poetics, involving as it does the whole issue of the relations between prose and verse and between artifice and reality. In Wain's case this seems less central an issue, though the poem does exhibit a variety of styles ranging from the elliptical and colloquial to the formality of the sonnet. His interest in this technique seems more nearly thematic. The quotations from *The Golden Bough* and others from Dostoyevsky, Johnson, Boswell, and eighteenth-century newspapers stress their subjects, which then are made the focus for poetic extrapolations, comments, comparisons, and allusions.

Precisely how this operates in the instance of *The Golden Bough* is best seen in the section near the middle of the poem entitled "Adventures of the Night-Self in the Age of the Machines." The poem as a whole—as the epigraph from Joseph Campbell's *Hero with a Thousand Faces* suggests—explores the twentieth century's concentration of wonder and mystery in man rather than in the natural world. It begins from Blok's poem of the Russian revolution "The Twelve," which epitomizes the clash of ego and society. Wain then develops the dialectic of day-self and night-self through which man works out his pattern of death by crucifixion and then of resurrection.

The poet engages in a sustained effort to relate the social and individual or personal issues of the age and to suggest their interaction. The section dealing with Frazer thus begins with a sonnet delivered by the possessed man who speaks to Jesus in the Gospel of St. Mark, and then moves on to deal with *Hamlet* and other topics that in a variety of ways develop the motif of kingship. Immediately following the initial sonnet, Wain declares:

> See now,
> the reverent burlesques begin.
>
> Man worships by parody.
> The outward miracles of Christ,
> the inward miracles of the Buddha:
> on the fourth day, the noose and the two razors.[65]

This inaugurates the theme of the king's office as simultaneously incarnational, sacrificial, and parodic. The English people of both the Renaissance and the eighteenth century are "crazed with their sufferings."[66] Hence they accept the king's proximity to the divinity as reason for regarding him as capable of magically healing their ills. For them, "The king is their best magic."[67]

Juxtaposition with passages from *The Golden Bough* suggests that the genesis and ground of this view lie in Frazer's discovery that primitive man held his king in both religious reverence and ruthless watchfulness. The king's vigor and good health were essential to the fertility of the land, the people, and their animals. When the king's health and virility began to fail, he was put to

---

[65] John Wain, *Wildtrack* (London: Macmillan, 1965), p. 21.
[66] Wain, p. 66.   [67] Wain, p. 67.

death. In this there is a profound indifference to the individual and his physical welfare for the sake of the larger communal good, and it is out of this context that the oblique reference to razors in the above passage is clarified:

> The piety of the Shilluk teaches how to disregard the flesh. If the king's soul leaks out through mouth or nostril, it wanders unattended. A sorcerer might trick and imprison it. And even without sorcerers, how can the people be sure the soul that keeps them safe will be transferred to the rightful body of the king's successor?

> In some tribes of Fazoqul the king had to administer justice daily under a certain tree. If from sickness or any other cause he was unable to discharge this duty for three whole days, he was hanged on the tree in a noose, which contained two razors so arranged that when the noose was drawn tight by the weight of the king's body they cut his throat. Frazer, *ibid*.

On the fourth day, the noose and the two razors.[68]

In a way this poetic technique represents a fusion of the two imaginative modes of poems like *The Waste Land*. The notes that Eliot later appended to his poem are here incorporated into the text itself. As a result the device of thematic and symbolic allusion is both used and identified, giving an increased sense of the imaginative interrelation of fact and poem. Eliot saw poetry as a dramatic distillation of experience and so conceived of the allusive technique as a means of condensing and multiplying literary contexts so as to achieve the maximum of imaginative power. Wain, however, as befits the 1960s, treats poetry less as a medium of concentration and more as an opportunity for imaginative reflection. Thus, immediately following the above passage, he goes on to observe:

> Primitives, of course. The seventeenth century looking back on the tenth. Edwardian Cambridge comparing the field notes of anthropologists.

[68] Wain, p. 23.

It is said that Frazer was allowed to keep his Cambridge fellowship just so long as he drew no conclusions from his evidence.

On the fourth day, the noose and the two razors.[69]

The reference to the seventeenth and tenth centuries suggests that *Hamlet*'s perspective involves a retrospective view of the period when Hamlet was supposed to have engaged in his own scrutiny and ritual of kingship. It leads on to and stands within the larger comparative view afforded by Frazer's contemplation of his ancient peoples from the ostensibly sophisticated vantage point of nineteenth-century English academic life. Both the poet and the anthropologists are, Wain suggests, detached chroniclers of man's ritual of survival and supremacy. In both cases the initial sense of cultural superiority is subjected to an ironic involvement which reveals its own subjection to the primitive ritual of adoration and sacrifice. Frazer as much as the primitive king of the Shilluk or Fazoql is subjected to taboos prescribing the kind of conduct requisite to his high office.

The net effect is to extend Frazer's ironies concerning the relation of primitive and higher cultures one century further, so that he himself is moved from his role of detached chronicler to that of ritual victim. Now it is the twentieth-century poet who surveys the cultural eddies and whirlpools of civilization's historical development. Thus, he carries the exploration of kingship as a socio-religious ritual on from the Renaissance into the eighteenth century of Swift and Johnson. And toward the end of the section, the poet renders his evaluative definition of the psychic structure of kingship and its magical base:

> belief in magic keeps
> humanity from devouring its
> own entrails.
>> Swift went
> mad because he saw too clearly
> where dreams end and wakefulness
> begins.

[69] Wain, p. 23.

> In a healing dream
> the lady in black touched Sam's face.
> He lived. Shilluk and Fazoql
> panoplied their kings in love and
> death. Their dream
> in the frightening jungle
> was no different from that licensed
> by Dr. Swinfen.
>
> Night-self and day-self!
> The ribboned ceremony and the dark
> creaturely sty of sleep,
> where motives are littered and
> tug at the ranged nipples in the mud!
>
> To have a king is to say:
> *We will dream of a magic person, and*
> *when we wake that person shall*
> *still, by our will, be magic.*
>
> Dean Swift,
>
> You never understood![70]

Here Wain suggests the similarity of magic and poetry or art. The figure of the king is the living fusion of the two selves (the night and day forms) in a realized prolongation of human desire that forestalls individual madness and societal catastrophe. It is the very imperative of magic coupled with its capacity to alter the world and man's perceptions of it that for Wain implicitly makes it a symbol of the poetic act, such as he is engaged upon in *Wildtrack*. Thus, his efforts to unify and reconcile the two selves through poetic meditation upon the cultural drift of the twentieth century is his form of magical exercise complementary to that of the ritual gestures and customs of the primitive tribes-man chronicled by Frazer in *The Golden Bough*.

[VI]

The final mode of mythopoeia to be considered is that by which the poet achieves a posture of existential detachment through an

[70] Wain, p. 30.

ironic perspective that enables him to view with a compassionate lucidity fact and metaphor, brute experience and myth, reasoned constraint and imaginative exuberance. Preeminent here is the poetry of Robert Graves, which adapts the patterns and figures of *The Golden Bough* to metaphors that enable the poet to attend simultaneously and with equal intensity to the immediacy of ordinary human experience and to the imaginative extrapolations by which he accommodates that experience. Graves, however, has been so closely identified with the world of myth and *The Golden Bough*, and his poems are such a seamless union of the human and the mythic, that it is difficult to show briefly how his irony affords detachment from existence and myth alike without alienation. A more manageable illustration of this way of handling of myth is found in the poetry of Louis MacNeice. Throughout his long career MacNeice's primary bent has been wryly topical, reflecting on social issues and the individual's relation to them. Consequently, even his use of mythopoeic materials is sceptical and detached, poetic rather than dogmatic, so that the prevailing temper of *The Golden Bough* was particularly congenial to him. This appears in incidental remarks, such as likening the Ionic columns of the British Museum to "totem poles— the ancient terror"[71] beneath which refugees from the contemporary barbarism of Hitler murmur sorrowfully, as well as in more sustained evocations of the world of myth and ritual. The two best instances occur in *Ten Burnt Offerings* (1952) and *Autumn Sequel* (1954).

The second poem in *Ten Burnt Offerings*, "Areopagus," adopts the basically Frazerian strategy of a comparative approach which ironically reduces religious and cultural claims of uniqueness. The Virgin Mary is likened to "those other Virgins/ Long brought down to classical earth," a parallel analogous to Frazer's of Mary and Isis and with much the same point.[72] The chief difference is that Frazer generally inclined to see the primitive genesis of Christian figures as evidence of their irrelevance to contemporary life. MacNeice, like many other mythopoeic artists, uses the

[71] Louis MacNeice, *Collected Poems*, ed. E. R. Dodds (New York: Oxford University Press, 1967), p. 161.
[72] MacNeice, p. 288.

comparison, on the other hand, to underline the effects of time in overlaying the past with ghosts that blur and dislocate the present. Thus, he suggests that Paul "scouring the market found an altar/ Clearly inscribed but between the words/ Was the ghost of a Word."[73]

The same essential point is made more concretely in the poem's next section where anemones and almonds, traditionally identified, as Frazer points out, with Adonis, are linked to Christ's crucifixion:

> After anemones, after almond,
> Pitiless heaven, enamelled sea;
> The Furies plumped the grapes with blood,
> Their living rock was the death of sea.
> As Christ's dead timber fired by blood
> Was to blossom bright as peach or almond.
>
> The Unknown God? Judge or saviour?
> The unknown goddesses—Cursing or kind?
> Shall we have neither? Either? Both?
> The dark prehistory of their kind
> Hung over Jews and Greeks and both
> Found, of their kind, a likely saviour.[74]

Here the images of crucified Christ, pagan dying gods, and natural vegetation are interrelated in a dramatic continuity that exactly matches the historical one developed by Frazer. In the poem the three images function to create a cycle whereby Christ, the most recent of dying gods, summons up the earliest emblematic form of the primitive deity, namely, the natural vegetative symbols of fertility. At the same time, the Frazerian comparative perspective of MacNeice creates a kind of Spencerian deity, a formative spiritual power that takes the shape demanded by the cultures in question. What differentiates MacNeice from Spencer in this regard is that the poet sees the spiritual form of the deity as generated by "the dark prehistory of their kind." That is, like Frazer, he finds the sacral character of the so-called high cultures determined by the events, compounded of ritual

[73] MacNeice, p. 288.   [74] MacNeice, p. 289.

173

and accident, of their primitive past. Thus, while both the poem and *The Golden Bough* seem to deal with the human necessity of having a deity, they also make it a wholly human and immanent affair. The god is generated out of the cultural context, which essentially consists of the phenomenological realities impinging on the imaginative consciousness of the individual. In neither poet nor anthropologist is there an assumption of transcendent reality's investing or incarnating itself in the natural order.

The chief difference between the two is that Frazer is more content, in theory at least, to accept a rational humanism, which looks forward to the ultimate disappearance of religion. MacNeice, on the other hand, recognizes that such a course is ultimately stultifying and disastrous for poetry since it would eliminate one of its richest sources of image and symbol. His solution is to base his beliefs and attitudes upon a poetics rather than a philosophy, upon the primacy of metaphor as a linguistic mimesis of an indefinite variety of ontological conditions. Essentially this is what he does when in the last section of "Areopagus" he declares: "The body may be a tomb/ Yet even the beggar's body is bread, is wine, is flowers in bloom."[75] Or when the Furies are associated with Christ and are called ripeners of "crop and flock" and "yeoman and bride" who ward off evil and blight.

The same basic deployment of metaphor to make real and viable some of the central myths endemic to the primitive mind of mankind appears also at the end of the volume. In a poem directed to his wife and her primacy in his world, he observes that "what was/ The earliest corn-and-fire dance is your hair."[76] Here the metaphor assists in the identification of primitive fertility ritual with a contemporary human being in a transformation of action into an entity. It also suggests the metamorphosis of ritual function between the ancient past and the present world. This knife-edge of difference broadens elsewhere to a full-scale sense of the imaginative diminution separating past and present, the extraordinary and the normal:

[75] MacNeice, p. 290.   [76] MacNeice, p. 323.

> Back to normal; the ghosts in the pinetrees
> Have dwindled to lizards; primaeval brows
> Lined with a myriad drystone terraces
> Smiles in the sun; the welded blue
> Of sea and sky is the tenure of legend;
> Far; near; true.[77]

The most sustained instances of Frazer's and myth's shaping force on MacNeice's topical and historical verse probably occur in *Autumn Sequel* and the third poem, "Cock o' the North," in *Ten Burnt Offerings*. The former deals with a number of MacNeice's friends, especially Dylan Thomas. MacNeice, however, is at pains to render the historical incidents and experiences in an archetypal or mythic pattern, and invokes a number of primitive deities, like Isis, Thor, and Pan, as symbols of man's drive for life and truth. And in Canto VIII, it is from the midst of the historical preciseness of September 25, 1953, and the facticity of an art gallery that he articulates the inexpungibility of the mythical quality from the human heart:

> When painters changed their theme
> From myth to bistro, something mythical
> Still dogged their hands like an abandoned dream
>
> That dares come back in daylight; rational
> Behaviour may ignore the cloven hoof
> But hoof prints in the heart remain indelible.[78]

Such a conviction, of course, squares with the evidence if not the contentions of *The Golden Bough*. Given this conviction, however, it is understandable to find Thomas represented as the archetypal poet and to learn that at least some of his imaginative entourage are mythic and Frazerian:

> The poet will not be bought, he has powerful friends
> Who are his own inventions—the one-eyed hag
> Whose one is an evil eye, the maiden goddess who sends
> Her silver javelin straight, the Knave of Fools
> Who cocks his snook and blows his dividends.[79]

[77] MacNeice, p. 304.   [78] MacNeice, p. 362.   [79] MacNeice, p. 338.

Hag and maiden, as Robert Graves has argued frequently in both verse and prose, are forms of the great female fertility deities whose rituals and myths are elaborately traced in *The Golden Bough*. For Thomas, or Gwilym as he is called in the poem, to have them as "powerful friends" suggests that he is a fusion of the poet and the dying god, the consort of the fertility goddess. When we take into account Thomas' biographical escapades, we are not surprised to find his early loves being called "deep-bosomed goddesses of corn" and he a "bow-tied Silenus" who was "well aware/ That even Dionysus has his day/ And cannot take it with him."[80]

Yet because *Autumn Sequel* is essentially in the same topical vein as *Autumn Journal*, it never really seeks to establish the identification of history and myth, of Thomas' twentieth-century life and Dionysus' archetypal pattern. Instead it explores the possibility of observing the similarities and parallels and of entertaining their relationship as metaphor. Consequently, the poem as a whole introduces both the connection and the disparity between Thomas and Dionysus so that the reader sees not only the individual given an archetypal definition but also the mythic figure redefined to achieve a more concrete and less remote quality. Back of this is the implication that the myth figure stands forth less as a historical phenomenon than as a more-than-historical creature, who lives in history but who so seizes the imagination that he assumes an aura larger than life. In effect, the mythopoeic process MacNeice inaugurates here implicitly leads, as Wallace Stevens shows us, to a dramatic description of the mythopoeic process itself as it unfolds in the human imagination.

Ten Burnt Offerings is of a more formal and reflective order, less determinedly chatty, of a tone that allows MacNeice to be more sustainedly archetypal or mythical when the situation warrants. The best instance of this is, as has been remarked, in "Cock o' the North," which deals largely with Byron and his death in Greece. Though much of the poem maintains the jaunty and ironical rhythms of the series, MacNeice also develops an imagery pattern that conflates Byron, Christ, Adonis, and Meleager into a single composite figure of sacrificial death. This

[80] MacNeice, p. 404.

is inaugurated in the conclusion of the first section of the poem where the advent of Easter is anticipated:

> Scarlet flowers from a far-off tomb,
> *Christos! Christos aneste!*[81]

In the second section Byron and Meleager are brought into conjunction through the ritual imagery appropriate to the myth —the boar, death by fire, and the life or soul deposited in the log. At the same time, MacNeice is careful to present the animal antagonist so as to make it possible for it to be associated with both Meleager and then in the next section with Adonis:

> The boar was black
> Like the after-life of an Ethiop; his tusks
> Flashed curving through the forest like the Milky Way
> And his small eyes were death.[82]

The deliberate multiplicity of reference achieved by this image is clearly indicated by the use of blackness. For not only does this intensify the sinister nature of the boar's role, but it also links it with the cropped black sow that figures so prominently in the Celtic world of both MacNeice and Yeats. Indeed, this creature is explicitly mentioned by MacNeice in *Autumn Sequel*. There the association with the Celtic antagonist is part of a childhood scene in which the children play their innocent games unaware of a more ancient realm that surrounds their cozy country kitchen. This same feeling of the boar and god as a part of a distant, departed era and of their at the same time being associated with childhood and its fantasies and dream terrors occurs in *Ten Burnt Offerings*:

> The boar is dark in the night of the wood,
> The boar is dead in the glens of myth,
> There is only a flame in the back of the mind
> Consuming a log . . . .
>
> . . . .
> The dogs i' the nicht are ill at ease
> For they snuff the boar i' the reed-banks.

[81] MacNeice, p. 291.   [82] MacNeice, p. 292.

His white tusks curve like a Turkish sword—
Back to the nightmare! Back to the nursery!
Our Lady o' Death has all assured
And her board is spread for Adonis.[83]

In the fourth section of this poem (as the above passage indicates) MacNeice assumes a dialect designed to point up Byron's Scots ancestry. It also identifies the speaker here as Byron himself, lamenting the death of Meleager and associating himself with those poets and gods who have sacrificially died for Hellas as a ritual act of triumph through death:

I maun burn my body to clear my een,
Yon withered bough maun blossom.
To fell yon boar means death by fire—
Calydon saved and Calydon ruined.[84]

It is in this linking of the poet, the dying god, and the legendary man that MacNeice finds his most sustained and most powerful deployment of *The Golden Bough*'s controlling image. To associate poet and god alone would be to adopt a more Romantic view of the dilemmas facing the poet in the modern world than MacNeice is prepared to accept. By the same token, to restrict the metaphor to god and human being would be to ignore his own central imaginative commitment—the art and act of writing poetry. It is precisely because MacNeice can see his affinities with all three, with the existential condition of mankind and with the imaginative states of poet and dying god, with ecstasy and dissolution alike, that he is able to carve out for himself a twentieth-century version of the middle style and an attitude that is one of mildly depreciatory irony toward both the benefits and liabilities of living.

[83] MacNeice, p. 294.
[84] MacNeice, p. 294.

CHAPTER VI

William Butler Yeats:
The Tragic Hero
as Dying God

[I]

T. S. Eliot's *The Waste Land*, together with its notes, first popularized *The Golden Bough* with literary audiences. But actually William Butler Yeats was, so far as can be ascertained, the first modern writer to register his awareness of *The Golden Bough* as relevant to the symbolic language of literature. In *The Wind Among the Reeds* (1899) Yeats has a long note to his poem "The Valley of the Black Pig" which shows clearly that he has been acquiring an intimate knowledge of anthropology and comparative religion. First there is an account of the merging of legend and politics in the folk prophecies of the future defeat of Ireland's enemies at the Valley of the Black Pig. Then Yeats goes on to set this belief in its anthropological context:

> The battle is a mythological battle, and the black pig is one with the bristleless boar, that killed Dearmod, in November, upon the western end of Ben Bulben; Misroide, MacDatha's son whose carving brought on so great a battle; 'the croppy black sow,' and 'the cutty black sow' of Welsh November rhymes ('Celtic Heathendom,' pages 509-516); the boar that killed Adonis, the boar that killed Attis; and the pig embodiment of Typhon ('Golden Bough,' II. pages 26, 31). The pig seems to have been originally a genius of the corn, and, seemingly because the too great power of their divinity makes divine things dangerous to mortals, its flesh was forbidden to many eastern nations; but as the meaning of the prohibition was forgotten, abhorrence took the place of reverence, pigs

and bears grew into types of evil, and were described as the enemies of the very gods they once typified ('Golden Bough,' II. 26-31, 56-57).[1]

And in this same note he reveals the beginnings of his assimilation of anthropological lore to his own interests, as when he takes over without acknowledgment Frazer's point about pigs' tails as fertility charms:

> It is possible that bristles were associated with fertility, as the tail certainly was, for a pig's tail is stuck into the ground in Courland, that the corn may grow abundantly, and the tails of pigs, and other animal embodiments of the corn genius, are dragged over the ground to make it fertile in different countries. Professor Rhys, who considers the bristleless boar a symbol of darkness and cold, rather than of winter and cold, thinks it was without bristles because the darkness is shorn away by the sun. It may have had different meanings, just as the scourging of the man-god had different though not contradictory meanings in different epochs of the world.[2]

The casual manner in which Yeats refers to Courland, as if it were in Ireland rather than Latvia, together with the easy accommodation of divergent interpretations in the last sentence, not to mention the Frazerian-oriented final analogy, all suggest that he was not only drawing on Frazer's material but was also approximating his general manner of looking at ancient myths and primitive customs.[3]

Just how much earlier than 1899 Yeats was acquainted with *The Golden Bough* is difficult to say precisely. From his letters and early prose, however, it is clear that he would have been receptive to its subject from the book's very first appearance in 1890. In a letter to John O'Leary dated 1888 by Allan Wade,

---

[1] *The Variorum Edition of the Poems of W. B. Yeats*, eds. Peter Allt and Russell K. Alspach (New York: Macmillan, 1957), p. 809.

[2] *The Variorum Edition*, p. 809. For Frazer's reference to the use of pigs' tails in Courland and elsewhere, see *GB*, VIII, 300. Yeats, of course, was using the 1890 first edition, but the material is substantially the same.

[3] This syncretistic inclination emerges even more clearly in the 1908 and subsequent versions of the above note. See *The Variorum Edition*, p. 810.

Yeats expresses interest in reviewing "professor Rhys' . . . book on Celtic religion," which, of course, is the same study he refers to in the 1899 note.[4] The liveliness of this interest is further attested to by the fact that Rhys's book *Lectures on the Origin and Growth of Religion as illustrated by Celtic Heathendom* only appeared in 1888, so that in this particular field Yeats was clearly keeping abreast. Nor is it implausible that he may well have done the same thing two years later when *The Golden Bough* made its first appearance. Encouraging this interest in religion and ancient custom was his own burgeoning concern with Irish folklore which issued in his editing of *Fairy and Folk Tales of the Irish Peasantry* (1888).

More than Irish folklore may have contributed to Yeats's attraction to *The Golden Bough*. Around 1887 he was emphatically condemning George Eliot's fiction because "she knows nothing of the dim unconscious nature, the world of instinct, which (if there is any truth in Darwin) is the accumulated wisdom of all living things from the monera to man."[5] Obviously Frazer did not share Yeats's suspicion of the rational, analytic habit of mind. Yet just as clearly much of his material exhaustively documents the poet's conviction that human wisdom is a matter of ancient responses made without conscious deliberation. Certainly a work which sees man groping intuitively toward truth and reality throughout the ages while never completely losing his earliest ways of viewing and reacting to the world would have had a profound fascination for Yeats. In addition, more personal influences may have also played a part. As early as 1888 Yeats knew as a family friend the Oxford historian and Icelandic scholar Frederick York Powell. Frazer's reliance on Powell's edition and translation of the Elder Eddas in connection with *The Golden Bough*'s treatment of the Balder myth reveals an important interest in common. Knowing Yeats's marked attraction to myth and

---

[4] *The Letters of W. B. Yeats*, ed. Allan Wade (London: Macmillan, 1954), p. 92. The letter has also been dated 1890, see p. 91, n. 1, by other hands—in which case Yeats may have been led by Frazer to Rhys rather than by Rhys to Frazer. This, however, seems unlikely in view of Yeats's strong attraction to anything with Celtic in its title.

[5] *The Letters*, p. 31.

folklore, Powell may possibly have called his attention to *The Golden Bough* when it appeared.[6]

Yeats may first have read *The Golden Bough* soon after its appearance in 1890. This possibility gains some support from letters and essays written between 1890 and 1899. Since this was the period of his writing and publishing his commentary on Blake, studying theosophy and magic, and exploring Irish myth and folklore, it is particularly difficult to isolate those remarks which can be exclusively or unmistakably taken as derived from *The Golden Bough*. In themselves the letters provide no thoroughly conclusive indication of the date of Yeats's initial contact with Frazer's work. What they do give is several hints as to how his other interests were supported by and conducive to a knowledge of *The Golden Bough*.[7]

When we turn from Yeats's letters to his published prose during these years we find a sharp increase in the evidence of his interest in myth, folklore, and primitive life generally. The essays and folk-tale reports of *The Celtic Twilight*, published in 1893, reveal a wealth of material that might have come as easily from *The Golden Bough* as from the Irish peasantry whose beliefs Yeats was then exploring.[8]

By 1897 and the appearance of *The Secret Rose, Stories of Red Hanrahan*, and *Rosa Alchemica*, the signs of *The Golden Bough* are more prominent and more speculative and at the same time more specifically anthropological.[9] The more steeped Yeats be-

[6] *The Letters*, p. 70, n. 2. Yeats was aware of Vigfusson's relationship with Powell and therefore presumably of their scholarly collaboration. In a letter in 1889, *The Letters*, p. 1132, Yeats mentions having the rooms formerly occupied by Vigfusson, "a friend of young Powell's." While this whole issue is admittedly speculative in the extreme, it would be highly surprising if friends with the similarity of interests found in Yeats and Powell did not exchange ideas, opinions, and information on ancient life in the course of informal conversations.

[7] See *The Letters*, pp. 88, 117, 211, 243 n.1, 246, 249-250, 263, 264 n.2, 265, 268, 278, 285, 305, 322, 324; *W. B. Yeats and T. Sturge Moore: Their Correspondence 1901-1937*, ed. Ursula Bridge (London: Routledge & Kegan Paul, Ltd., 1953), p. 114.

[8] See *Mythologies* (London: Macmillan, 1962), pp. 20, 38, 41, 78, 90.

[9] See, e.g., the taboo against the king's possessing any physical blemish in "The Wisdom of the King," the vagabond poet's suffering the death by crucifixion of the scapegoat, the golden boughs and defeated gods of "Han-

came in the comparative studies of myth, religion, and magic provided by Frazer, Rhys, Jubainville, and the rest, the more convinced he became of their relevance to poetry and of the need for a mythology in a world that did not possess an established one.[10] The great late nineteenth-century mythographers opened up, in Yeats's view, a whole range of knowledge by which man might find his way back to the fundamental relations between symbol and mind.[11] In addition, they encourage the comparativist and syncretistic attitudes toward symbolism of modern poets.[12] Writers from Wagner to Verlaine, Yeats declares, have come to accept all symbolisms, from that of the simple peasant to that of ancient priestly lore, from that of the human body to that of the natural seasons, all of which were part of an ancient pre-Christian religion.

From the foregoing it is clear that Yeats felt the impact of *The Golden Bough* keenly and subtly from early in his career. Precisely when he first read Frazer is, as we have seen from the available evidence, almost impossible to determine definitively. Nevertheless, we might hazard the informed guess that by 1895 he was already at least aware of Frazer's work and that between this date and the appearance of *The Wind Among the Reeds* in 1899 he extended his acquaintance with *The Golden Bough* and intensified his use of it for images and ideas relevant to the intellectual and poetic views he was already hammering into order. Among these were folk beliefs about ghosts, magic, and the human soul which he had already encountered directly among the Irish peasantry but which in a book like *The Golden Bough* would serve to corroborate his conviction that they represented a significant body of knowledge worth exploring.

Encountering elements of Irish lore interspersed among similar materials from a wide variety of other ethnic groups also encouraged Yeats to follow Frazer in developing a comparative method by which to approach his central problem, that of the re-

---

rahan's Vision," the sacred birds of Hera and the polite scepticism inherent in the comparative idiom found in *Rosa Alchemica*.

[10] See *Ideas of Good and Evil* (New York: Macmillan, 1961), p. 114.

[11] *Ideas of Good and Evil*, p. 116.

[12] *Ideas of Good and Evil*, p. 149.

lation of myths and rituals to literature and literary theory. Thus, the ordinary poetic license of being inspired by a Greek folk song to write "The Song of Wandering Aengus" is augmented by a quasi-anthropological conviction that "the folk belief of Greece is very like that of Ireland."[13] Similar Frazer-inspired notions that started to shape themselves at this time in Yeats's thought are those of such figures as the scapegoat, the king, the prophet, and the priest as well as the magician. Their continuing presence in his work attests not only to their fulfillment of a psychic need in the poet but also to the persistent importance of *The Golden Bough* to his thought and art.

In much the same way his early prose and poetry reveals him as beginning to struggle with subjects raised by Frazer as well as by his study of Celtic history and legend and theosophy and hermetic lore. He found, too, an endless fascination mingled with a certain melancholy in viewing the emergence of gods and spirits in all cultures; the problematic interaction of the mortal and immortal, the natural and the supernatural; the need to evolve efficacious rituals; the apparently ceaseless dialectic between the civilized and the primitive; and the awful power of symbols, whether existential or artistic, to move men and empires. All of these motifs and figures were beginning to stir in Yeats's mind during the 90s, when he must have read *The Golden Bough* for the first time. And until his death nearly fifty years later he never ceased to be absorbed in them, with what potent consequences for modern literature we now know.

Yeats's poetic career, obviously, began before the publication of *The Golden Bough* so that inevitably there are some poems apparently not marked by its impress. Yet curiously and significantly enough, in certain cases Yeats appears to have altered his original versions to take account of the affinities he later noted between his original inspiration and *The Golden Bough*. Illuminating instances of this process are found in the 1895 version of "The Madness of King Goll" as well as the same year's revised "The Wanderings of Oisin."[14] Though there was a limit to the

---

[13] *The Variorum Edition of the Poems*, p. 806.

[14] The original version of "The Madness of King Goll" describes the king as the bringer of the golden age. By 1895, after the first edition of *The*

changes he could effect in poems already written before the publication of *The Golden Bough*, this, of course, was not the case
with the verse written after 1890. He did not, however, immediately launch into full-fledged poetic transcriptions of Frazer's
compendium of primitive lore. Competing interests such as Madame Blavatsky's theosophy and the Hermetic Order of the Gold-
en Dawn antedated his acquaintance with Frazer's work and
largely overshadowed it, partly because they seemed to afford a
greater measure of system and certitude than could be derived
from *The Golden Bough*. As a result, the poems published
through the next decade reflect most clearly his engrossment with
Eastern wisdom, Kabbalistic magic, and Irish legends and folklore.

Although for Yeats *The Golden Bough* lacked both the esoteric
appeal and the nationalistic rationale of his other interests, it did
have considerable affinities with them. For one thing, both Madame Blavatsky and Frazer were adept at reasoning from analogy,
though Frazer's comparative method was soberly content to confine its arguments to written sources which could be scrutinized.
For another thing, while there was a world of difference between the sweeping generalizations about man and the universe
provided by Madame Blavatsky and the views espoused by Frazer, nevertheless *The Golden Bough* too was capable of presenting Yeats with an extensive world-picture. It as well as the
theosophical tomes he perused provided him with large, though
simpler, generalizations, with the sense of aeons of both change
and continuity, with compelling images and actions, and with
narratives that aroused the most powerful emotions.

The same general sort of relationship obtained between the
Kabbalistic magic of the Golden Dawn and Frazer's more de-

Golden Bough was available to Yeats, he is made the tribal protector against
the Northern cold. This identification of the seasonal image with Irish
legend is due in part to Frazer's treatment of the dramatic and ritualistic
struggle of Winter and Summer personified as human antagonists.

In "The Wanderings of Oisin" the 1895 version identifies Niamh as "born
where the sun drops down in the tide," an image which follows *The Golden
Bough*'s interrelation of birth and death, man and nature. Later the poem
follows *The Golden Bough*'s attention both to the legendary battle of gods
and giants and to E. B. Tylor's concept of "high gods."

scriptive treatment of primitive magic. If it is true that magic offered Yeats a reinforcement of his belief in the power of the word or symbol to evoke an otherwise inaccessible reality, then surely *The Golden Bough*'s treatment of the special languages employed by ancient man, and his conviction that actions and other forms of empirical reality can be occasioned by the words naming those phenomena, afforded Yeats another perspective on the magical power of language to create a world of concrete immediacy. An even stronger relationship obtained between the hermetic order and Frazer by virtue of the dominant interest of both in ancient rituals, especially those of initiation. Yeats was particularly touched by the central ritual myth of the Golden Dawn, the death and resurrection of the initiate, which seemed to him to embody a beautiful profundity of universal significance. His encountering of the same ritual pattern in a variety of forms in *The Golden Bough* could not have helped making that work take on a peculiarly vital relevance to himself.[15]

As a result of these and other affinities, the poetry of the 90s shows Yeats weaving together the ideas and images of intuitive occultists, nationalistic folklorists, and the rationalistic anthropologists to enunciate some of his most enduring themes. In most cases *The Golden Bough* motifs operate as a minor chord behind the theosophical and Irish material. This is what occurs, for instance, in "The Dedication to a Book of Stories Selected from the Irish Novelists." There a green branch hung with bells magically soothes all contentions, whether of merchant, farmer, or warrior.[16] Irish nationalism merges with Frazerian primitivism in a dim foreshadowing of the fusion of politics and myth that we find in "Parnell's Funeral." Similarly, "To the Rose upon the Rood of Time" develops an anthropological resonance through its implicit juxtaposition of Frazer's King of the Wood and the Venus-Adonis

[15] Richard Ellmann, *Yeats: The Man and the Masks* (New York: Macmillan, 1948), pp. 95-96.

[16] The greater vividness of natural imagery over that in "The Wanderings of Oisin" suggests that Frazer's treatment of tree worship and the use of bells for repelling evil forces may have entered into Yeat's shaping of the lines.

myth near the end of the first half of the poem.[17] And in "The Two Trees" *The Golden Bough*'s extensive treatment of ancient tree-worship and its modern European relics affords in some measure an exoteric level of interpretation to balance the esoteric one stemming from the Kabbala and MacGregor Mathers' commentary on it.[18]

[II]

When we turn to the poems collected in *The Wind Among the Reeds*, we can be sure that they all were, in principle, subject to the impact of *The Golden Bough*. An interesting reflection of this impact occurs in the opening poem in the volume, "The Hosting of the Sidhe." Yeats remarks in his notes that the Sidhe "journey in whirling winds, the winds that were called the dance of the daughters of Herodias in the Middle Ages, Herodias doubtless taking the place of some old goddess."[19] This substitution of one figure for another as mythology adapts to varying historical and cultural circumstances is an integral part of *The Golden Bough*. It seems likely therefore that Frazer's numerous references to unbound hair and its magical and religious significance also figured in the 1899 revision of Niamh's chant.[20] A loosely related alteration, perhaps inspired by the dominant temper of *The Golden Bough*, occurs in "The Unappeasable Host." Originally Yeats proclaimed that "the unappeasable host/ Is comelier than candles before Maurya's feet," but in a 1906 edition the last line is

[17] The poet invokes the presence of the Rose, emblem of Adonis as well as of Ireland and occult qualities, while singing "the ancient ways." He discovers "Eternal Beauty," a Platonized image of Venus, beneath "the boughs of love and hate," which merge the scenic properties of Adonis' death and the fierce ritual of the King of the Wood.

[18] Like the poem, Frazer makes certain trees sacred or holy, populates them with spirits, associates them with vegetative and by implication human fruitfulness, sees trees and people as double manifestations of a single spirit, and finds certain trees unlucky, associated with demons and evils, including death.

[19] *The Variorum Edition of the Poems*, p. 800.

[20] The 1893 version has Niamh calling "For breasts are heaving and eyes a-gleam; / Away, come away, to the dim twilight," but the 1899 collection has been changed to read "Our cheeks are pale, our hair is unbound, / Our breasts are heaving, our eyes are agleam."

changed to read "at Mother Mary's feet." The effect is to align Yeats more closely with Frazer, whose comparative method with its genetic emphasis tends to make earlier religious practices preferable to the modern absurdity of man's bowing down to Christian superstitions.

Less glancing and equivocal an adaptation of *The Golden Bough* appears in "He mourns for the Change that has come upon him and his Beloved, and longs for the end of the World." Here the speaker, realizing that fulfillment and self-realization are impossible, identifies himself with Mongan, an ancient Celtic priest-king.[21] He heroically aspires to confront that extinction of life whose mythic image is the product of the Yeatsian imagination brooding over the works of Rhys and Frazer:

> I would that the boar without bristles had come from the West
> And had rooted the sun and moon and stars out of the sky
> And lay in the Darkness, grunting, and turning to his rest.

In the 1899 version of the poem's note Yeats remarks: "I have made the boar without bristles come out of the west, because the place of sunset was in Ireland, as in other countries, a place of symbolic darkness and death."[22]

Two significant changes occur in this version: one is the reduced explicitness of the Celtic reference and the other is the addition of the comparative allusion to other countries. Together they indicate the growing pressure exerted by *The Golden Bough* to urge Yeats toward a more universal, archetypal deployment of his images and symbols. He himself announces the reason for this in the same 1899 note when he declares: "The image . . . is an eternal act; but our understandings are temporal and understand but a little at a time."[23] In the face of the parochial character of Celtic mythology considered as a self-contained and self-sufficient body of symbols, Yeats recognizes the need of broadening his scope so that as many temporal understandings as possible may be brought to bear on the elucidation of the mysteries of existence. To this end Frazer's compara-

---

[21] *The Variorum Edition of the Poems*, pp. 153, 177.
[22] *The Variorum Edition of the Poems*, p. 807.
[23] *The Variorum Edition of the Poems*, p. 807.

tive method, with its proliferation of similarities that issued in a series of related narratives, provided Yeats with both additional images and a model for their effective utilization. Hence the last lines of the poem provide in the boar an emblem of basically Celtic origin but one which in the light of Yeats's reading and Mongan's role as wizard and king expands to include those savage antagonists of the dying god whom *The Golden Bough* interprets in naturalistic terms.

With this expansion the tone and import of the poem is subtly altered. What had hitherto seemed a strange combination of the poet's self-pity coupled with a longing for a kind of *Gotterdäm-merung* destruction of the universe now appears as a mythically informed determination that the ritual of the dying god be completed correctly and with due formality. As a priest-king, Mongan becomes for Yeats the human representative of the dying and reviving god who in this case, as the boar's presence makes clear, is equated with Adonis. On this level, the poem is transformed from an expression of wounded vanity and petulant anger. It becomes an affirmation of the necessity of completing the downward cycle of life, of enduring the symbolic death by means of which alone the rebirth of the individual, the reappearance of the reviving god, can be effected. The transmutation of the disappointments and hard pain of life into a fierce and courageous joy, which Yeats was to effect so brilliantly in poem after poem in his later years, is here achieved, at least on a thematic level, through the use of Frazer's central myth.

It is this use of myth to transcend personal dilemmas that in large measure is responsible for the tone of calm acceptance that pervades "The Valley of the Black Pig," a poem that illustrates the difference between moving toward the myth and already being deep within it. In the preceding poem the protagonist enters the world of myth through his animal metamorphosis after which he desires the completion of the dying-god ritual. Here, though the language is heavily weighted with the misty shimmer of the Celtic Twilight, the theme is clearly man's religious acceptance of material and spiritual necessities.

Purely from the standpoint of *The Golden Bough*, the black pig, who has been transformed into the master of the flaming door, stands revealed as a demonic deity who controls that form of death which is a ritual of nature as well as a transition to something beyond nature achieved through the purging of those aspects of existence subject to "shadowy decay." To bow down to him is to acknowledge an inevitable segment of the life cycle of man and god, history and myth secure in the knowledge that it will inaugurate a revival of the man-god into a world of supranatural immutability. The destruction of the world in the battle of the black pig, then, is the prelude to regeneration rather than the world-weary anarchism of *fin-de-siècle* disillusionment.

In contrast to *The Wind Among the Reeds* the poems of the early years of the century which were collected for *In the Seven Woods* show, for the most part, a less explicit use of nature myths and fertility rituals. The chief exceptions are "Under the Moon" and "Red Hanrahan's Song about Ireland" both of which focus on Celtic rather than primitive materials. The latter, interestingly enough, was first published in 1894 and before its appearance in *In the Seven Woods* had undergone several drastic revisions. The version that appeared in the 1897 edition of *The Secret Rose* is more nearly Frazerian than either earlier or later forms, as the final stanza shows. When he refers to "the Fall of the Oak trees" and capitalizes it for emphasis, Yeats is endeavoring to bring Frazer's treatment of the oak to bear on the ancient and present sorrows of Ireland. In *The Golden Bough* the oak is a sacred tree dedicated to the god of sky, thunder, lightning, and rain, and so the home of the golden bough or mistletoe. The disasters so frequently visited on the oak, according to Frazer, serve Yeats as a symbol or nature myth of the political and cultural defeats suffered by Ireland. Nor is the choice of the oak purely arbitrary, for in reading *The Golden Bough* Yeats could not have missed noticing and being delighted by the fact that ancient Ireland used to possess numerous sacred oak groves.

"Under the Moon" makes an even heavier use of Celtic mythology with its references to Brycelinde, Lancelot, Uladh, Naoise, Branwin, Niamh, and others, so that it is more directly indebted to O'Grady and Rhys than to Frazer. Yet by its accumulation of legendary scenes and characters that share certain qualities of atmosphere or fate, the poem reflects also the shaping impact of

Frazer's comparative approach to myth. Both in Frazer and in Yeats the piling up of examples serves not only to indicate the diversity within the sameness of human experiences but also to give added force to the argument being developed. The poem's final lines explain the attitude that pervades the earlier enumeration of legendary scenes of love, enchantment, and sorrow:

Because of a story I heard under the thin horn
Of the third moon, that hung between the night and the day,
To dream of women whose beauty was folded in dismay,
Even in an old story, is a burden not to be borne.[24]

Here is perhaps the closest Yeats comes to allusive reliance on *The Golden Bough* at this stage in his career. For the story heard is not simply one of frustrated and unrequited love, of Maude Gonne's rejection of him and her marriage to Major MacBride. It also involves the moon-god whose dismemberment and burial are performed as the moon wanes into its crescent shape.[25] With this the poet brings his reading and personal experience to a focus in poetry that enunciates his anguish at the same time that it enables him to bear it. In short, Yeats's imagination fuses the death and dismemberment of the dying god with the agony of losing Maude Gonne irretrievably.

The remainder of *In the Seven Woods* shows the impact of *The Golden Bough* in a more general manner, as a force contributing to a reinforcement of thematic concerns rather than to innovation in imagery. Thus, the shaping of "The Folly of Being Comforted" owes something to Frazer's relentless but varied documentation of the recurring appearance of representatives of those beautiful and fateful consorts of the dying god like Venus, Astarte, Ishtar, and Aphrodite as well as to Yeats's preoccupation with the great Celtic heroines of the past. Similarly, the motif of play in "Never Give All the Heart" reflects both his current experience in the

---

[24] In *Later Poems* (1922) the first two lines are altered to read "the famished horn of the hunter's moon." See *The Variorum Edition of the Poems*, p. 210. The sharpened emphasis on hunger and human survival under primitive conditions suggests how *The Golden Bough* could operate on the poet's imagination to intensify the contrast between the ostensibly idyllic Joyous Isle and the mysterious, insupportable story.

[25] *GB*, VI, 130.

theater and Frazer's revelations about the sacred nature of ancient and primitive ritual drama. For it is clear that the women's "offering their hearts up to the play" is a dedicatory rite by which they approach their own reason for existence. And in moving toward his escapist cherishing of dreams, Yeats finds encouragement in folklore of the sort recorded by *The Golden Bough*. This is the burden of the titular paradox in "The Withering of the Boughs." There the speaker declares that boughs unaltered by winter storms "have withered because I have told them my dreams." Such an expression combines the conventional asseverative exaggeration of the romantic lyric and the Frazerian folk motif that fatigue and illness could be transferred to the branches of trees or bushes by contact and voice.

Of Yeats's earlier efforts to absorb *The Golden Bough* into his poetic the least extensive occurs in *The Green Helmet and Other Poems*. Nevertheless, this collection does possess several notable features. One of these occurs in the first poem, entitled "His Dream," which describes a vision of the author. In it the poet guides downstream a gaily decorated ship in the middle of which there rests a figure on a bed. In answer to the crowd's inquiry he identifies the figure as Death. Though the style is faintly Tennysonian, the basic narrative pattern is resolutely Frazerian. It follows *The Golden Bough*'s accounts of the funerary rituals of Osiris, primitive scapegoat expulsions of sickness, and the European peasant custom of carrying out Death. When all three of these are considered, it is clear that Yeats's extravagant admiration of the figure is something more than *fin-de-siècle* morbidity. With Frazer's aid, Yeats saw that he could praise, honor, and dignify Death because it symbolized the dying god who could face, suffer in, and return from the underworld, all with the dignity that men long for but seldom attain. The poem uses the dying god's ship-of-death pattern in order to reverse the poem's initial impression of being a mannered invocation to a romantic and unreal Death.

Another aspect of the volume is its development of the theme of the tree image in such a way as to fuse Yeats's hermetic knowledge with that acquired from *The Golden Bough*. Thus, in "The Fascination of What's Difficult" what is distinctive is the explicit association of tree and man. Hitherto the tree has functioned as an emblem or natural surrogate in whose condition man might read his own. But now man is a tree while still remaining a human being, so that he in effect becomes a kind of Frazerian tree-spirit in reverse, outwardly human but with an inner nature that strives for organic fruition. The manner in which this is achieved can be seen from "The Coming of Wisdom with Time," which is an advance in insight as well as a development in the elaboration of the tree image:

> Though leaves are many, the root is one;
> Through all the lying days of my youth
> I swayed my leaves and flowers in the sun;
> Now I may wither into the truth.

Through the experience and the contemplation of it the poet achieves an experiential truth to set beside the phenomenal beauty enshrined in the flowering tree of youth. Aiding him in this was Frazer's contention that primitive tree-worship, relics of which still exist in modern Europe, was based on the notion that the whole world is animate. Such a view would certainly have been very sympathetic to Yeats, all of whose studies in theosophy, hermetic lore, comparative religion, and astrology were concerned with discovering not only a hidden or forgotten reality but also a dynamic, continuous existence in which all things are woven together in a cosmic unity.

The acceptance of the possibility that one may "wither into the truth" leads, of course, to the great poems of Yeats's later years. Similarly his early celebration of the tree as a symbol of man and the aspirations of the artist is a natural adumbration of his great later symbol of the tower, which first began to appear in *Responsibilities*. Both are complex renderings of the poet's sense of the interplay of nature and art, the sacred and the secular, the indomitable and the embattled, being and becoming. And both are derived in some measure from *The Golden Bough*'s emphasis on the natural and supernatural attributes with which earliest man invested the tree. Preeminent among these was the identification of the tree-spirit as the original form out of which developed the anthropomorphic god of the woods who in turn was one manifestation of the dying and reviving god. The associations Yeats confers on his trees are substantially those Frazer records as attributed by his primitive worshippers: fertility, beauty and awe, magic, natural misfortunes, and sacrifice. Taken together, all these suggest clearly why the tree became a crucial symbol in the Yeatsian canon.

The final major contribution made by *The Green Helmet* to Yeats's effort to incorporate *The Golden Bough* into his poetic is the introduction of his prime symbol of the anti-self in "The Mask." What Frazer says about the role of the mask in early life affords an illuminating insight into Yeats's ability to transmute while retaining symbolic functions. Yeats, of course, did not develop his theory and practice of the mask exclusively from Frazer; a large part evolved from his struggle with his own personality and his recognition that society consisted largely of role-playing individuals. Frazer, however, gave Yeats an extensive historical sanction for finding in the mask more than a device for promulgating social hypocrisy and disguising personal insecurity. Among other things, he pointed out that masks were worn by kings, people personating gods, women, actors, and members of secret societies, and that they were employed in religious performances, fertility rituals, and scapegoat ceremonies. They also were designed to represent demons, gods, or spirits generally, including those of fertility, the dead, and totemic animals. Sensitively and imaginatively interpreted, the beings represented by the masks could reinforce and sanction Yeats's wish to assume a wide range of personalities or selves, from the demonic to the divinely omniscient.[26] His delight in the hereditary past and tradition, his absorption in the religious world of supernatural sanctions, and his sense of the magical power resident in heraldic emblems of great antiquity all found fulfillment in the mask-beings of *The Golden Bough*.

These efforts to acquire a new unity of self through becoming what one sets out by imitating continue in *Responsibilities*, whose publication coincided with the beginning of World War I. Yet there are significant differences in the mythic areas explored by

[26] See his unpublished letter written c. 1921, cited by Ellmann, *The Identity of Yeats* (New York: Oxford, 1954), p. 170.

this volume and that immediately preceding it. For one thing, *Responsibilities* shows a persistent interest in the theme of death and rebirth as well as in the dramatic interplay of mortality and immortality. "The Mountain Tomb" celebrates the famous legend of the miraculous 120-year preservation of Father Christian Rosencreuz, the alleged founder of the Rosicrucians, an account incorporated into the initiatory rites of the Golden Dawn. The legend itself apparently involved no rebirth for its protagonist, though it did in Golden Dawn ceremonies. Particularly interesting is the extent to which the poem attaches to the Rosicrucian legend rituals and customs drawn from *The Golden Bough*'s discussion of the funerary rites of the dying god. Observing the death of a revered leader by drinking, dancing, and sexual passion does not square with most modern ideas on the subject, but it does with primitive celebrations of the god's demise. Though there is plentiful and extreme mourning, there are also ceremonies of a releasing, sexually stimulating character. The latter both reflect and predict the return, revival, or rebirth of the god whose death is being witnessed. In short, Yeats fuses his Rosicrucian and Frazerian patterns so that the celebration of Rosicross' attained perfection merges with that of the death and resurrection of the god.

Where "The Mountain Tomb" stresses death and the present, "The Magi" emphasizes birth and the past. But both link their themes to the temporal cycle whose imaginative quality is what releases it from time and projects it into eternity. The figures of the poem are seen "in the mind's eye," which notes that they have performed their role before and that they hope "to find once more, / . . . / The uncontrollable mystery on the bestial floor." The death of the Christian god with its violence and turmoil has left them "unsatisfied" because they, like Yeats and Frazer, grasp his descent from a long line of primitive dying and reviving gods. In this respect, the most striking thing about "The Magi" is the way in which Yeats, almost as though he were deliberately copying Frazer's technique, is able to merge Christian and pagan or primitive rites without doing violence to either. This is achieved largely through the subtleties of the last line. From a Christian perspective, "uncontrollable" testifies to the supreme power of

God working through the mystery of conception and birth, while "bestial" is an unsentimental means of rendering the stable scene. To one familiar, as Yeats was, with *The Golden Bough* and related studies, the two terms convey the ceaselessly recurring arrival of new gods and the fundamental, non-human processes from which they originate.

[III]

When we turn to *The Wild Swans at Coole*, two distinct features occur in connection with Yeats's relation to *The Golden Bough*. The first is that there is less explicit concern with the death-rebirth theme as such; the stress falls rather on the soul's endurance and exploration of its human or bodily condition and on the moon symbolism of cyclicity and periodicity being evolved in connection with *A Vision*. The second interesting aspect of the volume for our purposes is that there is a greater correlation between the poems of major significance and those showing Frazer's impact. At the same time there is a marked increase in the number of poems incidentally utilizing images or concepts that are of a Frazerian cast.

Of the major poems shaped by *The Golden Bough* the first in the volume is "Lines Written in Dejection." This poem's closest link is with "The Realists," for both powerfully render the loss of mythopoeic consciousness as an epistemological and cosmological diminution of major proportions. The poet no longer sees "the dark leopards of the moon" or "the wild witches," much less "the holy centaurs of the hills." In their place he is left with "nothing but the embittered sun," the symbol of rational thought and perception whose lack of boldness is to provide the natural accompaniment of his old age. These symbolic images of mythic life carry a greater weight than merely their surface color and bizarre form. They point to the specific character of Yeats's loss and its roots in the ancient customs and beliefs detailed in *The Golden Bough* and other studies of the primitive life of man. Thus, leopards were associated with wizards and magicians as well as royalty, and were thought to inspire oracular revelations.[27] In addition, they were thought to contain the external

[27] *GB*, IV, 84-85; XI, 202.

souls of persons and in general to have their lives bound up with those of human beings.[28] As a symbol of beauty the leopard benefits from Frazer's linking of it to classical accounts of gods who assume animal form in order to carry out a sexual liaison with a human being.[29] This in turn is regarded as a story reflecting the custom of a Sacred Marriage ritually dramatized. The leopard envisaged by Yeats is the imagination's creative drive roaming darkly in search of expression. Its bravery, however, was legendary and was sought through communion rites by many primitive peoples, including those described in *The Golden Bough*.[30] This quality of ruthless courage Yeats also attaches to the leopard, who thereby becomes an animal form of one of the masks he sought to fashion for himself and whose absence he laments.

Even more obviously related to *The Golden Bough* is the image of "the wild witches." When Frazer talks about their sinister habits and magical powers and records folk beliefs from Europe and elsewhere, he is speaking of matters that Yeats felt he knew personally and intimately. As an Irishman, he had, as it were, a vested interest in spirits both benign and demonic, including witches. This interest was sufficiently strong for him to devote one of the sections of his *Fairy and Folk Tales of the Irish Peasantry* to witches, whom he is careful to designate as receiving their powers from "evil spirits and [their] own malignant will."[31] On the subject of witches and witchcraft Frazer provided Yeats with its tradition and evidence of its universality, so that he naturally felt encouraged to use them seriously and without embarrassment as symbols of a past and perhaps still persisting reality. In magic, omniscience and omnipotence are exquisitely related capacities, and to a poet who could achieve both only through language seen as a kind of incantatory spell the lure was irresistible. Another and related reason for Yeats's sympathy to witchcraft and magic is perhaps suggested by his remark that "the central notion of witchcraft everywhere is the power to

---

[28] *GB*, XI, 201-207.   [29] *GB*, IV, 83-84.

[30] *GB*, VIII, 141ff.

[31] W. B. Yeats, ed., *Fairy and Folk Tales of the Irish Peasantry* (London: Walter Scott Ltd., n.d.), p. 146.

change into some fictitious form."[32] From Frazer he could gather the heartening declaration that magical changes of shape were perfectly credible to primitive man. When to this he added theosophical notions about the lost wisdom of ancient peoples, he had what he regarded as the requisite intellectual justification for magic and witchcraft. It is precisely this aspect that Yeats's humorously affectionate salute to witches renders in "Lines Written in Dejection."

Unlike the Romantic ode for lost poetic powers, "Lines Written in Dejection" attempts no consolation. The absence of "heroic mother moon" prevents the heroic gesture in the face of the imagination's diminution. The nature of that gesture, however, is movingly conveyed in "Her Courage," the sixth in the "Upon a Dying Lady" cycle based on the pathetic end of Mabel Beardsley. What makes this poem a particularly significant expression of the stance of the tragic hero is its straightforward association of the attitude with mythic paradigms that recall Frazer even as it utilizes a minuscule version of the comparative method to extend myth into history. Thus, in anticipating Mabel Beardsley's death, Yeats avowedly uses the language of myth:

> When her soul flies to the predestined dancing-place
> I have no speech but symbol, the pagan speech I made
> Amid the dreams of youth.

In copious detail Frazer traces the flight of the soul from the body after death to primitive beliefs.[33] That Yeats was not unaware of this is suggested by "Another Song of a Fool," which employs the image of the soul as butterfly, described by Frazer.[34] Similarly, by alluding to symbolic pagan speech such as he learned when young he is acknowledging that his poetic language derives from the matrix of folktale, myth, and comparative religion into which he plunged in the 90s and whose most extensive form was *The Golden Bough*.

Further, "the predestined dancing-place" may very well owe more than a trifle to Frazer's accounts of dancing's forming "a conspicuous feature of the great festival of the dead" so that "the

[32] *Fairy and Folk Tales of the Irish Peasantry*, p. 148.
[33] *GB*, III, 30ff. [34] *GB*, III, 41, 51.

festival which began so lugubriously ends by being the merriest of the year."[35] The parabola of Mabel Beardsley's life exactly accords with the emotional progression of Frazer's great festival. And like Frazer too, Yeats seems in this series of poems to have been struck by the dialectical continuity obtaining between Catholicism and the primitive religions out of which it grew.

When we turn to *The Wild Swans at Coole* we see Yeats starting to unfold the emblems and themes that later receive more starkly abstract exposition in *A Vision*. The dominant symbol is the moon, whose phases and powers largely determine for Yeats the nature of the individual and history. As both "The Phases of the Moon" and *A Vision* make apparent, it is the changing appearance of the moon that provides the controlling metaphor for Yeats's cyclical theory of history and human development. Both Yeats's persistent eclecticism and his long familiarity with *The Golden Bough* played a significant role in shaping this theory. Frazer's narrative of the turning wheel of myth and nature forcibly suggests that the human mind is irresistibly drawn to imaginative visions of cosmic cycles. In this regard Frazer's great advantage for the poet is that he presents cyclical history not as an abstract theory but as a series of concrete observations which create a subsumptive and controlling image.

What makes the impact of Frazer's concrete cyclicity substantial is his treatment of the moon as a central force in primitive and ancient belief. He sets forth individual folk beliefs such as that sun and moon are wedded to one another and that the moon is particularly connected with birth, and these notions are skillfully adapted by Yeats in poems like "Under the Round Tower" and "On Woman."[36] He also develops at considerable length, especially in the chapters "Osiris and the Moon" and "The Doctrine of Lunar Sympathy," the view that the moon controls nature and man alike.[37] In the first of these chapters Frazer enumerates a number of points in Osiris' myth and ritual which link him to the moon, including his reputed twenty-eight-year reign. To Yeats such an identification would have been particu-

[35] *GB*, VI, 52, 55.
[36] *GB*, II, 146; IV, 71, 73-78, 87-89, 90, 92, 105; II, 128; X, 75ff.
[37] *GB*, VI, 129-150.

larly encouraging, for it would link the natural and, in his eyes, historical cycle to myth with its radical use of image in symbolizing those levels of the mind on which spiritual, social, psychological, and natural knowledge are not discriminated among because they are all imaginatively relevant to the experience. And in seeing the cycle associated with a dying and reviving god, he may possibly have felt that he was drawing close to the vision of Blake, his great master, that nature and the external world ultimately consist of a gigantic human body.

A third attraction for Yeats in the identification of moon and deity is Frazer's conclusion:

> If in one of his aspects Osiris was originally a deity of vegetation, we can easily enough understand why in a later and more philosophic age he should have come to be thus identified with the moon. For as soon as he begins to meditate upon the causes of things, the early philosopher is led by certain obvious, though fallacious, appearances to regard the moon as the ultimate cause of the growth of plants. In the first place he associates its apparent growth and decay with the growth and decay of sublunary things, and imagines that in virtue of a secret sympathy the celestial phenomena really produce those terrestrial changes which in point of fact they merely resemble.[38]

While, as we have seen, Yeats follows Frazer in attaching vegetative and fertility interpretations to his image of the black pig, he also was drawn to the more abstract speculations of philosophers. Hence when in a passage such as this he sees an already attractive notion linked to a "more philosophic age," it takes on an added appeal, especially since Frazer follows the above remarks with quotations from classical authors like Pliny, Macrobius, and Aulus Gellius, who take the power of the moon very seriously indeed. Yeats, like Eliot, Graves, Pound, and Joyce, had more than a touch of the scholar in his nature and loved not only to refer learnedly to obscure and ancient authors but also to peruse their works with a kind of imaginative ecstasy. At the same time, like Lawrence, he very much liked to think of himself as a bold and independent thinker so that, as in the above pas-

[38] *GB*, vi, 131-132.

sage, he could take particular pleasure in rejecting Frazer's conviction of the fallaciousness of the identification while drawing heavily on *The Golden Bough*'s description of it. In a poem such as "The Phases of the Moon," many of these notions and forces appear overtly.[39] In this way Yeats justifies and exalts two things that dominated his vision almost from the very beginning: the old age he could not avoid and the idealist, suprarational modes of thought epitomized by the occult interests he would not relinquish.

These two interests are continued, though with a rather different emphasis, in *Michael Robartes and the Dancer*. For present purposes, the most impressive thing is not the perpetuation and development of theme but rather the extraordinarily resourceful use of anthropological elements to focus the meaning and measure the emotional weight of individual works.

Effective instances of this occur in "Michael Robartes and the Dancer." There Yeats deepens his memory of particular paintings of St. George and the Dragon by recalling *The Golden Bough*'s identification of the legend as the medieval counterpart of the Perseus-Andromeda myth. Both in turn are regarded as civilized versions of the ancient widespread custom of "sacrificing human beings to water-spirits," especially in "the form of making over a woman to the spirit to be his wife, in order either to pacify his fury or to give play to his generative powers."[40] Similarly the image of the lover who turns "green with rage/ At all that is not pictured" indicates that Yeats is aware of Frazer's tracing of the knight to primitive leaf-clad mummers designed to stimulate fertility.[41]

Much the same merging of several contexts takes place in "Sol-

[39] Representative instances are the scornful exposure of the limitations of scholarship by Aherne and Robartes, the "twice-born" hero, the soul's entry into a labyrinth, and the images of burning arrow and wagon-wheel as counters to declining energy.

[40] *GB*, II, 163. The poem's witty ironic tone—directed both at the female speaker, the dancer, and at the educational or experiential convention of the world—might lead us to speculate also whether it was not partly shaped by Frazer's account, on the same page, of the Bavarian mummers' play called the Slaying of the Dragon which involved a rude sort of irony and what might almost be labelled a kind of archetypal comedy.

[41] *GB*, II, 74-78, 97; VII, 95.

omon and the Witch." Sheba's identification of the setting as "the forbidden sacred grove" establishes it as Eden seen from the outside, perfect sexual fulfillment whose impossibility only underscores its religious and symbolic function. But love's tests of the lover culminate in murder after which "the bride-bed brings despair." As a result the grove also takes on the lineaments of Frazer's sacred grove at Nemi in which two aspirants to the office of priest of Diana warily circle one another seeking the advantage that will allow one to triumph and gain ultimate realization at the expense of the death of the other. This second context substantially alters the point of Sheba's rapt enthusiasm for aspiring once more to Eden. Striving toward prelapsarian Adam and Eve may result in the emergence of the sinister killer-priest and his would-be successor. This is a knowledge not likely to have been conveyed as economically yet powerfully without the image and custom detailed by *The Golden Bough*.

A much more explicit use of Frazerian significance in a poem's controlling image is to be found in "The Rose Tree." This poem demonstrates Yeats's growing capacity to fuse history and myth, present and past into an imaginative vision of the tragic nature of man. The concern with natural fertility and the identification of it with national survival recall some of the central themes of *The Golden Bough*. Thus the final stanza makes it clear that Yeats is finding the rationale for human political sacrifice in the ancient customs described by Frazer. Blood offerings were long thought to be the most efficacious means of assuring the fertility of trees held sacred to a race and linked with their own survival and perpetuation as a people.[42]

On a personal level, "A Prayer for my Daughter," the last major poem in *Michael Robartes and the Dancer*, illuminates another aspect of Yeats's growing skill in fusing the particular and the universal, what is immediate and what is remote, both temporally and spatially. For at crucial junctures in the poem, he introduces images and motifs appearing in *The Golden Bough* that epitomize the conflicting forces of life with which the poet is struggling. The first of these occurs in the second stanza when after contemplating his infant daughter's helplessness before the

[42] GB, II, 13, 16, 19, 34, 44, 47, 367.

sea-created winds of the present, the poet turns to prayer and the future:

> Imagining in excited reverie
> That the future years had come,
> Dancing to a frenzied drum,
> Out of the murderous innocence of the sea.

The images of drum and dance point up affinities between the present and a past in which, as Frazer shows, human sacrifices, executions, and ritual murders, as well as unbridled fertility rites, were prefaced by emotion-heightening dances and music.[43]

Yeats clearly expected the future to be if anything worse than the present. It is significant therefore that *The Golden Bough* should note that dances and drumming are for some primitive peoples respected means of magically controlling the wind and especially of allaying storms.[44] Such a custom (a crucial word in the poem) reveals the frenzy of the drum and dance as man's furious attempt to quell the gathering storm that is about to burst upon him from "the murderous innocence of the sea." In such a context, both drum and dance are clearly metaphors for the magical coercing of human nature. In relation to his own personal case, that is, his concern for the future of his daughter, the focus of these metaphors is the poem-prayer itself, which, he hopes, carries its own kind of magic for at least one individual. Thus, the recurrent invocatory "may she" construction supported by the rhyme, intensified as it is by the heavy use of masculine couplet rhymes, functions as the repetitive, emphatic rhythm of the drum. It provides the basic pattern to which the images of horn, wind, tree, and house and the concepts of beauty, courtesy, serenity, innocence add the verbal equivalent of the dance in all its elegant variations.

The image of drum and dance, developed out of *The Golden Bough*, essentially captures the destructive threat of the wind and man's response to it. In contrast, the image of the tree— which first appears at almost the exact middle of the poem—pro-

---

[43] As an extension of Frazer's point Jane Harrison's discussion of the dance of the Kouretes, *Themis*, pp. 13-27, is both stimulating and a possible influence on Yeats's use of the drum and dance image here.

[44] *GB*, I, 328.

vides a symbol of organic stability, peace, and nobility with
which to counter the "assault and battery" of the "angry wind"
that represents the strident future of modern man:

> May she become a flourishing hidden tree
> That all her thoughts may like the linnet be,
> And have no business but dispensing round
> Their magnanimities of sound,
> Nor but in merriment begin a chase,
> Nor but in merriment a quarrel.
> O may she live like some green laurel
> Rooted in one dear perpetual place.

Pretty clearly the laurel image extends beyond the classical
token of victory in its significance for Yeats, for it delineates not
merely the hope of triumph but also the very shape it is to take.
And it is *The Golden Bough*'s treatment of the laurel in ancient
times that provided Yeats with the conjunction of associations he
could adapt to his own ends. One of these associations was derived from the great sanctity with which the sacred groves or
sanctuaries were invested. Punishment for their violation was
stern and no exceptions were tolerated. In particular the grove
of Dia near Rome contained laurels which were so revered that
expiatory sacrifices had to be offered when even "a rotten bough
fell to the ground, or when an old tree was laid low by a storm
or dragged down by a load of snow on its branches."[45] Such an
intensity of concern and reverence would particularly impress
Yeats because, as Frazer makes clear in his very next paragraph,
such an attitude was not confined to the peasantry but rather "the
feeling was shared by the most cultivated minds in the greatest
age of Roman civilisation."[46] This claim Frazer supports by,
among other things, a quotation from Pliny that could not have
helped setting Yeats's mind racing by its use of some of his favorite images: " 'we adore sacred groves and the very silence that
reigns in them not less devoutly than images that gleam with gold
and ivory.' "[47] Thus, to pray—in itself grounds for invoking an
image associated with a holy place—that his daughter should
exist like a holy tree of antiquity, a member of a sacred grove,

[45] *GB*, ii, 122.   [46] *GB*, ii, 123.   [47] *GB*, ii, 123.

"rooted in one dear perpetual place" is to seek for her much more than a serene and lengthy secular life. It is to envisage for her a paradisal world of eternal and intimate values that is the natural equivalent, as Pliny suggests, of the splendors of artifice.

Adding to this primary association is Frazer's concern in this section of *The Golden Bough* with Diana as a fertility goddess and with the idea of the sacred marriage as an ancient custom.[48] Her traditional nature of virginal innocence, though modestly qualified by Frazer, is entirely appropriate to Yeats's envisagement of his grown daughter. *The Golden Bough*'s concept of the sacred marriage celebrates both the reproductive opulence of nature or the horn and also the central sacrament of mankind which by its very reliance on choice entails a limitation imposed on nature's abundance:

> And may her bridegroom bring her to a house
> Where all's accustomed, ceremonious;
>
> .   .   .   .
> .   .   .   .
>
> How but in custom and in ceremony
> Are innocence and beauty born?
> Ceremony's a name for the rich horn
> And custom for the spreading laurel tree.

The equation developed in the last two lines of the poem bears out *The Golden Bough*'s concept of the sacred marriage as a reconciliation of the conflicting impulses of desire and restraint, nature and man.

Yeats submerges the primitive origins of the idea in the imagery of the contemporary world so that we are left with a sense of a civilized tradition that has refined its rude beginnings almost out of existence. Fertility rituals, which are the bodily enactment of the horn symbol, are diffused into the more general concern of human behavior as an intricately elaborated series of hieratic rites and gestures. In the same way, a transformation is wrought on the reverential awe, which is response rather than action, originally felt for the sacred laurel and its female form, Diana, the virginal object of worship. It becomes the habit of tradition,

---

[48] *GB*, I, 40, 120ff.; II, 115, 120ff., 378.

which makes a convention of respect out of the ancient roots of *religio*, the feeling that certain things are more than ordinary and to be treated with particular care. Thus, Yeats is able to adapt the primitive world of *The Golden Bough* to the exigencies of the modern postwar world while still retaining the charismatic powers originally thought to reside in the tree and the spirit animating it.

[IV]

In his subsequent volumes, *The Tower*, *The Winding Stair*, and *Last Poems*, the poet demonstrates the full extent of his control over these two worlds. He shows the power of his vision, which is capable of holding two such temporally distant scenes in dramatic and fruitful tension so that each illuminates the other. Thereby they reveal that continuity of tradition Yeats had sought for all his life, the tradition of phenomenological man's search for and creation of transcendence. It is to the exploration of one aspect of this tradition that Yeats turns in "Sailing to Byzantium," where the Frazerian impact, though somewhat attenuated, is still crucial.[49] In the first three stanzas the controlling images of natural fertility, the voyage of exploration, and fire-bound sages are related to comparable scenes in *The Golden Bough*. With the last stanza, in which Yeats declares that his eternal, supernatural form is to be that of a golden bird "set upon a golden bough" the relation is almost intrusively underlined. Nor would Yeats have to feel that he was being arbitrary in linking the Byzantine tree of artifice with Frazer's natural bough. For in discussing why the mistletoe was called the Golden Bough, Frazer remarks that "on the principles of homeopathic magic there is a natural affinity between a yellow bough and yellow gold."[50] Thus, not only does Frazer provide Yeats with a tradition for linking nature and arti-

---

[49] For instance, both *The Golden Bough* and the first stanza of the poem are dominated by sex and death and both testify to the disparity between sensual experience and intellectual comprehension. Similarly, the magnificent monuments of the second stanza call to mind not only Byzantine culture but the great ancient religions and customs delineated by Frazer; both authors use the image of a sea voyage for their basic quest, as well as the purification of the wise man by fire.

[50] *GB*, xi, 287, see also J. L. Allen, Jr., "The Golden Bird on 'The Golden Bough,'" *The Diliman Review*, xi (1963), 168-221.

fice, but he also gives him the very method most likely to appeal to the lifelong practitioner of magic. Hence, Yeats had what he would have considered two of the very strongest warrants for reading his Byzantine symbolism in terms of the vegetative fertility motifs of Frazer.

Such a reading would necessarily find a greater significance in the golden bird and golden bough than merely that of a rapturous delight in sumptuous splendor and aristocratic self-possession, though this too is an integral part of the world Yeats aspires to. Both the bird and the golden bough are images of the external soul, that aspect of the living creature upon which his continued existence depends. And clearly the poet's determination to assume such a form on such a branch "once out of nature" is dictated by his virtually lifelong interest in immortality. The same is true of his passionate absorption in the spirits of the dead and their capacity to affect human life materially. These convictions find satisfaction and inspiration in the bird's being a form of those who lived in the past and who in this shape continue to impinge on the living. And in the bird as corn-spirit he would have an image of Tammuz or Adonis, the dying and reviving god upon whom man is dependent for his life and in whose rites he might read the nature of his own destiny. This identification is made even more attractive by Frazer. He observes that in a particular Egyptian funerary scene on the tomb of Osiris "a bird is depicted among the branches with the significant legend 'the soul of Osiris,' showing that the spirit of the dead god was believed to haunt his sacred tree."[51] And just as Yeats's golden bird sings, among other things, of what is to come, so in his section on the corn-spirit as a bird Frazer stresses that the cry of the bird is prophetic.[52]

While in the bird image Yeats had to apply Frazer's material to the Byzantine metallic bird, in the case of the bough emblem no such adaptation was necessary. The penultimate chapter of Frazer's monumental study is entitled "The Golden Bough" and

[51] *GB*, VI, 110-111.
[52] Interestingly enough, the immediately following section is "The Corn-Spirit as a Fox," which Yeats might have connected with the fox who serves as the hero's guide and helper in Grimm's "The Golden Bird."

in it appear a number of points immediately apposite to Yeats's poem. First, the golden bough of the Balder legend represents the depositing of the individual's external soul in an object which then is instrumental in his death.[53] Thus, both bird and bough are repositories of the souls of both gods and man; they are simultaneously the means by which life may be prolonged or terminated. In short, they symbolize the crux of existence itself. What in the Byzantine context alone is a construct designed to amuse a bored and drowsy emperor becomes in the mythic scene an emblem capable of goading even a sleepy ruler into wakefulness through its pregnant relevance to his own condition.

Connected with the Balder association of the golden bough is the King of the Wood at Nemi, the figure with whom Frazer opens his book. The crucial significance of this figure for Yeats here is probably contained in the following passage. Frazer says: "before he could be slain, it was necessary to break the Golden Bough. As an oak-spirit, his life or death was in the mistletoe on the oak, and so long as the mistletoe remained intact, he, like Balder, could not die."[54] Such notions would serve as an emblem for Yeats that the golden bough is a potently ambivalent symbol, embracing as it does the possibilities of life and death. It is simultaneously the hero's death weapon, the assurance of his continued life, the talismanic protector of his underworld descent, and the sign of his admission to the priesthood of Diana.[55] As such, it seems to summarize in a single quintessential image the hero's life insofar as it is based on the myth of the dying and reviving god. Thus, when the bird, the carrier of the mistletoe seed according to Frazer, sings "of what is past, or passing, or to come," he is celebrating, on one level, the myth of the man-god in its eternal recurrence. In pointing to this, the golden bough fulfills its role, recorded in Frazer as being hallowed by the folk customs of many lands, of identifying and revealing treasure.[56] For the wealth that comes with knowledge of the scope and meaning of the dying and reviving god is the only kind that Yeats ultimately aspired to. And in the context of the poem, the motifs of immortality, the past, and the dying god come together in the

---

[53] GB, XI, 279, 283.

[54] GB, XI, 285.

[55] GB, I, 11; II, 379; X, 1; XI, 279ff.

[56] GB, XI, 287, 291.

image of the golden bough. For Yeats it becomes what Frazer declared it was for Aeneas and Orpheus and Adonis, a means by which "to unlock the gates of death," and so to attain what Osiris was said to offer his worshippers, "a blissful eternity in a better world hereafter."[57]

Despite the aesthetic promise of the golden bough, the themes of age and the problems it gives rise to continue in "The Tower," the next poem in the volume. Here again images and ancient trees play an important role. His initial scene mirrors Frazer's mention of the oracular capacities of trees and the spirits of the dead.[58] Later in the poem he follows the primitive mind as outlined in *The Golden Bough* in thinking that dreams are a form of reality containing revelations provided by the spirits of the dead who appear to the living through this medium. And though the Great Memory is Yeats's own concept, such ancient beliefs so widely diffused among mankind would certainly have struck him as excellent evidence in support of his view that such an overriding, subsumptive memory was operative in the world.

Later in the poem Yeats suggests that Hanrahan's life after death has resulted in what might be called the education of a hero:

> you have
> Reckoned up every unforeknown, unseeing
> Plunge, lured by a softening eye,
> Or by a touch or a sigh,
> Into the labyrinth of another's being.

This same image is repeated in the next stanza where it is described as "a great labyrinth." Yeats's habit of loading his images with a full weight of associative reference suggests that he means this one to be seen in relation to the myth of Theseus and Ariadne. Classical though the myth is, the fact that it is discussed by *The Golden Bough* in connection with ritual dances performed prior to a death by fire suggests that here too Frazer may well be exercising his impact on the meaning of the poem.[59]

---

[57] *GB*, VI, 114.
[58] *GB*, II, 9, 43, 358; VI, 167, 171-172; XI, 89ff.
[59] *GB*, IV, 75.

The labyrinth is created out of the consequences of a passionate human-animal love. It threatens death to the explorer of its intricacies and tests the courage of the hero whose triumph is also due to love and a woman won. As such, it is a virtually inevitable image for Yeats's exploration of the regrets of old age at adventures not pursued to their culmination. His mind, imbued as it was by the patterns of *The Golden Bough*, however, saw the hero as something more significant than human perfection and connected him with the divine king, the human representative of the dying and reviving god, whose power must be renewed periodically if his reign is to persist and the god is to remain vigorous and productive for his people. Frazer suggests that it was precisely this with which the tribute to Minos and the labyrinth-shrouded Minotaur was concerned.[60] The sacrifices enacted in the labyrinth were performed, he speculates, "in order to renew the strength of the king and of the sun, whom he personated." Failure to complete the sacrifice would issue in the diminishment of both king and sun, the human and natural sources of order and fertility. This is how Yeats sees it too. This is apparent from the lines and addressed to Hanrahan which urge the admission that if memory of the woman lost recurs, then "the sun's/ Under eclipse and the day blotted out." The choice of this metaphor derives unmistakably from Frazer's suggestion that the labyrinthine dance performed at Cnossus "may have represented the ecliptic, the sun's apparent annual path in the sky."[61]

Both "Sailing to Byzantium" and "The Tower" stress the poet's concern with finding his way to a state or condition that tran-

[60] *GB*, iv, 71-77.

[61] *GB*, iv, 77. Elsewhere Frazer records the custom of shooting burning arrows into the air at the eclipse of the sun (*GB*, i, 311) and the belief that eclipses were due to a monster's attacking the sun (*GB*, x, 70, 161 n.2), both of which would have greatly interested Yeats. It is worth noticing too, perhaps, that the sun's eclipse here is balanced by his earlier references to the disastrous confusion of moonlight and daylight (ll. 45-46) and to his hope that they may "seem/ One inextricable beam" (ll. 54-55). These images would seem also to derive from Frazer's report that the primitive belief of the marriage of the sun and the moon is reflected in the myths of Zeus and Europa, of Minos and Britomartis (*GB*, iv, 71-73), and of Pasiphaë and the bull. The inference clearly is that the above lines symbolize the desirable but disastrous experience of the mysteries of love which old age regrets both having had and having lost.

scends the mortal and the mutable. At the same time they recognize apparently that death must be endured if it is to be achieved. Indeed, there is a sense in which this same pattern or aspects of it are worked out in so many of the major poems in *The Tower* that the endurance of death and destruction for the sake of creating "Translunar Paradise" might well be said to be the controlling theme of the collection. This is best seen in "Meditations in Time of Civil War," "Nineteen Hundred and Nineteen," and "All Souls' Night." In the first of these Yeats has a dream-like vision of "phantoms of hatred and of the heart's fullness and of the coming emptiness." The second sees the historical realization of that vision in the "dragon-ridden days" of Irish civil strife and merges it with the legendary apparitions and evil spirits of early Ireland to give an unrelentingly somber view of the triumph of evil, death, and destruction. To this "All Souls' Night" affords an answer based on contact with the spirits of the dead and with thoughts so rapt in self-absorption that they can remain oblivious to the world's destruction.

In all these, to greater or lesser degree, *The Golden Bough* serves as a central shaping factor. Thus, in the "Meditations" poem "frenzies bewilder, reveries perturb the mind;/ Monstrous familiar images swim to the mind's eye." This statement accurately describes Yeats's own passion over historical events, his occult and theosophical visionary habits and experiences, and the behavior of shamans and medicine-men he may have remembered from reading Frazer.[62] He further declares:

---

[62] Frazer admittedly does not stress the ecstatic, hallucinatory quality of the shaman's experience as much as subsequent investigators like Mircea Eliade, Joseph Campbell, and others, perhaps because of his inclination to view the behavior rationalistically as almost wholly fraudulent. He does, however, give some indication of the medicine-man's capacity for a state of self-induced ecstasy. See, e.g., *GB*, v, 77; viii, 72. Interestingly, in *Taboo and the Perils of the Soul*, which contains the most extended treatment of the shaman in *The Golden Bough*, Frazer describes a shaman turning himself into a hawk and stealing the soul of another in order to save his patient (iii, 57) and later (iii, 59) mentions certain demons' being called "celestial agencies bestriding galloping horses." The first of these may be relevant to Yeats's vision here of unicorns and beautiful women being transformed into "brazen hawks," just as the second would reinforce his use in "Nineteen Hundred and Nineteen" of the image of "Herodias' daughters" as evil coming to a head.

> No prophecies,
> Remembered out of Babylonian almanacs,
> Have closed the ladies' eyes.[63]

Here he rejects excessive intellectuality in almost the same fashion as Frazer does with the same metaphor. Arguing that the ancient Indo-Europeans were quite capable of noting and correcting by observation the discrepancy between solar and lunar time, Frazer declares: "they were not, as has been suggested, reduced to the necessity of borrowing the knowledge of such simple and obvious facts from the star-gazers of ancient Babylonia. Learned men who make little use of their eyes except to read books are too apt to underrate the observational powers of the savage."[64] Yeats, it is true, is not inclined to prize the savage *per se*, but he certainly would see the connection between Frazer's point and his own ideal of unselfconscious knowledge and natural intelligence.

The second section develops an oblique comment on the present cultural disaster and culminates with an unmistakable reference to the world so assiduously described by Frazer:

> When Loie Fuller's Chinese dancers enwound
> A shining web, a floating ribbon of cloth,
> It seemed that a dragon of air
> Had fallen among dancers, had whirled them round
> Or hurried them off on its own furious path;
> So the Platonic Year
> Whirls out new right and wrong,
> Whirls in the old instead;
> All men are dancers and their tread
> Goes to the barbarous clangour of a gong.

Yeats obviously was not in need of Frazer to learn about the great year of Plato. Nevertheless, he could scarcely have inter-

---

[63] This image resembles that in "The Dawn":
> the withered men that saw
> From their pedantic Babylon
> The careless planets in their courses,
> The stars fade out where the moon comes,
> And took their tablets and did sums.

[64] *GB*, IV, 326.

preted its role as he does here without subjecting it to what he learned from *The Golden Bough*. It associates the great year with the custom of octennial tenure of the kingship, whose conclusion was celebrated by festivals in which, Frazer conjectures, "the priestly kings, who personated the god, slew their predecessors in the guise of dragons, and reigned for a time in their stead."[65] Yeats simply reverses the Frazerian pattern so that the triumph of the dragon, suggested in the first half of the stanza, constitutes the success of the old. What this success entailed is seen from the last lines of the stanza: "All men are dancers and their tread/ Goes to the barbarous clangour of a gong." The present historical barbarism is associated with Frazer's primitive men who danced themselves into a destructive ecstasy as part of a religious ritual whose blood-lust held human life and its sacrifice cheaply: "Man is in love and loves what vanishes." The dance thus becomes a symbol of the ordered and cyclical destructiveness of human history.

Significantly enough, Yeats makes clear through the gong image that this destructiveness follows not from intellectual or moral perversity but from the natural impulses of the human condition. The dance is performed in accord with "the barbarous clangour of a gong," a fact that is strikingly illuminated by *The Golden Bough*. For at the famous sanctuary of Zeus at Dodona there were "bronze gongs which kept up a humming in the wind round the sanctuary."[66] These, Frazer suggests, were designed to imitate the thunder that was equated with the voice of the god and that reputedly raged more often there than anywhere else in Europe. This coupled with the oracular nature of the gongs and the gloomy setting of Dodona provides Yeats with a power- ful symbol of the supernatural order that controls mankind and makes it and history revolve in destructive patterns. Like Frazer, he here asserts that man is a creature of patterned activity, that part of it encompasses violent destruction, and that this answers to a supra-personal compulsion exerted by forces outside the individual.

"Nineteen Hundred and Nineteen" concludes with a vision of the world overwhelmed by anarchy and "the blood-dimmed tide"

[65] *GB*, IV, 82.　　　　　　　　[66] *GB*, II, 358.

in accord with the destined revolutions of the Platonic Year. The desolate prospect it holds out would be insupportable were there no possible solution or answer to the seemingly inevitable savagery of man. Such an answer is found in "All Souls' Night," which, significantly enough, became the epilogue to Yeats's extended meditation on human history and human nature, *A Vision*. Here *The Golden Bough* is meaningful largely in relation to the ritual occasion celebrated in the title. The bulk of the poem does not invoke imagery of a Frazerian note. There are, however, nodal clues that indicate that the poet's mind is shaping the poem in terms of the anthropologists' comments concerning primitive and Christian festivals of the dead. Among these are the sound of "the great Christ Church Bell/ And many a lesser bell," the date and the hour, and the drink set out. All testify to Yeats's treating this as a modern version of the immemorial custom of reserving a period of the year in which to mourn, honor, and beseech the spirits of the dead, especially those of friends and relatives.[67]

The recurrent references to "mummies in the mummy-cloth" and "mummy truths" further link the poem to *The Golden Bough*. Frazer's extended discussion of the world's festivals of the dead occurs as part of a chapter on the Egyptian god Osiris' official festivals, a deity, incidentally, one of whose functions was to serve as god of the dead. The dead alone have the fineness of perception to respond ecstatically to Yeats's "mummy truths" and to his vision of "where the damned have howled away their hearts,/ And where the blessed dance." The precise nature of these truths Yeats never quite enunciates in the course of the poem. For these and the "marvellous thing" he has to say, *The Golden Bough* is virtually indispensable. In the same chapter Frazer devotes a section to the resurrection of Osiris and during a discussion of a number of bas-reliefs and funerary effigies he draws attention to representations of "the dead body of Osiris with stalks of corn springing from it" and to corn-stuffed figures of Osiris "bandaged like mummies."[68] These, he suggests, serve as magical symbols of the god's resurrection designed "to quicken the dead, in other words, to ensure their spiritual immortality."[69]

[67] *GB*, IV, 98; VI, 51ff., 81; X, 223ff.
[68] *GB*, VI, 91.   [69] *GB*, VI, 91.

For, according to Frazer, "from the death and resurrection of their great god the Egyptians drew not only their support and sustenance in this life, but also their hope of a life eternal beyond the grave."[70]

To this should be added *The Golden Bough*'s discussions of the rebirth and reincarnation of the dead, the identification of the Egyptian dead with the god Osiris, and the basing of the worship of the dead on the theory of the human soul.[71] From them we see how Yeats came to find his answer to the devastation of "Nineteen Hundred and Nineteen" in the spirits of the dead. His reading told him that this had been man's course since earliest times and what his own race had presciently created for the world. For in *The Golden Bough* he found that "among peoples of Aryan stock, so far back as we can trace them, the worship and propitiation of the dead seem to have formed a principal element of the popular religion" and that from that belief the custom of All Souls "has come down to us from dateless antiquity."[72] This would seem even more emphatically irrefutable when he could read in Frazer that "the festival of All Souls on the second of November originated with the Celts, and spread from them to the rest of the European peoples."[73] That is, his own people in the dimmest reaches of time brought to Europe the ritual answer to the perennial threat of death, darkness, and destruction. Such a discovery would afford Yeats conclusive evidence of the rightness of his view.

[V]

The crucial nature of Yeats's concern with the spirits of the dead is fully revealed in the volumes following *The Tower*, that is, in *The Winding Stair, From "A Full Moon in March,"* and *Last Poems.* "Blood and the Moon," for instance, stands as a fuller conspectus of the themes and symbols developed at the end of *The Tower*. For one thing, it utilizes those symbols of labyrinth and pig that we have already seen to be related to *The Golden Bough*. To these Yeats adds another when he says of the great satirist: "Swift beating on his breast in sibylline frenzy blind/ Be-

---

[70] *GB*, VI, 90.
[72] *GB*, VI, 67.

[71] *GB*, III, 365ff.; V, 82ff.; VI, 15-16; VII, 181.
[73] *GB*, VI, 81.

cause the heart in his blood-sodden breast had dragged him down into mankind." The ecstatic rapture of the seer is more Virgilian than Frazerian, but with the "blood-sodden breast" image the weight shifts in the other direction. In discussing the Sibyl, *The Golden Bough* provides two distinct but related contexts that are highly pertinent to the image and Yeats's interpretation of Swift. Frazer's very first volume connects the King of the Wood ritual not only with the Golden Bough Aeneas picked before descending to the underworld but also with "the bloody ritual which legend ascribed to the Tauric Diana" in which "every stranger who landed on the shore was sacrificed on her altar."[74] And in the penultimate volume of *The Golden Bough*, the visionary prophecy by the Norse Sibyl of Balder's death is quoted and Balder is described as "the bloody victim."[75] Such contexts suggest that Yeats viewed Swift both as a reluctant but helpless humanist and, perhaps more importantly, also as an instance of incarnation through suffering and sacrifice. To become a victim, even only of powerful and lacerating emotions, such as pity and anger, is to suffer that involvement of the spirit with the body which Yeats regarded as the incarnation of the divine in the human. It is, for Yeats, "the heart in his blood-sodden breast" that establishes Swift as the ritual human victim whose slaughter mimes the sacrificial incarnation of the deity through the observance of which resurrection and transcendence become possible. Such wisdom he regards as "the property of the dead,/ A something incompatible with life." Only those who have passed beyond the limits of the physical and its rational concomitants apprehend the truth of the metaphor of the dying and reviving god. They do so because their persistence as spirits testifies to their continued existence despite their death.

A more fully developed treatment of the themes of incarnation and the spirits of the dead appears in "Byzantium." Its imagery reveals the extent of Yeats's increased apprehension of the closeness of the ties binding man and the divine, the natural and the

[74] *GB*, I, 11.
[75] *GB*, X, 102. The translation Frazer used is that of Yeats's old friend F. York Powell in his *Corpus Poeticum Boreale*.

supernatural, the temporal and the eternal. Having declared the superhuman to be an aesthetic vision of the unified duality of the spirits of the dead, the poet turns directly to providing an example of it in terms of his own symbolic conventions:

> Miracle, bird or golden handiwork,
> More miracle than bird or handiwork,
> Planted on the star-lit golden bough,
> Can like the cocks of Hades crow,
> Or, by the moon embittered, scorn aloud
> In glory of changeless metal
> Common bird or petal
> And all complexities of mire or blood.

The miraculous bird is part of a group of symbols that creates a context in which the human (Aeneas and the Priest of Nemi) and the divine (Balder) are commingled just as are Hades (the underworld in which the dead reside) and the cock-crow (the sign of resurrection and revival of life). In addition, the golden bough, as we have already seen, represents the myth of the dying and reviving god. The bird itself is associated with the human soul, which must endure the scapegoat experience so that it may be identified with the miraculous dead who like the corn-spirit transcend their fate. By having this creature capable of either the crow of revival and resurrection or the embittered scorn of the natural and the human, Yeats dramatically reveals his growing awareness that the immortal and the supernatural are dynamic rather than static. It is this new insight that constitutes the central difference between this poem and "Sailing to Byzantium." Now the spirits of the dead who have endured the purgatorial fire are carried to their paradisal realm "astraddle on the dolphin's mire and blood." The dolphins are linked with the gong as symbols of the violent physicality and animality of human life and nature.

The choice of the dolphin as a symbolic figure owes much to Eugénie Strong's *Apotheosis and After Life*. Yet even here *The Golden Bough* may contribute to the image. In Strong's book Yeats read that the dolphins were associated with "the purifying power of water and to the part assigned to the watery elements in Mithraic and solar cults."[76] His interest in the symbolic significance of the dolphin was also stimulated by a cast at the Victoria and Albert Museum, by Raphael, and by the Swedish sculptor Carl Milles. Thus it would seem probable that he was receptive to dolphins wherever they occurred in his experience.[77] And in *The Golden Bough* he could read Frazer's account of Melicertes, the founder of the Isthmian games, who was transformed into a sea god and pictured riding on a dolphin's back.[78] Thus, the motifs of metamorphosis and transcendence were immediately present in Frazer and so influenced Yeats's choice of image when he came to deal with the same themes in the same general context of violence and death.

In "Vacillation," "Her Vision in the Wood," and "Parnell's Funeral" we see how Yeats applies the wisdom inherent in the myth of the dying and reviving god to his three principal concerns: the individual or the self, the beloved or the other, and Ireland or the meeting-ground of the other two.

"Vacillation" opens with a declaration that explicitly indicates the importance of death and the dead to the course of human life:

> Between extremities
> Man runs his course;
> A brand, or flaming breath,
> Comes to destroy
> All those antinomies
> Of day and night;
> The body calls it death,
> The heart remorse.
> But if these be right
> What is joy?

Here Yeats shows unmistakably that all those antinomies he had discovered and struggled with through a long life can be

[76] Cited by Ellmann, *The Identity of Yeats*, p. 284.

[77] See Ellmann, *The Identity of Yeats*, p. 284 and G. Melchiori, *The Whole Mystery of Art* (London: Routledge & Kegan Paul, Ltd., 1960), p. 212. The latter also stresses, pp. 162-163, how important things seen or read in early life were to Yeats.

[78] *GB*, IV, 93, 103, 162.

resolved through the purgative action of a deathlike remorse. For the first time, he links death with remorse so that the metaphoric nature of the image becomes transparent. To do so, however, raises the problem of the nature of joy, how it can exist in a world devoid of antinomies and dominated by the sorrow of regret. Joy, for Yeats, is an essential quality in life, linked as it is with the pleasure of experiential acceptance, the heroic transcending of the strictures imposed by the fate of being human, and the delight of rejecting through scorn, irony, and satire all that demeans the possibilities of heroism. Consequently, it is essential for him that he determine what joy can be in a world dominated by death and remorse.

The answer is presented in the second stanza through the archetypal image of tree and hanged god:

> A tree there is that from its topmost bough
> Is half all glittering flame and half all green
> Abounding foliage moistened with the dew;
> And half is half and yet is all the scene;
> And half and half consume what they renew,
> And he that Attis' image hangs between
> That staring fury and the blind lush leaf
> May know not what he knows, but knows not grief.

The magical tree of the *Mabinogian* blends with the pine described by *The Golden Bough* as sacred to Attis and emblematic of him. This allows Yeats to connect Celtic myth with Phrygian and Asiatic worship, the natural with the miraculous, and the purgatorial with the revivificatory. Contrasting though the flame and green are, the central point is that together they compose but a single tree. They are an organic unity transcending their own respective natures. The same is true even when considered independently, for "half is half and yet is all the scene." The mathematic form of the antinomy is admitted, but the consequences drawn are unique to this period of Yeats's career.

Instead of striving to turn one or the other halves of existence into a totality, the poet here accepts its incompleteness while seeing that its very antinomical character logically implies the wholeness that it does not itself have. The qualities of magic, miracle, and purgatory are meaningfully defined only in relation to the natural, organic, and fertile. Each is essential to the continuity of the other, a point Yeats underscores by insisting that "half and half consume what they renew." To Frazer's stress on the natural cycle of seasonal decline and growth Yeats adds his own occult emphasis on magic or miracle as instants or periods obliterating the ordinary or natural world. The result is a vision of the two that squares with Yeats's sense of the movement of the gyres of history as well as with Frazer's massive documentation of the religious response of mankind to the waxing and waning of vegetation. In both, the movements of creation and destruction are exquisitely balanced.

With this unequivocal recognition of the cycle's subsumption of the antinomies, Yeats turns in the last part of the stanza to its most complex and universal form, the myth of the dying and reviving god. The attachment of the god's image to the two-natured tree by his priest or worshipper is an emblem of the wisdom resident in ritualistic ignorance. In not fully comprehending the meaning of his worship of Attis, the priest or poet nevertheless does not ultimately experience grief or sorrow or remorse. Frazer's accounts of the dying god rituals continually make clear that the mourning of the worshippers is ritualistic rather than instinctive, affected rather than sincere. They are playing their parts in the great drama of death and resurrection just as is the person miming the dead god, and their exhibitions of grief are qualified by their knowledge that the god will revive. Consequently, their underlying emotion in the presence of the dead god is one of joy because as a divine being he will enact the miracle of resurrection by which death and remorse are transfigured. The self has united the images of artifice and nature, of tower and tree, into the one form that can imaginatively encompass both, namely, the transfigured human body, which, of course, as Yeats knew from Blake, is man aware of his divinity, an eternal, immortal being.

It is primarily in this collocation of tree, tower, and body that Yeats's reason for explicitly referring to Attis emerges. Among Frazer's dying gods he, more nearly than the others, fits the archetypal image of the self that Yeats is exploring in this poem. His death through the sacrifice of his procreativity would have appealed to Yeats.[79] It affords a violent metaphor for the cost his art exacts of the artist, though by this stage in his career Yeats was less concerned than was an earlier generation of English and Continental Romantics to see the artist as a maimed figure. Even more attractive to Yeats would have been the alternative account of Attis' death. Like Adonis, he suffered death from the attack of a wild boar, an event suggesting that the self too must face death from the black pig of the external, natural world.[80]

Even more important is Attis' role as the hanged god whose body was suspended from a sacred tree.[81] Attis blends perfectly with the tree imagery so important to Yeats. Further, as Frazer emphasizes, the hanging of his effigy from the sacred tree also introduces the motif of resurrection or a life after the destruction of the antinomies. Yeats needs this here to provide a counterweight for the sense of responsibility that weighs so heavily on him in the fifth section. *The Golden Bough*'s linking of Attis with the Phrygian satyr Marsyas and the Scandinavian god Odin would also have helped make Attis attractive as the medium of transcendence. Marsyas' role as a musician, who "had a soul for harmony even in death," and Odin's self-sacrifice, by which he acquired "divine power by learning the magic runes," would give Yeats a subtle way of plotting the relation of the self, the artist, and the victim to their own transcendence.[82] Self-sacrifice, spiritual harmony, and the magic of words are all essential if man is to surmount death and remorse and achieve the blessedness of joy. And all these are, as Yeats discovered, resident in the myth of the dying and reviving god Attis as interpreted by *The Golden Bough*.

A particularly apt illustration of the usefulness of the dying god for Yeats occurs with "Her Vision in the Wood," the eighth poem in the "A Woman Young and Old" series. With the resolution of the self's antinomies in "Vacillation" through the medium of the Frazerian dying god the way was cleared for a similar clarification of the nature of love. And in "Her Vision in the Wood" this is achieved when the old woman past the age for love (which in Yeats always involves sexuality) sacrifices herself into

---

[79] *GB*, v, 264ff., 283.
[81] *GB*, v, 264ff., 288ff.

[80] *GB*, VIII, 22.
[82] *GB*, v, 289-290.

seeing the mourning procession of the dying god Adonis fatally wounded by the wild boar:

> And after that I held my fingers up,
> Stared at the wine-dark nail, or dark that ran
> Down every withered finger from the top;
> But the dark changed to red, and torches shone,
> And deafening music shook the leaves; a troop
> Shouldered a litter with a wounded man,
> Or smote upon the string and to the sound
> Sang of the beast that gave the fatal wound.
>
> All stately women moving to a song
> With loosened hair or foreheads grief-distraught.

This vision is heavily indebted to Frazer's account of the ritual of Adonis. This is clear from Yeats's making the red stream of blood the means of recalling the god's wound and demise just as Frazer declares that the discoloration of the river Adonis "with a blood-red hue" is the signal for the celebration of the Phoenician festival of the god.[83] And only a page later Frazer remarks on the coinciding of an Athenian military expedition with the festival of Adonis: "As the troops marched down to the harbour to embark, the streets through which they passed were lined with coffins and corpse-like effigies, and the air was rent with the noise of women wailing for the dead Adonis."[84] In this perhaps lies the original impetus for Yeats's use of the troop image as well as his stress upon its female composition.

Similarly, his description of the music as both stringed and deafening as well as its grief-inducing hysteria reflect Frazer's account both of Adonis' funeral music and the role of music in religion generally. Frazer distinguishes between the Greek and Hebrew attitudes toward string music. Nevertheless, he allows that the lyre's mythical associations suggest that "in early days its

---

[83] *GB*, v, 225. In the same passage Frazer observes that "the crimson stain was believed to be the blood of Adonis," a remark that Yeats might have found of equal dramatic appropriateness to his heroine.

[84] *GB*, v, 226. *The Golden Bough* reiteratively emphasizes the female lamentations for Adonis as much as it does his identification with the color red. See, e.g., *GB*, v, 9, 17, 30, 224, 225, 230, 231.

strains may have been employed by the Greeks, as they certainly were by the Hebrews, to bring on that state of mental exaltation in which the thick coming fancies of the visionary are regarded as divine communication."[85] Or, as he says more objectively elsewhere, string music in Greek and Semitic ritual, such as that of Adonis, may have been used to induce inspiration or prophetic ecstasy.[86] Certainly it is this role that Yeats gives to it in the poem. To round off his indebtedness to Frazer for this ritual scene, Yeats pointedly describes the women as "moving to a song/ With loosened hair." This detail clearly derives from *The Golden Bough*'s accounts of the custom of so wearing the hair during magical and religious ceremonies.[87]

As we have seen, the middle two stanzas are permeated by details of the ritual absorbed from *The Golden Bough*. By the very explicitness of their allusions they suggest the extent to which Yeats now finds the dying god an image and symbol of unequivocal centrality to his whole poetic vision. But this emphasis upon rich narrative detail, while building up the physical density of the scene, does not allow Yeats to delineate clearly the meaning or role played by the dying god in love. For this, we must turn to the first and last stanzas. The first places the old woman in a context that is both appropriate and contributory to her vision:

> Dry timber under that rich foliage,
> At wine-dark midnight in the sacred wood,
> Too old for a man's love I stood in rage
> Imagining men. Imagining that I could
> A greater with a lesser pang assuage
> Or but to find if withered vein ran blood,
> I tore my body that its wine might cover
> Whatever could recall the lip of lover.

The sacred wood in which the bloodletting and vision take place is probably the grove of Diana in which the goddess rules as a fertility deity. In addition, Frazer argues from analogy that the

---

[85] *GB*, v, 55. Samples of the dirges sung over the Babylonian Adonis, Tammuz, appear on pp. 9-10 and may have contributed to Yeats's choice of "malediction" as the term to describe the song of the troop of women.

[86] *GB*, v, 52, 54ff., 74.   [87] *GB*, III, 310ff.

sacred marriage of Diana and her consort Virbius was observed there.[88] Consequently it would be particularly appropriate in Yeats's mind as the setting to which the old woman might return (perhaps through the memory of the Anima Mundi) when she is no longer invited to participate in such mimetic rituals.

To explain readily the vision that follows on the bloodletting we must turn to *The Golden Bough* and its accounts of blood's being a means of producing prophetic inspiration, achieving purification, and attaining communion with the deity.[89] There are some indications in this first stanza that Yeats conceives the woman as a modern figure who out of her anguish recovers the archetypal scene which alone can give her solace and understanding of her lost love. The last stanza, with its turn from the aged woman to the perennially young and doomed dying god, brilliantly shows how Yeats has transmuted his view of love. From the cynical embitterment of personal disappointment it has moved to that pity and terror aroused and released by the truly tragic scene:

> That thing all blood and mire, that beast-torn wreck,
> Half turned and fixed a glazing eye on mine,
> And, though love's bitter-sweet had all come back,
> Those bodies from a picture or a coin
> Nor saw my body fall nor heard its shriek,
> Nor knew, drunken with singing as with wine,
> That they had brought no fabulous symbol there
> But my heart's victim and its torturer.

As the stanza opens, the woman, though "in grief's contagion caught," still regards the scene as part of a dramatic vision at which she is a more or less detached spectator. Epithets like "thing" and "beast-torn wreck" even suggest a certain fastidious disdain for the emotionally remote figure of the dying god. But with the meeting of their eyes the drama becomes intensely her own and personal. She is swept by a surge of memory, a re-experiencing of the generic sense of "love's bitter-sweet," conjured up by the vision of the *pathos* of the handsome young lover

[88] *GB*, II, 129.
[89] *GB*, I, 381ff.; III, 104, 115, 219; VIII, 316.

prematurely doomed. She also, and more importantly, experiences the tragic *anagnorisis* in which the identity of the dying god is revealed as that of her own lover.

Just as the dying god dissolved the antinomies of selfhood in "Vacillation" so here he affords a similar resolution to the tensions and conflicts in love. The anguish over the indifference of men to her body with which the woman began is here purged by the bloody vision of the lover's premature death. In short, the archetypally dominant note in love is loss. Once this is grasped as the essence of the relationship, the question of whether it occurs early or late becomes irrelevant. At the same time, the antinomy of the human and the divine is also destroyed through the incarnational metaphor of the dying god. The divine lover, Adonis, enters into, literally becomes, the human figure remembered and longed for by her body. Thus she is brought to recognize simultaneously that all human love is divine—that is, preordained and not subject to accidents of time and circumstance—and as such inevitable in its course. Seeing her lover as the god dignifies even as it intensifies the tragedy of her loss, while seeing the god as her lover reconciles her to that loss. The cyclic myth of the god, marked by the inevitability of his death, removes her experience from the realm of the fortuitous. The myth assimilates it to an eternal world that is both rooted in "blood and mire" and subject to change but that also transcends secular love's antinomies of victim and torturer.

It is through this action that the further antinomy, of art and nature, is also dissipated. The eternal world that emerges here is one grounded in nature and revealed by art, unlike the earlier one of "Sailing to Byzantium" which sought to divorce the two. Insofar as the dying lover is victim and torturer he is natural and human, and insofar as he is symbol he is fundamentally an artistic revelation.[90] And that he is both is clear from the last three stanzas of the poem. With this, Yeats shows that he has fully

[90] This interpretation only *seems* to contradict the declaration that "they had brought no fabulous symbol there." The line is not denying the symbolic character of the dying lover but affirming that it is neither unbelievable (i.e., "fabulous") nor incredibly remote from the deepest interests of the woman.

overcome the divisive dead end of nineteenth-century symbolism's effort to create a wholly pure art, which he had entertained
in "Sailing to Byzantium." Now art feeds ravenously on nature
and its products that it may recreate their intrinsic character in
a perceivable shape. And in doing so, as the last four lines of the
final stanza show, it renders meaningless or pointless what was
perhaps the greatest antinomy in Yeats's artistic life, that between
knowledge and ignorance. His plunge into theosophy and occult
experiments, his steeping himself in folklore and comparative religion, his ransacking of history and philosophy, his deliberate
exposure to politics and social affairs and even perhaps to the
passions of love were all multi-faceted efforts to transform into
knowledge—a wisdom compensatorily greater than, profounder
than, that of other men—what his shy introspective nature told
him was ignorance.

All these come to fruition in the final complex image of the unconscious body of the woman. Now she knows the interdepend-
ent identity of both lover and dying god and of the troop
of "bodies from a picture or a coin" who, intoxicated with their
poignant ritual laments, remain ignorant of the personal and individual dimensions of the myth they enact and honor. Yeats's
conclusion is not that one is preferable to or more valuable than
the other. In any case the central figure, the dying god, is destined to die, and love is to be lost. Thus, the tragic experience is
unavoidable for both the troop and the woman—in sum, for man
whether in art or nature. Knowledge and ignorance come to the
same thing—suffering—and what matters is the way in which we
grapple with this tragic fact and shape the tragic experiences that
await us all.

It is to precisely this issue that Yeats addresses himself in "Parnell's Funeral." There, amid the antinomies of history itself, he
defines the archetypal nature and ancestry of the tragic hero. Beginning with the falling star reputedly seen by mourners at Parnell's funeral, Yeats invests it with a welter of significance drawn
from *The Golden Bough*. Like the blood in "Her Vision in the
Wood," it moves the experience unto a mythical level. This both
intensifies its seriousness and defines the needs of any community
or nation necessary to survival and flourishing:

> a brighter star shoots down;
> What shudders run through all that animal blood?
> What is this sacrifice? Can someone there
> Recall the Cretan barb that pierced a star?

In his chapter "The Killing of the Divine King," Frazer records numerous examples, drawn from ancient Greece, primitive tribes, and modern Europe, of beliefs concerning the significance of falling stars. Among them are that the falling star signals the death of a man, particularly a chief; the passage of a dead soul, especially that of someone who has been murdered or eaten, to the other world; and the sinning of the king against the deity for which he must be deposed or slain.[91]

The first two of these accord perfectly with Yeats's feelings about Parnell. The former emphasizes the fate of him whom his followers called "the Chief."[92] The latter underscores the loss occasioned by his departure from the world and subtly anticipates the poem's later charges of murder and cannibalism. At first sight, the third of these beliefs does not seem appropriate to an admirer of Parnell. But taken in conjunction with the shudders felt in the crowd's animal blood, the star may retrospectively allude to the adultery, which in the eyes of the Church and its followers warranted Parnell's dismissal and persecution. That is, the crowd's shudders record both its awed sense of bereaved loss and its apprehensive awareness of its own guilty responsibility, themes which Yeats develops more explicitly later in the poem. Additional support for this view appears with the line which asks "What is this sacrifice?" It suggests that the falling star symbolizes a deliberate ritual act as well as a fortuitous event. And to a Parnellite like Yeats the act necessarily partook in some measure of the scapegoat sacrifice in which the dying god came to be involved.

The last lines of the first stanza complete the transmutation of historical event into mythic symbol. "The Cretan barb that pierced a star," as the second stanza makes clear, does not de-

[91] *GB*, IV, 58ff.

[92] See A. Glasheen, "Joyce and the Three Ages of Charles Stewart Parnell," in *A James Joyce Miscellany*, ed. M. Magalaner (Carbondale: Southern Illinois University Press, 1959), pp. 151-178.

scribe an action but reveals a symbol. How the falling star image opens out into the complex symbol of the dying god in whom Yeats finds Parnell's ultimate meaning is set forth with beautiful iconographical compression in the second stanza:

> Rich foliage that the starlight glittered through,
> A frenzied crowd, and where the branches sprang
> A beautiful seated boy; a sacred bow;
> A woman, and an arrow on a string;
> A pierced boy, image of a star laid low.
> That woman, the Great Mother imaging,
> Cut out his heart. Some master of design
> Stamped boy and tree upon Sicilian coin.

The effect of the whole, unlike that of "Vacillation" and "Her Vision in the Wood," is richly and deliberately syncretistic in both setting and character. The "rich foliage" places us once again in the sacred grove, where the ritual *agon* is always enacted, while the glittering starlight recalls that of Babylonia, which "brought/ A fabulous, formless darkness in." The one looks toward the aloof, isolated figure of the priest-king of Nemi and the other toward Christ's crucifixion. Similarly, "a frenzied crowd" clearly presages the ecstatic delirium described by Frazer with which the worshippers of Attis greet and emulate his sacrifice.[93] Moreover, the "beautiful seated boy," the "pierced boy" is a composite of Apollo, Adonis, and the nameless young consorts of the Great Minoan or Cretan Goddess whom Yeats saw stamped on ancient coins. The "sacred bow" further identifies the boy with Apollo and the nameless consorts even as it links the woman with Artemis, whom some mythological sources make responsible for Adonis' death by the boar. And finally the woman's act of cutting out the dying god's heart establishes him as also representing Dionysus. He, as Frazer says, not only had his heart removed but "was cut to pieces by the murderous knives

[93] In this connection one may also wonder whether the star imagery may not afford a transition from Parnell to dying god and from Christ to Attis since Yeats likely knew from *GB*, v, 284 that the celestial aspect of Attis was suggested by his star-spangled cap supposedly given him by Cybele, the Great Mother.

of his enemies,"[94] a description that Yeats would have found peculiarly appropriate to Parnell's fate.

From the welter of mythological detail and identification provided by this stanza, it is, however, impossible to adduce an argument of the sort employed by the other poems of this group. Yeats's strategy is radically different here. He does not single out the myth and ritual of a particular dying god with which to illuminate the archetypal nature of a specific aspect of life. Instead he amasses emblems of as many such deities as possible so as to create a kind of iconographic syncretism. The main reason for this change in technique is that he is dealing primarily with the individual's relation to society rather than to the self or another individual, and this cannot be reduced to a single mythic form. Each of the mythic figures introduced has, however, a distinct contribution to make to the total effect. Thus, Apollo suggests the intellectual and aesthetic nature of Parnell, Adonis his handsome vulnerability, Dionysus his scapegoat-like sacrificial dismemberment, and so on. In this way, Yeats builds up a composite picture both of the nature of the tragic hero and of the reasons for the crowd's attack.

In the latter half of the first section of the poem Yeats turns from the hero and dying god to Ireland, society, his antagonist. And as in some of his earlier works, he makes the image of drama function mythically by suggesting its genetic roots in rituals of sacrifice. The earlier age "when strangers murdered Emmet, Fitzgerald, Tone" is cast as a contemporary play, a form almost of entertainment in that the audience-player dichotomy is rigorously preserved and so the deepest living emotions not engaged: "What matter for the scene, the scene once gone:/ It had not touched our lives." In sharp contrast, the drama of Parnell's political, social, and personal tragedy is not entertainment but primitive ritual drama. In it the audience become participants, and the illusion of "a painted stage" is exchanged for the dynamic reality of sacrificial communion. Unfortunately, this communion is abortive, for the devourers of Parnell's heart are motivated by "popular rage,/ Hysterica passio," not by the desire to acquire his heroic traits. Consequently, the last stanza of this section levels

[94] *GB*, VIII, 13.

a bitter accusation at all of Ireland, including Yeats himself. In it the contempt of the moment broadens out to include an oblique, mythopoeic characterization of society's intrinsic relationship to the tragic hero:

> Come, fix upon me that accusing eye.
> I thirst for accusation. All that was sung,
> All that was said in Ireland is a lie
> Bred out of the contagion of the throng,
> Saving the rhyme rats hear before they die.
> Leave nothing but the nothings that belong
> To this bare soul, let all men judge that can
> Whether it be an animal or a man.

The first response to whether the naked soul of Ireland is animal or man is that it is the former. The weight of this and the preceding stanzas indicates that Irishmen have by their hatred of Parnell been debased to an animalistic level. In view of the poem's heavy freight of anthropological lore, it is unlikely, however, that Yeats wished the image to remain on the level of purely contemporary metaphor. From nearly his earliest poems he has followed *The Golden Bough* and similar works in viewing the divine king's enemy as an animal, a wild boar or black pig who savagely gores the hero to death. It is likely, then, that he would see the soul of a country that has destroyed the leader upon which all its hopes depended as the dying god's animal enemy. Once the lines have moved us unto this mythopoeic level, however, the disjunctive antinomy of "an animal or a man" appears less clear-cut. The dying god is destroyed at the hands of a human being, as in the cases of Osiris and Balder, as well as by an animal. What is constant is the murderous assault against the heroic divine king. Thus, the antinomy of man and animal is destroyed since the crucial issue is the role of antagonist to the dying god. In short, to say that Parnell's murderers are animals not men is an evasion of the ultimate truth enshrined in the myth of the dying god. They are both and are as ready to spring upon their victim as they are to lure him to death by deceit and lies. Set and Loki equally with the wild boar are the furious enemy of the god.

The first section of the poem closes with a crystallization of the nature of the god's antagonist. The second carefully develops the ultimate nature of the dying god or tragic hero. In so doing, it brings the theme of society around to that of the individual and the self, which was plumbed in "Vacillation," thereby revealing the interrelationship of these dominant themes. Yeats opens this section by listing what the differences to Ireland and its people would have been had its leaders "eaten Parnell's heart" and thereby, in accord with the belief stressed in *The Golden Bough*, acquired his qualities:

> The rest I pass, one sentence I unsay.
> Had de Valera eaten Parnell's heart
> No loose-lipped demagogue had won the day,
> No civil rancour torn the land apart.
>
> Had Cosgrave eaten Parnell's heart, the land's
> Imagination had been satisfied,
> Or lacking that, government in such hands,
> O'Higgins its sole statesman had not died.

The focus here is exclusively political, social, and contemporary. The tone builds toward accusatory bitterness and a demand for vengeance that would keep the antinomies of history fluctuating instead of resolving them. But in the final stanza Yeats abruptly abandons this attitude—as if recognizing its ultimate futility—and turns directly to Parnell and the mythic origins that comprise his contemporary uniqueness:

> Had even O'Duffy—but I name no more—
> Their school a crowd, his master solitude;
> Through Jonathan Swift's dark grove he passed, and there
> Plucked bitter wisdom that enriched his blood.

Parnell enters Swift's dark sinister sacred grove because he too is dragged down into mankind by his heart and the struggles of the self. Once there he finds that his kinship is not only historical but mythic, for like the successful challenger in the grove at Nemi he seizes the talisman that commits his life to a violent religious devotion and preordained fatality. The golden bough Parnell

plucks is the knowledge not only that he has become the defend-
er of the sacred grove of Ireland but that he has embarked on a
mimetic ritual enactment of the dying god myth in which he will
be confronted by the violence, treachery, envy, and hate of those
around him. Despite the bitterness that comes with the loss of
communal anonymity, the acceptance of a public role, and the
submission to a fatal necessity, this wisdom also strengthens and
invigorates him. For in it he also finds that he is superior to
other men by virtue of his assuming the role, that his identity is
more sharply outlined, and that his capacity for acceptance is
now unlimited. This is reflected in the triumphant, almost exult-
ant tone of the last two lines. When coupled with the revelatory
narrative effect of the simple past tense of the verbs, the tone suggests that this wisdom also extends to the poet and all who read
him carefully. For them the bitter wisdom is primarily the recognition that the tragic hero is substantially and unchangeably different from other men and that they cannot ever, even by eating
his heart, assume his position. This is not to say, however, that
certain men are marked out as heroes and others are not. Rather
whoever assumes the role is going to face an awesome adversary
that as the ritual unfolds more and more takes on the appearance
of society seen as a ravening animal or treacherous friend.

Such a result ostensibly seems to commit us to the historical
and social antinomies of leader and opposition, savior and
enemy, hero and antagonist. Actually, as the last two lines suggest, the passage through the dark grove is an imaginative act of
choice in which man creates the mythic images and story of
guardian priest and rival, dying god and adversary. Thus, in effect, he creates those antinomies in terms of which his life
is lived. They are generated out of the solitude of selfhood in
which man begins, and to be capable of creation is also to be able
to destroy. Dying god and his slayer, Parnell and his opponents
are both ultimately developed out of and resolvable back into the
bare soul. It is out of the security of this perception that Yeats
can finally envisage the tragic joy and exultation of both Parnell
and the archetypal dying god and find therein the resolution of
the antinomies of self, love, and society with which he had struggled furiously all his life.

CHAPTER VII

T. S. Eliot:

The Anthropology

of Religious

Consciousness

[I]

Of all literary acknowledgments of *The Golden Bough* none is
more famous than that made by T. S. Eliot in 1922 in his notes on
The Waste Land. Yet this is not, in fact, Eliot's first reference to
Frazer and his part in the climate of opinion of the early twentieth century. A number of the poet's early reviews suggest that
he was acquainted with and well-read in contemporary anthropology, psychology, and classical scholarship. One of the first of
these, a review of C.C.J. Webb's *Group Theories of Religion and
the Religion of the Individual*, appeared in the summer of 1916.
In it he shows his familiarity with the thought of the Cambridge
School, including Frazer, the French sociologists such as Durkheim and Lévy-Bruhl, and Freudian analysts of mythology.[1] A
year later Eliot reviewed Wundt's *Elements of Folk Psychology*,
a work whose connection with Frazer has already been indicated.[2] And a few years later, in an essay berating Gilbert Murray for his Greek translations, Eliot carefully distinguishes between the translator and the scholar, between the poet who is
insignificant and the Hellenist who is most important.[3] The latter
he recognizes to be part of a central and salutary movement in
the interpretation of the classics and the Scriptures. Of the other

[1] *New Statesman*, VII (1916), 405-406; reprinted in *International Journal
of Ethics*, XXVII (1916), 115-117.
[2] *International Journal of Ethics*, XXVII (1917), 254.
[3] *International Journal of Ethics*, XXVIII (1918), 445-446.

chief members of the Cambridge School he declares: "Few books are more fascinating than those of Miss Harrison, Mr. Cornford, or Mr. Cooke, when they burrow in the origins of Greek myths and rites."[4] Similar references indicate that he was also acquainted with E. B. Tylor, Robertson Smith, and Heinrich Zimmern.

From these allusions it is not surprising that the essay should have been included in a volume entitled *The Sacred Wood*, a title that derives from the account of the priesthood at Nemi contained in the first chapter of *The Golden Bough*. Elizabeth Drew has suggested that Eliot employs the title "as a symbol for the immortal poetic tradition, always dying and being reborn."[5] This is assuredly part of its significance, but the nature of the ritual itself may further illuminate Eliot's choice of titles. The priest-king who guards the sacred grove ruled so long as he could defeat in ritual combat anyone who chose to oppose him.[6] When we remember that the volume is subtitled "Essays in Poetry and Criticism," and when we regard the composition of the volume—beginning with "The Perfect Critic" and ending with Dante, the perfect poet—it seems clear that if poetry is the sacred goddess, then criticism is her warrior-priest who defends her honor and sanctity, and whose function is to prevent inferior poetry and criticism alike from usurping unworthily the role of deity or of priest and attendant.

Two years after *The Sacred Wood* the appearance of *The Waste Land* and its notes made it quite explicit that Eliot had read at least two volumes of the third edition of *The Golden Bough*. His admission that he was "indebted in general" to Frazer's monumental study together with his tantalizing remark that he had "used especially the two volumes 'Adonis, Attis, Osiris'" suggests that perhaps he had read other volumes of the third edition.[7] The following year Eliot reviewed Olive Busby's study of

<hr>

[4] *The Sacred Wood* (New York: Knopf, 1930), p. 75.

[5] Elizabeth Drew, *T. S. Eliot: The Design of His Poetry* (New York: Scribners, 1949), p. 43.

[6] *GB*, I, 9.

[7] *Collected Poems, 1909-1935* (London: Faber & Faber, 1936), p. 78. It is perhaps worth recalling also William Empson's remark that Eliot "did not consider he had 'read' a book unless he had written copious notes

the Fool in Elizabethan drama, drawing on Cornford's *Origin of Attic Comedy* for an alternative interpretation of the Fool.[8] The same review also exhibits a knowledge of Frazer's predecessors and influences such as Darwin and Maine as well as of current works, like W.O.E. Oesterley's *Sacred Dance*, that follow paths opened by *The Golden Bough*.[9] How persistent the influence of anthropology and comparative religion was is hinted at in the fact that the title of this review is "The Beating of the Drum" and that a decade later, in the conclusion to *The Use of Poetry and the Use of Criticism*, Eliot remarks: "Poetry begins, I dare say, with a savage beating a drum in a jungle."[10] And in the same volume, when discussing recurring symbolic images, he refers to an anthropological article, "Le symbolisme et l'âme primitive."[11]

Even more directly concerned with Frazer and *The Golden Bough* is a newsletter Eliot wrote for *Nouvelle Revue française* in 1923. In it he discusses Henry James, F. H. Bradley, and Sir James Frazer in terms of their intellectual and stylistic influence. Of *The Golden Bough* he says:

> It is a work of no less importance for our time than the complementary work of Freud—throwing its light on the obscurities of the soul from a different angle; and it is a work of perhaps greater permanence, because it is a statement of fact which is not involved in the maintenance or fall of any theory of the author's.
>
> Yet it is not a mere collection of data, and it is not a theory. The absence of speculation is a conscious and deliberate scrupulousness, a positive point of view. And it is just that: a point of view, a vision, put forward through a fine prose style, that gives the work of Frazer a position above that of other scholars of equal erudition and perhaps greater ingenuity, and which gives him an inevitable and growing influence over the contem-

---

about it and so on." See *T. S. Eliot*, ed. Richard March & Tambimuttu (London: PL Editions Poetry London, 1948), p. 37.

[8] "The Beating of a Drum," *Nation and Athenaeum*, xxxiv (October 6, 1923), 11-12.

[9] *Nation and Athenaeum*, xxxiv, 11.

[10] *The Use of Poetry and the Use of Criticism* (Cambridge, Massachusetts: Harvard University Press, 1933), p. 148.

[11] *The Use of Poetry and the Use of Criticism*, p. 141.

porary mind. He has extended the consciousness of the human mind into as dark a backward and abysm of time as has yet been explored. And—with the other scholars whom I have mentioned—he has given a new vision of classical studies. And this will not fail to have a profound effect upon the literature of the future.[12]

And in trying to suggest the nature of that sensibility which Frazer helped to shape, Eliot distinguishes it from that of Bernard Shaw, Anatole France, or Thomas Hardy by declaring "it is something infinitely more disillusioned than any of these who are chosen because they have so little in common with each other; it may be harder and more orderly; but throbbing at a higher rate of vibration with the agony of spiritual life."[13] Bearing out this interest in *The Golden Bough* in the years following is the famous article, " 'Uylsses,' Order, and Myth," a series of reviews of works dealing with comparative religion and ritual behavior, and a translation of an article on Fustel de Coulanges, a scholar whose studies of ancient cultures antedated those of Frazer.[14]

From the foregoing it is clear that Eliot possessed a well-developed and persistent interest in psychology and anthropology, particularly as they applied to comparative religion. Precisely when this interest was first aroused is hard to say. It may have begun during the years when Eliot was a Harvard undergraduate or a graduate studying philosophy and literature in Paris, that is, in the period from 1906 through 1911. It is not inconceivable that at this time Eliot should have read *The Golden Bough* in either of its first two and less encyclopedic editions. Yet from the few reviews written during this period there is no indication that he was acquainted with Frazer.[15] Perhaps a more likely date

---

[12] *Vanity Fair*, XXI, 29.   [13] *Vanity Fair*, XXI, 98.

[14] " 'Ulysses,' Order and Myth," *Dial*, LXXV (November, 1923), 480-483; *Criterion*, II (July, 1924), 489-491; *Athenaeum*, 4668 (October 17, 1919), p. 1036; *Criterion*, III (April, 1925), 441-443; *Criterion*, VIII (December, 1928), 350-353; *Criterion*, XV (January, 1936), 363; *Criterion*, VIII (December, 1928), 258-269.

[15] This statement is qualified by the fact that not all Eliot's periodical contributions have been available for examination. Nevertheless, none of the articles prior to 1916 cited by Donald Gallup, *T. S. Eliot: A Bibliography* (New York: Harcourt, Brace, 1953) suggests a likelihood of references to Frazer.

for Eliot's initial acquaintance with Frazer and Frazer-influenced works is from late 1911 or early 1912 through 1915.[16] For one thing, a number of the important studies of myth and ritual receiving their orientation from *The Golden Bough*—such as Freud's *Totem and Taboo*, Jung's *Psychology of the Unconscious*, Miss Harrison's *Themis*, Cornford's *From Religion to Philosophy* and *The Origin of Attic Comedy*, and Murray's *Four Stages of Greek Religion*—did not appear until 1912 or later. Coupled with this is the fact that from 1911 through 1915 Eliot was reading Sanskrit and philosophy at Harvard and in Europe.[17] Both the subjects and his instructors, especially James Woods, could easily have intensified his familiarity with the Cambridge School, *The Golden Bough*, and comparative religion generally. In any event, his formative intellectual years were those when *The Golden Bough* and all it stood for were creating their greatest academic interest and achieving their widest scholarly influence.

Interesting though they may be, the fact and date of *The Golden Bough*'s impact on Eliot are of less significance than the precise nature it assumes in his poetry. One of the permanent effects of *The Golden Bough* on Eliot's poetry is its contribution to a poetic technique which conveys his subtle insights with a powerful immediacy. Eliot's abrupt transitions from topic to topic and his juxtapositions of apparently ironic materials have commonly been traced to his admiration of poets like Laforgue and Corbière.[18] Yet without denying either the priority or the power of this influence, we can see, too, that Eliot had an equally suggestive model nearer to home. This was the famed comparative method of the classical school of anthropology, especially in the form in which it was utilized by Frazer in *The Golden Bough*. He more than any other writer of his time spoke through his illustrations. His theories, almost without exception, were simply and briefly stated; their elaborations and qualifications were embodied in the copious examples. These illustrations were by and

[16] Eric Thompson, *T. S. Eliot, The Metaphysical Perspective* (Carbondale: Southern Illinois University Press, 1963), pp. 5-6.

[17] Herbert Howarth, *Notes on Some Figures Behind T. S. Eliot* (Boston: Houghton Mifflin, 1964), pp. 199-214.

[18] See, for instance, Warren Ramsey, *Jules Laforgue and the Ironic Inheritance* (New York: Oxford University Press, 1953), pp. 192-203.

large self-contained scenes which exhibited certain similarities and parallels, parallels which as often as not consisted of variant solutions to identical problems. The irregular overlapping of these scenes produced so jagged an outline as to appear almost to be dissolving into chaos. With this intellectual vision, we are probably as close to the metaphysical wit so admired by Eliot as the Victorian mind could go. Not in style, to be sure, but in the panoramic view of man's variety and disparities, irony, incongruity, and insight are welded together as firmly as in the poetry of Donne, Marvell, or any other of those who thought with their fingertips. The variations and elaborations in technique that develop from "Burbank with a Baedeker: Bleistein with a Cigar" and "Whispers of Immortality" through "Mr. Eliot's Sunday Morning Service" and "Sweeney Among the Nightingales" to "Gerontion" speak for themselves. The manners of Laforgue and Corbière have been assimilated into the comparative method, which came increasingly to assume the status of a poetics. The one was a rhetorical embodiment of a series of poses or attitudes; the other became an expanding vision of the complexity inherent in the central thesis of *The Golden Bough*.

With the publication of "Mr. Apollinax," there appears somewhat clearer evidence of Eliot's interest in combining the anthropological and classical worlds as Frazer had already done. The poem's extremely close-knit texture is based on references to art, vegetative and marine deities, and creatures of classical legend. The narrator's first impression of Mr. Apollinax relates him to a painting by Fragonard, which acts as a scenic focus for the poem. This same technique of using a painting to convey an attitude or to illuminate an insight is, of course, also used by Frazer. For instance, he uses Polygnotus' frescoes of Orpheus to suggest that legendary figure's connection with both Aeneas and Adonis.[19] This is particularly striking in that Mr. Apollinax, too, is linked to a deity, Priapus, a minor Roman god of vegetation and wine who recalls Dionysus by his lubricious and orgiastic rites. Clearly, the "buried life" of the fertility deity, so vaguely remembered in "Portrait of a Lady," has been revived.

Since Mr. Apollinax is a god of what Frazer delights in calling

[19] *GB*, XI, 294.

"increase," it follows almost as a matter of course that his laugh should be that of "an irresponsible foetus." The driving force of conception exults in its own riotous growth and rejects the stultifying existence of the drawing-room. Even in that palace of art belonging to Mrs. Phlaccus there lurks a chthonic deity whose libidinal energy unsettles the dunces and pundits of polite society. By equating Mr. Apollinax, whose torrential vigor is partly social and partly intellectual, with a fertility deity, Eliot adjusts to his own satiric purposes Frazer's account of the identification of sexual and social fertility. Under his hands, the fertility deity becomes a symbol of the man who, whatever his absurdities and shortcomings, is vigorously alive. Thus, the point of the satire is that Mr. Apollinax's audience is as disconcerted and outraged at social vitality as they would be at the intrusion of sexuality into the desiccated impeccability of their drawing-room. Overwhelmed by his Nereus-like laughter, they feel themselves to be "the worried bodies of drowned men" who have encountered something more powerful than they, who have been taken beyond their depth.

In view of this, it is perhaps interesting to notice the way in which images of Mr. Apollinax's head suggest distinct stages in the myth of Dionysus, the Greek forebear of Priapus. When the narrator looks for the head "rolling under a chair," he recalls to mind Dionysus' dismemberment by the Titans. The contemporary titans, however, are giants only in the realm of finance and conversation. The dismemberment of an individual is now a matter of surreptitious dissection through language, and Mrs. Phlaccus, Professor and Mrs. Cheetah, and the others can kill Mr. Apollinax's vitality only within their own limited world by picking him to pieces, by reducing him to their own level of fragmented awareness, by viewing him in clichés which merely reflect their own moribundity. But the mirrors of the titans are no longer able to trap the deity. Hence, the narrator balances his initial vision with a second one, that of Mr. Apollinax "grinning over a screen/ With seaweed in his hair." This resembles the god's resurrection and return from the underworld via water mentioned by *The Golden Bough*.[20] The parallel is made even

[20] *GB*, v, 237, 273; VII, 15; XI, 114ff.

more emphatic by Frazer's notes to his translation of Apollodorus, a work that could not, however, have influenced Eliot. In it, Frazer remarks that "an actor, dressed in the vine-god's garb, may have emerged dripping from the pool to receive the congratulations of the worshippers on his rising from the dead."[21] Clearly, Mr. Apollinax suggests a contemporary version of that ancient actor, though modified by his ironic grin at his audience's inability to carry out what they would like to do to him.

As a consequence of this return, the narrator is drawn back into the drawing-room: "I heard the beat of centaur's hoofs over the hard turf/ As his dry and passionate talk devoured the afternoon." In likening the visitor's conversation to "the beat of centaur's hoofs," the narrator may be linking Mr. Apollinax with Chiron who, as Frazer notes, taught human beings how to survive by their own resources.[22] In a sense, perhaps Mr. Apollinax's "dry and passionate talk" is also an attempt at teaching his audience something they need to know. An added connection between the centaur image and Mr. Apollinax is based on his name, which can mean "son of Apollo." The only son of Apollo connected with a centaur was Aesculapius, who was raised by Chiron and taught the arts of hunting and healing. The gentleness and compassion of Aesculapius is hinted at in the association of Mr. Apollinax with "that shy figure among the birchtrees." In balancing Fragilion against Priapus the narrator is recognizing both the Apollonian and the Dionysian aspects of the visitor and fusing the knowledge of the one and the vigor of the other for the satiric purpose of effecting a conquest by mockery.

A more compassionate lament for mankind occurs in "La Figlia Che Piange," published in the same year as "Mr. Apollinax." The weeping girl calls to mind a figure such as Persephone or perhaps Eurydice. The sunlight, the flowers, the hair, and the garden urn all contribute to the impression of vegetative growth and beauty represented by the Corn Maiden.[23] The weaving of the sunlight in her hair is obviously an act designed to heighten the appealing beauty of the girl. It is also a request that she bring fertility to the

---

[21] James G. Frazer, ed. & trans., *The Library* by Apollodorus (London: Heinemann, 1921), I, 333, n.2.

[22] *GB*, I, 19.   [23] *GB*, VII, 36-37, 40, 42-44.

world, a fertility of the spirit and sensibility rather than of the body or nature. In effect, Eliot uses the images of physical fertility as symbolic metaphors for a revival of sensibility, of the ability to feel precisely and deeply. This revival is presented immediately and dramatically in the elegiac celebration of the necessary isolation of the heroine whom the hero has failed:

> So he would have left
> As the soul leaves the body torn and bruised,
> As the mind deserts the body it has used.

The loss of love is for her an unredeemable death. Unlike the mythic death toward which she turns with the approach of autumn, this death leaves behind no figure capable of resurrection but only the mortal corpse, "the body torn and bruised."

To convey the full impact of this, Eliot uses both an ancient and a contemporary image of death, and in so doing illuminates the past and present associations of the girl. According to *The Golden Bough*, ancient peoples thought of death as the permanent absence of the soul from the body. They also regarded the soul as a man existing within the body.[24] For the girl, death is equated with the departure of her soul who is, indeed, a man, her lover. For the strange notion of the soul, the contemporary world substitutes the abstract concept of the mind. In the one case, death is the departure of a creature; in the other, the cessation of an action. Yet by their juxtaposition, the loss of love is seen to have the same effect on sensibility in all times. Henceforth, the girl lives only in art, as the statue for which Eliot is reported to have searched Italy in vain,[25] and in myth, as Persephone. But on this level, she does continue to weave the sunlight of life and growth in her hair, for her mythic existence is identical with her ability to compel the imagination.

The poems published in 1918 and 1919 continue to reveal Eliot's familiarity with *The Golden Bough* while providing a further development in technique. The abrupt shifts of perspective common to Prufrock and the lady are merged with the enigmatic

[24] *GB*, III, 26ff.
[25] Helen Gardner, *The Art of T. S. Eliot* (London: Cresset Press, 1949), p. 107.

allusiveness of "Mr. Apollinax." Each mode intensifies the other so that these poems take on added depth and subtlety. Transitions are more numerous and more bewildering. Similarly, allusions to historical figures, books, theological arguments, geographical locations, astronomical myths, classical figures all contribute to the multiplication of complex perspectives. Representative here is "Sweeney Among the Nightingales." It is an ironic and elegiac survey of the original form of religion, that is, of the fertility cult. It is at once a lament for the dead and for unfulfilled love. What the scene, like *The Golden Bough*, reveals most clearly is the presence in modern society of cultural survivals from another age and the irony each provides for the other. The blend of satire and elegy in this poem is designed to present the death of the hero. Agamemnon is the hero whose death is viewed elegiacally; Sweeney is the mock-hero whose death is celebrated satirically.

Though the poem clearly deals with the theme of fertility,[26] it does not simply develop a contrast between fertility and sterility in terms of past and present, Agamemnon and Sweeney. Rather it seeks to show the ways in which both heroes are threatened with betrayal and deprived of participation in a life of fertility by the world in which they live. It does so through an intricately combined set of images a considerable measure of whose significance is provided by Frazer and *The Golden Bough*. Thus, the moon is worshipped as responsible for life-giving moisture and its departure thought to entail decay.[27] And in the poem its departure leaves Sweeney alone facing Death and the Raven. The raven, in turn, was thought to expose persons guilty of infidelity, a point particularly apposite to the Agamemnon story,[28] and was also frequently held to visit blight and sterility on the land.[29] The absence of fertility is further borne out by the veiling of Orion and the Dog, for according to Frazer, Orion was a signal for the commencement of sowing, while the rising of Sirius, the Dog-Star, marked the beginning of the sacred Egyptian year.[30] In the light

---

[26] See D.E.S. Maxwell, *The Poetry of T. S. Eliot* (London: Routledge & Kegan Paul, Ltd., 1952), p. 83.

[27] *GB*, VI, 132, 137-138.   [28] Apollodorus, *Library*, II, 15.

[29] *GB*, II, 107ff.   [30] *GB*, V, 290; VI, 35.

of this failure to achieve fertility, the waiter's bringing in of various fruits is a contemporary substitution for the fertility rituals described in *The Golden Bough*.[31] The final ironic rendering of the way in which fertility and sterility both mock and mime one another occurs with the image of "the Convent of the Sacred Heart." Originally, as Frazer makes clear, the sacred heart was that of Dionysus, the god of fertility, but now this spirit of fecundity is imprisoned in a Christian temple dedicated to celibacy.[32] As a result, when the nightingales, emblematic of Philomela and her barbaric revenge, sing near the convent, they gain further revenge by mocking the inability of man and god alike to demonstrate or exercise their powers of fertility.

[II]

The majority of Eliot's early poems that show indications of employing the materials and ideas of *The Golden Bough* are predominantly ironic and satiric. With *The Waste Land*, however, anthropological details and methods are used less for overt satire than for exploration of the human soul. This was the first poem in which he explicitly admitted the influence of *The Golden Bough*. That it should also be a major work is of crucial significance both for Eliot's own poetry and for those poets who came afterward. More than any other poem of Eliot's, *The Waste Land* is a Janus-figure looking both backward and forward, summing up the verse of the past and anticipating that of the future. And nowhere else in Eliot's work does the impact of *The Golden Bough* emerge so clearly and unequivocally. Indeed, in a very real sense, it may have been Sir James Frazer who, ironically enough, brought Eliot to the Anglican Communion and an acceptance of orthodox Christianity. For though it did not create it, *The Golden Bough* did accentuate the pattern of death and resurrection with which Eliot was overwhelmingly concerned.

Eliot, however, undeniably saw the religious significance of Frazer's work in a different light from that of its nineteenth-century rationalist author. Frazer saw himself as slowly drawing into place siege guns (the image is his own) to be directed against the forces of hidebound tradition and superstitious religions. Eliot

---

[31] See Maxwell, p. 84.   [32] *GB*, VII, 13-15.

himself, however, saw *The Golden Bough* as a work "throwing its light on the obscurities of the soul," while of its author he declared: "He has extended the consciousness of the human mind into as dark and backward an abysm of time as has yet been explored."[33] Clearly Eliot would have agreed with the late John Peale Bishop in thinking that far from being destroyed, Christianity actually gained by being linked with Adonis and the other dying gods. In speaking of Christ, Bishop remarked that "His divinity is to be found precisely in those attributes which He shares with these and other older incarnate gods."[34] The gain for Christianity is found to consist in the revelation of its having a longer and wider tradition than heretofore known, one as old as man himself.

In *The Waste Land* this tradition is invoked to convey the theme of the growth and recovery of religious consciousness by man throughout his history. With it Eliot's poetry ceases to represent the quest for a hero and instead deals with the quest of a hero. Here "Gerontion" plays a mediating role, detaching the poet from his excoriation of mock-heroes and introducing him to a protagonist who will embark upon the life-saving quest. Gerontion himself is not the protagonist but the maimed priest-king living in a personal waste land, and, in consequence, all he can do is recount the legend of his old age. But *The Waste Land* presents a more likely candidate for the protagonist's role. In one sense, the entire poem is a series of trials calculated to determine whether or not the protagonist is a true hero. As a result of these trials, the protagonist successfully establishes his right to the role. He hears and understands the three divine injunctions: "Datta. Dayadhvam. Damyata." Thus, the poem presents simultaneously man's introduction to and reclamation of the knowledge of religious consciousness. The successive modes by means of which the human race became aware of a power greater than itself are presented obliquely and in compressed form.

In essence, *The Waste Land* presents a threefold quest of which the first is that of the Grail quest itself. This aspect of the quest pattern is fundamentally a ritual of action; it exhibits a pat-

[33] *Vanity Fair*, XXI, 29.
[34] John Peale Bishop, *Virginia Quarterly Review*, XII, 437.

tern of public behavior. Here Eliot's protagonist is the Grail knight whose adventures and temptations in the Waste Land test his right to knowledge of the Grail. He is, however, a Grail knight whose experiences are presented in a manner reminiscent of the dissolving perspectives and fragmented order of the *Satyricon*. The second quest is primarily a ritual of knowledge which not only recapitulates but reenacts the evolution of religious consciousness. Just as the Grail romances constitute the source of the first quest pattern, so Jessie Weston's *From Ritual to Romance* provides the basic form for the second quest. Miss Weston declared that she was concerned with "comparative religion in its widest sense"[35] and the same attitude controlled Eliot's selection of materials in *The Waste Land*. In both cases nature myths, fertility rituals, mystery cults, and the Grail legends are seen as progressive stages in the gradual evolution of man's religious consciousness. These observances and their records reveal increasing degrees of abstraction in their conception of what constitutes, in Miss Weston's phrase, "the secret sources of life."[36] At the same time, their respective rituals progress from forms of imitation to forms of knowledge.

The first quester moves from place to place in the timeless present of literature, while the second, following the pattern of history, journeys from the past to the present. In the third quest, the direction of history is reversed; the starting point is the present and the protagonist, who is modern man, works back into the past. Here the theme is not so much the evolution as the clarification of religious consciousness. The psychology of rediscovery replaces the history of discovery; the progressive unfolding of man's spiritual nature constitutes a ritual of wisdom. Beginning in that darkness which is characteristic of all human societies, the protagonist ultimately recovers the original mythic distinction between the sacred and the profane. With this he sees what is truly illuminating, namely, the vision of death and resurrection, the supreme ritual in the life of mankind. On this third level, the literary source comparable to the Grail romances and *From*

[35] *From Ritual to Romance* (Cambridge: Cambridge University Press, 1920), p. vi.
[36] *From Ritual to Romance*, p. 191.

245

Ritual to Romance is Sir James Frazer's *Golden Bough*. Frazer's study of the beliefs and institutions of primitive man plunges into "those dark ages which lie beyond the range of history"[37] in quest of the origins and nature of mankind. In so doing, it provides an exact image and analogue of the protagonist who as modern man searches the past of his race for knowledge relevant to his own conduct and attitudes.

The Golden Bough's role in *The Waste Land* is not confined, however, to serving as prototypical source for one of the quest patterns. Its ideas and material also permeate and shape *From Ritual to Romance*. Included in its material are even some medieval legends such as that of Lancelot's being forced to assume the role of sacrificial king. Thus, Frazer, as well as Miss Weston, provided a suggestive bracketing of primitive ritual and medieval romance for Eliot. In addition to contributing to the shaping of the threefold quest pattern, *The Golden Bough* also provided the poem with its underlying archetypal figure, the protagonist. As Frazer points out, the hero-savior of a culture or society is traditionally regarded as a representative of his people, as, in some sense, a microcosmic equivalent of the nation or tribe.[38] That is to say, he is more than an individual; he is the spirit of a community or even of mankind. By the same token, the salvation sought by the protagonist for his community is not only physical but also spiritual and psychological. It is precisely these attributes and pursuits that characterize Eliot's protagonist in *The Waste Land* whether he appears as priest-king, Grail knight, or modern explorer. Through witnessing the poem's various scenes, with their details of primitive ritual, past history, and contemporary incident, he recognizes that his is a role, a function that belongs to all men; hence he is inevitably a protagonist and committed to an active role. Needless to say, both points, the universality and the performance of a function, are underscored by *The Golden Bough*'s numerous accounts of sacred kings who participate in the ritual drama of sacrifice that reenacts the myth of the dying and reviving god.

Both the structure and the central figure in the poem derive substantially from *The Golden Bough*. They do so, however, pri-

[37] *GB*, I, xxiv.   [38] *GB*, IV, 21, 27.

marily by virtue of images, scenes, allusions, and their interrelations. In short, *The Golden Bough* is as important for incidental
details and setting as for overall plan and approach, and it is to
an elucidation of this material that we shall now turn. The first
point is the epigraph and its connection with the poem as
a whole. Though Eliot draws his epigraph from the *Satyricon*,
Petronius' account of the Sibyl is also discussed by Frazer. And
in the course of his discussion he finds an analogue to the Sibyl
story in the folk tale concerning a girl in London who wished to
live forever and whose wish was granted.[39] Eliot also creates a
link between Cumae and London, past and present, by showing
that London contains its own contemporary Sibyls in the persons
of the nameless lady of "A Game of Chess," Lil, and the typist.
Each in her own way is confronted by an endless vista of misery,
despair, and boredom. Each is a mute prophetess dramatizing
the doom of a single aspect of the social order, a doom that is
not physical death and dissolution but unending life and
degradation.

The Sibyl's concern with death is elaborated in "The Burial of
the Dead" section, which opens with an account of the interrelation of death and life on the vegetative level:

> April is the cruellest month, breeding
> Lilacs out of the dead land, mixing
> Memory and desire, stirring
> Dull roots with spring rain.
> Winter kept us warm, covering
> Earth in forgetful snow, feeding
> A little life with dried tubers.

In a very real sense, these lines are hung between the two poles
of birth and death. As a result, a feeling of foreboding is mingled
with one of watchful anticipation. The paradoxical quality of
April as the cruellest month is clarified by *The Golden Bough*
and the anthropological context in which Eliot's mind was moving. Thus, Frazer remarks that "from the middle of April till the
middle of June the land of Egypt is but half alive, waiting for the

[39] *GB*, x, 99.

new Nile."[40] Clearly such a time does not call for rejoicing on the part of the land and its inhabitants. Indeed, while primitive man's reactions to spring might be "a secret joy" yet "it was essential that he should conceal the natural emotion under an air of profound dejection."[41] From this it is obvious that the opening lines of *The Waste Land*, a poem related by the author to vegetative rites, constitute a clearly defined part of ritual behavior in accord with age-old traditions.

We cannot, of course, deny that to contemporary ears the attributing of cruelty to April is an arresting and somewhat puzzling idea. But stated most simply, the reason for describing April as the cruellest month is that it marks the point at which the vegetative and human cycles both intersect and contradict one another. Vegetation begins to bloom at the time of the crucifixion and death of Christ, the man-god. Inevitably in such a situation man's attitude is one of bewilderment and uncertainty, for he is compelled to face the complexities of his world. This feeling that April is a time of great crisis is also reflected in *The Golden Bough*'s discussion of a number of April rituals designed to protect people from the evil and destruction in the world.[42] Coupled with this is April's connection with burial ceremonies. The reference to the office of "The Burial of the Dead" reminds us that the death of Christ occurred in the spring, according to many accounts in this very month. In addition, festivals of mourning for the dead Adonis often took place in the spring.[43] By these allusions implicit in April's cruelty, Eliot links Christ and Adonis to suggest that both their deaths were part of those ritual celebrations that protected man from the overwhelming power of evil. And since Adonis was a vegetative deity it is inevitable that his departure should be matched by a "dead land" filled only with "dull roots" and "dried tubers."

April, then, seeks to awaken man and the world to her crucial nature and to the death and burial of the god. It is to this end that lilacs bloom and roots are vivified by rain. The lilacs are a symbol not only of the miracle of birth in a dead land but

[40] *GB*, VI, 31.   [41] *GB*, VI, 45.
[42] *GB*, II, 330, 335; IX, 149-150, 158ff.
[43] *GB*, V, 225-226, 231.

of memory, even as the symbol of desire is found in the hyacinths of the garden. And through the lilacs themselves we recall the dying and reviving god, Attis, whose return from the dead was foreshadowed in the appearance of lilac-colored blossoms at the very beginning of spring.[44] Thus, the lilacs and the rain appear as symbols of the revival and awakening of the human consciousness to its religious dimensions.

The "dull roots" are a vegetative analogue to human history and myth; both stretch back into "the abysm of time" which Eliot found illuminated by *The Golden Bough*. The ironic human equivalent to the "little life" of "dull roots" and "dried tubers" is found in the line: "I read, much of the night, and go south in the winter." Going south in the winter is an unconscious mimicry of the death and disappearance of the god. It is the physical, not the symbolic and spiritual, warmth of spring and summer that is sought. At the same time this endeavor to maintain perpetually the season of life and growth constitutes an implicit denial of the cyclic order of existence. In this, Eliot again reveals what he has learned from Frazer. The anthropologist showed that myths and rites often have a significance other than that normally attributed to them; the poet suggests that people's behavior and remarks often carry archetypal implications that they themselves do not recognize.

With the collocation of the images of the roots and branches, the pitiless sun, the dead tree, the cricket, the dry stone, the red rock, its shadow, and the handful of dust, the waste land itself is presented in detail for the first time. As both Eliot and his critics have made abundantly clear, its name derives from Miss Weston's *From Ritual to Romance*. Yet in both this study and earlier works such as *The Quest of the Holy Grail*, she is very chary with her descriptions of the land, usually contenting herself with adjectives such as "waste and desolate."[45] More nearly resembling the concreteness and precision of Eliot's description are certain passages in the Bible and *The Golden Bough*. To take but one example from a number, Frazer describes the land dur-

---

[44] *GB*, v, 264.

[45] *The Quest of the Holy Grail* (London: G. Bell & Sons, 1913), p. 34; cf. *From Ritual to Romance*, pp. 19, 21.

ing the dry season when the level of the river drops in the following fashion:

> Egypt, scorched by the sun, blasted by the wind that has
> blown from the Sahara for many days, seems a mere continua-
> tion of the desert. The trees are choked with a thick layer of
> grey dust. A few meagre patches of vegetables, watered with
> difficulty, struggle painfully for existence in the immediate
> neighbourhood of the villages. Some appearance of verdure
> lingers beside the canals and in the hollows from which the
> moisture has not wholly evaporated. The plain appears to pant
> in the pitiless sunshine, bare, dusty, ash-coloured, cracked and
> seamed as far as the eye can see with a network of fissures.[46]

Here is an unequivocal picture of the inferno-like waste land.
Here the protagonist must endure his exile while struggling to restore the land by healing the king and to approach the deity by
recovering his religious consciousness. Indeed, this passage mirrors the desert motif of much of the poem. It reflects not only the
"heap of broken images" of the poem's opening but also the third
part where "the wind/ Crosses the brown land, unheard" and the
Fisher King sits by "the dull canal" that is still edged by vegetation, as well as part five with its "sandy road," its arid "endless
plains" of "cracked earth," and its "empty cisterns and exhausted
wells."

Beginning with the song from *Tristan und Isolde*, the protagonist embarks on his quest for the Grail, the dying god, and his
own soul. Each of the three remaining scenes of this section offers
him a means of achieving the ultimate vision. But if he fails to
grasp the significance of what is offered, then both the offering
and his own actions become debased and meaningless. Only by
increased awareness can the journey from imitative fertility
rituals to the spiritual symbolism of Christianity, and from the
present to the origins and sources of human life, be performed.
The first of these scenes, that of the hyacinth garden, presents
several instances of disappointed love. One involves Apollo and
Hyacinth, the aboriginal vegetative deity. The hyacinths in the
girl's arms represent the love of a god for man and the return of

[46] *GB*, VI, 31.

the god to the world of mankind. In ritual terms, this is represented by the sacred marriage. But the protagonist does not see this. As a result, he fails to connect his attraction to the hyacinth girl with the higher love that is "the attraction towards God."[47] He cannot even detect the sacred marriage which the girl, who is a priestess of the god, is offering him. Her offer is one of knowledge and initiation on the lowest level of the quest; the mystery of human and vegetative fertility as symbolized by the sacred marriage is within the protagonist's grasp. But lacking the higher love, he sees in the sacred marriage "simply the coupling of animals."[48] The hyacinth is the flower of desire, but of unfulfilled desire. "Looking into the heart of light, the silence," the protagonist sees in the flower not so much a resurrection as a lament for the death of the god. It becomes for him, as for the ancient warriors from Hyacinth's own home, an omen of death.[49] His failure is, in effect, the failure of the dying god to achieve rebirth; both are "neither/ Living nor dead" and hence in a critical state of transition.

The alternative states of life and death are vividly rendered in this section by the juxtaposition of the waste land and the Hyacinth garden. This structural balancing of images is due, at least in part, to specific passages in *The Golden Bough*. For, according to Frazer, just such a sharp contrast in scene actually existed in parts of Asia Minor which were centers of worship for father and son fertility deities embodied in vegetation and water.[50] One of these places was approached by a road running through a range of mountains "torn here and there by impassable ravines, or broken into prodigious precipices of red and grey rock"[51] and stood "at the mouth of a deep ravine enclosed by great precipices of red rock."[52] Of the area just beyond the valley Frazer says: "all is desolation—in summer an arid waste broken by great marshes and wide patches of salt, in winter a broad sheet of stagnant water, which as it dries up with the growing heat of the sun

[47] T. S. Eliot, *Selected Essays, 1917-1932* (New York: Harcourt, Brace, 1932), pp. 234-235.

[48] Eliot, *Selected Essays*, pp. 234-235.

[49] *GB*, v, 314. [50] *GB*, v, 119, 152.

[51] *GB*, v, 120. [52] *GB*, v, 121.

exhales a poisonous malaria. To the west, as far as the eye can see, stretches the endless expanse of the dreary Lycaonian plain, barren, treeless, and solitary, till it fades into the blue distance, or is bounded afar off by abrupt ranges of jagged volcanic mountains."[53] In contrast to this, he observes that "with its cool bracing air, its mass of verdure, its magnificent stream of pure ice-cold water—so grateful in the burning heat of summer—and its wide stretch of fertile land, the valley may well have been the residence of an ancient prince or high priest."[54] Equally significant for *The Waste Land* as a whole is the fact that "the place is a paradise of birds"[55] where "the thrush and the nightingale sing full-throated."[56] And as if the contrasting scenes are not themselves sufficiently startling, Frazer explicitly calls attention to their relationship by remarking that "the sight of the rank evergreen vegetation at their bottom, fed by rivulets or underground water, must have presented a striking contrast to the grey, barren, rocky wilderness of the surrounding tableland."[57]

Having failed to accept the offer of the Hyacinth girl, the protagonist turns to Madame Sosostris, the famous clairvoyante, for assistance in determining the direction to be taken by his quest. Accordingly, she shows him certain symbols, while confining her interpretation of them to dark and oracular hints. Though her use of the Tarot pack links her to topics discussed by Miss Weston in *From Ritual to Romance*, she and her symbols also derive from *The Golden Bough*. In the first place, as a modern fortune-teller, she illustrates Frazer's point that "magic regularly dwindles into divination before it degenerates into a simple game."[58] At the same time, the images on her cards obviously bear some ancient significance. Thus, the title "Lady of the Rocks" may serve to identify Belladonna with the great Asiatic goddess of fertility whose figure was sculptured on the rocks surrounding her sanctuary.[59] She was of the same general type as that discussed in connection with the Hyacinth garden. And by the name "Belladonna" the protagonist may be receiving an implicit warning that the orgiastic rites of this deity function as a

[53] *GB*, v, 123.　　[54] *GB*, v, 122.
[55] *GB*, v, 122.　　[56] *GB*, v, 123.
[57] *GB*, v, 159.　　[58] *GB*, vii, 109 n.2; see also x, 336.
[59] *GB*, v, 128, 137.

narcotic and anodyne whether practiced in the past or the present, and that her worship entails the personal sacrifice of virility.[60]

The next image, "the man with three staves," Eliot says, is arbitrarily identified with the Fisher King of Miss Weston's book. Yet the significance of this identification is not quite so simple or devoid of logical connection as it appears to be. In an earlier work Miss Weston points out that "there is a persistent tradition of three Grail Kings" which she then associates with the dying and reviving god.[61] And an authority on the Tarot pack says that the man with three staves is "an Egyptian relic having relation to the triple Phallus which represents the recovery of Osiris."[62] Whether or not Eliot was sufficiently familiar with the history and significance of the Tarot pack to know this is not vitally important. He could have made the association himself as a result of reading *The Golden Bough*'s account of the funeral rites of Osiris which "set forth the nature of Osiris in his triple aspect as dead, dismembered, and finally reconstituted."[63] As a result of these associations, it would appear that the full implications in the figure of the Fisher King are not realized by treating him simply as the maimed and impotent king. He is also the youthful prince whose accession restores the kingship to its original power, Ferdinand succeeding his apparently dead father. In short, the man with three staves, like the dying and reviving god, follows a cyclical pattern of sacrifice, death, and resurrection.

Of the other symbols presented to the protagonist, not all are connected with *The Golden Bough*. Thus, the one-eyed merchant is Mr. Eugenides, who is a contemporary version of the Syrian disseminators of the Mystery cults discussed by Miss Weston. Any association with Frazer's one-eyed buffoon who served as a mock or temporary king during winter holiday ceremonies, though an interesting possibility, is difficult to accept in terms of the total poetic context. The image of the Wheel, however, ap-

[60] See *GB*, v, 268, 278-279.
[61] *The Quest of the Holy Grail*, pp. 93-94.
[62] H. T. Morley, *Old and Curious Playing Cards*, cited in E. M. Stephenson, *T. S. Eliot and the Lay Reader* (London: The Fortune Press, 1946), p. 23.
[63] *GB*, vi, 87.

pears rather more dependent on *The Golden Bough*. Frazer cites
a number of cases in which a wheel is used in purificatory ceremonies which seek to restore fertility by removing the evils preventing its appearance.[64] Credence is given to this function of the
image in *The Waste Land* by the wheel's recurrence in the
"Death By Water" section, which intimates that man's purification depends on a knowledge of the direction in which his life is
moving and of the fate to which he is as liable as those who have
already suffered it. In terms of the protagonist's total spiritual development, the conjunction of the wheel and the death by water
scene recalls Frazer's account of an effigy of Death being fixed to
a wheel and then thrown into the water.[65] At the same time Frazer also points out that the effigy of Death was often thought to
possess "a vivifying and quickening influence" on all forms of
life.[66] In short, the protagonist's perception of Phlebas' mortality
permits him both to cast off his fear of death and to recognize
how death can be a stage in the sacred cycle of existence. The
antithesis of this attitude is that expressed by Madame Sosostris
who warns the protagonist to "fear death by water." Her attitude, *The Golden Bough* suggests, was characteristic of the ancient Egyptians with whom she is also associated by her name.[67]

The final image is that of the Hanged Man, who Eliot says is
directly connected with the Hanged God of *The Golden Bough*.
According to Frazer there was a widespread custom of sacrificing a man by hanging and crucifixion to encourage the growth of
the crops, the multiplication of animals, and the fertility of wom-
en.[68] The victim represented the dying and reviving deity, Attis,
who was thought of as a father-god as well as a tree-spirit. His association with the hooded figure of the last section of the poem
is clearly part of Eliot's attempt to suggest the antiquity of
Christ's tradition as a dying and reviving god. At the same time
the reappearance of the god on the road to Emmaus indicates
that not only Christ but Attis as well is resurrected by the protagonist's gradually expanding religious consciousness. This is

[64] *GB*, x, 116ff., 345.   [65] *GB*, iv, 247.   [66] *GB*, iv, 250.

[67] *GB*, v, 185; vi, 119. Though her name seems to have been borrowed
from a character in one of Aldous Huxley's novels, it nevertheless still
recalls the Egyptian conqueror Sesostris mentioned by Frazer.

[68] *GB*, v, 288-297.

borne out by the association of the life-giving water with the place "where the hermit-thrush sings in the pine trees," for the pine tree was traditionally identified with Attis and his sacrificial death.

By calling the hanged figure a man rather than a god, Eliot continues the use of the Tarot pack, thus preserving the verisimilitude of the fortune-teller. This also links the figure to the protagonist by intimating that the sacrificial death which results in rebirth must be undergone by man as well as by gods. The mimetic ritual described in *The Golden Bough* becomes in Eliot's hands a device for suggesting a sophisticated view of the spiritual and psychological trials confronting the individual who wishes to gain a renewed sense of life. And that Madame Sosostris does not find this figure, while the protagonist does, is a clear indication of their respective natures and of the extent of their interest in restoring the waste land and its inhabitants to fertility. It also demonstrates the inadequacy of the magical attitude toward the world as compared to the fully awakened religious consciousness.

Despite the seeming defeat or failure of the Hyacinth girl and Madame Sosostris, the protagonist is led to the first stage of realization. He is able to see that the people are a reflection of the land, whereas previously he had seen nothing but "a heap of broken images," heard nothing but scraps of equally broken conversation. Now he is able to connect the two with each other and with death. Confronted by this terrifying vision of the complicated interrelation of life and death, the protagonist responds eagerly to the sight of a familiar face, that of Stetson who was with him "in the ships at Mylae." The proximity of the references to Mylae and the sprouting corpse suggests that Stetson may be one of those warrior-priests who worshipped Mars as a god of vegetation and who performed his rites to quicken the growth of vegetation.[69] Additional support for this identification is found in *The Waste Land*'s use of Grail figures and scenes and in Miss Weston's suggestion that the Salii or warrior-priests of Mars constitute the real origin of the Grail Knights.[70] At one time the pro-

[69] *GB*, IX, 231-233; Weston, *From Ritual to Romance*, pp. 86-88; Harrison, *Themis*, pp. 194-202.
[70] *From Ritual to Romance*, p. 95.

tagonist, too, may have been a warrior-priest, but he has forgotten the rites of the cult. Thus, by his questions he is making a confused plea for guidance; in Stetson he sees the repository of the secret knowledge of the Mysteries and also a possible way of achieving the quest. He can associate the idea of death and possible rebirth with Stetson, who represents Miss Weston's Mystery Cults. As yet, however, he is incapable of grasping the significance of the mystery ritual itself. His grouping of "corpse" with "sprout," "bloom," and "sudden frost" assimilates the human and vegetative forms of the god. Yet his primary interest seems to be that they be kept buried rather than revived, hidden in man's memory rather than revealed in his religious consciousness.

The corpse clearly is Osiris, who is not only a vegetative deity like the other dying gods but also a culture hero. He provided his people with laws, redeemed them from cannibalism by introducing the cultivation of grains and fruits, and in general diffused civilization throughout the world.[71] His death, then, means not only the withering of vegetation but also the decline of civilization. As a symbol of the cultural crisis that perennially confronts man, the corpse of Osiris is particularly apposite. The planting of the corpse in the garden recalls the ceremony of ploughing and sowing enacted on the opening day of the god's festival which is described in *The Golden Bough*.[72] The reference to its sprouting and blooming recalls the habit of burying effigies of the god made of earth and corn in the god's "garden," which was really only a large flower-pot, and in his final resting place, a subterranean sepulchre. Similarly, the carefully balanced references to "last year" and "this year" point to the yearly celebration of Osiris' burial.

At the same time, all these phrases and images are part of a careful interrelation of Osiris and Christ, an association that is inaugurated by "the dead sound on the final stroke of nine." Thus, though this line is suggestive of Christ's Crucifixion, it also recalls Frazer's account of the burial of Osiris: "On the twenty-fourth of Khoiak, after sunset, the effigy of Osiris in a coffin of

[71] *GB*, vi, 7; Weston, *From Ritual to Romance*, p. 7.
[72] *GB*, vi, 87.

mulberry wood was laid in the grave, and at the ninth hour of the night the effigy which had been made and deposited the year before was removed and placed upon the boughs of sycamore."[73] In removing the previous year's effigy, the worshippers, like the protagonist, were concerned to see whether the grain had sprouted in it. If it had, then, as Frazer remarks, this was "hailed as an omen, or rather as the cause, of the growth of the crops. The corn-god produced the corn from himself: he gave his own body to feed the people: he died that they might live."[74] Nor is this parallel to Christ's sacrifice restricted merely to the material and vegetative level. Similar effigies were placed in the tombs of the dead in Egyptian cemeteries with a view to quickening the dead and ensuring their spiritual immortality.[75] In short, the protagonist is brought by his meeting with Stetson to articulate the worry implicit in "April is the cruellest month"—whether time and the god are being reborn.

Because of his concern, he enjoins Stetson and all men to be on their guard and to "keep the Dog far hence, that's friend to men,/ Or with his nails he'll dig it up again!" In these lines Eliot fuses Webster and Frazer to reflect the protagonist's ambiguous attitude toward the blooming of the corpse. As we have seen from *Sweeney Among the Nightingales*, the image of the dog is associated with Sirius, the Dog Star, which possesses both a benevolent and malevolent aspect. As the former, it signals the rising of the Nile and the return of fertility to the land.[76] As the latter, on the other hand, it was supposed to wither the crops and to cause the intense heat of the Mediterranean summers.[77] Given this first sense, it would appear that the protagonist wishes to avoid the star's fertility role lest the god be reborn. The second sense, however, suggests that he seeks to prevent the baleful star from disturbing the corpse lest its process of growth and regeneration be interrupted. In short, the protagonist simultaneously desires and fears the resurrection of the god. While it will restore his fertility, it will also involve him in a painful and dangerous experience since his own rebirth is connected with that of the deity.

[73] *GB*, VI, 88.   [74] *GB*, VI, 90.   [75] *GB*, VI, 91.
[76] *GB*, VI, 34.   [77] *GB*, VII, 261; X, 332.

[III]

At first sight, "A Game of Chess" appears entirely concerned with the contemporary world. Yet it too has a mythic setting and significance reflecting familiarity with *The Golden Bough*. Particularly in the boudoir scene elaborate descriptions intimate more than merely the physical existence of their objects. The whole of this section is not only an indictment of life in the present but also an elaborate ritual of inversion. "A Game of Chess" parodies, with tragic overtones, a cohesive world that is primitive only in the sense of being primary. It reverses the mind that sees all species of existence as interchangeable forms and past, present, and future as versions and translations of each other. It mirrors that mind which reduces existence to a series of self-contained compartments and then limits its focus to one straitened object at a time. It is this mind and this world that is being revealed in the boudoir and tavern scenes. Nor is it any accident that as we move from the description of the boudoir to the tavern monologue, the focus narrows down solely to men and women in the present. Save for the Ophelia refrain, the whole tavern scene is a matter of surface, permitting no interplay between the various forms of life and time. Its characters suggest not so much the decline of civilization as the rise of barbarism and the transformation of human beings into mechanical dolls. They fail to see a sacred connection between themselves and other living kinds. Hence they unwittingly establish a profane relation, one which gives them the status of highly sophisticated animals, capable of discussing mental, social, and sexual problems with equal aplomb.

While the general pattern and significance of this section are dependent on *The Golden Bough*, there are also specific images that seem to rely on Frazer's accounts of primitive ritual and belief. One of the first of these is contained in the fire-place:

> Huge sea-wood fed with copper
> Burned green and orange, framed by the coloured stone,
> In which sad light a carvèd dolphin swam.

The dolphin recalls both the hero, Antony, and the sea-god described by Frazer as riding on a dolphin.[78] Appropriately

[78] *GB*, v, 113.

enough, it appears in a "sad light," for, according to Frazer, the deity suffered both death by water and death by fire.[79] The burning of the sea-wood, then, foreshadows not only Phlebas' revelatory fate but also the protagonist's submission to the fires of lust and purgation. The image, however, serves a purpose other than foreshadowment. It also helps define the lady's limitations, for she fails to connect the sea-wood and the dolphin with the sacrificial death of the god. By not seeing the emblematic significance of the image, she bars herself from attaining the true meaning of fertility. For her, the "fruited vines" continue to be a graven image of the reviving god, and the "sylvan scene" pictures not human fecundity but its depravity by substituting the rape of Philomela for "the loveliest pair/ That ever since in loves imbraces met."[80]

Another image that may derive from *The Golden Bough* is that of the woman's hair. Linking it with "words" suggests that the woman still is connected with the mystery of the fertility rituals. But now she cannot reveal its message and the silence is no longer "the heart of light" but is instead of a savage nature. This corruption of the woman as a fertility figure is borne out by the contrast between her hair and that of the Hyacinth girl. The latter's was a symbol of beneficent, life-giving fecundity, for it was "wet with rain." The woman's, however, is indicative of a need for a purgative ritual since it is "spread out in fiery points." The ritual of sex has become a series of meaningless gestures whose result is destruction rather than the creation of life. Consequently, her threat to "walk the street/ With my hair down" conveys the contemporary social repugnance but not the ancient religious awe for the prostitute. The woman whose religious devotion was stronger than her fear of indiscriminate sexuality is the antithesis of the lady in the boudoir and Lil.

That they and the rest of their world are corrupt is emphasized by the significance *The Golden Bough* gives to the man's remarks that they "are in rats' alley/ Where the dead men lost their bones." Frazer suggests that rats were often linked with sinners

---

[79] *GB*, iv, 93; v, 110.
[80] John Milton, *Paradise Lost*, iv, ll. 321-322.

and in certain myths with the origin of death.[81] Bones, on the other hand, were regarded as essential to resurrection by the primitive peoples discussed in *The Golden Bough*.[82] These two points illuminate the contrast between the reference to rats and bones in "A Game of Chess" and that in "The Fire Sermon." In the former, the rats are the corrupt sinners of the boudoir and tavern who have denied dead men the means of resurrection. In the latter, the protagonist overcomes his fear and revulsion of the rat and so is able to confront the fact of man's death in its ugliest form. The difference is due to the protagonist's increased consciousness of his own role in the sacred drama of life. As a result, the bones are preserved from year to year "in a little low dry garret" where they await resurrection. This state is achieved in the last section of the poem when the protagonist recognizes that the bones' garret is in the Grail chapel, which preserves them not only from physical but also spiritual decay. Here Eliot parallels not only Frazer's point about the part played by bones in resurrection but also his assertions that they were employed in rainmaking ceremonies and that moral virtues could be acquired through contact with them.[83] For immediately following the Grail chapel scene there occurs the cock-crow of the dawn's daily resurrection, the beginning of rain, and the moral injunctions of the Upanishads. And in the line "dry bones can harm no one" Eliot embodies Frazer's idea that historically man passes from magic to religion. The protagonist is in this statement recording his disavowal of voodoo, charms, and fetishes and his acceptance of faith.

In "The Fire Sermon" and "Death by Water" the protagonist undergoes the two chief forms of ritual purgation and purification, both of which are dealt with in detail by *The Golden Bough*. The former opens with a river scene in which the contemporary nymphs "and their friends, the loitering heirs of city directors" reveal the tawdry vulgarity of a life devoid of fertility. The reason for this degeneration is found in the opening lines:

[81] *GB*, VIII, 299; Frazer, *The Belief in Immortality*, I, 67.

[82] *GB*, VIII, 259-260. The fact that the preserved bones were suspended in baskets from trees may suggest the Sibyl reference again.

[83] *GB*, V, 22; VIII, 153 *passim*.

The river's tent is broken: the last fingers of leaf
Clutch and sink into the wet bank. The wind
Crosses the brown land, unheard.

The image of leafy fingers suggests that the scene is that of the death by water of the vegetative god, an event that inaugurates a period of mourning and even, on occasion, of sterility. Life has already withdrawn from "the brown land" and is now preparing to leave even the heart of fertility, the tree by the living waters. The river is no longer the seat of worship of fertility deities as, according to *The Golden Bough*, it once was for many peoples.[84] Instead it is the Midsummer receptacle for the refuse of a civilization. Eliot's view of this twentieth-century "sweet Thames" and all it represents may well have been shaped by such observations in *The Golden Bough* as "men of old saw the hand of God and worshipped him beside the rushing river with the music of its rumbling waters in their ears," a stream which for them carried a "glad promise of fertility and life."[85] At the same time, the god's death is not, to the true believer, an irredeemable catastrophe and tragedy. As Frazer remarks in the chapter entitled "The Killing of the Tree-Spirit," the death of the god is "merely a necessary step to his revival or resurrection in a better form. Far from being an extinction of the divine spirit, it is only the beginning of a purer and stronger manifestation of it."[86] Historically, this is borne out by the first explicit appearance of Christ in "What the Thunder Said." After the Adonises, Attises, and Osirises of the world he comes as the "stronger manifestation" of divinity, the Christian dying and reviving man-god.

There is clearly an implicit contrast between the uses of the river in the past and in the present. Nevertheless, Eliot still continues to suggest some parallels designed to point up the continuity of human motives and the similarities of the human mind in all times and places. Thus, the line "white bodies naked on the low damp ground" is part of the death motif surrounding the Fisher King. But it also recalls the nymphs of the summer and their enactment of the traditional sacrifice of their virginity to the river prior to their marriage.[87] Both the ancient Greek maidens

[84] *GB*, v, 160.   [85] *GB*, v, 289.   [86] *GB*, iv, 212.
[87] *GB*, ii, 162.

and the modern Thames nymphs suffer the fate, described by Frazer, of those who bathe or loiter by the river: "occasionally, it would seem, young men took advantage of the practice to ravish the girls, and the offspring of such a union was fathered on the river-god."[88] Here Eliot again subtly reflects Frazer's interest in the ways "the sexual instinct has moulded the religious consciousness."[89] And, as a result, it would seem that part of what he is suggesting in *The Waste Land* is that the present is to be criticized not so much for letting sexual relations degenerate into a mere automatic physical activity as for its failure to see how such casual promiscuity as that of the nymphs, Sweeney and Mrs. Porter, and the typist can be fitted into a religious perspective.

Thus, in the Tiresias scene the protagonist witnesses the perfunctory vulgarity of contemporary sexual intercourse. He also views a kind of sacred marriage which brings him closer to the fullness of religious consciousness. The scene is not simply a summary of what has gone before but is also an epiphany of the complexity of existence in which the divine, the human, and the beast all contribute to the fertility rhythm of birth, death, and regeneration. Naturally therefore *The Golden Bough* is pertinent to the scene. This is suggested both by the reference to Tiresias and by Eliot's remark in the Notes that "the whole passage from Ovid is of great anthropological interest." Were the shoddiness of modern sexual mores Eliot's sole concern, the scene could have stood by itself, and there would have been no need to introduce Tiresias or to point out the anthropological significance of his experience. Clearly the typist and the "young man carbuncular" are to be equated with the coiling serpents seen by Tiresias. These serpents represent two apparently disparate but related powers—the corruption of mortality and the fertility of life. According to *The Golden Bough*, snakes are associated with the souls of the dead.[90] With this, Tiresias' reason for calling the clerk "one of the low" and for saying that he himself "walked among the lowest of the dead" becomes apparent. As snakes, the typist and clerk are dead; and as dead, they have the form of snakes. Here Eliot dramatizes the sterility of sex alone by sug-

[88] *GB*, II, 162.   [89] *GB*, VII, viii.   [90] *GB*, VIII, 293-294.

gesting that its participants are walking corpses and by identifying human and animal intercourse. And, in both instances, the
illustrative ideas were derived from *The Golden Bough*.

Yet to see only this aspect of the serpent is to shrivel into the
dead-end of mortality and despair. Having faced this aspect of
the serpent, the protagonist, if he is to continue his quest, must
find in this emblem of death the very seeds of life itself. In this,
he further bears out the anthropological interest mentioned by
Eliot. Snakes, says Frazer, were often worshipped as sacred creatures, and they were often employed in phallic ceremonies in order to promote fertility.[91] Thus, in the coiling serpents, the protagonist is witnessing the sacred marriage in its most primitive
form, the mating of a human being with a spirit of fertility. Since,
however, the snake represents both fertility and death, it follows
that the controlling concept to emerge from the Tiresias scene is
the necessity of mating with death, of being indissolubly wedded
to one's own mortality. Hence, the protagonist realizes that the
serpent is, as it were, the totem of humanity, the guarantee of its
perpetuity as well as the emblem of its failure and mortality. And
in realizing that fertility and immortality are dependent on the
sacrificial death he mirrors one of the central notions documented by *The Golden Bough*.

In essence, this sacrificial death is a purging of that which is
old, corrupt, or sterile in the individual so that he may emerge
with a new life. Such a purgative and purificatory process is carried out in "The Fire Sermon" and "Death by Water." Interestingly enough, *The Golden Bough* is pertinent here not only for
the rites involved but also for the structural parallel it contains
to the end of the third and the beginning of the fourth sections
of the poem. In view of Frazer's account of the midsummer festival named after St. John the Baptist, it is interesting to learn from
Eliot's Notes that the water party on the Thames at which Elizabeth and Leicester engaged in their love-game was held on St.
John's Day. The collocation of the Tiresias scene, Elizabeth and
Leicester, the Thames maidens, and the Augustinian and Bud-
dhistic purgatorial fires may have been suggested in part by Fra-

[91] *GB*, VIII, 287, 316; Harrison, *Prolegomena*, pp. 122-124, 133; Harrison,
Themis, pp. 266, 268.

zer. His description of a pagan festival on the same day includes references to gay boating parties on the river, their licentious conduct, watery rites of purification and baptism, and concludes that "the great Midsummer festival has been above all a festival of lovers and fire."[92] The same structure appears in *The Waste Land*: first the saturnalian river festivities of Elizabeth and Leicester; then the consuming fires of Augustine and Buddha; and, finally, the resurgence of the water ritual which has been transformed from a ceremony of license and pleasure into the dread discipline of death and rebirth undergone by Phlebas the Phoenician.

A similar developing pattern may be seen in the fact that, according to Frazer, "the three great features of the midsummer celebration were the bonfires, the procession with torches round the fields, and the custom of rolling a wheel" into water.[93] The bonfires clearly approximate the cauldron in which the protagonist finds himself at the close of "The Fire Sermon," and the procession with torches appears at the opening of "What the Thunder Said." These two are linked by the less precise but still relevant image of the wheel in "Death by Water." With the elaborately realized image of death in the fourth section of the poem, a further parallel to *The Golden Bough* is suggested. In discussing beliefs associated with St. John's Day, Frazer notes the tradition that "this day will have three persons; one must perish in the air, one in the fire, and the third in the water."[94] And in Eliot's poem the death by fire occurs in "The Fire Sermon," the death by water in the section so entitled, and the death by air in the Christian ritual of crucifixion alluded to in "What the Thunder Said."

The concept of death by water is an integral part of the dying god ritual described by Frazer. Nevertheless, the details of the fourth section of *The Waste Land*, apart from the image of the wheel, do not derive from *The Golden Bough*. In effect, Eliot emphasizes in this section that the sacrificial death of the god is a mimetic rite observed by men in a number of ways. Thus, the death of Phlebas, like that of the god, is presented as a physical

[92] *GB*, II, 272-273.   [93] *GB*, X, 161.   [94] *GB*, XI, 27.

fact, a rite of transition, and a memorial event calling for contemplation. The inference is that all men who participate in the ritual form of the god's death take on its characteristics whether or not they believe in the myth of death and resurrection. Phlebas, then, as Eliot's Note suggests, is something of an everyman figure whose death is the human equivalent of that of the fertility deity because it occurs at a time when the protagonist is capable of seeing its significance.

It is only in "What the Thunder Said" that the ritual death of the god becomes central and explicit, thereby balancing and giving point to the mimetic death of the god's human representative. Indeed, it is no accident that the injunction "Consider Phlebas" should lead directly into the scene of the god's death. Here, for the first time, the poem focusses on Christ rather than the older dying and reviving man-gods. The central image, that of the garden, is obviously based on Gethsemane. At the same time Eliot is concerned to show that the older vegetative deities and their observances are implicit in Christ and his death. Thus, "the torchlight red on sweaty faces" is an imaginative extrapolation from the Gospel accounts of Gethsemane. It also identifies Christ's Crucifixion with the custom, dealt with in *The Golden Bough*, of using torches in gardens as a part of fertility and purificatory ceremonies.[95] In this way the function of the "sweaty faces" of the Pharisees is defined, for by their action they contribute, ironically enough, both to the flowering of Christianity and to the revelation of their own corrupt antagonism toward Christ.

Similarly, in the line about "the frosty silence in the gardens" the plural form of "gardens" indicates that more than simply Gethsemane is involved. It suggests that there is a connection between the scene of Christ's betrayal from which his journey into death begins and the gardens of Adonis, those little pots of vegetation whose rapid forced growth was intended to encourage the revival of life.[96] This interrelation of Christ with the dying and reviving gods of *The Golden Bough* is further developed by "the shouting and the crying" phrase. It links the boisterous noises of the soldiers and the lamentations of the women of Jerusalem with

[95] *GB*, VIII, 249; IX, 110 *passim*; X, 107 *passim*.
[96] *GB*, V, 236 *passim*.

the sounds of mingled grief and joy accompanying the ritual death and revival of the pagan vegetative deities.[97] And the immediately following images of prison and palace encompass Christ's progress from Caiaphas to Pilate, which, as Frazer suggests, reflects the primitive ritual of the scapegoat by which a criminal is transformed into a mock king.[98] The connection of Christ with the scapegoat role of the older dying and reviving gods can also be seen in the phrase "the agony in stony places." It embodies not only the suffering of Christ at Golgotha but also that of the scapegoat who is left to wander in the wilderness.[99]

At the same time, Christ's connection with these ancient fertility deities is not confined to the ritual death they all undergo. There is also an indication in the death itself that the god is destined to revive and return to the world. This is supplied by the phrase "reverberation/ Of thunder of spring over distant mountains," which announces simultaneously the death and the revival of the god. The god's demise is found in the Bible's record of a violent storm accompanying Christ's death, while his return derives from *The Golden Bough*'s statement that "the first peal of thunder in spring announces the reviving energies of nature."[100] From the foregoing, it is clear that the assertion "He who was living is now dead" refers to both Christ and the fertility deities of *The Golden Bough*.

The protagonist now longs for the restoration of this whole long tradition of death and revival. This has already been suggested in the earlier identification of the pine trees with Attis and of the hooded figure with the Hanged God. Added evidence is provided by the image of the thrush which through its association with the mistletoe recalls Balder, the Scandinavian dying and reviving god.[101] And "the sound of water over rock," which the protagonist regards as the quintessence of fertility, recalls those deities who were worshipped by a mountainous stream, such as the father and son gods of Ibreez mentioned earlier. Here the protagonist's desire for the restoration of fertility has mingled with his memory of the sacrificial death central to the life of man, beast, and land alike. As a result, he can observe without

[97] *GB*, v, 254.　　　　[98] *GB*, IX, 414ff.　　　　[99] *GB*, IX, 193, 195.
[100] *GB*, VIII, 121.　　　　　　　　[101] *GB*, X, 101ff; XI, 316, n.1.

fear the disintegration of the unreal cities, the participation of the woman with the long hair in one of those ambivalent celebrations focussed simultaneously on life and death,[102] and his own confrontation of the Chapel Perilous.

Following this final trial, he hears the voice of the thunder who is the lord of creation. He learns that its three dicta are not isolated maxims but cumulative and related indications of the right way through the maze and of the ultimately successful conclusion of the quest. In consequence, the protagonist grasps what the poetic scenes have revealed, namely, the underlying pattern exhibited by the religious consciousness of mankind. And in formulating this pattern poetically, Eliot follows Frazer's statement of it while modifying and extending its ironic view to effect a reversal of *The Golden Bough*'s underlying intention. This is clear when the total form of *The Waste Land* is set against the following summary made by Frazer:

> Thus religion, beginning as a slight and partial acknowledgment of powers superior to man, tends with the growth of knowledge to deepen into a confession of man's entire and absolute dependence on the divine; his old free bearing is exchanged for an attitude of lowliest prostration before the mysterious powers of the unseen, and his highest virtue is to submit his will to theirs: *In la sua volontade e nostra pace*. But this deepening sense of religion, this more perfect submission to the divine will in all things, affects only those higher intelligences who have breadth of view enough to comprehend the vastness of the universe and the littleness of man. Small minds cannot grasp great ideas; to their narrow comprehension, their purblind vision, nothing seems really great and important but themselves. Such minds hardly rise into religion at all.[103]

[IV]

The Golden Bough is indisputably a more powerful factor in *The Waste Land* than anywhere else in Eliot's poetry. Nevertheless, there is a discernible connection between his later work and Frazer's anthropological studies. Thus, the opening lines of "The

[102] *GB*, III, 141, 297, 310.   [103] *GB*, I, 240.

Hollow Men," with their image of straw-filled creatures, recalls *The Golden Bough*'s account of the straw-man who represents the dead spirit of fertility that revives in the spring when the apple trees begin to blossom.[104] Similarly, the disguises of "Rat's coat, crowskin, crossed staves" are clearly anthropological as well as religious. *The Golden Bough* describes how sacred animals and birds are sacrificed and their skins preserved "as a token or memorial of the god, or rather as containing in it a part of the divine life."[105] By seeking to put on these strange garments, the speaker approximates another ritual pattern described by Frazer, that of a man's dressing himself in the skin of a creature that has suffered a sacrificial death.[106] A neat rounding-off of this ritual pattern is provided by "the stone images" in the lines immediately following. Frazer notes that the change from an annual to a permanent image was easily achieved by substituting more lasting substances, such as stone, for the skins.[107] As a result, in "The Hollow Men" "the stone images" constitute the permanent and enduring form of the "rat's coat, crowskin, crossed staves" and hence of both the dead god and the speaker's misdirected worship of idols.

Only when the speaker has made this admission and performed the purgative ritual that empties him of life does he realize that "the perpetual star" and "multifoliate rose" constitute "the hope only/ Of empty men." The nature and object of this hope are illuminated by the poem's intricate star symbolism which seems to be developed in accord with certain ideas found in *The Golden Bough*. According to Frazer, the shooting star which, like that of "The Hollow Men," becomes "a fading star" is traditionally associated with the souls of the dead and the death of an individual.[108] This suggests that "the twinkle of a fading star" may be heralding the death of the speaker and his world. Yet, it may be argued, "a fading star" may not necessarily

---

[104] *GB*, VIII, 6. This association of the apple tree with fertility may also have been suggested to Eliot by this ritual. In *Ash Wednesday* it is the sterile and "withered apple-seed" that marks those who "are terrified and cannot surrender." Similarly, in the *Four Quartets* "the children in the apple-tree" are at the life-giving stream's point of origin.

[105] *GB*, X, 173.   [106] *GB*, III, 68-69; *GB*, IX, 288.

[107] *GB*, X, 174.   [108] *GB*, IV, 64-67.

be a shooting star. It may merely be fading in the sense of disappearing with the approach of dawn. In this connection, Frazer observes that in ancient lore healing was often performed as the stars were disappearing from the sky and suggests that this was so that "the ailment might vanish with the stars."[109] As the poem makes clear, the sickness from which the speaker is suffering is that of ennui or a lapse in religious consciousness. Hence, *The Golden Bough*'s two interpretations of the star give a single, coherent meaning to the same image in the poem. For the speaker to be healed, he must submit to the ritual death and destruction of himself and his world, from which he can then be reborn into the renewed wisdom of religious consciousness.

Even more than "The Hollow Men," the "Journey of the Magi" emphasizes the dying and reviving god's connection with the natural and vegetative cycles. The poem is clearly dramatizing the birth of Christ, the young god-like successor to Attis, Adonis, Osiris, and Dionysus. The powers of rebirth are first encountered in their natural and vegetative form:

> Then at dawn we came down to a temperate valley,
> Wet, below the snow line, smelling of vegetation;
> With a running stream and a water-mill beating the darkness,
> And three trees on the low sky,
> And an old white horse galloped away in the meadow.

When we recall *The Golden Bough*'s descriptions of the lush valleys and proliferating vegetation in which the temples devoted to the worship of Adonis and similar deities were located, it is clear that the present scene embodies the rebirth of the god in nature.[110] The "running stream" is both the scene where the priest-king is buried and the symbol of divine life.[111] The water-mill in which Tammuz was ground and so dismembered is a reminder that death is the price of rebirth.[112] That this process is both endless and implicit in the birth of the new god is suggested by the last two images in the passage. The presence of the three trees foreshadows the fate of the Christian dying god, while the

---

[109] *GB*, I, 83, n.2. [110] *GB*, V, 121-161. [111] *GB*, III, 15; V, 9.
[112] *GB*, VII, 258.

white horse recalls both the sacrificial beast of primitive and classical times and the triumphant conqueror of Revelation.[113]

That death is implicit in birth and that the dying and reviving god appears in a succession of forms is made even clearer by the next scene:

> Then we came to a tavern with vine-leaves over the lintel,
> Six hands at an open door dicing for pieces of silver,
> And feet kicking the empty wine-skins.

The image of the men "dicing for pieces of silver" clarifies that of the "three trees on the low sky." In calling to mind Christ's betrayal by Judas, it also anticipates the Crucifixion. Yet just as the dying and reviving god moves from birth to death, the "tavern with vine-leaves over the lintel" and "the empty wine-skins" suggest that as he draws near to the birthplace of the new god, Christ, the mage finds himself passing through the abode of the old Dionysus, the spirit of the vine.[114] The birth of the one entails the death of the other.

Indeed, the whole verse paragraph elaborates this succession with respect to the major forms of the dying and reviving god. Thus, the "temperate valley" which is "smelling of vegetation" approximates Adonis who was originally the representative of wild vegetation.[115] The "running stream" and the "water-mill" suggest Tammuz whose name means "true son of the deep water" and whose fate was to be ground to death in a mill.[116] The "three trees on the low sky" connect with Attis through his having been a tree-spirit, a hanged god, and a sky-deity.[117] And, finally, in "the meadow" reference there is perhaps the faintest of associations with Osiris who moved his people from a nomadic to a pastoral and agricultural stage of existence.[118]

The contemplation of death and rebirth, the death of man and the triumphant rebirth of the god, is continued in "A Song for Simeon." Here too the concern with ritual death is reflected on the natural level in the opening verse paragraph:

[113] *GB*, I, 27; II, 174 n.2.   [114] *GB*, VII, 2.
[115] *GB*, V, 233.   [116] *GB*, V, 8, 230, 246; VII, 258.
[117] *GB*, V, 277, 282-283, 288-289.   [118] *GB*, VI, 7.

Lord, the Roman hyacinths are blooming in bowls and
The winter sun creeps by the snow hills;
The stubborn season has made stand.

But here it is not nature as a whole that has entered its spring
phase of fertility but only "the Roman hyacinths." These once
again recall the myth of the hero-god whose death was memorialized by the flower bearing his name. According to Frazer, the
hyacinth, like the flowers associated with the other dying gods,
"heralded the advent of another spring and gladdened the hearts
of men with the promise of a joyful resurrection."[119] Thus, in this
poem the flowers announce both the god's salvation or resurrection and Simeon's own death from which comes his rebirth into
the company of the Saints. This continuity of belief in the myth
of the dying and reviving god which extends from pagan to
Christian is suggested in the poem by the fact that the hyacinths
which Simeon, the Christian, observes blooming are referred to
as "Roman." Further evidence for this continuity of worship between differing religious modes is found in the phrase "blooming in bowls." It recalls the tiny Gardens of Adonis grown in baskets, pots, or bowls.[120]

Though the notion of resurrection is implicit in the hyacinth
reference, the poem's emphasis is upon the death which must
precede the rebirth:

My life is light, waiting for the death wind,
Like a feather on the back of my hand.
Dust in sunlight and memory in corners
Wait for the wind that chills towards the dead land.

This is not a neurotic wish for annihilation nor a world-weary
sigh of despair. The significance *The Golden Bough* gives to the
wind and feather image is relevant here. In discussing the Egyptian king's role as Osiris and his part in a festival designed to renew the king's divine energies and to provide him with a new
lease of life, Frazer quotes Flinders Petrie's comment: "The os-
trich feather received and bore away the king's soul in the breeze

[119] *GB*, v, 313.   [120] *GB*, v, 236 *passim*.

that blew it out of sight. This was the celebration of the 'end,' the *sed* feast. The king thus became the dead king, patron of all those who had died in his reign, who were his subjects here and hereafter. He was thus one with Osiris, the king of the dead."[121] From this it is clear that Simeon's death is the ritualistic one of the god. It will take him into the land of the dead, "the twilight kingdom," and from it he, like Osiris, will return to his rightful home.

"Animula," as a result of its contemporary setting, is less intimately related to *The Golden Bough*. Yet running throughout the poem are a series of mythic details which Frazer's materials embedded in a context of society, civilization, and culture. Thus, the pleasures of the chase which led to the death of Adonis are seen as "running stags around a silver tray." The "kings and queens" of myth, legend, and history are confined to "playing-cards." Similarly, the child, in being fascinated by "what the fairies do and what the servants say," is enveloped in material of interest to *The Golden Bough*. In Frazer's eyes, popular superstitions and customs are "by far the fullest and most trust-worthy evidence we possess as to the primitive religion of the Aryans."[122] Further, the soul, as in *The Golden Bough*, is identified with shadows and related to spirits which hover about man when they are dissatisfied and unpropitiated.[123] The culmination of this undercurrent of myth and folklore occurs in the final lines where it breaks through to the surface in clear, unmistakable images: "Pray for Floret, by the boarhound slain between the yew trees,/ Pray for us now and at the hour of our birth." The death of Floret recalls that of Adonis and Attis in whose ritual prayers for the dead merge with those for rebirth.[124]

With *Ash Wednesday*, as the title indicates, Eliot's themes and the tone of his verse become predominantly Christian. There still remain, however, images and phrases that recall the central issues of Frazer's work. Thus, in seeing himself as "the agèd eagle," the speaker is reminding himself, however diffidently, of his guardian spirit who ultimately will carry his soul heavenward on "unbroken wings."[125] In this way the Christian longing is con-

---

[121] *GB*, VI, 154-155.   [122] *GB*, I, xi-xii.
[123] *GB*, III, 51, 67-77.   [124] *GB*, V, 120.
[125] *GB*, I, 200; V, 126.

veyed by a pagan image, thereby graphically conveying the permanence of the religious impulse beneath the multitudinous forms of worship. Similarly, the beauty and savagery of the leopards who consume the protagonist's body represent a fusion of the Christian Communion with sacred animal rites practiced by classical civilizations and primitive barbarians alike.[126] And "at the first turning of the third stair," the speaker is greeted with a scene which relates his own Christian nature to the vegetative fertility motif that is so central to *The Golden Bough*:

> Was a slotted window like the fig's fruit
> And beyond the hawthorn blossom and a pasture scene
> The broadbacked figure drest in blue and green
> Enchanted the maytime with an antique flute.

Frazer explicitly identifies the fig tree and its fruit with fertility rites and suggests that the process of fertilizing the trees constitutes a form of vegetative marriage and hence is analogous to the sacred marriage performed by the god and goddess.[127] The fig is also traditionally associated with Dionysus, a point which serves to identify "the broadbacked figure" with "the garden god" who is the deity of the vine himself.[128] Since "the broadbacked figure" possesses "an antique flute," he may also be linked with Pan. The two deities are, however, but different aspects of the same essential form, the creative and fertilizing god of vegetation. The fig, the flute, Pan, and "maytime" all come together in Frazer's discussion of the scapegoat, which may suggest that the speaker contains within himself both the scapegoat and the image of the deity.[129]

The Rock reveals this interrelation of Christianity and earlier forms of religion as a developing phenomenon of history. Beginning with the creation of the world and man, the Chorus sketches human history in terms of the evolution of religious consciousness while regarding the whole as a *praeparatio Christi*:

> And when there were men, in their various ways, they
> struggled in torment towards GOD

.   .   .   .

[126] *GB*, IV, 83.   [127] *GB*, II, 314-315.
[128] *GB*, VII, 4.   [129] *GB*, IX, 255-256.

Worshipping snakes or trees, worshipping devils rather
    than nothing: crying for life beyond life, for ecstasy not
    of the flesh.

. . . .

And men who turned towards the light and were known of
    the light
Invented the Higher Religions; and the Higher Religions
    were good
And led men from light to light, to knowledge of Good
    and Evil.
But their light was ever surrounded and shot with darkness

. . . .

And they came to an end, a dead end stirred with a
    flicker of life,
And they came to the withered ancient look of a child
    that has died of starvation.
Prayer wheels, worship of the dead, denial of this world,
    affirmation of rites with forgotten meanings

. . . .

Then came at a predetermined moment, a moment in
    time and of time,

. . . .

Then it seemed as if men must proceed from light to light,
    in the light of the Word,
Through the Passion and Sacrifice saved in spite of their
    negative being;
Bestial as always before, carnal, self-seeking as always
    before, selfish and purblind as ever before,
Yet always struggling, always reaffirming, always resuming
    their march on the way that was lit by the light;
Often halting, loitering, straying, delaying, returning,
    yet following no other way.

And in its own fashion *The Golden Bough* provides eloquent
testimony to the enduring quality of man's religious impulse. Frazer vividly exhibits the multitude of forms in which it manifests
itself, ranging from the Higher Religions to the worship of

snakes, trees, devils, and the dead, and perpetuated by the observance of rites whose original significance has long since been modified or forgotten.[130]

In *The Family Reunion* the primitive religious customs discussed by Frazer are linked to the individual's awareness of death and efforts to be reborn. Harry observes:

> The eye adjusts itself to a twilight
> Where the dead stone is seen to be batrachian,
> The aphyllous branch ophidian.

In seeing the identity of animal and vegetative forms, he begins on the initial level of religious consciousness which consists of "worshipping snakes and trees." By the same token he is able to recognize the primitive religious features attached to the spring season, all of which, significantly enough, are described in detail by *The Golden Bough*:[131]

> Spring is an issue of the blood
> A season of sacrifice
> And the wail of the new full tide
> Returning the ghosts of the dead
> Those whom the winter drowned
> Do not the ghosts of the drowned
> Return to land in the spring
> Do the dead want to return?

In so doing, he reflects his awareness of the fact that relief from his insane world can be attained only by going back to the origins of man's religious impulse, "To the worship in the desert, the thirst and deprivation,/ A stony sanctuary and a primitive altar,/ The heat of the sun and the icy vigil."

While *The Family Reunion* stresses the fact that spring, "the season of birth/ Is the season of sacrifice," the form of the year as a whole is made explicit only with *Murder in the Cathedral* and the *Four Quartets*. There the theme of the cyclic nature of existence is given its fullest development. It is this vision that the *Four Quartets* elaborate in philosophical terms. Indeed, the phil-

---

[130] *GB*, I, 163, 382; II, 8ff.; VIII, 316ff.; IX, 89ff., 97.
[131] *GB*, II, 364; IV, 266ff.; IX, 400.

osophical and anthropological myths, the beginning and end of
Eliot's mature poetry, are linked in "Burnt Norton." The philosophical vision, expressed in "the still point" passage, succeeds
the anthropological perspective contained in these lines:

> We move about the moving tree
> In light upon the figured leaf
> And hear upon the sodden floor
> Below, the boarhound and the boar
> Pursue their pattern as before
> But reconciled among the stars.

Thus Adonis and his wild animal antagonist, Osiris and his malevolent brother, are absorbed into the all-embracing dance
which occurs "at the still point of the turning world." A number
of other details and images reveal Frazer's continued relevance
to Eliot's poetic thought. In addition to "the boarhound and the
boar" passage in "Burnt Norton" already mentioned, there are
explicit references in "East Coker" to fertility charms discussed
by Frazer, such as dancing, leaping over bonfires, midsummer
festivals, and human sexual intercourse in order to influence the
growth of vegetation.[132] And in a later section of the same poem,
the Christian Crucifixion and Communion are alluded to in terms
which recall the savage rites of Dionysus and Attis: "The dripping blood our only drink,/ The bloody flesh our only food."
These rites, like the Christian Communion, were calculated to
purify man and bring him into contact with the deity and divine
life. A somewhat different form of the primitive deity appears at
the opening of "The Dry Salvages" which declares that "the
river/ Is a strong brown god . . . almost forgotten/ By the dwellers in cities." Though he is ignored by most people, he continues,
according to the poem, to exhibit the qualities ascribed to him by
The Golden Bough such as expecting sacrificial offerings of animals and human beings to propitiate and allay his destructive
powers.[133] A human rather than a natural image similarly concerned with death, sacrifice, and scapegoat offerings is found in
the "broken king" of "Little Gidding" who has reached "the end

[132] *GB*, I, 137; II, 98-101, 106; V, 251; X, 107, 119, 161, 204.
[133] *GB*, I, 151; II, 16, 76; V, 160; IX, 27; XI, 26.

of the journey." Eliot here is crossing history and myth, for he views Charles I as the sacred king of *The Golden Bough* who, when he can no longer rule, accepts the death imposed upon him: "I think of a king at nightfall,/ Of three men, and more, on the scaffold."

For the primitive mind in all periods of history there is an overwhelming urge to know how to control or at least placate and cajole the powerful gods, spirits, and forces which rule man and his world. The nostrums and techniques for wielding power without troubling to gain the true wisdom of spiritual presences constitute magic. Since at least as early as "A Cooking Egg" Eliot was interested in, scornful of, fascinated and disturbed by this manifestation of the human mind. With Madame Sosostris of *The Waste Land* and Dusty and Doris of "Sweeney Agonistes" this theme assumes a major place in Eliot's poetry. By the time of *The Family Reunion*, magic, the antagonist of religion in Frazer's eyes, has absorbed virtually an entire family. The Chorus, composed of Harry's relatives, stands over against him and his newly acquired religious insight and declares:

> We know various spells and enchantments,
> And minor forms of sorcery,
> Divination and chiromancy.

In the *Four Quartets* the whole rigmarole of magic is threatening completely to absorb the attention of an entire society, for its practices "are usual/ Pastimes and drugs, and features of the press." Here Eliot shows how the impulse to religious consciousness is being corrupted and warped into the opposite of itself. It is threatened with stultifying perversions which reduce the cycle of existence to a flight from life through hallucinations both conscious and unconscious. That this situation can be changed is shown by *The Confidential Clerk*. Lady Mulhammer begins by believing in all the paraphernalia of magic and witchcraft, but as she moves toward the astounding reality of her own child, these trivial yet dangerous occupations of the mind drop away from her.

Magic, according to Frazer, was calculated not only to provide one with desired material things but also to protect one from the perils of the souls, both external and internal, which were ever ready to beset the unwary individual. On one level, it is for precisely this reason that Eliot's poetry so dramatically indicts magic. Only by facing rather than evading its perils can the soul enact the myth of the dying and reviving god through which alone existence is transformed into the eternal life of the imagination. At the same time, Eliot mocks magic because it fails to protect the soul. It guards the soul against isolated evils while permitting it to be corrupted and destroyed by a greater and more subtle evil—the habits of mind and modes of action which give rise to magic itself. Imbedded in the very heart of *The Golden Bough* and the creative myth of the dying and reviving god is the malevolent spirit of the magic art. Nor is it impossible that this fact should have been part of what Eliot had in mind when in *East Coker* he observed that "as we grow older/ The world becomes stranger, the pattern more complicated/ Of dead and living." This awareness of the increasingly complicated pattern of existence testifies to the continued fascination that *The Golden Bough*'s myth of the dying and reviving god has exercised on the poet and his work.

Nowhere is the continuing character of Frazer's impact more subtly yet centrally exhibited than in Eliot's last work, *The Elder Statesman*. Here the poet integrates his concern over the spiritual clarification of the individual's true self with his interest in the nature of the soul viewed as a historically developing phenomenon. The former represents the dominant theme of the later plays, while the latter reflects his earlier anthropological concerns. In both he is preeminently concerned with the perils to which the soul is subject. Throughout *The Elder Statesman* Eliot's characters are made to ring all the changes on the dangers, effects, and implications of changing personal names.

The last chapter of Frazer's "Taboo and the Perils of the Soul" is wholly given over to a discussion and cataloguing of tabooed words, among which personal names, those of relations, the dead, and gods are most prominent. Eliot utilizes several of Frazer's points in his sophisticated and urbane adaptation of the idea of taboo. In addition to the terror evoked by the contemplated or actual loss of one's name, he finds relevant to his theme the possible temporary character of the personal-name prohibition, the substitutive adoption of relatives' names, the basing of some of these taboos on a fear of ghosts, and the belief that utterance of the names of gods disturbs the order of nature.[134] Needless to say, Eliot does not merely take over these notions and customs baldly and in their primitive form or context. He shows how these ancient feelings continue to permeate modern, civilized man's responses to experience although expressed in phrases and accents redolent of twentieth-century upper- and middle-class life. Eliot is convinced that barbaric and confused notions of taboo, sacrifice, and supernatural powers cannot be ignored or denied with impunity. What he was interested in is the slow, subtle process of transformation by which human insights and acts are clarified to the point of actual spiritual illumination. As a result, though recognizing the ultimate falsity of taboo and related concepts, he sees it as the historical and psychological ground of man's contemporary feelings and beliefs and so worthy of respectful attention. In substantial measure this view is in accord with and may be traced to one enunciated by Frazer in *The Golden Bough*. In his lifetime Eliot's conception of what constituted fundamental ideas obviously changed and deepened. Nevertheless, he always saw them emerging from what in 1923 he called their crude forerunners. This, for him, was a constant conviction and one based in substantial measure on his assiduous study of the light thrown on human history by *The Golden Bough*.

[134] *GB*, III, 354, 365ff., 387ff.

CHAPTER VIII

D. H. Lawrence:
The Evidence of
the Poetry

[I]

As a major talent in twentieth-century literature, D. H. Lawrence ranks with Yeats, Eliot, and Joyce. He is also preeminently a writer whose sympathies were fully engaged by the material discussed by turn-of-the-century leaders in English studies of comparative religion such as Frazer, Jane Harrison, Gilbert Murray, and Cornford. Lawrence's interest in myth and ritual cannot escape even the most casual reader of his work. Precisely when this interest first crystallized cannot be pinpointed with complete accuracy, but there is sufficient evidence, of both external and internal orders, to indicate that it occurred fairly early in his career. As early as 1911, in a letter to Edward Garnett, he alluded to "the seated statues of the kings of Egypt,"[1] a point which perhaps suggests Frazer's observation about portrait statues containing the souls of the deified Egyptian kings.[2] More unequivocal, however, are his references to the works of the Cambridge

---

[1] *The Collected Letters of D. H. Lawrence*, ed. Harry T. Moore (New York, Viking, 1962), I, 87.

[2] *GB*, XI, 157. If this possibility seems tenuous, stronger links may be found in such works as C. P. Tiele's *History of the Egyptian Religion* (1882), J. H. Breasted's *A History of the Ancient Egyptians* (1908), Sir E. A. Wallis Budge's *Egyptian Religion* (1900) or *The Gods of the Egyptians* (1904), Sir W. M. Flinders Petrie's *The Royal Tombs of the Earliest Dynasties* (1901) or *The Religion of Ancient Egypt* (1906). All these were drawn upon and referred to by Frazer, who may thereby have directed Lawrence's attention to them. Budge and Petrie in particular were beginning at this time to enjoy a considerable vogue in England. Interestingly enough, several of these works, such as Budge's *Egyptian Religion*, contain illustrations of deities or kings seated upon thrones.

School from 1913 on. Late in October of that year, Lawrence acknowledged from Italy the gift of books sent by his old teaching friend, A. D. McLeod. In his letter he remarked that he preferred Jane Harrison's just-published *Ancient Art and Ritual* even to *Tristram Shandy*, which "I love." For "I am just in the mood for it. It just fascinates me to see art coming out of religious yearning—one's presentation of what one wants to feel again, deeply."[3] And in December of the same year he told McLeod, "You have no idea how much I got out of that *Ritual and Art* book—it *is* a good idea . . ." though at the same time he indulged in his rapidly growing habit of evaluating the author as a personality behind the book when he observed that it was "a schoolmarmy woman who writes it."[4] In addition to Lawrence's interest in the religious source of art, his letters from this point on suggest that Miss Harrison, who learned it herself from Frazer's *Golden Bough*, may also have shown him that the individual goes through critical stages of transition which are analogous to the death and rebirth of vegetation.

Having sampled the anthropological diet through Miss Harrison's little introductory survey and found it to his liking, Lawrence was now ready for more ambitious efforts. In 1915 he met Bertrand Russell, whose gift of John Burnet's *Early Greek Philosophy* led him to write that "These early Greeks have clarified my soul. I must drop all about God" and "I am rid of all my Christian religiosity."[5] Perhaps because of the antiquity of this influence or the desire to find new grounds for his ineradicable religious impulse or the awe he felt for Russell's erudition, together with an attendant spirit of emulation, Lawrence turned to pondering one of the most influential works of the twentieth century. In a letter to Russell on December 8, 1915, Lawrence remarked that he had been reading both Frazer's *Golden Bough* and his *Totemism and Exogamy*.[6] With characteristic casualness he fails to give any hint as to which of the three possible and, on points, quite different editions of the former work he was reading. What its impact was, however, he makes quite clear: it substantiated his own views on a variety of subjects and gave impetus to his own speculative

---

[3] *The Collected Letters*, I, 234. [4] *The Collected Letters*, I, 249.
[5] *The Collected Letters*, I, 352. [6] *The Collected Letters*, I, 393.

bent. The specific nature of this effect is best seen when, after announcing his study of Frazer, Lawrence declares:

> Now I am convinced of what I believed when I was about twenty—that there is another seat of consciousness than the brain and the nervous system: there is a blood-consciousness which exists in us independently of the ordinary mental consciousness, which depends on the eye as its source or connector. There is the blood-consciousness, with the sexual connection holding the same relation as the eye, in seeing, holds to the mental consciousness. One lives, knows, and has one's being in the blood, without any reference to nerves and brain. This is one half of life, belonging to the darkness. . . . Now it is necessary for us to realise that there is this other great half of our life active in the darkness, the blood-relationship: that when I *see*, there is a connection between my mental-consciousness and an outside body, forming a percept; but at the same time, there is a transmission through the darkness which is never absent from the light, into my blood-consciousness: but in seeing, the blood-percept is perhaps not strong. On the other hand, when I take a woman, then the blood-percept is supreme, my blood-knowing is overwhelming. There is a transmission, I don't know of what, between her blood and mine, in the act of connection. So that afterwards, even if she goes away, the blood-consciousness persists between us, when the mental consciousness is suspended; and I am formed then by my blood-consciousness, not by my mind or nerves at all.

Similarly in the transmission from the blood of the mother to the embryo in the womb, there goes the whole blood-consciousness. And when they say a mental image is sometimes transmitted from the mother to the embryo, this is not the *mental* image, but the *blood-image*. All living things, even plants, have a blood-being. If a lizard falls on the breast of a pregnant woman, then the blood-being of the lizard passes with a shock into the blood-being of the woman, and is transferred to the foetus, probably without intervention either of nerve or brain consciousness. And this is the origin of totem: and for this reason some tribes no doubt really *were* kangaroos: they contained the blood-knowledge of the kangaroo.—And blood knowledge comes either through the mother or through the sex —so that dreams at puberty are as good an origin of the totem as the percept of a pregnant woman.[7]

As if to round out his acquaintance with the Cambridge School, Lawrence the following year read both Gilbert Murray and Frazer's great mentor Sir Edward B. Tylor. His letter to Lady Morrell gives no hint of which of Murray's books he had read. But in view of his then current interest in anthropology, most probably he is referring to *Four Stages of Greek Religion*. But if there is some uncertainty as to the exact book in Lawrence's possession, there is none whatever as to his estimate of its content and its author: "Thank you for the Gilbert Murray book. I liked it. But I wish he were a little less popular and conversational in his style, and that he hadn't put so many layers of flannel between him and his own nakedness. But the stuff of the book interests me *enormously*."[8] Just how much it interested him is perhaps best indicated by his having turned to its expanded version, *Five Stages of Greek Religion*, in the last years of his life and during the writing of *Apocalypse*.[9]

Even more enthusiastic was his reaction to Tylor's *Primitive Culture*, for here he found no occasion to protest the nature of the man behind the book. To two different correspondents he expressed his preference for it over *The Golden Bough* while describing it as "a very good sound substantial book" and "*most interesting*."[10] The length of Frazer's work, its almost endless multiplication of examples, its reticence about providing a theo-

[7] *The Collected Letters*, I, 393-394; cf. I, 416.

[8] *The Letters of D. H. Lawrence*, ed. Aldous Huxley (London: Heinemann, 1932), p. 328; italics his. This letter is not included in the Moore edition.

[9] A. & E. Brewster, *D. H. Lawrence, Reminiscences & Correspondences* (London: Martin Secker, 1934), p. 305. Cf. Tindall, pp. 98, 122, who minimizes the importance of Murray's book in the later period by failing to consider that Lawrence probably read it early in his career when much of its material would have been new and striking to him. At any rate, Tindall does not suggest an alternative Murray volume available to Lawrence in 1916.

[10] *The Collected Letters*, I, 446, 463; italics his.

retic framework or analytic categories, and its looser organization probably all contributed to Lawrence's attitude, which more
often than we are accustomed to recognizing aligned itself with
one form or another of orthodoxy. And in this particular opinion
he is but anticipating the views of subsequent anthropologists.[11]
Nor did he limit his criticisms of Frazer to private correspondence. His article "Aristocracy" apparently alludes to Sir James's
study habits or to what Lawrence conceived them to be.[12]
Though far less savage than his reported remark to Dorothy
Brett,[13] the tenor is the same: a repetition of the charge hurled
at Frazer much earlier by Andrew Lang when he dubbed his
work the Covent Garden school of anthropology.

A similar feeling is expressed in *Apocalypse*, where Lawrence
refers to *The Golden Bough* as though it were a repository of
symbols possessing but a single meaning each.[14] He appeals for
a recognition of the inexhaustible, plurisignificative character of
symbols and expresses his fear that the lazy and indifferent may
rest content with Frazer's catalogue of identified symbols rather
than attending to their profound emotional and spiritual rever-
berations. In one sense, his own *Apocalypse* represents an attempt to write a book which, like *The Golden Bough*, deals with
the great primary symbols of mankind but which also generates
in the reader a sense of the original mystery and power of these
same symbols. Thus, though his comments on Frazer are not always wholly sympathetic, it would be unwise to regard these too
seriously, for as William York Tindall has put it, "he generally
condemned what he found most useful."[15] More important to an
estimate of *The Golden Bough*'s impact on Lawrence is his actual
literary practice, his use of symbols, images, concepts, and ideas
enunciated by Frazer and the other members of his school.

[11] Kroeber, *The Nature of Culture*, p. 145.
[12] See *Phoenix II*, eds. W. Roberts & H. T. Moore (New York: Viking,
1968), pp. 479-480.
[13] Dorothy Brett, *Lawrence and Brett* (Philadelphia: J. B. Lippincott,
1933), pp. 81-82.
[14] *Apocalypse* (Florence: G. Orioli, 1931), p. 284.
[15] W. Y. Tindall, *D. H. Lawrence and Susan His Cow* (New York:
Columbia University Press, 1939), p. xi.

[II]

In virtually all his literary efforts Lawrence made extensive use of material from anthropology and comparative religion. The majority of his works through image, scene, action, or allusion embrace nearly every major notion concerning myth and ritual to be found in *The Golden Bough*. The point here is not that Frazer's great study constitutes Lawrence's only source, though it is undeniably one of the most important, but that it is the most encyclopedic treatment of primitive life available to the English-speaking world and the one that lies behind the bulk of twentieth-century interest in the subject. As such it may justifiably be regarded as playing a controlling part in Lawrence's immersion in ancient modes and manners of life. For so widespread was Frazer's impact on other thinkers that even when Lawrence drew directly on other studies of primitive thought and belief, he was also indirectly absorbing the impress of Frazer's views. Assimilating his reading to his own temperament and thought resulted in the manifestation, in both his poetry and his fiction, of a concern with primitive beliefs and images of the most varied kinds.

The best way into this complex and sustained concern is probably through Lawrence's poetry. Its various strands parallel elements in the fiction and its corpus is briefer in scope. On both counts, therefore, it serves as a useful introduction to Lawrence's imaginative response to *The Golden Bough* and the world it has so impressively represented to the twentieth-century consciousness.[16] We have already seen that Lawrence's first explicit references to the Cambridge School were made just before and during World War I. His first poems, however, were written in 1904, a fact which immediately presents the interesting question as to whether the poetry affords any significant internal evidence of Lawrence's awareness of *The Golden Bough* before 1915.[17]

One of his first published poems, "Discipline," appeared in Ford Madox Ford's *English Review* for 1909. At the end of a re-

[16] See my " 'The Golden Bough' and Modern Poetry," *Journal of Aesthetics and Art Criticism*, xv (1957), esp. pp. 277-282.

[17] *The Complete Poems of D. H. Lawrence*, ed. V. de Sola Pinto & W. Roberts (New York: Viking, 1964), ii, 849, 1026.

flective assessment of the real and ideal relations between pupil and teacher, Lawrence enunciates an aspect of the natural cycle of the soul or self. Like Frazer's primitive men, Lawrence instinctively notes the intimate analogies obtaining between man and nature, and also the ineluctable cyclic return of fecundity. Small wonder that when he did encounter *The Golden Bough* he should find it copiously endorsing many of his earliest convictions and revealing the historical and prehistorical genesis of many of his central metaphors. A number of other poems published in *Love Poems and Others* (1913) also show suggestive traces of reading in sources like if not identical with *The Golden Bough*.

A poem like "The Appeal," for instance, addresses the beloved in language that combines Frazerian and classical imagery to define the relation of love in ancient and mythic terms:

> You, Helen, who see the stars
> As mistletoe berries burning in a black tree,
> You surely, seeing I am a bowl of kisses
> Should put your mouth to mine and drink of me.
> Helen, you let my kisses steam
> Wasteful into the night's black nostrils; drink
> Me up, I pray; of you, who are Night's bacchante,
> How can you from my bowl of kisses shrink?

Though not conclusive, perhaps, the naturalistic form of the mistletoe image seems to develop into an anthropologically weighted symbol through both its conjunction with "a black tree" and its metaphorical "burning." Frazer cites scientific authorities to the effect that one species of mistletoe is most frequently associated with the black poplar.[18] In addition, this species possesses bright yellow rather than greenish-white berries, a point that might seem to be more accurately rendered by the "burning" image.[19] Nor should it be forgotten that this image carries with it at least some overtones of the Druidic worship of the mistletoe and practice of sacrificial burnings, behavior described in the same volume of *The Golden Bough*.[20]

By the time of his next volume of poems, *Amores* (1916), Law-

[18] *GB*, XI, 318, n.6.   [19] *GB*, XI, 318-320.   [20] *GB*, XI, 32-33.

rence has made explicit his acquaintance with Frazer and *The Golden Bough* and the incidence of anthropological lore has increased. Thus, in "Mystery" he sharpens one of the central images of "The Appeal" and in so doing reveals an even more specific mythic context for it. The speaker confides:

> Now I am all
> One bowl of kisses,
> Such as the tall
> Slim votaresses
> Of Egypt filled
> For divine excesses

and the mystery ritual of which he speaks is clearly sexual. "The Virgin Mother" involves a reference to double birth, which is a part of initiation rituals described at length by both Frazer and Miss Harrison: "Once from your womb, sweet mother,/ Once from your soul."[21] In "this rare, ancient night" beneath "The Yew-Tree on the Downs," the poet pleads:

> Lie down, and open to me
> The inner dark of the mystery,
> Be penetrate, like the tree.

This invocation may hint at the birth of Adonis from a tree-mother as well as request initiation into the knowledge of life's source. The image of the sacred tree is again used in "Under the Oak" but with greater emphasis on its mythic nature:

> Beneath this powerful tree, my whole soul's fluid
> Oozes away from me as a sacrifice steam
> At the knife of a Druid.
>
> .   .   .   .
>
> Above me springs the blood-born mistletoe
> In the shady smoke.
>
> .   .   .   .
>
> What have you to do with the mysteries
> Of this ancient place, of my ancient curse?

[21] *GB*, v, 274ff.; vi, 153, 155ff.; xi, 225, 247, 251, 256-257, 261.

Similarly, trees outside the window in "Late at Night" impel the mind back to ancient images which provoke disturbing questions:

> Tall black Bacchae of midnight, why then, why
> Do you rush to assail me?
> Do I intrude on your rites nocturnal?
> What should it avail me?
> Is there some great Iacchos of these slopes
> Surburban dismal?
>
> Have I profaned some female mystery, orgies
> Black and phantasmal?

Here the psychological terrors of modern life are personified in classical and primitive terms; in "Autumn Sunshine" an escape from these terrors is found by merging a classical observance with Frazer's concept of the vegetative character of deities. The poet contemplates and participates in a ritual libation such as both Miss Harrison and F. M. Cornford describe:[22]

> All, all Persephone's pale cups of mould
> Are on the board, are over-filled;
> The portion to the gods is spilled;
> Now mortals all, take hold!
>
> .   .   .   .
>
> And take within the wine the god's great oath
> By heaven and earth and hellish stream,
> To break this sick and nauseous dream.

One result of this escape is found in "Don Juan." The protagonist begins and concludes with the conviction that "Isis the mystery/ Must be in love with me," a point which if true identifies him with Osiris, the dying and reviving god of Egypt. The "Hymn to Priapus" develops the implications of this in contemporary terms and crosses it with the traditional death of the cereal god:

[22] Cornford, *From Religion to Philosophy* (London: Edward Arnold, 1912), pp. 23-25.

> The warm, soft country lass,
> Sweet as an armful of wheat
> At threshing-time broken, was broken
> For me, and ah, it was sweet!

The result is that actions in the present become symbolic of past actions which ostensibly are of an entirely different character. Love and its fulfillment become a harvest image that invokes and contains both death and life.

On the other hand, separation from woman and love prompts a prayer to chthonic deities, deities which Jane Harrison had declared were psychologically and culturally earlier and more important than the Olympian sky gods: [23]

> dark Gods, govern her sleep,
> Magnificent ghosts of the darkness, carry off her
> decision in sleep,
> Leave her no choice, make her lapse me-ward, make her,
> Oh Gods of the living darkness, powers of Night.

Yet with the woman returned, certain crucial times of the year, such as "New Year's Night," demand religious offerings and her sacrifice:

> You're a dove I have bought for sacrifice,
> And tonight I slay it.
>
> .   .   .   .
>
> Now I offer her up to the ancient, inexorable God,
> Who knows me not.
>
> .   .   .   .
>
> I sacrifice all in her, my last of the world,
> Pride, strength, all the lot.

That this is a sacrifice of and for love is underscored by Frazer's point that doves were sacred to Aphrodite and Astarte and were burned at the funeral of Adonis.[24] The sacrifice of life to death makes rebirth possible. The centrality of this theme to Lawrence's poetry is inescapable, and equally inescapable is the fact

[23] Harrison, *Prolegomena*, pp. 11, 28-31.
[24] *GB*, v, 33, 147.

that *The Golden Bough* provides the most explicit definition of this theme as well as the bulk of its images.

The volume *Birds, Beasts and Flowers* (1923) develops naturally enough the vegetative and animal aspects of the myth of the dying and reviving god. The eating of "Medlars and Sorb-Apples" is linked with "Orpheus, and the winding, leaf-clogged, silent lanes of hell," and the poet declares:

> I say, wonderful are the hellish experiences,
> Orphic, delicate
> Dionysos of the Underworld.

The result of his experience is "Orphic farewell, and farewell, and farewell/ And the *ego sum* of Dionysos/ The *sono io* of perfect drunkenness/ Intoxication of final loneliness." Lawrence links the two deities by their identical fates of dismemberment and their connection with the dead in order to convey the peculiar quality of his feeling about the essential loneliness of the individual.

In addition to "Cypresses" and the aforementioned poems on the yew tree and the oak, Lawrence's own version of the primitive worship of trees, a subject treated at length in *The Golden Bough*, is further elaborated in "Bare Fig-Trees," "Bare Almond-Trees," and "Almond Blossom."[25] In "Purple Anemones" he declares that "it is Pluto,/ Dis,/ The dark one./ Proserpine's master," not Jesus or Apollo, who is the god of flowers. With Frazer he links the appearance of vegetation with the return of the deity, in this case, Proserpine, from the underworld:

> When she broke forth from below,
> Flowers came, hell-hounds on her heels.
> Dis, the dark, the jealous god, the husband,
> Flower-sumptuous-blooded.

Similarly, "St. Luke" hints at the Christian saint's association with the bull-god of antiquity, while "Snake" recognizes the reptile as a divine king of the underworld. In "Lui et Elle" the male tortoise is identified with the dismembered dying god and both are

[25] *GB*, ii, 8ff., 59ff.

emblems of the tortures sexual awakening produces in the adolescent:

> Poor little earthy house-inhabiting Osiris,
> The mysterious bull tore him at adolescence into pieces,
> And he must struggle after reconstruction, ignominiously.

And in one of the last poems in the volume, "Autumn at Taos," Lawrence while riding through a canyon on his horse, sees "the golden hawk of Horus/ Astride above me." In this, Lawrence is accurately imitating the Egyptian custom, described by Frazer, of identifying the hawk with the sun and both with the king.[26] As a sun worshipper, Lawrence clearly was placing himself under the protection of the appropriate deity.

This concern with the myths and rites of ancient and primitive peoples was by no means restricted to a single phase of Lawrence's career. Like Yeats, he seems to have invoked the myths expounded in *The Golden Bough* as his talisman for the descent to the underworld during his last years. In *Last Poems* (1933), "Middle of the World" describes the approach of "the slim black ship of Dionysos" which advances "with grape-vines up the mast, and dolphins leaping." In this image the poet follows Frazer's report of the ancient identification of Dionysus and Osiris and then transfers Osiris' death-voyage to Dionysus.[27] The image of Dionysus' ship recurs in "They Say the Sea is Loveless," a title that is disproved by the fact that "the sea is making love to Dionysos/ in the bouncing of these small and happy whales." Despite the gay phallicism of the voyage of the god, his death is inevitable. Hence in "Stoic" the great gods and goddesses such as Artemis, Aphrodite, Cronos, and Ares have died. Nevertheless, lamentations for them are unnecessary, "for perhaps the greatest of all illusions/ is this illusion of the death of the undying," a conviction that is at the very core of Frazer's treatment of the dying god.

With this there begins an exploration of the nature of death and the character of evil. "Doors" develops Miss Harrison's thesis concerning the chthonic deities by insisting that "not the ithy-

[26] *GB*, IV, 112; see also I, 29; VI, 8, 21ff.
[27] *GB*, VI, 113; VII, 3.

phallic demons/ not even the double phallus of the devil himself/ with his key to the two dark doors/ is evil."[28] This concern with evil, which runs throughout a number of the later poems, is further defined in "Evil is Homeless":

> Hell is the home of souls lost in darkness,
> even as heaven is the home of souls lost in light.
> And like Persephone, or Attis
> there are souls that are at home in both homes.

Because, as one title declares, death is not evil, Lawrence, like Yeats, can follow Osiris to "The Ship of Death" and "the longest journey, to oblivion" which is "the long and painful death/ that lies between the old self and the new." Here life is seen as a cycle of decline and resurgence which contains a death phase that must necessarily be endured. For Lawrence, this death is, in a sense, a divestiture from the contemporary categories of thought and modes of perception. The new self possesses a noncerebral mode of thought focussed upon a phallic worship through which sex becomes a way of life and a form of intuitive apprehension.

In "What are the Gods!" and "Name the Gods!" we learn that as a consequence of this divestiture the gods are nameless and without form and yet they live "in a great full lime-tree of summer," in a woman washing herself under a tap, and in the new-mown "tall white corn." Unconsciously perhaps but nonetheless significantly, Lawrence repeats Frazer's stress upon the tree, the woman, and the corn as objects of religious awe and veneration. And like Frazer's primitive men he refuses to distinguish between the animate and the inanimate, the human and the vegetative; all are seen as spirits possessing sacred potency.[29] This conclusion is made explicit in "All Sorts of Gods":

> every god that humanity has ever known is still a god
> today
> the African queer ones and Scandinavian queer ones,
> the Greek beautiful ones, the Phoenician ugly ones, the
> Aztec hideous ones

---

[28] Harrison, *Prolegomena*, pp. 333-334, 337; *Themis*, pp. 260, 270-271, 279.
[29] *GB*, VIII, 206ff.

goddesses of love, goddesses of dirt, excrement-eaters
    or lily virgins
Jesus, Buddha, Jehovah and Ra, Egypt and Babylon
all the gods, and you see them all if you look, alive
    and moving today,
and alive and moving tomorrow, many tomorrows, as
    yesterdays.

As a result of the continuing presence of man's many gods, the
poet records in "For a Moment" how persons with whom he
comes in contact stand revealed as Hyancinthus, Io, Isis, or
Chiron the Centaur. Similarly, in "Maximus" the poet meets
Hermes, and in "The Man of Tyre" Aphrodite coming out of the
sea.

By the same token, as we learn from "Be It So," one can oneself
become "one of the gods, Jesus or Fafnir or Priapus or Siva."
"Man is More than Homo Sapiens" and "Two Ways of Living and
Dying" add to this list of gods incarnate in man such names as
Ashtaroth, Huitzilopochtli, Baal, Krishna, Adonis, and Balder all
of which appear in *The Golden Bough*.[30] The essential relationship between gods and men, or between the divine and mortal
aspects of man, is made clear by "The Old Idea of Sacrifice":

sacrifice is the law of life which enacts
that little lives must be eaten up into the dance and
    splendour
of bigger lives, with due reverence and acknowledgement.

This statement from Lawrence's final years underscores the fact
that the basic co-ordinates of his version of the dying and reviving man-god are the necessity of death, the acceptance of a sacrificial communion, and the attainment of a new life.

[30] *GB*, I, 284, 406; II, 26; IV, 75, 167ff., 195; V, 3ff., 15-16, 26ff., 223ff.; VIII,
86ff., 95; IX, 300; X, 102-104; XI, 87, 94, 101ff., 243.

CHAPTER IX

D. H. Lawrence:
The Mythic Elements*

[I]

Turning from Lawrence's poetry to the central basis of his literary reputation, his fiction, is to confront the full extent and depth of his involvement in a mythopoeic vision grounded in substantial measure in the figurative patterns of *The Golden Bough*.

To begin with, his work, like *The Golden Bough*, is filled with a number of incarnational human forms. Unequivocally anthropological and religious are the names of Isis, Osiris, Adonis, Dionysus, Astarte, Bacchus, Pan, Venus, Persephone, Baal, Ashtaroth, Artemis, Cybele, and Balder. All these are leading characters in Frazer's drama of the dying and reviving god and his wife-mother-lover so that their appearance in such stories as "The Lady Bird," "St. Mawr," and "The Man Who Died" as well as *The Rainbow, Women in Love, The Lost Girl, Kangaroo*, and *The Plumed Serpent* makes this drama one of Lawrence's major *leitmotivs*. On occasion, as when Gerald Crich is likened to Dionysus in *Women in Love*, the references suggest a dual level on which the characters are operant: as human beings with roots in Lawrence's own experience and as mythical figures whose very names define the incarnation of qualities and actions otherwise inexplicable to mankind. That Lawrence's acquaintance with Frazer sharpened his sense of man's participation in the divine is suggested by comparing his first novel, *The White Peacock*, with those written after his avowed reading of *The Golden Bough*. Although the later novels make a sustained functional use of mythical figures, *The White Peacock* shows not only Lawrence's sense of the duality of his characters but his uncertainty

* *Modern Fiction Studies*, © 1959, by permission of Purdue Research Foundation, Lafayette, Indiana.

as to how to convey it dramatically. Thus, he contents himself with allusions whose significance rarely extends beyond the immediate scene. Most of these are drawn from the commonplaces of classical reading as characters are likened to Bacchantes, Hippomenes, Narcissus, Jove, and Charon, among others.

Not all the references to the great deities of comparative religion, however, are designed to underscore the archetypal role of his characters. They also serve at times to define the mental state of a character and so to relate that state to larger cultural issues either drawn from Lawrence's reading or from the world scene as it was at the time of the novel's composition. In Ursula Brangwen's early religious gropings in *The Rainbow*, for example, she becomes convinced that "she moved about in the essential days, when the sons of God came in unto the daughters of men."[1] And as a result of this vision, she denies the validity of the Frazerian comparative method for her: "Nor would any comparison of myths destroy her passion in the knowledge" (274). Jove, Pan, Bacchus, Apollo are rejected because they are not of her culture and because she has, in effect, dedicated herself to the Sons of God. Later, however, under the pressure of events, Ursula, with the help of Winifred Inger, her lesbian teacher, moves toward a position advocated by many just prior to World War I. Having eliminated the dogmas and falsehood of religion and humanized it, Ursula now is convinced that "all the religion she knew was but a particular clothing to a human aspiration. The aspiration was the real thing,—the clothing was a matter almost of national taste or need. The Greeks had a naked Apollo, the Christians a white-robed Christ, the Buddhists a royal prince, the Egyptians their Osiris. Religions were local and religion was universal. Christianity was a local branch. There was as yet no assimilation of local religions into universal religion" (340). And in accepting this view, she is following Jane Harrison and Gilbert Murray, both of whom were impressed by religion as a form of human aspiration. She also accepts an analysis of religious motives at least partly inspired by *The Golden Bough*. Like Frazer, Ursula and her friend regard fear as one of the central motives

---

[1] D. H. Lawrence, *The Rainbow* (London: Heinemann, 1950), p. 274. Subsequent references will be indicated in the text.

in religion, and feel superior to it. At the same time they recognize that what was feared was not necessarily all evil and that fear could be transformed into reverence.

Yet Lawrence does not confine himself simply to the major deities and fertility cults of the Semitic, Egyptian, Greek, and Scandinavian worlds. The nature and temperament of his characters are continually being defined with reference to maenads, dryads, fauns, and satyrs, out of whose coalescence the greater deities emerged, according to Frazer.[2] In one sense, Lawrence even seems to parallel this development of deities out of nameless spirits in his fiction. In *The White Peacock* George Saxton and Lettie Beardsall sit by an oak tree amid great purple hyacinths— both of which Frazer identifies as emblems of the dying god— while the latter longs for the existence of fauns and hamadryads so that their real emotional relation to one another might be defined and realized apart from the contemporary social world which has warped them and is now about to separate them.[3] The Dionysian passionate quality George shares with Gerald Crich is here felt only vaguely and left undefined in contrast to its specific identification in *Women in Love*. The difference is an index of Lawrence's increased familiarity with *The Golden Bough*, in which he found terms and concepts that clarified his intuition of the mysteries of human personality. The way in which Lawrence was moving is most clearly illustrated by that scene from *The Rainbow* in which Fred Brangwen's wedding is prepared for. Ursula's unformed nature, just awakening to the sensuous realities of nature and the human body, is caught in all its quicksilver elusiveness by being likened to "a frightened dryad" (306). At the same time her Uncle Tom, whose character is fixed and clear, receives a static definition as "the cynical Bacchus" (306) that is in keeping with his relatively minor role.

Actually, we can almost determine a character's importance to the action by the ways in which he is described. If he is a peripheral figure, appearing for but a scene or two, he is invariably described as one of the nameless spirits of nature. One such is An-

---

[2] *GB*, IV, 253; V, 233; III, 213.
[3] *GB*, I, 42; II, 361, 370ff.; V, 313; XI, 89ff.

thony Schofield of *The Rainbow* who fleetingly excites Ursula by his faun-like manner and satyr eyes. Another is little Dora Crich who appears as a small dryad who is devoid of a soul. When the character is a minor one but possesses some measure of importance in defining central themes or characters, he is often likened to a major deity, thereby providing, in effect, a shorthand description of a stock character. Such is the case with the previously mentioned Uncle Tom. Variations of this technique appear in the cases of Diana Crich, who choked her lover as they drowned, and Lady Artemis Hooper of *Aaron's Rod*. For major characters Lawrence employs both modes, as when Gerald Crich is aligned variously with a Nibelung, an undefined incarnation, a furious and destructive demon, as well as with Dionysus and Hermes.

Such references to nameless spirits serve a further purpose in Lawrence's fiction. In them we see the anthropological dimension with which Lawrence's concept of the spirit of place is endowed. Thus, in "St. Mawr" the New England woman and Louise Carrington feel that the landscape lives and that it possesses a spirit which senses the sacred nature of the female sex. And in this conviction the spirit of place embodies the interrelation of vegetative and human fertility and the primitive worship of both.[4] The beginnings of this notion, as of so much in Lawrence, can be seen in his first novel, *The White Peacock*, when Cyril, the narrator, sentimentally likens snowdrops to "forlorn little friends of dryads" and then associates them with some old, wild, lost religion such as that of the Druids.[5] A more typical attitude, however, is Alvina Houghton's in *The Lost Girl*, for she recognizes that not all places have friendly spirits or ones which will accommodate themselves to our habits and perspectives. Before she can enter "the pre-world, . . . the old eternity" on the edge of the Abruzzi,[6] she has to see that "there are places which resist us, which have the power to overthrow our psychic being. It seems as if every country had its potent negative centres, localities

---

[4] *GB*, I, 37; V, 39, 112ff.

[5] D. H. Lawrence, *The White Peacock* (London: Heinemann, 1950), p. 197. Subsequent references will be indicated in the text.

[6] D. H. Lawrence, *The Lost Girl* (London: Heinemann, 1950), p. 345. Subsequent references will be indicated in the text.

which savagely and triumphantly refuse our living culture"
(343).

In effect, Lawrence utilizes Frazer's concept of taboo as negative magic and as a dangerous physical power that needs to be
insulated. For Lawrence, it is a means of emphasizing both the
living quality of the natural world and also the protective nature
of space in creating geographical isolation.[7] The terror aroused
when a man sensitive to such primitive feelings comes in direct
contact with such a potent, negative center is most graphically
and sustainedly presented at the very beginning of *Kangaroo*.
Somers, confronted with the Australian bush, is roused to see the
trees as corpses and aborigines, to feel the mythic power of the
moon, and to sense the existence of a mysterious and unseen but
full-bodied presence that "not tired of watching its victim . . . was
biding its time with a terrible ageless watchfulness."[8] By skillfully
keeping this brooding presence in the forefront of the novel,
Lawrence endues the spirit of place with an added function. It
serves as a mythically aware audience before which the totemic
drama of the kangaroo, simultaneously animal, man, and country,
is enacted.

Objects of human veneration and respect such as spirits and
deities are not the only things upon which both Lawrence and
Frazer concentrated their attention. Intensification of mood,
clarification of character, and deepening of theme are all
achieved by invoking such creatures as devils, demons, and
ghosts. Sometimes they are mentioned only casually, as in "The
White Stocking" where the watchful husband is likened to
a ghost, or as in "Tickets, Please," which finds the spirit of the
devil in cripples and hunchbacks. The same is true of *The White
Peacock* and *The Trespasser* where the rich possibilities of calling Annable, the gamekeeper in the former, "a devil of the
woods" (224) are not exploited, and the trifling make-believe of
Helena in the latter results only in fanciful visions of dream
spirits.

At other times, however, they become central to the story as

---

[7] *GB*, I, 111ff.; x, 6ff.

[8] D. H. Lawrence, *Kangaroo* (London: Heinemann, 1950), pp. 9-10. Subsequent references will be indicated in the text.

with the title image of "The Captain's Doll," which is not only magical but is regarded by the Captain as a male devil arousing both fascination and repulsion. In "St. Mawr" Frazer's point about the variety of forms possessed by supernatural beings is illustrated by associating demons, devils, and ghosts with human beings (Mrs. Witt), animals (St. Mawr himself), and vegetation (the pine tree of Las Chivas).[9] Beginning with *The Rainbow* and continuing through to *The Plumed Serpent*, there is scarcely a Lawrence hero who is not at some time or other described by other characters or the author as a demon, devil, or ghost. Will Brangwen, Birkin, Lady Hermione, Gerald Crich, Cicio, Lilly, Somers and Harriet, Don Ramon, and Cipriano all are so presented as Lawrence endeavors to heighten and intensify his readers' appreciation of the evanescent moods and states of the human personality either as it appears to others or as it is when reacting to tensions and pressures generated by the external world.

As we would expect of an author familiar with Frazer's point about the potency of such beings, these descriptions are employed in two ways. At times they underscore the sudden powerful eruptions of the psyche to which so many of Lawrence's characters are prone. Such is Don Ramon's devil-like rage at the realization of his future betrayal by mankind. On other occasions, the descriptions reveal the monolithic inflexibility of society's perspectives and in so doing show the continued necessity of a readjustment of values. Here we think immediately of the struggle between Birkin and Hermione in *Women in Love* and of their characterizing each other as devils. Like Blake, Lawrence intimates that those most frequently said to be of the devil's party may in fact be touched with divinity, while the smooth faces of the established religion of society mask the diabolic nature that seeks to thwart, pervert, and destroy life. In situations where the thwarting and perversion have continued unchecked the result is what we see in "The Princess." There two human beings gradually metamorphose until at the end of their encounter they appear like two demons watching each other.

[9] *GB*, II, 33, 35, 42; VII, 270ff.; IX, 170ff., 213-214, 235; XI, 196ff., 201ff.

While many of these metaphoric identifications are of vicious, unpleasant persons, there are others which suggest that Lawrence shares Jane Harrison's view of the spiritual worth of the chthonic powers of the underworld.[10] For both Frazer and Lawrence they reflect one of man's deepest impulses and one which is fundamentally religious in character.[11] Thus, there is a world of difference between the sadistic Pauline of "The Lovely Lady" or the diabolic Ethel Cane of "None of That" and a representative miner like Mr. Pinnegar in "Jimmy and the Desperate Woman." In this connection, it is particularly interesting to note how often Lawrence's miners—the perfect image of the contemporary underworld—possess that inexpugnable quality of life and personal power that Frazer and Miss Harrison attribute to chthonic deities. This is recognized most fully by Alvina Houghton of *The Lost Girl* when she returns to the daylight world from her first visit to a mine:

> She watched the swing of the grey colliers along the pavement with a new fascination, hypnotised by a new vision. Slaves— the underground trolls and ironworkers, magic, mischievous, and enslaved, of the ancient stories. But tall—the miners seemed to her to loom tall and grey, in their enslaved magic. Slaves who would cause the superimposed day-order to fall. Not because, individually, they wanted to. But because, collectively, something bubbled up in them, the force of darkness which had no master and no control. It would bubble and stir in them as earthquakes stir the earth. It would be simply disastrous, because it had no master. There was no dark master in the world. The puerile world went on crying out for a new Jesus, another Saviour from the sky, another heavenly superman. When what was wanted was a Dark Master from the underworld (57).

This perception, however, is not something arrived at readily and at first glance. More often, as in the case of Gudrun Brangwen of *Women in Love*, the miners' world appears a ghostly rep-

---

[10] Harrison, *Prolegomena*, pp. 259-260, 340-344.
[11] *GB*, v, 88, 278; VII, 37.

lica of the real world peopled by ghouls and marked by sordidness. Yet its power is not to be denied. Ultimately Gudrun finds the difference between the mining town of Beldover and other cities to reside in its atmosphere of "a resonance of physical men" which she finds both "potent and half-repulsive."[12] These underworld men give off "a wave of disruptive force" that arouses both desire and callousness and is strangely in keeping with "their strange, distorted dignity, a certain beauty, and unnatural stillness in their bearing" (119). For Lawrence, the tragedy is that these descendants of the old chthonic powers have been warped into a mold that drains off enough of their ancient vitality to make them amenable to a machine-like life as "half-automatised colliers" (119). No "dark master" is likely to emerge from the pits.

The power of the underworld is not confined purely to the physical manifestation of the mines. There is, for Lawrence, also a psychological and personal underworld of awesome depths and potent influences. It is into this that Will Brangwen of *The Rainbow* is plunged when his bride seeks to return to the outside world of society and tea-parties from the sensual intimacy of their honeymoon. Both here and in the case of Gerald Crich, when he accepts marriage as a condemnation to the underworld, it is more nearly the classical concept of the underworld that is invoked, that which is conjured up by earlier references to Eurydice, Charon, and the Styx. But the psychological underworld also has its affinities with the phallic power and awesome mystery of the chthonic realm as seen by Miss Harrison. Nowhere is this more graphically revealed than in that scene in which Gudrun and Gerald struggle with Winifred's pet rabbit. Here they gain an "underworld knowledge" (253) of their joint passion of cruelty which evokes an unqualified sensuality devoid of personal regard. But because they are representative products of their age, they cannot accept the potency of such a world. Thus, though they are "implicated with each other in abhorrent mysteries," this association is "abhorrent to them both" (254). To

[12] D. H. Lawrence, *Women in Love* (London: Heinemann, 1950), p. 119. Subsequent references will be indicated in the text.

Gerald it means "letting through the forever unconscious, un-thinkable red ether of the beyond, the obscene beyond" (254) which is the psychic equivalent of those chthonic powers that lie, according to Miss Harrison, below and prior to the serene and rather cerebral Olympians.[13]

While the miner as chthonic power is a particularly striking example, it is by no means the only instance in which Lawrence's characters derive their primary significance from their function rather than from their individual personalities. One of the most important individuals to function archetypally is the stranger who, as in *The Golden Bough*, is a disturbing figure because of his aura of fertility and his apparently magical powers to influence others.[14] Such stories as "Odor of Chrysanthemums," "Samson and Delilah," "The Fox," and "The Border Line" testify both to the importance of this figure and also to the variety ascribed to it by Lawrence. In "The Fox," Lawrence, like Frazer, deals with the appearance of an actual physical stranger and the rites of propitiation and purification by which he is incorporated into the communal life of the farm. But elsewhere he uses the concept of the stranger as a mysterious power to illuminate the extent to which circumstances create strangers out of those most familiar to us. A wife confronted by the body of her dead husband finds that death has made him a stranger possessed of his own power of finality and completeness. Another faces her runaway husband who has returned, and despite her indignation capitulates to the potency resident in his appearing to the group as a stranger. Circumstances are not alone, however, in multiplying the number of strangers in our lives. To those people who live out of the deepest resources of their being, it is apparent that in some ultimate fashion individuals are always at bottom strangers to one another. Thus Kate Leslie finds that both as a sexual partner and as a person Cipriano cannot be grasped as a known entity: "She could not *know* him. When she tried to know him, something went slack in her, and she had to leave off. She had to let be. She had to leave him, dark and hot and potent, along with the

[13] Harrison, *Prolegomena*, pp. 11, 28-31.
[14] *GB*, III, 102; VII, 217, 225, 230, 253.

things that *are*, but are not known. The presence. And the stranger. This he was always to her."[15]

Men, however, are not the only ones who function archetypally as the stranger. Women, too, embrace this role both in their own right and in the minds of their men. The particular direction this action takes is charted most clearly in *The Rainbow*. There Tom Brangwen, who seeks in a woman "the embodiment of all his inarticulate, powerful religious impulses" (14), first meets a voluptuous woman and a foreigner of ancient breeding neither of whose names he knows, and then encounters Mrs. Lensky, his wife-to-be, who is not only a stranger but belongs to "another world of life" (27). And like the stranger of Frazer's primitive peoples, she is believed to possess "a curious communion with mysterious powers" (57), a quality that she never loses throughout her life and that impresses even her grandchildren.[16] So compelling is her power, her "potent, sensuous belief" (99), that she is able to envelop her husband in "a mystery of life and death and creation" (99) which is a ritual form of the Sacred Marriage that both Lawrence and Frazer see as the key to human fertility.[17]

Wrought up in this complex of the woman as stranger and the interrelation of divine and human fertility is a concept largely alien to Western and contemporary minds—that of the sacred prostitute who serves her god by submitting to strangers.[18] Lawrence utilizes this notion both to explore the inner recesses of the marital temper and to deepen his rendering of the man's reactions to the woman as stranger. With respect to the latter, Tom Brangwen is shown to fear what he does not know not because of his ignorance but because he dimly senses its archetypal lineaments: "His heart always filled with fear, fear of the unknown, when he heard his women speak of their bygone men as of strangers they had known in passing and had taken leave of again" (175). By a verbal *tour de force* Lawrence here conveys

---

[15] D. H. Lawrence, *The Plumed Serpent* (London: Heinemann, 1950), p. 421. Subsequent references will be indicated in the text.

[16] *GB*, III, 102, 112.   [17] *GB*, II, 120ff.; IV, 71, 73.

[18] *GB*, V, 36ff., 59.

the subtle interrelation of archetype and realism so that what emerges is the suggestion that to husbands wives may always be thought to have played the sacred prostitute with the men of their earlier life. This inability to fuse the religious and the sexual is most strikingly embodied in Julius Halliday of *Women in Love*. He alternates between religious mania and obscenity and so cannot see that Minette in acting as the harlot is actually also the object of his real worship which has nothing in common with his *fin-de-siècle* deluded longings for purity and abasement. When, however, the man is sufficiently integrated to accept these two apparently disparate modes, he can experience their fusion without anxiety or revulsion. Hence, Somers in *Kangaroo* recognizes in Victoria Callcott's smile something "like an offering—and yet innocent. Perhaps like the sacred prostitutes of the temple: acknowledgement of the sacredness of the act. . . . She seemed like an old Greek girl just bringing an offering to the altar of the mystic Bacchus. The offering of herself."[19] Yet the figures of stranger and sacred prostitute do not always function outside of marriage. For example, when Will Brangwen returns home after a period of tension with his wife Anna, she instinctively grasps the new dimension in their relationship: "All that had gone before was nothing to her. She was another woman, under the instance of a strange man. He was a stranger to her, seeking his own ends" (232). Under this image Lawrence probes the depths of marriage in order to show how it is bound up with the extremes of sensuality in which both parties abandon the ordinary moral position and seek "gratification pure and simple" (232).

Prominent as the stranger archetype is in Lawrence's fiction, there are others whose symbolic natures possess an equally profound anthropological orientation. One such is the virgin, who figures prominently in stories such as "The Virgin and the Gypsy" and "The Princess" as well as in *Sons and Lovers*, *The Lost Girl*, *Kangaroo*, and *The Plumed Serpent*. In effect, Lawrence here uses what he has learned from *The Golden Bough* about the religious role, the sacrificial character, and the fertility associations

[19] The "sacred prostitute" reference unequivocally reveals Frazer's impact. See *GB*, v, 36-39.

of virgins to a twofold end.[20] On the one hand, he endeavors to picture contemporary virgins who possess just these qualities so that the sense of regarding life with reverence, awe, and delight, as he thought Frazer's early civilizations did, will be borne in upon his readers. On the other hand, he also sketches pitilessly the virgins of the modern world who lack the divine potency of their predecessors and whose lives are therefore compounded of hesitant timidity and self-centered arrogance. In his total canon, the two types are juxtaposed so that Kate's regaining of her virginity through marriage to Huitzilopchtli is the logical extension of Yvette Saywell's encounter with the stranger. Both point up the lack of fulfillment and the inadequacy of Miriam and her bitterly satirized concomitant, Dollie Urquhart.

Another archetypal figure is the witch or magician, who hovers in appropriately vague and sinister fashion over the action of "Wintry Peacock" or "Mother and Daughter," for example. Unlike the other types, however, these are for Lawrence of a lesser order of reality, perhaps as a result of his announced antipathy to magic.[21] In any event, his identification of characters as witches or magicians is consistently more metaphorical than literal. The aim is to catch some particular aspect of a person's physical appearance that eludes more ordinary comparisons, as when Paul Morel likens Lily to a youthful witch-woman because of the daisies in her hair, or Gudrun's voice is called witch-like in *Women in Love*, or Julia Bricknell of *Aaron's Rod* is seen as a witch because of her habit of sitting in a hunched position. Or else it is to isolate some specific but intangible quality of the individual's personality, to serve as a kind of preliminary and groping definition of his essential nature. It is this that Paul is doing when he ponders why red berries in Miriam's hair would make her look "like some witch or priestess, and never like a reveller."[22] The same is true of Alvina Houghton's discovery that the little Alexander Graham, even though absent, is capable of

---

[20] *GB*, I, 38, 155; II, 155, 198, 229, 326; V, 60.
[21] *The Collected Letters*, I, 550.
[22] D. H. Lawrence, *Sons and Lovers* (London: Heinemann, 1950), p. 222. Subsequent references will be indicated in the text.

appearing before her as "terribly large, potent and magical" (32). An even more breathtaking awesomeness is encountered by Ursula when she feels that Birkin's dancing is aided by some form of black magic.

Other important archetypes are those of the hanged man and the scapegoat. The former is particularly useful in tracing Lawrence's development, in seeing the manner in which the complexity of an image evolves. "A Fragment of Stained Glass," "The Thorn in the Flesh," and "The Man Who Died" chart the manner in which first Christian and then ancient religious associations of divinity accrue to the stark figure of the hanged man. Similarly, stories as different as "England, My England" and "The Princess" together illuminate the duality of the scapegoat figure as well as its capacity for sustaining irony. And back of these figures, bulking large in *The Golden Bough*, too, are the warriors, hunters, farmers, peasants, and primitive savages whose social and personal needs give rise to the myths and rituals found in Lawrence and Frazer.[23] Indeed, in "The Man Who Loved Islands" there is even a satiric portrait of the sort of person who was one of Frazer's earliest and most avid readers. And though Sir Compton Mackenzie was Lawrence's actual target, the picture of the gentleman scholar who possesses a vast knowledge about a number of practical subjects, is interested in the classics and aware of bygone ritual combats and sacrifices such as those in the grove at Nemi also calls to mind the author of *The Golden Bough* and Lawrence's attitude toward him.

[II]

Densely populated as Lawrence's work is with the figures of comparative religion, this is not its only affinity with the primitive world of *The Golden Bough*. Time and again the characters exhibit those mental phenomena, those modes of thought and belief that Frazer chronicled with such a wealth of illustration. Levels of consciousness from the rational to the most intuitive are as graphically presented in stories like "Glad Ghosts," "St. Mawr," "The Rocking-Horse Winner," and "The Blind Man" as they are

[23] *GB*, I, 109, 211, 236; II, 104; III, 157ff.; VI, 30, 218; VII, 169, 204; VIII, 274ff.; IX, 98; XI, 224ff.

in *The Golden Bough*. The same is equally true, of course, of the novels, many of which may be viewed, at least in part, as patterns of tension between the ordinary, common-sense mode of consciousness and the blood-consciousness which, as we have already seen, Lawrence linked so closely to the contents of Frazer's work. In point of fact, the same tension inheres in *The Golden Bough* itself, for set against the calm, sceptical, rationalistic temper of the author is an abundance of evidence that the human mind is capable of operating or at least of being conceived as operating in terms of prophetic foresight, shamanistic trances, mass psychology, and the denial of common-sense categories of thought.

The White Peacock shows a man unable to articulate his sensuous perceptions, who is identified as a "primitive man" (31), being sacrificed in a psychological dismemberment that is in keeping with the heroine's view of him as a bull, a dumb beast whose death feeds others. Similarly, death awaits Siegmund of *The Trespasser*, who demands of the anemone that he get "a sympathetic knowledge of its experience, into his blood" (81) before he will be satisfied. For him suicide is inescapable, for he confronts a world that denies his gropings for a deeper awareness of the rhythms of life. At the same time he faces a woman whose characteristic form of consciousness is only a civilized and affected dabbling with the powers of sensuous perception, whose chief delight is to think that "the rippling sunlight on the sea was the Rhine maidens spreading their bright hair in the sun" (51). Like Frazer, Lawrence sees that some manners of thinking go back to the dimmest reaches of man's existence and that they persist dimly and confusedly into the present.[24] In *The Lost Girl* Alvina Houghton's "ancient sapience went deep, deeper than Woodhouse could fathom" (29). And as a result of "her mediumistic soul" (344) she is able to gain in Italy "a sense of ancient gods who knew the right for human sacrifice" (344). The strongest concentration of primitive awareness is found, however, not in the urban bourgeois but in those folk whose manner of life is the lineal descendant of their ancestors. The surpassing capacity for "blood-intimacy" exhibited by the Brangwens derives from

[24] *GB*, I, 236; III, 419ff.

their having lived for generations in a natural environment that reiterates with a murmurous insistence the primitive awareness of vegetative, animal, and seasonal cycles and rhythms. What they lack is the energy and desire to explore the nature, functions, and significance of this kind of consciousness. This is left to the Lawrence hero whose name is variously Birkin, Aaron, Somers, and Don Ramon.

Another particularly striking aspect of this matter of levels of consciousness is the idea of spells and magic in general. Lawrence probably describes more characters as "spell-bound" and does so more repeatedly than any other writer of recent times. Through their recurrent use, especially in contexts of great dramatic intensity and mythopoeic overtones, he refurbishes such time-worn phrases and invests them with some of their original potency. "Daughters of the Vicar," "The Captain's Doll," and "The Border Line," all have characters who exercise and react to spells that are both deliberately imposed and the by-product of the impact of one personality on another. These spells usually exist between a man and a woman who are aware of one another as desirable but unknown and therefore dangerous, but they also obtain between parent and child, as in "The Christening" and "England, My England," and *The Rainbow*. When a character behaves as though under a spell but there is no human agent, he is exhibiting the state of possession in which, according to Frazer, he is in the power of a spirit who may be either divine, evil, or human but dead.[25] Such is the state in which *The Rainbow* pictures Ursula during the climactic scene with Skrebensky on the moonlit beach.

Other aspects of magic used in Lawrence's work to reveal relationships, the incalculable nature of the human mind, and the mystery of the natural but living world further demonstrate the extent to which he was imbued with the material of *The Golden Bough*. Frazer's point that talismans and amulets serve both as protection against evil spirits and as a place of safekeeping for one's soul underlies the image of the thimble in "The Lady Bird."[26] Similarly, the magical use of images appears in the man-

[25] *GB*, IV, 25ff.; V, 66, 68, 72ff.; VI, 192ff.; XI, 186.
[26] *GB*, IX, 95; XI, 155.

nikin or puppet in "The Captain's Doll" and *Sons and Lovers* as well as in the bloodstone of "A Fragment of Stained Glass" and the picture of "The Primrose Path."[27] The role of special languages for particular occasions and the magical significance of names and sounds are touched on in *The Lost Girl*, *The Plumed Serpent*, and *The Rainbow*.[28] Figuring more or less prominently in "The Captain's Doll" and "St. Mawr" is the capacity for second sight, while trances, either imposed or induced, momentary or prolonged, reflect the psychic state of characters in "Jimmy and the Desperate Woman," "The Rocking-Horse Winner," *Women in Love*, and *The Plumed Serpent*.[29] And, finally, we find mediums together with all the other apparatus of spiritualism, as in "Glad Ghosts" and "The Lovely Lady" or *The Lost Girl*. Included are sinister physical transformations such as the metamorphosis of the policeman's foot into a clubbed limb "like the weird paw of some animal" in "The Last Laugh."

Beyond their physical and mental qualities Lawrence's characters share other things with Frazer's primitive peoples. Like Frazer, Lawrence possessed a deep and persistent interest in those human actions whose importance derives as much from their being performed by the majority of people as from their being essential to human existence. He focussed on death, marriage, fornication, initiation, dancing, sacrifice, departure and arrival, and many other actions not merely because the conventions of fiction demand a kind of loose realism but because they are performed, consciously or not, in ritualistic fashion. The very manner of their performance testifies to their connection with the sacred existence, that is, the order in which the mysterious potency of life itself resides. Typical of Lawrence's use of ritual actions are those works that revolve around death or sex. In "The Prussian Officer," for example, the struggle between the two men occurs in a grove whose trees are likened to human bodies and whose presiding spirit is a horse. The parallels with the ritual combat in the grove at Nemi between the warrior-priest and the runaway slave in which victory entails a new and unknown life

[27] *GB*, I, 55, 70-74; III, 26ff., 53ff., 62ff., 96; 419ff.; IX, 187.
[28] *GB*, III, 358ff., 375, 380, 396-413.
[29] *GB*, I, 187ff.; IX, 380.

that leads to a final defeat are both obvious and significant. Even more deliberately ritualistic is the sacrificial death undergone by the central figure in "The Woman Who Rode Away." Similarly "The Last Laugh" shows the swift retribution visited upon the man who penetrates the mystery of the god's existence and approaches too closely to the divine but dangerous power.

In the novels it is such powerfully ritualistic scenes that carry the burden of thematic development as well as of narrative progression. Thus, in *The Rainbow* the end of one stage in the life of the Brangwen family is signalled by Tom's death by drowning during a great flood whose realism never obscures its mythic significance. This dual nature of the flood is reflected in his wife's reactions to his death. At first, she is overcome with terror and horror at the transformation death has wrought in her husband "who had been to her the image of power and strong life" (247). Then, as his body lies naked and washed, the ritual of divestiture and purification exerts its power so that what emerges before her consciousness is "the majesty of the inaccessible male, the majesty of death. It made her still and awe-stricken, almost glad" (248). Particularly interesting here is the fact that Lawrence has the wife and son take antithetical attitudes toward the death, which reflect Frazer's distinction between European and primitive views. According to him, the former is marked by a fear of death, the reaction of Fred who cries tearlessly "like a stricken animal" (247) and regards the death as murder.[30] Lydia, on the other hand, approximates the primitive response which treats death as an event to be accepted with an equanimity bordering on indifference.[31] And it is because of this response that she can share with Frazer's ancient peoples the belief in man's natural immortality and rest content in the conviction that "he had made himself immortal in his knowledge with her. So she had her place here, in life, and in immortality" (256).[32]

As for those scenes involving a ritualistic approach to sex, the most formal are those in *The Plumed Serpent* between Kate and Cipriano. In the chapter entitled "Malintzi" the earlier marriage of Cipriano and Kate is consummated in the wedding of

[30] *GB*, IV, 135ff., 146.　　　　　　[31] *GB*, IV, 9ff., 136ff.
[32] *GB*, IV, 1.

the deities Huitzilopochtli and Malintzi, just as Frazer pointed out that ancient cultures were fond of having human beings fulfill in dramatic ritual the mythic functions of their deities.[33] But what is even more significant in this chapter is the degree to which ritual overshadows the sexual act itself. Cipriano's request, the dress of the goddess, the saluting of the gods, the lighting of the god's lamp, and the silent waiting on the thrones, all are dwelt on in detail and presented in Lawrence's most incantatory prose. In contrast, the focal point of these rites, the consummation itself is tacit, occurring in the unspoken silence intervening between two sentences: "She closed her eyes, and was dark. Then later, when she opened her eyes and saw the bud of flame just above her, and the black idol invisibly crouching, she heard his strange voice" (420-421). Such a proportion clearly is Lawrence's method of stressing the importance of the ritual, of the manner in which human beings approach their most critical experience. The function of ritual, as this scene demonstrates, is not to furnish opportunities for spectacle but to inculcate the emotions and states of mind appropriate to the situation.

Less elaborately but with equal intentness, the sexual encounters of Miriam and Paul in *Sons and Lovers* are presented with ritualistic overtones such as those of sacrifice, immolation, baptism, and initiation. And what is touched on only fleetingly by Paul is developed at length by Ursula in *The Rainbow*, namely, the complex and profound connections between death and sex. During her brother Fred's wedding she and Skrebensky wander outdoors amid a darkness "which seemed to breathe like the sides of some great beast" (315). Against a background of the dance which is "a vision of the depths of the underworld, under the great flood" (316) and beneath a moon whose watchful presence arouses her desire for communion and consummation with it, Ursula and Skrebensky enact their ritual of the destructive power of sex. Despite his fear and terror of the moonlit stacks of corn, Skrebensky follows Ursula seeking to impose his will and to compel her psychic submission.

What follows, however, is Lawrence's ironic version of the

[33] *GB*, v, 110, 223, 285ff.; IX, 386.

myth of Dionysus' death at the hands of the Bacchantes. Her initial ecstatic desire "to let go" (315) intensifies to the point where
"her feet and hands beat like a madness" (316) and she is on the
verge of flinging away her clothing and fleeing over the hills to
the moon. But Skrebensky stands in her way, a burdensome persistent presence, and as a result, "a sudden lust seized her, to lay
hold of him and tear him and make him into nothing" (319). The
sexual combat, centering in the kiss, ends with "her soul crystal-
lised with triumph" while he is "the victim, consumed, annihilated" (320). At this point, she returns from the dark consciousness of transcendent myth to the "temporary warm world
of the commonplace" (321) and is overwhelmed with fear and
horror of her deepest nature so that she embarks on a fresh stage
of the myth of Dionysus, that in which his resurrection is
enacted.

Here Lawrence again follows Frazer, who draws attention to
the similarity between the rites of Dionysus and Osiris.[34] For Ursula, in her determination to "bring him back from the dead"
(321), assumes the manner of Isis who brought back Osiris from
the dead by collecting the fragments of his dismembered body.[35]
Thus, she, like Isis the ideal wife,[36] does "him homage of loving
awareness" and is "his servant, his adoring slave" until "she restored the whole shell of him. She restored the whole form and
figure of him" (321). Nor does the parallel end here any more
than Lawrence's irony does. Just as Isis was unable to recover a
vital portion of Osiris' body so Ursula's efforts cannot alter the
fact that in Skrebensky "the core was gone" (321). And like Frazer, Lawrence seems to record that it was the man's genital organs that were missing, for he says: "as a distinct male he had no
core. His triumphant, flaming, overweening heart of the intrinsic
male would never beat again" (321).[37] The punishment meted
out to Skrebensky because of the fact that he "never loved, never
worshipped, only just physically wanted her" (315) is as psychologically severe as the physical suffering of Dionysus and Osiris
and is as rooted as they are in The Golden Bough. For as Frazer
insists, ancient peoples scrupulously affirmed the interrelation of

[34] GB, VI, 113, 127.
[36] GB, VI, 117ff.

[35] GB, VI, 10-13, 50, 85; VII, 262.
[37] GB, VI, 10, 102.

the divine and the human and worshipped the two simultaneously as parts of an integral whole.[38] It is just this that Skrebensky has failed to do and he envies the barge-man, his "worshipping the body and spirit of the girl, with a desire that knew the inaccessibility of its object, but was only glad to know that the perfect thing existed, glad to have had a moment of communion" (314-315).

Lawrence, then, as well as Frazer, was aware of the fact that danger attends not only contact with sacred or divine persons but also participation or involvement in sexual relations.[39] From the behavior of many of his characters it is apparent they would agree with Ernest Crawley's remark in his study of primitive marriage, *The Mystic Rose*, that "all persons are potentially dangerous to others, as well as potentially in danger, in virtue simply of the distinction between man and man."[40] Stories such as "Daughters of the Vicar," "Second Best," and "The Horse Dealer's Daughter" develop with considerable power this feeling of the danger inherent in love and entrance into the marriage state. Similarly, in *The Rainbow* Tom Brangwen feels terror in the presence of his wife because of her strangeness, and despairs of being able "to yield himself naked out of his own hands into the unknown power" (53) which she embodies. And as if to stress Frazer's point about fear as a source of religion, Lawrence introduces as the key image in the scene one from Christian ritual: "The time of trial and his admittance, his Gethsemane and his Triumphal Entry in one, had come now" (53).

Women in Love continues this theme with elaborations of its own, for through the relation of Gudrun and Gerald is defined the nature of sexual attraction: "her passion was a transcendent fear of the thing he was" (350). It also borrows from *The Golden Bough* the form in which it finds this dangerous power manifesting itself. To describe the primitive concept of sacred power Frazer invokes the idea of a psychic or spiritual electricity.[41] Gerald

[38] *GB*, I, 373ff; II, 177; IX, 278 *passim*.
[39] *GB*, III, 132ff; XI, 277ff.
[40] Ernest Crawley, *The Mystic Rose*, rev. ed. by T. Besterman (New York: Boni & Liveright, 1927), I, 39. The same passage appears in the first edition of 1902.
[41] *GB*, I, 371.

confronting Minette and recognizing in her a victim feels himself possessed of a "turgid and voluptuously rich" electricity by which he will be able "to destroy her utterly in the strength of his discharge" (66). And later Gudrun finds that "her soul was destroyed with the exquisite shock of his invisible fluid lightning" (351).

Frazer attributes this power not to individuals but to certain classes or groups of persons.[42] Lawrence locates this quality in many of his more important male characters, though with the difference that he implies that it is available to all men would they but discover it within themselves. Gerald is not the only one in *Women in Love* who possesses this power; Birkin, too, has it and in even greater and deeper measure. As the result of actual contact, of touching him, Ursula discovers that "it was a dark flood of electric passion she released from him, drew into herself. She had established a rich new circuit, a new current of passional electric energy, between the two of them, released from the darkest poles of the body and established in perfect circuit" (330). Here, however, it is one of the sons of God and a daughter of men who approach one another with ritual gestures of worship; consequently, the dangerous power is channeled into new and creative forms.

Lawrence also utilizes *The Golden Bough*'s accounts of men who have lost touch with their divine source of strength and power as a background for a quest of recovery.[43] This appears most notably in *Aaron's Rod*, where Aaron had been existing only by denying and suppressing his own virile power. But after playing his flute for the Marchesa and restoring her to a fullness of being, he finds his own power released and restored to him so that "he moved about in the splendour of his own male lightning, invested in the thunder of the male passion-power. He had got it back, the male godliness, the male godhead" (270). By identifying this power as "royal, Jove's thunderbolt" (270), Lawrence also underscores his awareness of Frazer's observation about lightning being regarded as the descent of a god.[44] At the same time he links it with what he had learned from the anthropologist

[42] *GB*, III, 131-138.   [43] *GB*, IV, 14ff., 21ff.; VI, 154, 163.
[44] *GB*, XI, 298-299.

314

and his own intuitions concerning the primacy of phallic observances in human life.[45]

Dangerous as the relation between the sexes may be, it is not seen by Lawrence as inspiring only terror and spiritual annihilation. Stories such as "The Shades of Spring" and "Sun," for example, reflect Frazer's emphasis on the beneficent custom of human beings' miming the rite of the Sacred Marriage in which male and female fertility deities guarantee the perpetuation and flourishing of all forms of life.[46] So, despite its initial terrors, does Tom Brangwen's marriage in *The Rainbow*. Ultimately he and his wife, gaining a full knowledge of the rite's significance, find it "the entry into another circle of existence, it was the baptism to another life, it was the complete confirmation" (91). They realize that this is because the god, who for them has a Christian form, has both incarnated himself in them and revealed this to them. It is toward some sense of this divine union that occurs behind the tangible human marriage that Birkin is groping early in *Women in Love* when he asserts that " 'there remains only this perfect union with a woman—sort of ultimate marriage—and there isn't anything else' " (59). But he is hampered in his understanding of this rite by his denial of the monotheistic God of society. Later he finds his kinship with the Egyptian Pharoahs, who, Frazer points out, were both deified and the ritual enactors of the myth of Osiris, including his resurrection.[47] With this he shares their "immemorial potency" which is "magical, mystical, a force in darkness, like electricity" (335). Then he is able to celebrate the real union, apart from any civil ceremony, in which he finds "his resurrection and his life" (390).

An even clearer perception of the nature and rationale of this belief is expressed by Somers who learns in *Kangaroo* of the great danger inherent in human love and how to counteract it. The solution lies in "the God who is the source of all passion," for "once go down before the God-passion and human passions take their right rhythm. But human love without the God-passion always kills the thing it loves" (222). To acknowledge the dependency of human life on maintaining a ritual concord with the di-

---

[45] *GB*, II, 97-98ff., 284, 287.   [46] *GB*, II, 120ff.
[47] *GB*, I, 148ff; VI, 151, 153, 155ff.

vine image of fertility is an abstract formulation of one of the central beliefs propounded in *The Golden Bough*. The concrete embodiment of this belief in the necessity and vitality of a Sacred Marriage is found, as we have seen, in *The Plumed Serpent*, where the full pomp and splendor of ancient celebrations of the rite are captured.

Not all the ritualistic actions of Lawrence's characters, however, are of such an unusual order; many are concerned with human behavior in the face of practical problems in daily life. Perhaps the best example of this is the miner's method of cleaning himself after a day underground. The practice of kneeling on the hearthrug, stripped to the waist, and washing in a large basin is one to which Lawrence often refers in *Sons and Lovers*, *The Rainbow*, and elsewhere. Three stories in particular, "Daughters of the Vicar," "A Sick Collier," and "Jimmy and the Desperate Woman," chart both its recurrence and Lawrence's own developing comprehension of its ritualistic character. The first two stories stress the habitual, unconscious movements involved, the feelings of awe and fear aroused, and the underlying phallic core of object and attitude. The last emphasizes the hypnotic fascination it generates and defines its anthropological role by repeatedly calling it a ritual.

Other actions whose ritual quality Lawrence assumes attain a significance by virtue of their number and in so doing attest to the degree to which his mind was permeated by the point of view of *The Golden Bough*. Even the most ordinary and commonplace of incidents are touched with it, as when in *The White Peacock* Lettie plucks flowers "as if it were a rite" (199) or in *Women in Love* Gudrun's brushing of her hair is called "part of the inevitable ritual of her life" (437). In such cases, Lawrence adapts Frazer's notion that ritual is dramatized myth, for in these actions there resides the quintessential story of the character's nature and life.[48] The same is true of Gerald's party behavior, which Gudrun describes as being " 'a whole saturnalia in himself' " (416). By this remark she seeks to convey his underlying dissatisfaction with the life and world he is dedicated to advancing.

In other instances, however, the ritual is magical and designed

48 *GB*, x, 105.

to protect the performer or the subject. Thus, Siegmund of *The Trespasser*, like Frazer's mock kings, enjoys a five-day exalted interlude from his ordinary life before his death.[49] During it he removes, he thinks, all his past spiritual and psychological afflictions by bathing in the sea. For him it is a "purification" and he is once again "a happy priest of the sun."[50] A similar purgative act on the part of Mrs. Morel is suggested by the chapter heading in *Sons and Lovers*, "The Casting Off of Morel—The Taking On of William." More deliberately ritualistic, dominated by rhythm, incantation, and rapt participation, is Lilly's massaging of the lower half of Aaron's body in order to free his soul and restore to him the spark of life.

The most sustained form of ritual participation in Lawrence, however, is found in the variety of dances whose significance is so heavily stressed throughout his work. From the solitary dance of worship directed to the Unknown Creator by the pregnant Anna Brangwen, through that commanded by Hermione and that performed before the cattle by Ursula and Gudrun, and on to the mass participation found in *The Plumed Serpent*—all involve the enacting of a drama of individual or communal emotion by means of gesture and motion. In each case, the participants become aware of or worship a divine power by celebrating or miming events they feel to be true and important. The result is invariably a transcendence of each one's normal range of perception and a merging of personal feelings with something larger.

A third class of rites in Lawrence have a different goal. These are rites designed to evaluate the performer. Instances that come to mind are the chapter title "The Test of Miriam" in *Sons and Lovers*, which summarizes the pattern of events the chapter delineates, and Gerald's watching his father die. Of the latter: "It was a trial by ordeal. Could he stand and see his father slowly dissolve and disappear in death, without once yielding his will, without once relenting before the omnipotence of death. Like a Red Indian undergoing torture, Gerald would experience the whole process of slow death without once wincing or flinching"

[49] *GB*, IV, 114; IX, 355, 357.
[50] D. H. Lawrence, *The Trespasser* (London: Heinemann, 1950), p. 72. Subsequent references will be indicated in the text.

(340). And perhaps the most sustained example of this function of ritual is found in the wrestling combat between Birkin and Gerald where the struggle serves, as do many of those recounted by Frazer, to initiate the combatants into physical intimacy, to test courage and endurance, and to determine the essential truth of the individual.[51]

<h2 style="text-align:center">[III]</h2>

Complementing the mythic and ritualistic qualities of Lawrence's characters and their actions is their physical background, the natural phenomena with which the author invests their world and to which they respond. Their associations with the fertility deities of the ancient world are accentuated by the images of vegetative fertility which run through many of the tales and novels. In "The Prussian Officer," one of Lawrence's earliest and best stories, the woman, the golden wheat, and the green corn coalesce into an image reminiscent of Frazer's Corn Goddess.[52] Throughout *The Rainbow* Frazer's association between vegetative and human fertility is dramatized by such events as the synchronization of the corn harvest with the last months of Lydia Brangwen's pregnancy, the relating of the sheaving to sexual attraction in the case of Will and Anna, and the juxtaposing of the autumnal harvest and the marriage of Fred Brangwen.[53] Similarly, in *Women in Love* Lawrence conveys Ursula's growing alienation from Gerald and Gudrun and the strange frozen world that is theirs by presenting her as passionately longing for direct sensuous contact with the earthy fecundity of vegetation.

The majority of these instances reveal the natural flourishing of lives that maintain contact with the underlying rhythms of the physical world. But like Frazer, Lawrence does not forget the profound symbolic effect the first signs of growth have on persons emerging from a winter world. Thus, the gradual revival and awakening of the woman in "Sun" is described in terms of ripening grapes and gourds, while her retreat is guarded by a single cypress tree which Frazer describes as sacred to the heal-

<hr />

[51] *GB*, I, 88ff.; II, 89ff., 322; VI, 17ff., 71, 77; VII, 74ff., 153ff., 219ff.
[52] *GB*, VII, 41, 42, 63, 263.
[53] *GB*, II, 489ff.; V, 39, 67; XI, 32, 42ff.

318

ing god's sanctuary.[54] Virtually the identical image appears in *The Plumed Serpent* when Kate first moves toward the world of legend and myth by travelling across the lake to Don Ramon's home. She recognizes in herself and her male Mexican boatmen a flowering of the soul which is the gift of grace from the greater mystery. What she experiences is "the fulfillment filling her soul like the fulness of ripe grapes" (115), and she contrasts it with love as she knew it with her husband by thinking that "this is the fullness of the vine" (116).

The vine and grape references suggest that Lawrence is using them with an awareness that Frazer linked them to Dionysus and his surrogates such as Pan and Bacchus.[55] In addition there are other images which show how extensively Lawrence saw his landscapes and natural settings with the eyes of the ancient peoples who appear in *The Golden Bough*.[56] Pine trees, for example, which are central to the rites of Attis and Osiris, appear as a mythopoeic vegetative form in "St. Mawr," "The Border Line," and "The Man Who Died."[57] Equally sacred to primitive Europeans and even more numerous, according to Frazer, are oak trees, which in both "A Fragment of Stained Glass" and "The Shades of Spring" as well as *The White Peacock* Lawrence associates with the hyacinth, the flower of the dead king.[58]

Catching up many of these images into a single complex is that scene in *Women in Love* where Birkin, naked, moves through a wild valley after Hermione has struck him with a paper-weight. Here he engages in a series of actions that are nonetheless ritualistic for being unpremeditated. He rolls his naked body amid hyacinths, covers it with handfuls of grass, stings his thighs and shoulders with fir and hazel branches, and clasps a birch tree to his chest. As the context shows clearly, this scene presents Birkin's withdrawal from the world of the present typified by Hermione and his endeavor to come into contact with something capable of fulfilling him. And when we remember Hermione's "drugged, almost sinister religious expression" (109) and her ecstatic manner, it is apparent that he is responding instinctively

---

[54] *GB*, II, 10; V, 81, 165.
[56] *GB*, VII, 2.
[58] *GB*, V, 313ff.

[55] *GB*, V, 166; VII, 2-3ff., 165.
[57] *GB*, V, 264 *passim*; VI, 108.

and with primitive acumen. He seeks out trees reputed to afford protection against witches, and performs actions, such as rolling on the ground and submitting to a kind of whipping, which variously constitute rituals of purification, protection, and fertility.[59]

The same sort of symbolic background is provided by recurrent references to anemones, almond blossoms, mistletoe, hyacinths, and ivy. All these *The Golden Bough* shows to be vegetative signs and representatives of the great fertility deities like Adonis and Dionysus.[60] The concentration of Siegmund of *The Trespasser* on anemones has already been mentioned. An even more mythic awareness of them is evidenced in *The Lost Girl* when Alvina recognizes the inevitability and desirability of a change in her relation with her old governess: "Black-purple and red anemones were due, real Adonis blood, and strange individual orchids, spotted and fantastic. Time for Miss Frost to die" (44). At the end of the same novel, Alvina, herself pregnant, sees spring in Italy come in a fashion that shows a firm sense of Frazer's treatment of the myths of vegetative deities. To her the scent of the wild narcissus is "powerful and magical" (362), reminding her of the green-clad caroler at Christmas, who echoes the leaf-adorned mummer of *The Golden Bough*.[61] The month of March brings a lavish flowering of violets, almond blossoms, lavender crocuses, and sprays of peach and apricot, all of which, Frazer observes, are emblematic either of major fertility deities or of rites of protection against harm.[62] Then, "she felt like going down on her knees and bending her forehead to the earth in an oriental submission, they were so royal, so lovely, so supreme" (363). In contrast to the Christian church, which is suffused with "the sense of trashy, repulsive, degraded fetish-worship" (364), the vegetative world is not only beautiful but significant. Against a background of flourishing corn, maize, and vines, hyacinths remind her of "the many breasted Artemis" (364) and the anemones of the tears shed by Venus for Adonis. Finally, Lawrence's first novel, *The White Peacock*, imitates the central core of *The Golden Bough*: it too poses the question of the significance of a

[59] *GB*, I, 207, 301; II, 54, 103-104; IX, 260, 270-271; XI, 185.
[60] *GB*, V, 226, 263ff., 313-315; VI, 112; XI, 76ff., 279, 283.
[61] *GB*, II, 75-76, 79, 343.　　　　　　[62] *GB*, V, 263, 267; IX, 146, 213.

scene in which a man and a woman enter a wood and while they feel themselves "in another world" (151), he breaks off a sprig of mistletoe. Less central to the story but fully as revealing is the wife's ironic identification, in "Two Blue Birds," of herself with the mistletoe as " 'the parasite on the British oak' " (738).

On the animal level, the mythic dimension of Lawrence's fiction is conveyed through the weight of significance given to such creatures as the horse, the snake, the fox, the rat, the scarab, the pigeon, the dove, the mole, the lamb, and the cock, each of which figures in the myths, rites, and superstitions explored by Frazer.[63] The same sort of stress is placed on the mythical nature and magical properties of such phenomena as the sun, the moon, water, and fire. In stories like "Sun," "The Horse Dealer's Daughter," "The Lady Bird," "The Woman Who Rode Away," and "The Man Who Died," and in novels like *The Plumed Serpent*, *Women in Love*, *The Rainbow*, and *The Trespasser* they become central to the meaning of the story. They are closely linked to the behavior of the characters, who see in them not so much objects as omens, talismans, ritual modes, and mythical beings that lead them to a further and deeper participation in the drama of existence.

The foregoing survey demonstrates that Lawrence's fiction contains a wealth of material drawn from Frazer's anthropology and comparative religion. Needless to say, however, certain myths and rites play a more important part than do others in shaping theme and structure. At the risk of oversimplification we can resolve Lawrence's fiction into six main categories, which constitute a progression from the obvious and apparent to the subtle and hidden presence of myth and ritual. At one end of the scale, representing a concealed anthropological dimension, is a story such as "England, My England" and novels like *The White Peacock*, *The Trespasser*, and, in part, *Aaron's Rod*, which are based on the myth of the scapegoat and the rites of passage leading to his expulsion. Equally interesting is the use to which Lawrence puts these beliefs and observances. His penchant for social,

[63] *GB*, I, 90, 151, 152, 200, 381; II, 149-150; III, 13, 226; V, 33, 147, 279; VII, 15, 276ff., 296ff.; VIII, 42ff., 143, 283, 287ff., 314ff.; IX, 191, 371; XI, 104, 138, 140, 199, 200, 209ff., 223.

cultural, historical, and spiritual jeremiads on modern life, especially that of the middle and upper classes, is as well known as it is important. Not much notice, however, has been taken of the way in which, as in "England, My England," he employs myth as a way of emphasizing his major criticism.[64] For him, myth functions as a satiric device by offering contrast between the mythico-ritualistic life of ancient man and that of contemporary man, which is profane because commonplace and ordinary. It also affords an ironic sense of the continuity between the two worlds that shows how the one may be both a degeneration and an adaptation of the other.

The second category deals with myths of the Andromeda type in which a virgin faces a sacrificial death and attains a salvation which, as Lawrence would insist, is only partly secular. The central rites here are those of purification and revivification by water and fire, a point made clear by the most obvious representatives of this type, "The Virgin and the Gypsy" and "The Horse Dealer's Daughter." In such stories and in *Sons and Lovers* and *The Lost Girl* Lawrence's use of myth and ritual is primarily structural: the myth serves as a concealed pattern which organizes the narrative into a ritual sequence. The third category reveals the presence of myth more directly and also fuses the two uses to which it has been put in the earlier categories. Both "St. Mawr" and "The Fox" exemplify Lawrence's treatment of the animal or totemic myth whose strangeness has, unfortunately, largely kept it from being taken seriously as an integral part of the tale. In "St. Mawr" the myth is more nearly satiric or critical in function, while that of "The Fox" operates as a concealed pattern, though, to be sure, there are elements of both in each. The most detailed formulation as well as the most complete fusion of the satiric and structural functions of myth is, of course, found in *Kangaroo*.

With the fourth category, which includes stories like "The Ladybird," "The Princess," and "Sun," myth is neither concealed nor employed as critical instrument. Instead, it operates as a kind of second story, almost a double plot, which illuminates the basic story by suggesting a link with man's earliest forms of belief and

[64] See my "Myth and Ritual in the Shorter Fiction of D. H. Lawrence," *Modern Fiction Studies*, v (1959), 70-77.

behavior. The relevant myth is that of the Sacred Marriage, while the rites of initiation, taboo or prohibition, and fecundation present a definition of the central character's reaction toward the myth itself. Consequently, we find here instances of Lawrence's using ritual as mythic reenactment, as a method of telling a past story through what is being done now. It is this that gives *The Rainbow* and *Women in Love* their unparalleled density of texture and *Lady Chatterley's Lover* its luminous clarity of outline. A related but distinct use of myth and ritual occurs in the fifth category where works like "The Man Who Died," "The Woman Who Rode Away," and *The Plumed Serpent* deal directly and as part of the narrative with the myth of the reviving god and his worship through rites of separation, initiation, propitiation, and ordination. Lawrence treats myth in these instances as a new version of an old story, a technique that links these stories to Graves's *King Jesus*, Mann's *Joseph* series, Gide's *Theseus*, and Faulkner's *A Fable*. In every case the author takes a well-established myth or legend and in the process of retelling it fleshes it out with his own imaginative extrapolations so that the final product is both a new tale and a commentary on the old one.

While in one sense these last works represent the fullest development of myth and ritual in Lawrence's fiction, there is also a sixth category which is important but stands a little to one side of the others. Significantly enough, none of the novels falls directly into this category, though they do, on occasion, utilize various of its characteristics. It does, however, embrace stories like "The Border Line," "The Last Laugh," "Glad Ghosts," and "The Rocking Horse Winner" that focus on the myth of a supernatural world populated by spirits of the dead, ghosts, and invisible divinities, and coped with by human beings through magical rites of propitiation and prediction as well as the hocus-pocus of spiritualism. In these stories, myth is again used to underscore a point, most frequently that of the mystery of existence, though as a by-product there are some satiric asides on human ignorance. Ritual, on the other hand, is equated primarily with contemporary habit patterns and as a result becomes, as it were, a satiric view of itself; for modern man's attempt to deal with the unknown is shown to be largely silly or disastrous. In effect, these "ghost" stories demonstrate a concomitant of the other tales' insistence on the importance of myth and ritual: they show that it is too vital a subject with which to trifle.

Finally, when we consider Lawrence's uses of myth and ritual in fiction, it is possible to see that not only did he write different kinds of stories but also that these kinds or classes together suggest an approximation to a mythic pattern. Broadly speaking, Lawrence's fiction contains four main kinds of story: those of endurance, of criticism, of combat, and of questing. The stories of endurance, are preeminently those that deal with the English miners and their lives and, more broadly, the simple folk of the villages and rural areas (e.g., *The Lost Girl*, *Sons and Lovers*, *The Rainbow*, "A Sick Collier," "The Christening," "Odor of Chrysanthemums," "Second Best," and "Jimmy and the Desperate Woman"). They stress the stoical, almost mindless determination of man to endure hardship, suffering, and subjugation without admitting defeat. The stories of criticism are those in which Lawrence drops the air of detached watchfulness for social, cultural, historical, and spiritual jeremiads and satires on modern life, especially that of the middle and upper classes (e.g., *The Trespasser*, *Aaron's Rod*, "Two Blue Birds," "The Man Who Loved Islands," "The Rocking Horse Winner," "The Lovely Lady," "The Blue Moccasins," and "Things"). Here the content, as distinct from the tone or attitude, reveals a world in the throes of degeneration and destruction and a people incapable of that self-sufficiency exhibited by the miners.

In the third group of stories, the attitude of indignation and rebellion against prevalent attitudes and beliefs is found not only in the author, as in the satires, but also in certain of the characters. Thus, these tales revolve around a combat or series of combats between individual characters and ways of life (e.g., *Women in Love*, *Sons and Lovers*, *Lady Chatterley's Lover*, "The Thorn in the Flesh," "Daughters of the Vicar," "The Virgin and the Gypsy," "England, My England," "None of That," "The Captain's Doll," "St. Mawr," and "The Princess"). For the most part, these struggles take place between a character who realizes or desires or possesses a more fulfilling mode of existence than is presently common in the world and a character unaware of the stultifying nature of his and society's life. Finally, the questing stories present a central character who is engaged in a search for what may best be called "wholeness," a sense of physical, emotional, and spiritual integration (e.g., *The Plumed Serpent*, "Sun," *Kangaroo*, "The Woman Who Rode Away," "The Man Who Died," "St. Mawr"). If these four groups are considered as a sequence, they exhibit a development similar to the myth of the dying and reviving god. Their characters—whose repeated recurrence and symbolic properties produce an archetypal dimension—are, like the god and his human representative, the hero or protagonist, subject to defeat, death, revival, and resurrection. And these four stages are mirrored in the four kinds of story. For Lawrence, man is an incarnate being capable of triumphing over the greatest indignities visited upon his spirit.

CHAPTER X

James Joyce:
From the Beginnings to
A Portrait of the
Artist as a Young Man

[I]

Unlike Yeats, Lawrence, and Eliot, James Joyce gives no explicit indication, apart from his creative work, of having been acquainted with *The Golden Bough* or the other work of Sir James Frazer. Most of the other writers considered provide external evidence to corroborate the signs of familiarity found in the literary texts, but in Joyce's case there is no mention of *The Golden Bough* in either his letters or critical essays. Despite this, most readers of his works, especially of *Ulysses* and *Finnegans Wake*, find in them a peculiar congruence with Frazer's ideas, images, and informing narrative patterns. Rooted as Joyce's writing is in his own biography and that of Dublin, and dedicated as the prose is to fictive specificity and the proliferation of concrete detail, in it there is still a powerful and sustained drive toward the generalizing and typifying stance of myth. And given the pervasive influence of *The Golden Bough* throughout the early years of the twentieth century when Joyce was sharpening his verbal cunning against the whetstone of exile, it would seem intrinsically plausible that much of his interest in what Eliot called the mythic method was stirred and directed by the insights of Sir James Frazer.

Certain kinds of interest and attitude might well have rendered Joyce susceptible to *The Golden Bough*. Preeminent is Ernst Renan, the great French polymath who at the end of the century made comparative religion popular at the same time that he was elevating historical scepticism to new heights of controversy.

Renan's affinities with Frazer have already been touched on in an earlier chapter. There we saw that Renan served as an over-lapping predecessor to Frazer in the adaptation of irony and art to the religious history of mankind, particularly to Christianity. In 1904 we find Joyce writing to his brother Stanislaus that he is reading Renan's *Souvenirs d'enfance et de jeunesse*, which was first published in 1883, and finding it emotionally and intellec-tually incomprehensible.[1] Despite this unfavorable judgment, scarcely a month elapsed before Joyce was again telling his brother about Renan and related scholars. This time he an-nounced that he was ordering the Frenchman's *Life of Jesus* and asking Stanislaus to send him a translation of Strauss's *Life of Jesus*.[2]

This interest in the person and history of Jesus and the will-ingness to canvass the opinions of those outside his nominal faith suggest that Joyce had more than a casual interest in the nature of the founder of Christianity and, by implication, in the forms of human history. Significant support for this view appears also in Marvin Magalaner's interesting discovery that Joyce had more than a passing familiarity with the works of Leo Taxil, especially his *Vie de Jésus* which appeared only a year after Renan's.[3] If Renan's work seemed urbane in its renunciation of the Church and its historical teachings, the same could not be said of Taxil's. His were deliberately blasphemous vulgarizations of the nine-teenth century's scholarly effort to demythologize Jesus as a re-ligious leader. For our purposes, however, what is particularly interesting is that, as Magalaner suggests, he professes to show, "anticipating Frazer's *Golden Bough*, that the beliefs and rituals of Christianity existed in recognizable outline long before Christ entered the world."[4] A young writer like Joyce, aware of his in-

---

[1] *Letters of James Joyce*, ed. R. Ellmann (New York: Viking, 1966), II, 72.

[2] *Letters*, II, 76; see also *Letters*, II, 82, 85, 110; III, 105; *Stephen Hero* (New York: New Directions, 1944), p. 189; *Ulysses* (New York: Modern Library, 1934), pp. 42, 332, 385, 509; Richard Ellmann, *James Joyce* (New York: Oxford University Press, 1959), p. 578.

[3] Marvin Magalaner, *Time of Apprenticeship: The Fiction of Young James Joyce* (New York: Abelard-Schuman, 1959), p. 54. For the full dis-cussion of Taxil's role in Joyce's work, see pp. 52-71.

[4] Magalaner, p. 52.

tellectual powers, passionately devoted to moral and imaginative truth, and with a growing sense of irony as a means of illuminating reality, would probably seize on *The Golden Bough* either as a companion piece during the same period or as a coda to the persistent critical cast of his mind first enunciated in his youth. If Renan's orotund emotionalism and Taxil's stylistic vulgarity could not help but alienate Joyce, Frazer's dispassionate objectivity and controlled irony might well have proved exactly to his taste.

Preceding Joyce's expressed interest in Renan are several critical essays indicating that he was already absorbing the atmosphere epitomized and in substantial measure created by *The Golden Bough*. The earliest of these is entitled "Royal Hibernian Academy 'Ecce Homo,'" written in 1899 when Joyce had just entered University College, Dublin. It is a highly appreciative response to the Hungarian painter Michael Munkacsy and his representation of the Passion of Christ. Some of Joyce's comments on the artist and his depiction of the scene are similar to those made by Frazer on similar subjects. Both emphasize Christ as a human being basically concerned with reform and revolution on the social and moral planes, and stress the theme of truth as centrally involved in Jesus' unhappy fate. It is obvious that at the very least their views derive from a jointly held intellectual tradition.[5]

A less religious, more broadly secular concern of the young Joyce follows directly from some of the essay's comments about drama. It marks an interest in the anthropological dimensions of ancient life which is exhibited in Joyce's very important essay of a year later, "Drama and Life." His dominant aim is to defend the appearance of a new drama epitomized by Ibsen which is anticonventional, dedicated to truth and freedom rather than to beauty and morality, and sensitive to the dramatic values of the

[5] *The Critical Writings of James Joyce*, eds. Ellsworth Mason & Richard Ellmann (New York: Viking, 1959), pp. 32, 35, 37; *GB*, I, xxv; IX, 422-423; XI, 304. Complicating the possibility of arguing for Frazer as a source for Joyce is the fact that the above passages from *The Golden Bough* closest in tone to Joyce first appear in the second edition, which did not come out until 1900, while Joyce's essay was written in September 1899.

commonplace. Nevertheless, it is significant that Joyce should also touch on points that link, at least implicitly, the new realism of Ibsen with older, more archetypal dramatic forms.[6] Coupled with this is his distinction between literature and drama and his elevation of drama to a position of superiority: "Human society is the embodiment of changeless laws which the whimsicalities and circumstances of men and women involve and overwrap. The realm of literature is the realm of these accidental manners and humours—a spacious realm; and the true literary artist concerns himself mainly with them. Drama has to do with the underlying laws first, in all their nakedness and divine severity, and only secondarily with the motley agents who bear them out."[7] In substance he suggests that drama may often be the expression of myth, that racial myths lose dramatic value when identified with religion, that society is founded on immutable laws, and that drama is essentially the embodiment of these laws in imaginative form.[8] It would, of course, be too much to suggest that *The Golden Bough* embraces all these ideas. Nevertheless, Frazer does make claims similar to at least some of them. Thus, in the cases of both Osiris and Dionysus, he singles out their myths as having formed the content of ritual dramas enacted at festivals like the Anthesteria.[9] The net effect for both Joyce and Frazer is to associate myth, drama, and those perennial forces and patterns that a later age calls archetypes. As a result, we find here those incipient factors that were to lead Joyce to link the *Odyssey* to dear, dirty Dublin, the individual human conscience to a *Walpurgisnacht* drama, and the whole of human history to a recurring cycle of giant forms ceaselessly rising and falling, dying and reviving. An excellent example of this "mythicizing" of the artist and the history in which he was rooted occurs in Joyce's treatment of the Irish poet James Clarence Mangan. Of Mangan he says: "In the final view the figure which he worships is seen to be an abject queen upon whom, because of the bloody crimes that she has done and of those as bloody that were done to her, madness is come and death is coming, but who will not believe that

---

[6] Cf. *The Critical Writings*, pp. 30, 43; *GB*, VI, 85-91; VII, 32.

[7] *The Critical Writings*, p. 40.

[8] *The Critical Writings*, pp. 40, 43.   [9] *GB*, VII, 32.

she is near to die and remembers only the rumour of voices challenging her sacred gardens and her fair, tall flowers that have become the food of boars."[10]

A measure of the importance Joyce attached to this metaphoric assessment is the fact that he repeated it almost exactly five years later when he lectured on Mangan in Trieste in 1907.[11] The mad queen recalls those female rulers of ancient times chronicled by *The Golden Bough* who, like Semiramis, for instance, won their position by brutal treachery and preserved it in the same fashion. Her sacred gardens and the boars, on the other hand, seem to point unmistakably to the Frazerian dying god, his fate, and the emblematic character of the natural scene. As a result, the passage assumes an added symbolic weight in Joyce's analysis of Mangan's fate.

Such, then, is the "evidence" from Joyce's own nonliterary works for his likely receptivity to *The Golden Bough* and the climate of opinion from which it emerged. Apart from occasional other references to Renan, Azrael the angel of death in Mohammedan mythology, the Mahamanvantara or great year of Hindu belief, Christianity as "the remnant of a Syriac religion," and the comparative method in folklore study, there is nothing in the letters and critical essays that unmistakably attests to Joyce's interest in the world of myth and primitive custom.[12] A modest addition to this admittedly slender body of documentation comes from the fact that Joyce's personal library contained copies of Jane Harrison's *Mythology*, Renan's *Les Apôtres*, Lucien Lévy-Bruhl's *L'Âme primitive* and *L'experience mystique et les symboles chez les primitifs*, and Heinrich Zimmer's *Maya der indische Mythos*.[13] In addition, Joyce, like Yeats, began his career with a substantial interest in eastern philosophy, mysticism, and theosophy, an interest that he gratified both by buying and reading books on the subject and by discussing it with George Rus-

---

[10] *The Critical Writings*, p. 82.

[11] *The Critical Writings*, pp. 185-186; cf. *GB*, v, 229-230, 236ff.; VIII, 22ff.

[12] *The Critical Writings*, pp. 81, 103, 152, 160, 165.

[13] Thomas Connolly, *The Personal Library of James Joyce: A Descriptive Bibliography* (Buffalo: University of Buffalo, 1955), pp. 15, 19, 24, 32, 42.

sell.[14] According to Richard Ellmann, despite religious reservations Joyce "was genuinely interested in such Theosophical
themes as cycles, reincarnation, the succession of gods, and the
eternal mother-faith that underlies all transitory religions."[15]
Theosophy itself formed no part of Frazer's interests and figures
not at all in *The Golden Bough* although these themes are for the
most part common to both Blavatsky and Frazer.

While the foregoing material scarcely warrants our regarding
the Joyce-Frazer relationship as more than a possible one, it is
important to remember that Joyce is rarely more detailed and
emphatic in declaring any of his other literary debts. Despite the
three weighty volumes of letters and the collection of his earliest
essays and lectures, both published and unpublished, we do not
find him spending appreciably more time discussing those authors and works which have demonstrably provided his major
works with much of their structure and many of their themes.
Bruno, Vico, and Homer are, it is true, mentioned, but scarcely
in such a way as would allow us to infer the extent of his indebtedness. So Frazer's receiving no mention whatever need not be
taken as firm evidence that Joyce neither knew him nor was
receptive to his impact. Though it would be immeasurably convenient for the critic, the writer is under no obligation to declare
all the forces that have gone into the crucible from which emerge
his imaginative works. And so long as the critic does not leap to
the assumption that absence of evidence constitutes a positive
discovery, he may properly proceed to look for other forms of
evidence with a wary but undespairing eye.

In such a spirit we now turn to Joyce's creative work, more
specifically his poetry, which constitutes his earliest published
efforts of imagination. At the outset, we are struck by the manner
in which *Chamber Music* and *Pomes Penyeach* preserve the
sense of a barely tentative relation to *The Golden Bough* without
destroying it utterly as a possibility. Even if Joyce had been
steeped in Frazer's ideas this early in his career, still a number

[14] *The Critical Writings*, p. 93, ed's. note; p. 83, n.1; Richard Ellmann,
James Joyce, p. 103.
[15] Ellmann, *James Joyce*, p. 103.

of literary factors conspire to conceal or at least blur the extent of *The Golden Bough*'s impact. The most notable of these factors, of course, are those that define the general poetic tradition in which Joyce was working. Essentially he was utilizing a combination of the Jonsonian and Cavalier lyric with the melodic harmonies of Verlaine and perhaps the early Yeats. Subtle and interesting though it may be from the standpoint of craft—both verbal and rhythmical—this kind of poetry does not lend itself easily to contemporary intellectual allusion. Its images and themes are largely established by past poetic conventions that render specific, direct references to the material of *The Golden Bough* blatantly anachronistic in attitude if not in content as well. The whole weight of this sort of verse is toward rendering a precise delicacy of sensibility rather than a density and magnitude of significance. Consequently, it could utilize the myths, rituals, and customs of a work such as *The Golden Bough* only tangentially and at a distance that would impose such remote generality on the images as to remove virtually every vestige of their origin. A representative example of this occurs in the very first poem in *Chamber Music*. It draws its own distinctive and unique image of the figure of Love from that matrix of comparative religion in which poet, lover, and dying god possess the generic traits of myth.[16] Other motifs of a similar order are the association of the beloved with the evening star in Poem iv, the mutual enhancement of beloved and "the merry green wood" in viii, the equating of unloosening hair with the movement from maiden to woman in xi, the clearly phallic role of "the dark pine-wood" of xx, the protective powers of the wren in xxiii, and the conjunction of willows with witchcraft in xxiv. For all these, at least approximate equivalents can be found in *The Golden Bough*. Yet none possesses the style, tone or thematic weight to testify unequivocally to the impact of Frazer.

[16] Interestingly enough, Joyce's brother said late in life that he had arranged the order of the poems "to be read as a connected sequence, . . . representing the withering of the Adonis garden of youth and pleasure." See William York Tindall, ed., *Chamber Music* (New York: Columbia University Press, 1954), p. 44. (A letter from Stanislaus Joyce to Professor Tindall, January 23 and February 6, 1953.)

[II]

If Joyce's early essays and poems hint only fleetingly and obliquely at the possibility of their having been conditioned by Frazer's work, so too do his first efforts in fiction. On the one hand, *Dubliners* gives no sign whatsoever of *The Golden Bough*'s ideas, themes, attitudes, or techniques. Dedicated as Joyce was to examining the moral paralysis of his native city and its inhabitants and to couching his impersonal epiphanic revelations of daily human behavior in a style of scrupulous meanness, it was inevitable that he should rigorously exclude the larger and more remote worlds of myth, primitive belief and custom, and historical development. *Dubliners* is the most relentlessly phenomenological of Joyce's works, offering surfaces of carefully controlled density that are their own end and justification. As such, its formal requirements preclude the extrapolative techniques of metaphor, allusion, and pun that figure so prominently in Joyce's later writing.

When we turn to *Stephen Hero* and *A Portrait*, the situation is significantly altered. Both works afford a number of instances of possible response to the impact of *The Golden Bough*.

Stephen Hero reveals certain historical and social attitudes that seem to bear some impress of *The Golden Bough*. Several characters, including Stephen himself, develop a strongly articulated critical rejection of Roman Catholicism whose foundation is that late nineteenth-century rationalism in which so much of Frazer's thought too was rooted. A natural concomitant of this view, both for his characters and for Joyce himself, is a concentrated reexamination of the figure of Jesus as a man and as a central focus for religious ritual. And finally, the third aspect of this nexus of Frazerian attitudes is Stephen's awareness of the ancient past as of shaping relevance to himself and his own time. The backward glance to Jesus, inspired, as we have seen, by Renan and Strauss, is carried into an even yet more remote era, one where, as in Frazer, the subject is classical and primitive life, ritual and art.[17]

To turn from *Stephen Hero* to *A Portrait of the Artist as*

[17] *GB*, II, 186; V, 275ff., 304ff.; VI, 59, 83; IX, 328, 412ff.

a Young Man is to encounter a quite different dimension of *The Golden Bough*. *A Portrait* is a completed work of art rather than a fragment and registers a subtle absorption of autobiographical experience into fictive texture. Consequently, it is almost completely devoid of the rather simple expression of personal belief and details that mark *Stephen Hero*. As a result Stephen emerges less as a representative rebel against society and much more as the artist archetypally divesting himself of whatever threatens to impede the realization of his creative nature. It is in his movement from child to young adult, from recorder of sense experience to shaper and creator of imaginative entities, that the impact of *The Golden Bough* is evinced subtly and pervasively. *A Portrait of the Artist as a Young Man* is structured, in the largest sense, about its hero's painstaking exploration of the concrete, given qualia of his existence through which he comes to a recognition of the expanding horizons of myth. Indeed, like *The Golden Bough*, it is polarized between the phenomenological and the mythological. By degrees Stephen moves from a preoccupation with sight, sound, feel, taste, and smell to an apprehensive trust in the myth inherent in his name. Substantially the same polarization occurs in *The Golden Bough*, though with the difference that Frazer does not link the two ontological attitudes by a narrative progression. Indeed, the structure of *The Golden Bough* is, in a limited sense, that of *A Portrait* turned inside out. That is, Frazer begins with a secular, human voyager who moves out into the largely uncharted seas of myth, ritual, and primitive custom and then after a series of adventures returns to his home port and the commonsense empirical realm from which he set out. The movement is from the ordinary to the mythical and back again, whereas in *A Portrait* the pattern is one of unrelieved and intensifying progression from one world to another. Nevertheless, *The Golden Bough* does embody the phenomenological and the mythological in such substantial profusion and density to make it a factor of considerable weight in the ultimate texture of Joyce's *Portrait*. There is, moreover, another relevant dimension of correspondence between Joyce and Frazer. That is the general approximation of the two species of the phenomenological. At first glance, the sights, sounds, smells, and feelings generated by early twentieth-century Dublin seem to have little connection with the scenes and sensations of ancient and primitive life registered in *The Golden Bough*. Yet a closer scrutiny of *A Portrait* reveals a number of significant instances in which Joyce approximates the primal details of the Frazerian vista, though displaced in such a manner as to render them an integral and credible part of the contemporary Irish context. One of the earliest of these in the novel is Stephen's anxious attraction to a rather sentimentalized peasantry while saying his evening prayers:

> That was a smell of air and rain and turf and corduroy. But they were very holy peasants. They breathed behind him on his neck and sighed as they prayed. They lived in Clane, a fellow said: there were little cottages there and he had seen a woman standing at the halfdoor of a cottage with a child in her arms, as the cars had come past from Sallins. It would be lovely to sleep for one night in that cottage before the fire of smoking turf, in the dark lit by the fire, in the warm dark, breathing the smell of the peasants, air and rain and turf and corduroy. But, O, the road there between the trees was dark! You would be lost in the dark. It made him afraid to think of how it was.[18]

Obviously Stephen's feeling has its genesis in Joyce's own Irish experience. Joyce, however, as much as any modern writer was prone to seek support for his impulses and beliefs in the ideas of others. It is far from irrelevant therefore to note Frazer's emphatic stressing that the peasant of his own day represented both a repository of ancient attitudes and an ignorant debasement of their original significance. *The Golden Bough* adamantly insists on the modern peasant's preserving, in more or less denatured form, the generic religious consciousness or sensibility of earliest known man. Equally stressed—indeed, one of the central contentions in Frazer's entire study—is the point that primitive religion was essentially nature worship and especially nature as vegetative fertility. These points of emphasis have their fictive reflection, adjusted to the requirements of the novel's specificity, as this passage indicates. They are found in the suffusion of Ste-

---

[18] *A Portrait of the Artist as a Young Man*, ed. R. Ellmann (New York: Viking, 1964), p. 18. Subsequent references will be indicated in the text.

phen's consciousness with the holy character of the peasants, the creative, almost maternal, qualities of the natural setting, the figures emblematic of the interrelation of human and natural fecundity, and even the brooding sense of being lost in the dark.

Having established for his hero the necessity of the dark and backward glance into human history and prehistory, Joyce continues to draw the material of *The Golden Bough* into Stephen's imaginative experience. Thus, immediately following the above passage Stephen's mind moves from the unnamed threats of darkness on the road to the peasantry to an imaginative shaping of the darkness of his dormitory into physical forms. Stories of ghosts of murderers and far-distant soldiers suffuse his mind, informing it with a complex sense of fear and wonder. This leads him to invoke a prayer which is the Christian equivalent of the primitive rites of exorcism and expulsion detailed by Frazer. The ghosts entertained by the child Stephen are obviously those of figures appropriate to his position as a late-nineteenth-century Irish boy of considerable sensitivity and imagination. Nevertheless, Joyce is clearly utilizing more than the Celtic awareness of a supernatural world. He is also approximating *The Golden Bough*'s recognition that the civilized world's response to ghosts, spirits, and the like derives from an older universe more redolent of spiritual presences, many of which are formless as well as insubstantial. In short, Joyce's pattern of having the child Stephen sense that human beings begin in a primitive condition of darkness, swarms of vague but powerful presences, and apprehensive awe and fear mirrors the conviction held by Frazer and other anthropologists of his era. They saw what they liked to call the primitive mind as dominated by fear and ignorance and fugitively groping its way through a universe surging with spirits of nature and the dead. These spirits possess only dimly ponderable natures which render them capricious creatures, alternately beneficent and malevolent, to be approached warily and to be fled from at the first sign of hostility.

To the peasant image of order and harmony the ghost figures add the aura of fear and apprehension that characterizes the young Stephen's attitude to the concrete real world. From these two images Joyce gradually fleshes out the mythopoeic awareness of Stephen in terms that *The Golden Bough* renders particularly intelligible. Motivated by fear and desire, those emotions that Frazer sees intertwining to invest sex and religion with the features of each other, Stephen steadily expands his awareness of anthropological reality. One of the first things he finds himself developing is a sense of the significance of the mythic icons of his people's traditions. Thus, as a child he finds the festal holiday of Christmas marked by holly and ivy, religio-political contests and, above all, the memory of a "dead king" who is neither fully dead nor exclusively a political monarch. Through this scene the young Stephen is first apprised of the fact that the social, political, and historical polarities surrounding him also have ancient and indeed archetypal associations. To the early Irish, holly was one of the "chieftain" trees whose destruction was most heavily penalized.[19] Ivy, on the other hand, was linked with several of those dying gods most exhaustively chronicled by Frazer.[20] The conjunction of the two vegetative emblems provides an educative challenge to Stephen. He has to grow iconographically so as to apprehend how these natural images encompass both the secular holiday of the present-day Christmas and also the human-divine personage whose death is so woefully ordained and whose archetypal genesis antedates his Christian representative. As the scene unfolds before the appalled but observant Stephen, the significance of the holly-ivy complex is clarified through the remembered figure of Parnell. The *agon* over his nature and role in Irish life quickly points up his resemblance to Frazer's priest-kings.[21] Not only are they figures drawing authority from both religion and secular politics but they are also one of the paradigmatic forms for subsequent leaders of society.

Another aspect of anthropological reality and folk tradition that Stephen explores is the meaning and significance of names and language. In the novel's opening school scene Stephen is confronted by the challenging response to his name: "What kind of

[19] P. W. Joyce, *A Social History of Ancient Ireland* (New York: Longmans, Green, 1903), II, 286-287.

[20] *GB*, II, 251; V, 278; VI, 112; VII, 4.

[21] See A. Glasheen, "Joyce and the Three Ages of Charles Stewart Parnell," in *A James Joyce Miscellany, Second Series*, ed. M. Magalaner (Carbondale: Southern Illinois University Press, 1959), pp. 151-178.

a name is that?" (8). He is unable to answer until very nearly the end of the book when the full sense of the mythic past invested in his surname flows over him and becomes virtually synonymous with his person. This experience has strong affinities with the attitude toward language and especially proper names found in primitive cultures, which Frazer considered in copious detail in the third volume of *The Golden Bough, Taboo and the Perils of the Soul*. Stephen is initially apprehensive when asked his name, then he turns to a contemplation of words like "suck" and "belt," and later in Cork feeling himself "beyond the limits of reality" (92), he both clings to names in his immediate situation and finds that of his childhood "he recalled only names" (93). All these responses indicate that he, as much as Frazer's primitive man, is fear-haunted, guilt-ridden, and a wanderer in the dark recesses of psychic terrors. For both, names are an inherent part of the universe and liable to irreparable damage unless handled with exquisite care and solicitude.

In the primitive world described by Frazer this concern produced the elaborate patterns of taboo that structured the society. In the aesthetic world explored by Stephen the same concern resulted in the artist's subtle and intense discriminations in description and definition. This led the young Stephen not only to cherish his word hoard privately but also to partake sedulously of the lore that passionately informed the society of his time: "Trudging along the road or standing in some grimy wayside publichouse his elders spoke constantly of the subjects nearer their hearts, of Irish politics, of Munster and of the legends of their own family, to all of which Stephen lent an avid ear" (62). No more than Frazer's tribesmen did Stephen view myth and legend as narratives of remote and esoteric powers of incalculable magnitude. *The Golden Bough* could provide the warrant for what Joyce already knew from his own experience, that myths are generated and perpetuated in the passionate tales of a community, whether it is located around a campfire or in a tavern.

Other passages in the novel indicate pretty conclusively that Joyce by this time had already seized upon the relevance of ancient myths to his artistic purposes. The first of these occurs early in the last chapter as Stephen walking by Trinity College sees "the droll statue of the national poet of Ireland" (180) and associates it with his peasant friend, Davin. The statue is cast as "a Firbolg in the borrowed cloak of a Milesian" (180), that is, as a member of one of the earliest races of Ireland clothed in the garb of a foreigner and a conqueror. Such an image shows the ironic relating of the legendary past to the prosaic present. What Joyce does here microscopically through a single image, Frazer does macroscopically. Joyce's temper on this topic is as ironic as Frazer's. This is clear from Stephen's subsequent development of Davin's association with the past of his native land: "the young peasant worshipped the sorrowful legend of Ireland. . . . His nurse had taught him Irish and shaped his rude imagination by the broken lights of Irish myth. He stood towards this myth upon which no individual mind had ever drawn out a line of beauty and to its unwieldy tales that divided themselves as they moved down the cycles in the same attitude as towards the Roman catholic religion, the attitude of a dullwitted loyal serf" (181).

Here Joyce is every bit as coolly aloof to the nature of myth and those who continue to respond to it with religious belief as is *The Golden Bough*. The rudeness of Davin's mental processes, the corrupt and therefore semicoherent character of myth and the slavish, myopic nature of Davin's belief in it, all conform to *The Golden Bough*'s presentation of the primitive mind and its responses to its own creations.

If his purpose in the foregoing passage is ironic, such is not the case in another passage which demonstrates his recognition that the stuff of *The Golden Bough*, myths of every sort and source, is germane to a master-builder of the imagination. Standing on the steps of the library observing the flight of a flock of birds, Stephen's mind is drawn to see himself ritualistically merging with the past: "And for ages men had gazed upward as he was gazing at birds in flight. The colonnade above him made him think vaguely of an ancient temple and the ashplant on which he leaned wearily of the curved stick of an augur. A sense of fear of the unknown moved in the heart of his weariness, a fear of symbols and portents, of the hawklike man whose name he bore soaring out of his captivity on osierwoven wings, of Thoth, the god of writers, writing with a reed upon a tablet and bearing on his narrow ibis head the cusped moon" (225).

Both Daedalus and Thoth are discussed in the course of *The Golden Bough*, but since Joyce mainly uses their traditional iconology, it is difficult to feel that Frazer is their only or central source. What is rather substantially more Frazerian is the establishment of a long panoramic vista of human contemplative questing for knowledge of the future. Frazer dramatizes the transmutations of setting and objects that nevertheless perpetuate the essentially similar archetypal functions. So Joyce has the library colonnade and the ancient temple, Stephen's ashplant and the ancient augur's curved stick merge into one another in the artist's imagination. Stephen's perplexed scrutiny of the soaring birds from among the portals of knowledge draws him into a diffused and generalized past of considerable remoteness. In doing so, it operates in the same fashion that Frazer does. On numerous occasions *The Golden Bough* moves from a specific present scene to reconstruct the spatial context in an earlier temporal order while preserving the sense of that order as one irremediably past. The effect is one of a doubled perspective. This doubling process has, in both writers, the effect of making the remote and primitive past appear not only real and immediate but also teleological. The past seems to exist only in order to become the present and to assume the forms of the contemporary.

Daedalus escaping from imprisonment in the labyrinth and Thoth the self-begotten, whom one scholar describes as "the personification of divine intelligence, omniscience and omnipotence, exercising his creative powers by divine utterance," between them comprise a mythic icon of Stephen's desires and Joyce's ultimate achievement.[22] In bringing together Daedalus and Thoth, Greek and Egyptian legends, human and divine, Joyce follows the comparative bent of *The Golden Bough*. By so doing he takes the first steps toward the intricately varied metamorphoses wrought on the figures populating *Finnegans Wake*. Similarly, he approximates Frazer's amused sense of gods and myths as be-

[22] E. O. James, *The Ancient Gods* (New York: G. P. Putnam, 1960), p. 205.

ing no more than emanations of the human mind by having Stephen think of the god's image as that of "a bottlenosed judge in a wig, putting commas into a document which he held at arm's length" (225). The reduction to a human level with the attendant note of wry comedy balances the fear-dominated mood of awe. This balance pays exact tribute to the total emotional reality of the scene, suspended as it is between convictions of folly and augury. Such a judicious and scrupulous rendering is of precisely the same order as Frazer's recurrent appraisal of the primitive myths and customs as simultaneously moving and erroneous. At the same time, Joyce is aware of the limitations inherent in nineteenth-century rationalism's perspective on myth. Indeed, Stephen comes to his Daedalian-Thoth matrix in which myth is both threat and potential salvation only after he has rejected the simplistic version of rationalism, which with MacCann argues that female beauty is grounded on capacities for reproducing the species. Stephen also extends his apprehension of anthropological reality to include his own religion. The first intimation that his religion and its rituals are susceptible to the comparative method is oblique but highly significant. The Belvedere School Whitsuntide play in which Stephen has a major role is performed in the chapel. Here the Christian occasion of the drama provides the symbolic action through which Stephen apprehends the ancient and pagan functional significance of ritual drama. The traditional descent of the Holy Spirit is here transformed into the perception of the drama as a mode of communion in which the individual members of the audience cohere into a unified body through the ritual sacrifice of the drama itself.

Stephen's recognition that drama is actually as mythopoeic as Frazer suggests leads him to expand this response to include representative aspects of his own actual contemporary world. Thus, at the end of chapter two he enters the brothel district of the city, an area that appears to him, significantly enough, maze-like. The immediate reality is quickly caught up in an imaginative metamorphosis in which the gasflames of the street lights are seen to be "burning as if before an altar" (100). With this Stephen sacralizes the world of prostitution in a way that provides a rationale for the romanticizing of the prostitute and his loss of virginity later in the same scene: "Before the doors and in the lighted halls groups were gathered arrayed as for some rite. He was in another world: he had awakened from a slumber of centuries" (100). Here the awakening is from the present and the world of historical reality, which are seen as a somnolent ignoring of the original ritual reality of the ancient world. To find himself in another world centuries old entails for Stephen the instinctive recognition that the loss of virginity is neither trivial nor moral but momentous and religious. In effect, for him the Dublin whore is not simply a contemporary streetwalker but a woman functionally similar to the sacred prostitute of *The Golden Bough* who serves the god of fertility by cohabiting with strangers, each of whom may be a manifestation of the god.

Though the prostitute is made a creature of great significance and symbolic weight by Stephen, she is not allowed to triumph unchallenged. Stephen's inherited regard for the Church and its emblems creates an imaginative confrontation between the prostitute and the Virgin Mary. Ultimately he is driven to see them as antithetical and antagonistic, but his first reaction to his loss of virginity is to see the two women as not in conflict over him. His response, "That was strange" (105), clearly renders his psychological puzzlement, but it also points toward a relationship that is historically curious as well. In the scene in question, two complexes particularly impress themselves upon Stephen's hypersensitive mind. One is the Virgin's religious manner, her traditional Christian quality. The other is her natural emblems: "spikenard and myrrh and frankincense, symbolising . . . her royal lineage, her emblems, the lateflowering plant and lateblossoming tree, symbolising the agelong gradual growth of her cultus among men" (104).

Clearly these images too are part of the Christian tradition surrounding the Virgin, but they also include the continuity between earlier religions, with their heavier reliance on a worship of nature and the powers of fertility, and Christianity. Significantly enough, it is the trappings of secular royalty and the symbols of nature worship which impress Stephen first. That is, it is precisely those elements associated by Frazer with the sacred rulers of primitive times which Joyce has Stephen struck by initially and to such a marked degree. In addition, Frazer carefully draws parallels between the Virgin Mary and the goddess Isis, especially by virtue of their joint emblematic identification with the morning star. Stephen insistently calls the same image to mind in connection with Mary. Tenuous though these connections may be, it does seem that Joyce may have delicately utilized Frazerian comparatist ideas and strategies to provide a rationale for Stephen's puzzlement over his linking of the Virgin and the prostitute. Actually Stephen is groping his way toward the recognition that, as *The Golden Bough* makes clear, these sacred and profane female figures are the same.

Only in the last chapter does Stephen fully sense the complex interweaving of the sacred and profane. In the scene with Davin, he is profoundly impressed by Davin's story of being asked to spend the night with the peasant wife who is alone in an isolated cottage: "The last words of Davin's story sang in his memory and the figure of woman in the story stood forth, reflected in other figures of the peasant women whom he had seen standing in the doorways at Clane as the college cars drove by, as a type of her race and his own, a batlike soul waking to the consciousness of itself in darkness and secrecy and loneliness, and, through the eyes and voice and gesture of a woman without guile, calling the stranger to her bed" (183).

It is Davin's *story singing* in his memory that moves Stephen, the fusion of narrative and music that fires his imagination. And what emerges from the account is an unmistakable, if implicit, intimation of the peasant woman's being a kind of secularized sacred prostitute. The specific woman's association with Frazer's archetype is underlined by her avowedly typological role, the emphasis on her welcoming sexual relations with a *stranger*, and by her soul's being construed under the bat image. This last is particularly meaningful, for it defines the racial soul in terms of anthropological symbolism. To Joyce, Frazer's linking of bats with the souls of the dead and the lives of men would have afforded a strikingly economical means of suggesting that for the Irish in general their lives are dead and their souls dominated by the past.[23]

[23] *GB*, VIII, 287; IX, 215ff.

In a later passage Stephen crystallizes the threat to himself and all creative figures into a single mythic image of devastating violence: "Ireland is the old sow that eats her farrow" (203). Yeats's Frazer-derived black pig is here modulated into a cannibalistic female destroyer of the son who is also her lover. Thus, Stephen's increasing bitterness at his stifling environment and his sense of personal embattlement are here broadened to take on mythopoeic lineaments. The artist-aesthete of the turn of the century is cast in the more inclusive role of the dying god sacrificed to a maternal Ishtar. By doing so, Joyce both intensifies and universalizes the significance of Stephen's highly personalized anguish and rebelliousness.

The sow image is one of a complex developed by Joyce in which myth is utilized for the purpose of religious irony and satire. It stands with the priest's looping the cord of the window blind into a noose and with Stephen's vision of a bovine god. The sow image, as we have seen, directs its irony at the terrible mother-figure of myth and the Irish nation of history. Both are the embodiments of the rapacious female whose lust is for the lover's annihilation. A similar kind of irony exists also in the other two images. The priest is a divine hangman, an institutionalized killer dedicated, at least in Stephen's mind, to the obliteration of the poetic imagination. It only remains similarly to expose the masculine deity for Joyce to have completed his parodic dissolution of the Christian religion in Stephen's mind. This he does in the scene following the rector's awesome announcement of the school's religious retreat: "His soul was fattening and congealing into a gross grease, plunging ever deeper in its dull fear into a sombre threatening dusk, while the body that was his stood, listless and dishonoured, gazing out of darkened eyes, helpless, perturbed and human for a bovine god to stare upon" (111).

In the immediate context of the passage it is obvious that Joyce is using the bovine image for its physical aptness. Both Stephen and his deity possess bovine properties. Stephen's fattening soul, his darkened eyes, and the general aura of dullness, listlessness, and helplessness all present him as a bovine victim whose anguished suffering is indifferently and impotently contemplated by a bovine god. Further, Stephen's role of bovine victim carries with it the illuminating epithet of "dishonoured," which alerts us to the added meaning the image holds for Joyce. For not only does he echo Frazer's attitude toward Christianity, he also had available to him *The Golden Bough*'s variable symbolism for bovine creatures. In Stephen's mind one of the most powerful is the bovine's serving as an emblem of the Father-God, for it serves ironically to link Stephen's physical father and the heavenly one whom hitherto he has respected.[24]

Similar ironic adaptations of the bovine god's anthropological associations complete the removal of the divine father's image from Stephen's consciousness. The most important of these associations are the bovine figure's roles as a sacrifice to the dead and as a fertility spirit.[25] The former functions ironically by capturing exactly the stunned, paralyzed moribundity of the past, reverence for which consigns the hero's realm to stultification in his own eyes. In contrast to this, the role of fertility spirit is inverted and made a complex appraisal of Stephen as well as a rationale for his current condition. That is, the imagery of the passage clearly attests to the impotence of man and beast, of artist and god. Through such Frazerian implications Stephen ultimately purges himself of the Christian God, who for him is an impotent father immobilized in a past that is dead. Only then is he able to move toward a realization of himself as an artist and a recognition of the mythopoeic as his true spiritual vocation. It would doubtless be excessive to say that *The Golden Bough* is the exclusive shaping force in Joyce's imaginative rendering of this early modern agnosticism. Nevertheless, given his affinities with Frazer's ironic chronicling of man's religious consciousness and its inherent aberrations, it seems certain that his rejection of Christianity would not have led him to locate its artistic surrogate in the expanding universe of myth had he not seen in *The Golden Bough* an instructive locus of metaphoric possibilities.

[24] *GB*, v, 164.
[25] *GB*, IV, 72, 95; V, 123, 163; VIII, 113.

CHAPTER XI

James Joyce:
Ulysses and the
Anthropological
Reality

[I]

As Joyce's techniques expanded in number and subtlety so did his sense of the intrinsic viability of myth and ritual for a truly twentieth-century literature. And when these techniques came to full efflorescence in *Ulysses*, his conscious deployment of the ideas, attitudes, and strategies of *The Golden Bough* followed suit. At the same time *Ulysses* demonstrates its relationship with the preceding works by its own variation on the threefold pattern of emphasis begun, as we have seen, in *Stephen Hero*. Thus, *Ulysses* extends the sense of the primal character of the phenomenological by accentuating even more boldly the anthropological reality inhering in that which has been given to man from the beginning, his own and the race's. It does so not simply by sedulous attention to the minutiae of ordinary daily existence but by interpenetrating those present qualia with ones from the past, with beliefs, attitudes, and actions that are immemorially Irish. The result, in effect, is a reconstitution of the relevance of what is truly folklore not only to literature but to life as well. The old woman who supplies milk to the tower is both a repository of and an emblem for the habitual thought of the Irish race throughout time. Joyce, however, does not seek to erect such figures and thoughts into images of surpassing wisdom or heroic action worthy of emulation. Instead, they are seen dispassionately but sympathetically as the constituent elements of the recurring human response to its inescapable situation. The ironic and the re-

gretful merge to give heightened expression to the comic romance of mankind's aspiration and achievement that Frazer
chronicled with equal detail, plangency, and austere humor in
The Golden Bough. In effect, *Ulysses'* use of folklore is neither
in the service of sentimental antiquarianism nor in modernist accumulation of the tangential.

The second pattern in *Ulysses* shaped by the cultural presence
of *The Golden Bough* is the generation of archetypes out of specific individual characters. In this, *Ulysses* accentuates *A Portrait's* exploration of the transmutation of phenomena into mythological entities. The chief difference between the two books in
this regard lies in the view of myth and the attitude taken to it.
Stephen's growth into his Daedalian nature in the course of *A Portrait* is, in a significant sense, a rendering of the euhemeristic
view of myth. As has been suggested, the opening of the novel
defines the child and putative artist phenomenologically—he is
virtually the sum of his sensations—and from this the alembic of
his imagination and external circumstance creates the mythic
namesake. Joyce points up this mythicizing of the concrete, historical individual by the shift in his character's naming process.
As a child more often than not he is called by his given name, but
as he grows and moves out into the world of school and university he is increasingly identified by his surname until ultimately
he equates himself with the hawk-like man who makes his cunning serve his desire for freedom.

In contrast to this euhemeristic drama with its inherently romantic attitude toward the function of myth, *Ulysses* seems to
present a more conceptual and functional view of myth, a view
that is more in keeping with the dominant tone of *The Golden
Bough*. Though Stephen, Bloom and the author scatter a substantial welter of mythological allusion throughout the book, the final
achievement is not their transformation into Odysseus or Christ
or Hamlet or even a God content to pare his fingernails. Rather,
the characters of *Ulysses*, both major and minor, are items or illustrations of anthropological archetypes. The four major characters, of course, receive the bulk of Joyce's attention, so that by
the end of the novel it is clear that they have taken on the lineaments of scapegoat, fertility goddess, priest-king and rational

intellectual. In doing so, they follow both Frazer's pattern and method.

Just like *Ulysses*, *The Golden Bough* masses details, scenes, and individuals to develop a subsuming concept that embraces them all under a loose, perhaps ahistorical, but functionally meaningful rubric. Frazer, for instance, passes before our eyes an interminable series of native chieftains, mythological beings, folk sayings and customs, and ancient rites in order to abstract from them the concept of the dying and reviving god or the scapegoat. Perhaps the clearest instance of Joyce's adaptation of this process of inductively creating archetypes comes in Molly Bloom's final soliloquy. There as her dreamy, ruminative associative flow unfolds and memories of past men jostle in her consciousness, antecedents for third-person singular pronouns get increasingly confused. Reminiscences superimpose and then coalesce into a mirror image of her ultimate role of fertility goddess dedicated to sexuality as the constituent motivation of life.

The final Frazerian pattern in *Ulysses* is a development of *A Portrait*'s concern with what has earlier been called the inductive perspective and comparative method. It is closely related to the formation of archetypal characters in that each of the three major ones becomes a vehicle for a distinct cultural metaphor. Each combines with the others to create a complex which sums up Joyce's mature vision of social history. It is clear both from Joyce's own comments and from the novel itself that *Ulysses* consists of several clearly distinguishable cultural strata. One is the classical world of Homer and the *Odyssey*, which can best be thought of as a pagan or pre-Christian culture. Another is the universe of Bloom and his heritage, the world of Jewish life and belief and custom. Finally, there is the Irish Celtic world whose Roman Catholicism establishes it as preeminently a culture of Christian symbols and rites. Molly, Bloom, and Stephen respectively epitomize in their characters the essential responses and dilemmas of these three cultures as envisaged imaginatively by Joyce.

Though Frazer draws on all three of these cultures for data and illustration, it is less this than his method of handling them that is pertinent to *Ulysses*. *The Golden Bough* distinguishes, for example, Balder, Attis, Adonis, Dionysus, Osiris, and Huitzilo-pochtli from one another. It does so not merely by describing their individual legends, rites, and customs but by locating their particular characteristics in a comparative context that simultaneously isolates and identifies them with a specific culture. The dreamy voluptuousness of Adonis stands out because of the puritanic sacrifice inherent in Attis' bloody rites of emasculation. And the dismemberments in the cases of Dionysus and Osiris can be differentiated by the frenzy of sexuality and death in the one as against the heroic civilizing aspirations of the other. The comparative method, in short, affords Joyce a means of surpassing dramatic economy for revealing not only the striking differences of character and attitude between, say, Bloom and Stephen, but their root origin in a particular cultural condition and racial heritage. Each responds differently to similar situations or persons or ideas because one is a lapsed Jew and the other a lapsed Catholic. That is to say, the cultural imagination of each is haunted by a different image of the godhead as well as by the possibility that the image is inoperative and so no more than an image.

At the same time, Joyce is not merely rendering *The Golden Bough*'s scepticism concerning the value of religious modes of life. He is also, and more importantly, suggesting something of the form in which the post-Christian world of the secular imagination is to be cast. At this juncture the full scope of that form exceeds our concern. But one aspect that is immediately relevant to the pattern under discussion is that of the three cultures alluded to above. The so-called mythical method of *Ulysses* manipulates temporal parallels and juxtapositions and cultural ones as well. As a result, the pagan world of Molly, the Jewish one of Bloom, and the Christian aura that dominates Stephen's universe are drawn together into a single multistratified universe that becomes a kind of secular surrogate for the religious mystery of the Trinity. And it is perhaps not wholly speculative to see, if not the model for this, at least a representative instance of it in *The Golden Bough*'s encyclopedic vision of human history with its many heterogeneous cultures slowly crystallizing into an age emancipated from both magic and religion yet retaining transmuted and vestigial remnants of both.

Both *Ulysses* and *The Golden Bough* reject the possibility of transcendent solutions in favor of a knowledge of the hard discriminations between things similar and dissimilar in the inescapable natural world of man's creation. Frazer's view, of course, was dominated by a naively simple trust in cultural evolution. Of this there is no trace in *Ulysses*. Instead, Joyce groups his three cultures so as to afford a conspectus of the possible ways in which mankind can shape the possibilities of the transcendent. Between them they define not a trust in evolution but a confidence in change and the capacities of the cultural imagination to bring into being whatever is requisite to the age.

[II]

From the foregoing it would appear perhaps that we are in reality a long way from *The Golden Bough* when reading *Ulysses*. In a sense this is true, but only if we are thinking of the uses to which Frazer's work is put by writers like Yeats and Robert Graves. They and others like them draw on *The Golden Bough* for textural elements as well as for overarching structural properties. Joyce in *Ulysses*, on the other hand, is largely content to find in Frazer habits of thought and imaginative methods whose essence he can utilize. This is not to say, however, that he is less responsive to the literary impact of *The Golden Bough*. Joyce's strategy is rather to reproduce Frazer in a dramatic mode, to create, in a sense, his own encyclopedia of myth, folklore, and cultural history informed by the temper and methods of *The Golden Bough*. The precise manner in which Joyce achieves this can probably best be seen by tracing in more detail some of the patterns in *Ulysses* as sketched in the preceding section.[1]

Recent criticism of *Ulysses* has emphasized the density of physical and even physiological texture that informs it, and there is no need to rehearse these findings. What is necessary, however, is to observe how Joyce's textural detail also has an anthropolog-

---

[1] The third of the patterns mentioned in Section 1 of this chapter will not be treated in further detail. As I have suggested, it is closely related to the issue of the formation of archetypal characters the discussion of which will necessarily touch upon a number of the same issues. This coupled with the amount of material relevant to the other two patterns dictates a certain foreshortening of perspective.

ical ambience that is particularly Frazerian. In their opening conversation atop the tower, Mulligan after observing to Stephen that "There is something sinister in you" goes on to declare him "the loveliest mummer of them all."[2] *The Golden Bough* contains a number of points about mummers that link Mulligan's ascription to other major themes in the novel. In a section on various Whitsuntide mummers throughout Europe, Frazer points out that they all involve a mock victimization of a member of the community known by such names as the Wild Man and the King.[3] Such material clearly squares with a number of motifs developed in connection with Stephen. Certainly his drinking companions and even Bloom are inclined to see him as a wild man in his intellectual convictions and social behavior. And just as certainly his view of himself as an artist and intellect carries a sense of royal superiority. Frazer's identification of these figures with the rites of Nemi also serves to underline Stephen's association with the priesthood. This is especially so since he continues to regard the office as a threat to his own way of life and a taking of service with a God who is an executioner, the sinister *dio boia*.

Elsewhere in *The Golden Bough* mummers are associated with the carnival season in a masked ritual calculated to encourage the fertility of crops.[4] An especially prominent figure in this mumming ritual is the Old Woman or Mother whose possession is hotly contested by the celebrants. Stephen's desperate concern with his own mother and his being described as a mummer here come into alignment and reinforce one another. He is a mummer not merely because he plays the comic buffoon to an imperceptive audience. In addition he masks himself behind it as a persona disguising his more serious struggle to come to terms with the archetypally beneficent presence of the mother. And in the process he is subjected to a comic form of the scapegoat ritual in his flight from the *Walpurgisnacht* trial scene of the brothel. During this his beating at the hands of the soldiers culminates with his loss of consciousness, which for the artist and intellectual is tantamount to a beheading.

---

[2] *Ulysses* (New York: Modern Library, 1961), p. 5. Subsequent references will be indicated in the text.

[3] *GB*, IV, 205-214. [4] *GB*, VIII, 333-334.

The second instance of Joyce's opening use of folk materials in a Frazerian manner occurs in the scene involving the old milk woman. Mulligan at breakfast enacts an old woman making tea and then comments: "—That's folk, he said very earnestly, for your book, Haines. Five lines of text and ten pages of notes about the folk and the fishgods of Dundrum. Printed by the weird sisters in the year of the big wind" (12-13). Then he turns to Stephen and continues: "—Can you recall, brother, is mother Grogan's tea and water pot spoken of in the Mabinogion or is it in the Upanishads?" (13). In all probability the primary target of Joyce's wit is the publishing projects of Yeats and his sisters, particularly their efforts to revive interest in Irish myth, legend, and folklore. But the jibe about "five lines of text and ten pages of notes" more accurately applies to professional scholars like Frazer and encyclopedic works like *The Golden Bough* than to the much slighter amateur efforts of Yeats and Lady Gregory. Joyce was too keen an appraiser of incongruity not to be hugely amused by Frazer's late-nineteenth-century penchant for the trappings of scholarship modelled on German exhaustiveness. Instead of the portentous and the sober Joyce was drawn to the ordinary and the comic.

A firm sense of this emerges from the appearance of the milkwoman in the tower and the responses of Mulligan and Stephen to her. When she attributes the beauty of the day to God, Mulligan comments in the ironic, sceptical accents of the anthropologist like Frazer: "—The islanders, Mulligan said to Haines casually, speak frequently of the collector of prepuces" (13). Both her religious faith and the nature of her deity are rendered quaint or curious and yet wholly natural. God is not a supernatural transcendent being of enormous power and awesomeness but a quasi-official eccentric amasser of useless bits of foreskin, a figure precisely analogous to *The Golden Bough*'s tribesman who carefully preserves hair and nail clippings.[5] And the old woman's traditional religious attitude is cast as a superstitious custom observed only in limited or remote regions; "the islanders" suggests Frazer's Pelew Islanders more than the residents of Ireland.

[5] *GB*, I, 57, 64-66; III, 268ff.

Stephen's response to the old woman is less condescending, but it too sets her in an essentially Frazerian context. As she pours their quart of milk, Stephen reflects: "Old and secret she had entered from a morning world, maybe a messenger. She praised the goodness of the milk, pouring it out. Crouching by a patient cow at daybreak in the lush field, a witch on her toadstool, her wrinkled fingers quick at the squirting dugs. They lowed about her whom they knew, dewsilky cattle. Silk of the kine and poor old woman, names given her in old times. A wandering crone, lowly form of an immortal serving her conquerer and her gay betrayer, their common cuckquean, a messenger from the secret morning" (13-14). She has been identified by critics both with Ireland and with Mentor in the Odyssean context, and certainly the Frazerian qualities of this passage do not contradict either of these. But they do suggest that the merging of the contemporary Irish with the classical pagan is achieved through the medium of *The Golden Bough*'s habit of fusing or relating disparate cultures. As "a witch on her toadstool," the old milkmaid clearly reflects the belief recounted by Frazer that witches were particularly prone to steal milk from cows on certain days of the year.[6] That one of these days was the Celtic holiday of Beltane Eve or Walpurgis Night suggests, of course, that Joyce may well have known this belief through experience rather than reading. But the added description of her as "a wandering crone, lowly form of an immortal" indicates that like Frazer he was concerned to link modern folklore with primitive beliefs. The goddesses of Homer's day have, as Frazer averred, dwindled to crones and milkmaids; the witch is the intermediary in the degeneration of immortality.[7]

The old woman's witchlike nature and role is Stephen's way of rendering the superstitious Joyce's sense of the artist's betrayal by Ireland. She is a threat to Stephen the artist both because she is the "common cuckquean" to the invader from England and the native materialist and because she does not acknowledge his superior healing and life-giving capacities: "She bows her old head to a voice that speaks to her loudly, her bonesetter, her medicineman; me she slights" (14). What *The Golden Bough* affords Joyce here is less the association of witches with cows than a gen-

[6] *GB*, ii, 52-55.   [7] *GB*, viii, 269.

eral thesis. Imaginatively deployed, it allows him to link immortal queens, contemporary peasant women, and sinister female workers of magic and spells in an image of the power of woman and her loss of it. The awesome lineage of the woman is rendered in a context of historical decline and diminution. The witchlike old woman is one with all those figures in *The Golden Bough* who illustrate Frazer's thesis about the dwindling of magic and its rituals into games and their degenerating into divination.[8] Whether Ireland or the classical Mentor, the old woman in Stephen's eyes represents them in a condition *manquée*.

As we read further in *Ulysses*, it becomes clearer that Joyce uses *The Golden Bough* and folklore as a means of intimating the decline of custom and belief in cultural meaningfulness and also as a way of defining the precise sensibility obtaining in the early twentieth century. As Stephen and Haines converse on the way to the beach, Stephen, like Frazer, reveals a legacy from the preceding age, namely, the conviction that religion is rationally untenable and the feeling that this creates a severe emotional loss. Following his ironic declaration of naturalistic faith, Stephen's mind moves in a stylistic and thematic mode that more nearly reflects the elegiac brooding of Pater and Frazer over what once was until they construct a reflective consciousness that provides a workable alternative: "The proud potent titles clanged over Stephen's memory the triumph of their brazen bells: *et unam sanctam catholicam et apostolicam ecclesiam*: the slow growth and change of rite and dogma like his own rare thoughts, a chemistry of stars" (20-21). Frazer's impact is concentrated precisely here, in Stephen's fascination with "the slow growth and change of rite and dogma." One of the things *The Golden Bough* never tires of is tracing the modifications and accretions in rites and myths in response to the all-powerful though dimly comprehended forces of cultural evolution.

Another important facet of the sensibility of the age Joyce is seeking to define is, as *The Golden Bough* makes extremely clear, the abundance of superstition, residual convictions of the supernatural that constitute the greater, if hidden, portion of the human mind even in modern times. The presence—obscure, pow-

[8] *GB*, VII, 110n.; X, 336.

erful, threatening—of the primitive in the civilized mind and world was a perception never far from the center of Frazer's consciousness. In significant measure it is just this insight that *Ulysses* dramatizes through a number of small but revelatory observations and practices. Just like *The Golden Bough*, *Ulysses* encompasses not only the educated mind's stance of amused intellectual superiority but also the common or illiterate sensibility's convictions regarding the constitution of the world, both seen and unseen. Thus, while returning from purchasing his morning kidney, Leopold Bloom makes one of his characteristic observations: "Watering cart. To provoke the rain. On earth as it is in heaven" (61). Imbedded here in the modern urban alertness of Bloom's mind is an adaptation of Frazer's point about the homeopathic nature of some forms of magic and more particularly of the numerous forms in which water was used as a rain charm.[9] Bloom's use of the notion differs in tone and attitude, as well as specific form, while remaining congruent with Frazer's primitive instances. Because of this it establishes both the uniquely modern habit of Bloom's mind at the same time as it unfolds the dependency of that mind on its earlier expressions.

Joyce carefully locates illustrations of modern and ancient ritual interdependency throughout *Ulysses*. The result is a cumulative impression of the perdurability of patterns of human behavior and of the quasi-vestigial persistence of customs and beliefs that no longer retain their original cultural function. Thus, at the opening of the "Hades" chapter, Bloom at Dignam's funeral contemplates the treatment of the body after death: "Never know who will touch you dead. Wash and shampoo. I believe they clip the nails and the hair. Keep a bit in an envelope. Grow all the same after. Unclean job" (87). Here Joyce is as relentlessly anthropological, as studiously dedicated to the study of man as Frazer. Obviously *The Golden Bough*'s delineation focusses on primitive cultures and ancient tribesmen rather than on modern settings. Yet both books vent their anthropological curiosity on the custom of preserving nail- and hair-clippings and the feeling that a dead body contagiously pollutes or defiles those who come in physical contact with it. In much the same way, Bloom touches

[9] *GB*, I, 248-251, 268, 278, 284-286; III, 154-155; V, 237-239.

on the custom of offering food sacrifices to the dead: "Beyond the hind carriage a hawker stood by his barrow of cakes and fruit. Simnel cakes those are, stuck together: cakes for the dead. Dog-biscuits. Who ate them? Mourners coming out" (100). It is the phrase "cakes for the dead" that generates the contextual allusion to *The Golden Bough*. The remainder of Bloom's reflection creates a species of colloquial comedy that neatly reduces the original idea of the food offering to absurdity. At the same time it demonstrates the mutations in the custom wrought by modern commercial civilization, so that it too stands revealed as ridiculous. And holding all these nuances together is a miniature representation of Bloom's characteristic approach to issues and problems. This approach might well be classified as essentially anthropological, for it starts from an observed or described custom, makes a preliminary identification, and follows that with a ritual or cultural interpretation, which generates further curiosity that is satisfied by continued exploration of the context.

This technique's scope for fusing both the comic and the pathetic is strikingly realized later in the same chapter, as Bloom contemplates death, its physical reality, and ritual beliefs: "Chinese cemeteries with giant poppies growing produce the best opium Mastianksy told me. The Botanic Gardens are just over there. It's the blood sinking in the earth gives new life. Same idea those jews they said killed the christian boy. Every man his price. Well preserved fat corpse gentleman, epicure, invaluable for fruit garden. A bargain. By carcass of William Wilkinson, auditor and accountant, lately deceased, three pounds thirteen and six. With thanks" (108). Here the primitive belief, strongly emphasized in *The Golden Bough*, that human blood had strengthening and fertilizing properties which made it worth sprinkling on fields is articulated more nearly as a piece of comparative folklore, as a recollected superstition, not an unequivocal conviction.[10] Bloom accommodates both his disbelief and belief, through the transposition of folklore as well as biochemistry, to the level of anthropological comedy. He is aware of the incongruity in his envisaged advertisement and creates out of or through it a persona that dramatizes the modern Odyssean men-

[10] *GB*, I, 85ff; VIII, 148-152.

tality's confrontation with an immemorial ritual. This meeting can be nothing other than comic since it involves two antithetical responses to the human condition—the sacred and the secular, the holy and the profane. Bloom too, however, accepts certain beliefs emphasized in *The Golden Bough* in an unquestioning manner that indicates that he has his own sense of the limits to the profane and of the mysteries lying beyond. An economical but revealing instance of this occurs just after his encounter with Gerty MacDowell. Musing on the physical and emotional changes in women at their menstrual period, Bloom merges speculation and superstitious conviction in a manner worthy of one of Frazer's savages: "Wonder if it's bad to go with them. Safe in one way. Turns milk, makes fiddlestrings snap. Something about withering plants I read in a garden" (369).

The Golden Bough, both in early and later volumes, dwells on the intricate and varied taboos with which many cultures surround menstruous women as a result of the dread and apprehension the condition inspires in the men. Among these are their being forbidden to handle milk or to be near crops and growing vegetation, both of which Bloom remarks on.[11] His reference to reading, an almost continuous source of misinformation for him, suggests too that his convictions are founded on more than simply indigenous folklore and that Frazer or someone like him was their source. Here, Bloom's attitude toward these beliefs seems one of respectful acceptance. The effect of this is to align him with primitive man in his fear of the danger generated in menstruous women. At the same time, because his gynecological information is sounder than that of primitives, he regards such women as an attraction because they are "safe in one way." Thus, here he fuses in himself the profane and sacred attitudes toward a single object.

[11] *GB*, x, 79, 80, 84, 96.

CHAPTER XII

James Joyce:

Ulysses and the Artist

as Dying God

The foregoing discussion of *Ulysses'* deployment of folklore materials is far from exhaustive, but it is sufficient to establish a significant point. Joyce does, it is clear, invest the texture of the novel with beliefs and customs that are essentially concrete manifestations of an immemorial past. As a result, the constituent experiential *données* in the book are concretizations of intricately related strata of time. This fact substantially explains why the major anthropological pattern in *Ulysses* is the generation of archetypal figures, characters who are simultaneously individual persons and anthropological archetypes, that is, general human functions recurring throughout many times and places. Thus, the presence in the novel of scapegoat figures and the like is a dramatic recapitulation of an earlier historical process of psychological projection. Given the use of folklore and related materials, Joyce could no more avoid producing characters of archetypal dimensions than he could escape dwelling on the fortunes and features of Dublin.

The actual manner in which *Ulysses'* major characters assume the stature of structural archetypes closely resembles those enunciated by Frazer in the pages of *The Golden Bough*. *Ulysses* opens with Stephen Dedalus and Buck Mulligan counterpoised in a hieratic ritual that is to Joyce's aesthetic eye no less sacred for being so emphatically profane. Stephen's mannered weariness and aloofness in the face of Mulligan's comic rituals show his dim sense that the role of the priest is both infinitely more complex than he had thought in *A Portrait* and not so easily put off. *Ulysses* is dedicated, on one level, to broadening Stephen's awareness of the lineage and function of the priest, and in the course of the novel he discovers what *The Golden Bough* had to teach him. He finds that the priest originally was a priest-king and has socio-political or secular dimensions as well as religious ones.

This effort in historical recovery is presented in miniature form on the very first page of the novel. The imaginative movement back through history is charted by three images—Mulligan's chant, his being seen as "a prelate, patron of arts in the middle ages" (3), and Stephen's name. On the same page Joyce also defines the archetypal basis of the relationship between Stephen and Mulligan in scenic terms borrowed from *The Golden Bough*'s paradigmatic metaphor. When Stephen appears first at the top of the staircase, he "looked coldly at the shaking gurgling face that blessed him, equine in its length, and at the light untonsured hair, grained and hued like pale oak" (3). Mulligan acts like a Roman Catholic priest, but his untonsured head denies it. His face looks like that of a horse while his hair recalls an oak. And toward him Stephen stands as "his watcher," silent, wary, determined. In their several ways these images serve to call attention to the grounding of the two characters' relationship in Frazer's opening scene of the priest at Nemi. There, the solitary priest ruled as King of the Wood and personated the oak-god until slain by his successor in hand-to-hand combat. Such is the nature of the relationship between Stephen and Mulligan, though naturally enough given an ironic inflection calculated to catch Joyce's persistent sense of the complexity of human relationships. Mulligan is the old priest-king under surveillance of his young successor endeavoring to fend him off with the verbal weapons of parody and irony but inevitably doomed to lose his life. This polarity comes to a head in Stephen's identification of Mulligan with a secular "medicineman" and himself, as in *A Portrait*, with the priest of the eternal imagination.

Essentially, Frazer's priest at Nemi and the whole archetype of the priest-king became a controlling metaphor for structuring Stephen's character and actions. A crucial part of this adaptation of Frazer to fictive reality is precisely the metaphoric character of the pattern. Joyce is not creating an absolute equation between Stephen, the embattled and arrogant Dublin artist, and the ancient priest-king; he is showing both how the one is the informing structural archetype of the other and also how that relationship is one of functional homologue rather than of identity. It is, on one level, exactly with Joyce's clear recognition that there is an immense gulf between the age of the priest-king and Stephen's world, a gulf charted by the stylistic economy of metaphoric ascription, that what Eliot was to celebrate as Joyce's mythic method came into being as a sustained structural technique.

This method, which is considerably more complicated than Eliot's account of it would suggest, orders a number of otherwise apparently random images and actions. At the breakfast scene in the tower Stephen ponders on himself, the history of the Church, and the inevitability of conflict:

> Words Mulligan had spoken a moment since in mockery to the stranger. Idle mockery. The void awaits surely all them that weave the wind: a menace, a disarming and a worsting from those embattled angels of the church, Michael's host, who defend her ever in the hour of conflict with their lances and their shields.
>
> Hear, hear. Prolonged applause. *Zut! Nom de Dieu!* (21)

One of the things *The Golden Bough* underlines is the weight of affect surrounding the figure of the stranger in primitive societies. He is dreaded, suspected of magical capacities, hedged about with numerous taboos, and on occasion killed or sacrificed.[1] Substantially the same welter of superstitions and vague, half-named apprehensions govern Stephen's response, so that he is prepared to make the stranger the issue in his staying in the tower or leaving.

Though Stephen here couches his thoughts in traditional Christian imagery, the final summary reflection shows that he has a thoroughly ironic stance toward it: "Hear, hear. Prolonged applause. *Zut! Nom de Dieu!*" In the final phrase there is a hint that Joyce is making the irony reach into the remote past too for its leverage. By invoking the name of God he possibly seeks to recall Frazer's point about the ancient conviction that there was a kind of magical virtue inherent in the names of the gods and for that

---

[1] *GB*, III, 101-113; VII, 217, 242.

reason the names were tabooed unless under exceptional circumstances.[2] It is as if Joyce were creating ironic depreciations of Stephen's Christian-phrased comments from the perspectives of both present and past. From the standpoint of the present, the moving contemplation of the perdurability of the Church is shrivelled into a rhetorical set piece, an oratorical *tour de force* eliciting only clichés. And from the standpoint of the ancient past, it is seen to have derived from a magical view of language and a superstitious belief in the efficacy and power of unseen beings.

In the same general scene at the beginning of the book, Stephen's importance is further attested to by Mulligan's insistence that of all the Martello towers "ours is the *omphalos*" (17). If the term invokes the theosophical speculations of Blavatsky and A. E. and Yeats, it also points toward Jane Harrison's less cosmic and more radically anthropological treatment of the same concept. Joyce's mature vision owes more to the literary empiricism of *The Golden Bough* than to the quasi-philosophical idealism of *Tertium Organum*. Consequently it is inherently plausible to think that in Miss Harrison's treatment of the *omphalos* he would find a moving counterbalance to the essentially ludicrous theosophical abstraction. For her, the center of the world from which sprang the quintessential forms of life was not only a womb emblem but a tomb symbol,[3] and the various artistic depictions of gods rising from the *omphalos* demonstrated that the site was also the tomb or burial ground of a dead hero. It was, in short, both a memorial and a source. From the dead hero emerged the living god. To Joyce, with his penchant for reconciling polarities, the prospect of an ancient figure, both solemn and slightly grotesque, that unites the ultimate modern antitheses of life and death, human and divine, would have proven irresistible. In the present context, the image begins as one of centrality, of pivotal importance, and then broadens out to an ironic revelation of that centrality's residing in the fact of death. The *omphalos* by including both Mulligan and Stephen is the ground of the priest-king's ritual combat in which one must perish. And it is over the issue

[2] *GB*, III, 384-391.
[3] Harrison, *Prolegomena*, pp. 322-362, 556-558, 560.

of Haines and the key to the tower that Stephen and Mulligan do clash and part.

Only much later in the novel is the creative, life-giving aspect of the image developed. Naturally, this occurs in the "Oxen of the Sun" chapter, which is given over to stylistic fecundity in all its forms. In the section parodying Addison's style, Mulligan is presented as an eighteenth-century gentleman about town who has just purchased an island as part of an extensive social project: "He proposed to set up there a national fertilising farm to be named *Omphalos* with an obelisk hewn and erected after the fashion of Egypt and to offer his dutiful yeoman services for the fecundation of any female of what grade of life soever who should there direct to him with the desire of fulfilling the functions of her natural" (402). Here the eighteenth-century diction and contemporary medical student's attitude are distanced and wrought into high comedy by those qualities of primitive ritual practice most accessible to Joyce in the pages of *The Golden Bough*. The phallus-shaped obelisk ("erected" functions as a calculated pun whose past participial form catches both the temporal remove and the architectural analogue of human action), the specific geographical location, and the sexual role all combine to suggest that Joyce is here utilizing Frazer's accounts of sacred obelisks in Egypt and elsewhere and of the ceremonies of ritual defloration.[4]

Given this apparent disjunction of the twin roles of the *omphalos*, it would seem to follow that Stephen would necessarily turn his mind to the imminence of his own ritual combat and hence confrontation with the experience of death. The first intimation of this is, of course, the introduction of the Hamlet motif, of the tragic hero who must perforce meet death. More immediately archetypal and Frazerian-derived, however, is the history lesson and the schoolroom scene. There, surrounded by references to "Lycidas," Stephen locates his mythic nemesis: "Fed and feeding brains about me: under glowlamps, impaled, with faintly beating feelers: and in my mind's darkness a sloth of the underworld, reluctant, shy of brightness, shifting her dragon scaly folds" (25-26). To face the dragon and either imprison or slay him

4 *GB*, v, 14, 36-39, 57-61.

is the task of the culture hero, as Frazer's detailed discussion of Cadmus makes clear.[5] Such an encounter, however, entails, as the "underworld" image indicates, a deathlike experience. For the artist of the modern world, it is wholly appropriate that this event be located in the deeper, more remote regions of the mind. And for Stephen, it is equally fitting that the creature faced be "a sloth," the precise rendering of that state of spiritual and imaginative inanition which first beset him in *A Portrait*. It is hard to say whether or not Joyce's labyrinthine associative mind fastened on Frazer's mention of the sloth's being imitated by a masked man.[6] Stephen has already been linked with a masked man through Mulligan's phrase "the loveliest mummer of them all." But should this prove to be the case, certainly we would feel no surprise.

In the immediately ensuing scenes this sense of Stephen's moving further and further into a world of struggle and death is intensified. The history lesson's account of death and defeat in the midst of victory counterpoints the mythic aura of Stephen's riddle and its answer: "The fox burying his grandmother under a hollybush" (27). In the riddle, the implication of resurrection and rebirth is uppermost. *The Golden Bough* would have told Joyce that the fox serves as an emblem of the individual's guardian spirit, that grandmother is both a title for the Mother of Ghosts and a name for the last sheaf, that burying her was an annual ritual expression of the death and revival of the vegetation, and that holly was used in ceremonies for expelling ghosts.[7] Obviously Joyce went through no elaborate, conscious, rational process of putting these details together to yield the requisite theme. By assembling them, however, in the context and manner he has done, he does emblematically testify to Stephen's desire to live and to his recognition that he can do so only by purging himself of the ghosts that haunt him, while preserving the spirit of fertility and creativity.

To articulate this perception in the oblique and impersonal

---

[5] *GB*, IV, 69-70, 78-92.   [6] *GB*, IX, 381.
[7] The first of these images may owe something to Frazer's account of the Egyptian "Eater of the Dead." See *GB*, VI, 14. For a somewhat different emphasis see *GB*, IX, 377.

form of the riddle is Stephen's first step: "Three nooses round me here. Well. I can break them in this instant if I will" (30). Here is the beginning of a dim recognition on Stephen's part that he is threatened, as Frazer described those singled out in primitive times, with having to mime a contemporary equivalent of the hanged god role.[8] The feeling of being hedged around with various forms of death is heightened in the next chapter in which Stephen meditates by the sea, the great symbol for him of fear and death and dissolution. From his walk there arises a whole series of sinister emblems that culminate in the reiteration of his hanged god role: "Unwholesome sandflats waited to suck his treading soles, breathing upward sewage breath. He coasted them, walking warily. A porter-bottle stood up, stogged to its waist, in the cakey sand dough. A sentinel: isle of dreadful thirst. Broken hoops on the shore; at the land a maze of dark cunning nets; farther away chalkscrawled backdoors and on the higher beach a dryingline with two crucified shirts. Ringsend: wigwams of brown steersmen and master mariners. Human shells" (41).

None of the details here derives directly or unmistakably from *The Golden Bough*. Frazer does, however, afford a suggestive model for structuring the scene and for locating the important in the ordinary. Thus, in microscopic fashion the scene recapitulates the larger passage from the phenomenological to the mythological. Perceptions of Dublin, sand, bottles, and hoops gradually yield to ones of a maze and emblematic crucifixion. Between them they sketch the alternatives between a primitive pagan myth and the Christian one, between a ritual of living entrapment and flight on the one hand and a ritual of sacrificial death and resurrection on the other. For Stephen, as for Joyce, the beginning of the life of the artist entails the selective syncretistic use of both myths: the forging of a pattern of flight that makes resurrection viable. A possible adumbration of this appears in the image of "brown steersmen and master mariners." The use of this image here may be due simply to the nature of Ringsend and the demands of verisimilitude. Nevertheless, it is interesting to note that *The Golden Bough*, as Eliot was quick to notice, draws attention both to the awe aroused in primitive days by the sea and

[8] *GB*, v, 288-293.

to the vital role played by sailors in disseminating religious customs and beliefs.[9]

A little later in the same chapter Joyce obliquely points up the mythological quality of Stephen's involvement. Recollecting his days as a student in Paris, Stephen remembers Patrick Egan, a political exile, but does so in terms that make him a rather sinister adaptation of an Andrew Lang fairy tale: "His breath hangs over our saucestained plates, the green fairy's fang thrusting between his lips" (43). And moments later Stephen interprets even as he records Egan's Paris conversations: "Lover, for her love he prowled with colonel Richard Burke, tanist of his sept." The last phrase aligns Egan with the ancient, almost legendary Irish role of chosen successor to the chief of the clan or tribe. In doing so, it conveys quite clearly the backward turn of Stephen's mind and sensibility, an almost deliberate reaching out toward the ancient and mythopoeic. Though Frazer himself does not deal with this particular custom, he obviously has a great deal to say about analogous observances. Significant portions of *The Golden Bough* are devoted to detailing the many instances in which the successors to chieftains are selected without regard to familial succession.[10] Hence Joyce would have had to be inexpressibly obtuse not to have connected the Celtic tanist with Frazer's accounts of older, more primitive, and culturally variegated means of choosing a leader.

To have done so would have associated the leader with the dying and reviving god, for Frazer's chieftains more often than not were regarded as representatives of the god.[11] Their replacement was usually a result of their lowered vitality or fertility, which was taken as a sign that the human representative was moving toward the dying god phase.[12] Some evidence that this sort of association was operative in Joyce's mind appears in Stephen's brooding on the rocks by the sea in accents simultaneously comic and folkloristic: "I'm the bloody well gigant rolls all them bloody well boulders, bones for my steppingstones. Feefawfum. I zmells de bloodz odz an Iridzman" (44-45). In the nursery tale of the

[9] *GB*, III, 9-10, 203-204. See also Jessie L. Weston, *From Ritual to Romance*, p. 160.

[10] *GB*, II, 292-323.   [11] *GB*, I, 373-421.   [12] *GB*, IV, 14-46.

bloodthirsty giant and the hero there lurks analogues both to the Homeric Polyphemus and to the Frazerian giant who figured in initiation ceremonies of young men.[13]

The same issue of death and succession is caught in a multiple historical context a few paragraphs later when Stephen's mind ponders his own role as a changeling and pretender: "Pretenders: live their lives. The Bruce's brother, Thomas Fitzgerald, silken knight, Perkin Warbeck, York's false scion, in breeches of silk of whiterose ivory, wonder of a day, and Lambert Simnel, with a tail of nans and sutlers, a scullion crowned. All kings' sons. Paradise of pretenders then and now" (45). When Stephen identifies the historical pretenders as "all kings' sons," he is not suffering from a lapse of historical imagination but attending to the office rather than the person. This, of course, is exactly what *The Golden Bough* does when it treats of the ancient phenomenon of temporary kings and of the practise of sacrificing the son for the father.[14] Bitter as Stephen's final comment is, it still contains in the Joycean ironic mode more than a hint of thematic release. To see "a scullion crowned" and therefore become a king's son, and to find a paradise today as well as in the past, is to recognize that meaning as well as deception resides in the concept of the role and that it is through the permutations of function that the archetypal emerges.

The concluding pages of the "Proteus" chapter bring Stephen's archetypal role into even clearer focus while at the same time bringing its pattern of imagery full circle. Moving from the prosaic act of micturation through a contemplation of the pattern of the sea in its ceaseless forming and reforming, Stephen comes to crystallize in a single perception the three main facets of his being, the literary, the quotidian, and the archetypal: "Five fathoms out there. Full fathom five thy father lies. At one he said. Found drowned. High water at Dublin bar. Driving before it a loose drift of rubble, fanshoals of fishes, silly shells. A corpse rising saltwhite from the undertow, bobbing landward, a pace a pace a porpoise. There he is. Hook it quick. Sunk though he be beneath the watery floor. We have him. Easy now" (50). The drowned man from Dublin, the old king of *The Tempest*, and the

---

[13] *GB*, XI, 243.　　　　　[14] *GB*, IV, 148-195.

young man of "Lycidas" coalesce into a vision of death that does justice to the archetypal without ignoring the full repugnancy of man's end: "Bag of corpsegas sopping in foul brine" (50). Fact, change, and restoration are simultaneously recognized in what is clearly Joyce's initial adaptation of Frazer's myth of the dying and reviving god. Stephen has earlier linked himself with the dying man: "A drowning man. His human eyes scream to me out of horror of his death. I . . . With him together down. . ." (46). And that he anticipates moving through the other phases of death is suggested by his ironic registering of the cyclical character of life: "God becomes man becomes fish becomes barnacle goose becomes featherbed mountain" (50). Out of such disparate materials Joyce formulates his own version of the mythic pattern to which Frazer devotes so much historical and anthropological attention.

Though the archetypal Frazerian stress upon reviving as well as dying is echoed in this scene, Joyce is careful to point up two other things he regards as crucial to Stephen's experience. One of these is his suffering the rebel's version of the fall: "Allbright he falls, proud lightning of the intellect" (50). The second thing central to Stephen is that his fall should be from life into the metaphor of death. This is conveyed in the chapter's final paragraph where Stephen endeavors to see whether anyone is observing him: "He turned his face over a shoulder, rere regardant. Moving through the air high spars of a threemaster, her sails brailed up on the crosstrees, homing, upstream, silently moving, a silent ship" (51). Instead of the watchful eye of an Almighty God he finds the serene disregard of a human creation, a vessel of trinitarian shape and crucifying function. In silently "homing" it is engaged in a voyage that cannot be other than into death so far as the consciousness of Stephen Dedalus is concerned. Implicit in this strangely powerful figure is the fact that Stephen's world is to be shaped by something that renders a voyage and a hanging inevitable and sustaining.

The next mythopoeically critical segment of the voyage occurs in the "Scylla and Charybdis" chapter. There Stephen undergoes the intellectual form of ritual combat appropriate to his archetypal priest-king role: he advances and defends his views about

Shakespeare and Hamlet. Almost at the outset Joyce indicates that the contest involves the very issue of religious and anthropological investigations of the order that Frazer and men like him pursued. After Eglinton has taunted Stephen as an Irish poet with not creating any character to match Hamlet, Russell observes: "—All these questions are purely academic, Russell oracled out of his shadow. I mean, whether Hamlet is Shakespeare or James I or Essex. Clergymen's discussions of the historicity of Jesus. Art has to reveal to us ideas, formless spiritual essences" (185). The irrelevancy of historical and biographical criticism is for the transcendental Russell absolute, so he equates literary criticism and comparative religion. Since Stephen is known to have a biographical theory about Shakespeare, the implication is that he is engaged in an enterprise resembling comparative religion and that he is committed to defending it as a fundamental approach to reality. Ironically, Stephen's attempt to escape the nightmare of history is made through the remotest reaches of history itself.

In this there is a fundamental insight into the value of *The Golden Bough* for Joyce. Frazer affords him a means of creating the universal out of and not in contradistinction to the particular. Both *The Golden Bough* and *Ulysses* are firmly grounded in the facticity of historical experience, and it is by the accumulation of a welter of details that each is able to elaborate the same central archetypes of the human condition. Comments like that of Russell's about the historicity of Jesus, or Best's remark about showing Haines "Jubainville's book" (186), or Bloom's hallucinatory distribution of a book like "Was Jesus a Sun Myth?" (485) alert us to the way in which to read the multiplicity of detail. Just as with *The Golden Bough*, the anthropological pattern and the archetypal figures are the consequence of an orderly and deliberate ranging of scenes, incidents, and persons so that by a process of superimposition and reiteration they create overriding and subsumptive composites of human experience.

Even apparently trivial or ironic details take on a larger importance than their individual contexts would originally seem to dictate. Russell's aligning of the *Volk* with the most significant movements in art and literature is representative: "The movements

368

which work revolutions in the world are born out of the dreams and visions in a peasant's heart on the hillside. For them the earth is not an exploitable ground but the living mother" (186-187). The ironic mimicking of the diction and sentimentality of Yeats and Lady Gregory conditions but does not refute Stephen's later feeling that "*Amor matris*, subjective and objective genitive, may be the only true thing in life" (207). The earth as the great mother of life is, of course, a notion accessible to Joyce from many sources, including Irish folklore. But it is also one to which Frazer devotes many pages and numerous examples.[15] When we look on to Molly's section of *Ulysses* and the giant natural forms of *Finnegans Wake*, we see that the metaphor uniting the maternal figure with the earth is a central one for Joyce. That he is able to satirize it in Russell's comment and celebrate it elsewhere is a testimony both to his flexibility and to his discrimination among the sources of the notion. The renascence of Irish folklore and ancient culture wrought by Yeats, Lady Gregory, and the rest was for Joyce inherently a distortion of reality through sentimentality. Hence it was to be criticized. In *The Golden Bough*, on the other hand, he could find a dispassionate and concretely grounded expression of this root-metaphor, which affirmed his sense of reality as experiential rather than projective.

Russell's comment generates in Stephen's mind a sustained consideration of the implications of the mother as beloved. Indeed, in a very real sense the archetypal, especially as embodied in the myth of Adonis, obliquely approaches involuted personal relations that Stephen could not cope with directly. His association of his mother and her death with Shakespeare's wife and her role as mother of his children suggests an Oedipal situation of considerable tension. The first stage in this conflict is to transpose it to the symbolic or archetypal or mythopoeic level where its full complexities can be traced and enacted. This Stephen does by a modern intellectual approximation to the primitive ignorance of paternity, a state which Frazer remarks on and, like Stephen, sees as the ground for theological speculation. Though couched in Stephen's most magisterial vein, the argument about paternity essentially celebrates his mind's movement toward the ancient

[15] *GB*, I, 283, 291; II, 128 n.4, 229; III, 247; V, 27, 90; VII, 245-250; VIII, 115.

realms of myth. To think that "paternity may be a legal fiction" (207) is to strip away at one gesture all modern conceptions of parenthood and the family. It projects us into what Eliot once spoke of as the dark and backward abysm of time where lack of knowledge and the need for certitude conspire in the formation of myths that simultaneously inform and reassure.

Joyce's selection of the myth of Adonis enables him to explore Stephen's priest-king dynamic of perennial combat. By this choice he is able to have the mythopoeic grow out of the literary or, as Joyce would prefer, the dramatic. The result is the illumination of both. Stephen locates Shakespeare's paradigmatic problem in his relationship with the woman who became his wife. Hence he inevitably turns to *Venus and Adonis* as offering the clearest illumination of the way life grows into art: "He chose badly? He was chosen, it seems to me. If others have their will Ann hath a way. By cock, she was to blame. She put the comether on him, sweet and twentysix. The greyeyed goddess who bends over the boy Adonis, stooping to conquer, as prologue to the swelling act, is a boldfaced Stratford wench who tumbles in a cornfield a lover younger than herself" (191). Certainly one of the most Frazerian things about this passage, apart from its use of the Adonis myth, is its association of myth and ordinary life through the medium of ritual that is not set apart from human behavior but is an expression of it. Just as *The Golden Bough* documents in a variety of forms, here the myths of the gods are enacted by human beings, who approximate in their essential actions the timeless patterns associated with the deities.

Joyce's characters are enacting personal dramas of frustration and fulfillment which are constitutive elements in the archetypal pattern elucidated by *The Golden Bough*. Different though they are, both Frazer and Joyce stress the way in which human and divine, literal and imaginative cohere one with the other through the medium of myth. Ann Hathaway seducing the young Shakespeare is for Stephen the archetypal love goddess transporting and mortally wounding the handsome young man doomed to shuttle ceaselessly between worlds of darkness and light. He is looking at the world with the mythopoeic eye requisite for the kind of artist he seeks to become. It operates not by changing an object into something else but by accruing to itself all the levels and qualities inherent in the object. In this way, the temptress is both Ann and Venus, both "a boldfaced Stratford wench" and a "greyeyed goddess." On close inspection the myth of Adonis bears a profound relation to the full nature of the artist as priest-king, which Stephen is concerned to apprehend in the course of *Ulysses*. The fifth volume of *The Golden Bough* devotes its first book to Adonis, his myth, ritual, and related observances. Clearly Joyce could not utilize all the material provided there. Still, he could find a number of relevant things not available through other common sources, like the classical accounts of Ovid or Apollodorus or the nineteenth-century adaptations such as those in Bullfinch.

At the same time, the classical title of Shakespeare's poem suggests that Joyce is conflating classical and primitive or pre-classical sources rather than opting simply for the Frazerian emphasis. Thus, the Ovidian humor at the *ars amatoria* is caught in the image of rural sexual romping, and its occurrence in "a cornfield" introduces *The Golden Bough*'s stress on Adonis as a corn god and fertility figure.[16] As if to alert us to the relevance of this last, Joyce has Mr. Best transform it into a "Ryefield" to accord with a poem he has been reading. Actually, of course, his allusion points up the interrelation of human and vegetative fertility so emphasized by Frazer, though distanced into a literary response by his attitude:[17]

> He murmured then with blond delight for all:
> *Between the acres of the rye*
> *These pretty countryfolk would lie.* (191)

With regard to *The Golden Bough*'s treatment of the myth proper, perhaps one of the chief points is its linking of human love and sexuality with more inclusive and extensive forms of fertility. The effect of this in *Ulysses* is to intensify the pathos of the classical version of the myth, which consists largely in the untimely and premature death of Adonis and the bereavement of the goddess. The Adonis myth, however, functions not simply as

16 *GB*, v, 229-230, 233.
17 *GB*, v, 39, 67; vɪɪɪ, 332 ff.

a poignant rendering of the emasculations of a young lover but as a study in the crippling psychic wound of the artist. Stephen articulates this in words that substantially apply to himself as well as Shakespeare: "Belief in himself has been untimely killed. He was overborne in a cornfield first (ryefield, I should say) and he will never be a victor in his own eyes after nor play victoriously the game of laugh and lie down. Assumed dongiovannism will not save him. No later undoing will undo the first undoing. The tusk of the boar has wounded him there where love lies ableeding" (196). Clearly, Joyce uses the great goddess' major functions of wife and mother to convey the respective artists' dilemmas.

The myth also affords an archetypal structure to other aspects of Stephen's existence. For one thing, it heightens the creative, fertile role of sexuality. In *The Golden Bough* the myth is less story than crucial ritual.[18] The love of Adonis and the goddess mimes the disappearance and return of those powers essential to the existence of man. For Stephen, these are essentially aesthetic. But they cannot be adequately manifested in him until he has apprehended the real nature of sexuality, particularly in his own being—grasped that his Adonis dimension links him with the dying-god archetype and underscores the redemptive or resurrective possibilities of his suffering and aesthetic extinction in two ways. First, it makes the matter of the death-experience an imperative in the logic of creation rather than a fortuitous by-product of personal history, and second, it clarifies the complex nature and function of the woman in relation to the artist-hero.

When we examine Stephen's relations with women, we find him moving among virgin, mother, and harlot with no clear sense of their connections with one another. Indeed, under the pressure of his upbringing and temperament Stephen regards these archetypes as antithetical each to the others. Until he is able to achieve some integrated vision of woman, he is consigned to enact over and over in a variety of forms the myth of the dying god whose fate is to be separated from the means of his own self-realization. For Stephen, the woman may be a source of sexual pleasure, of aesthetic contemplation, or of existential pity, but no

[18] *GB*, v, 3-11, 223ff.

one woman can cause all three in either fact or imagination. At this juncture *The Golden Bough*'s impact becomes crucial, for through Frazer's pages Joyce gained access to a dramatic and ostensibly historical (and therefore phenomenologically real) integration of these apparently disparate and contradictory roles of woman.

As part of his discussion of the cult of Adonis, Frazer develops in considerable detail the custom of what he calls sacred prostitution. Apparently female worshippers of the goddess linked with Adonis were required at some point in their lives "to prostitute themselves to strangers at the sanctuary of the goddess."[19] This custom included both virgins and married women, and was so religiously and socially sanctioned that some women even became professional harlots dedicating their lives to submitting to the embraces of strangers in the temple of the deity. Thus, all three roles—virgin, mother, and harlot—are unified in a single sexual ritual that is both a sacrificial and creative mystery. By finding a basis in which the ostensible contradictions of the archetypal woman are elided into a single comprehensive form uniting the extremes of secularity and sacredness, of the profane and the holy, Joyce makes it possible for Stephen to face and redeem his own fragmentation.

The scene in the library does not, of course, contain this form. Nevertheless, there are signs. The point of this identification of wife and mother appears unmistakably when Stephen describes Ann Hathaway's later years of spiritual anxiety: "Venus had twisted her lips in prayer. Agenbite of inwit: remorse of conscience. It is an age of exhausted whoredom groping for its god" (206). Ann's identification with the prostitute of myth and ritual serves to complete the unity: any woman who is seen by Stephen as a complete entity in her own right will be all three. The agony belongs both to her because of a fear of mortality and to him because of the need to see the necessary impurity of his mother, of her relationship to the sacred prostitute as well as to the wife and virgin. The full confrontation with this archetypal reality is finally attained in the "Circe" chapter. There Stephen is forced to see mother and prostitute in a dynamic tension which is a con-

[19] *GB*, v, 36.

flict of social manner but an identity of emotional intent and response.

Stephen, then, comes to see that the woman cannot be subdivided into mutually exclusive species of varying degrees of
moral and psychological use. This brings him to the crucial stage
of his ritual combat, that in which he is engaged with himself as
the ultimate adversary. His first response to this is to envisage
forms of evasion. This is what he does through the imaginative
rendering of Shakespeare's fleeing Ann: "Christfox in leather
trews, hiding, a runaway in blighted treeforks from hue and
cry. Knowing no vixen, walking lonely in the chase"(193). Since,
as *The Golden Bough* makes clear, the fox is one of those creatures whose name is tabooed and is also regarded as the guardian
spirit and as emblematic of the corn spirit, he would serve perfectly to carry the weight of mythic significance needed.[20] In this
there is an advance over Stephen as the artist functioning as the
archetypal priest-king, for when he becomes an expression of the
dying god himself, his fate is determined more precisely within
the context of ritual.

As we might expect, Stephen conveys his awareness of the
centrality of the dying god in oblique, ironic, intellectual fashion
as part of a discourse on the relation of art and life:

> Every life is many days, day after day. We walk through
> ourselves, meeting robbers, ghosts, giants, old men, young
> men, wives, widows, brothers-in-love. But always meeting
> ourselves. The playwright who wrote the folio of this world
> and wrote it badly (He gave us light first and the sun two
> days later), the lord of things as they are whom the most
> Roman of catholics call *dio boia*, hangman god, is doubtless
> all in all in all of us, ostler and butcher, and would be bawd
> and cuckold too but that in the economy of heaven, foretold
> by Hamlet, there are no more marriages, glorified man, an
> androgynous angel, being a wife unto himself (213).

Joyce does more than simply stress the hanging god as a figure
occurring in art and the world. He also makes life into a drama
and the creator into a playwright whom he then identifies as the

---

[20] *GB*, I, 200; III, 396-398; VII, 296-297.

"hangman god." In short, he imaginatively shifts Frazer's concept of the dying god from the realm of secular history to that of Christian ontology. The orthodox loving, forgiving father and creator is seen, by ingenious use of the "hangman" paradox, to be also the stern, inflexible judge and executioner. The "hangman god" is equated by Stephen with the bounds of human possibility. He is "all in all in all of us" so that in the empirical world he is both "ostler and butcher," taking care of creatures and also destroying them. Essentially, this is a humanist or naturalist view of god. It makes the god coterminous with his creatures so that whatever he does to or for them, he also does to or for himself. Thus, as the "*dio boia*, hangman god," he is both the hanger and the hanged, victim and victimizer.

With this, we can see how the dying god and the priest-king of the wood are subtly interrelated. Indeed, the dual aspect of the *dio boia* is exactly rendered in *The Golden Bough*'s phrase "the hanged god." Frazer uses this to refer to those deities who both demanded sacrificial death by hanging of their worshippers and also suffered it themselves. In the chapter entitled "The Hanged God" he suggests that "in old days the priest who bore the name and played the part of Attis at the spring festival of Cybele was regularly hanged or otherwise slain upon the sacred tree."[21] A similar custom was observed in connection with the Scandinavian deity Odin so that he was called "the Lord of the Gallows or the God of the Hanged." Moreover, "he is said to have been sacrificed to himself in the ordinary way" according to Frazer, who emphasized the reflexive nature of the self-sacrifice by quoting the verses from the *Havamal* which conclude "Wounded with the spear, dedicated to Odin,/ Myself to myself."[22] This sacrifice of the self for the sake of the resurrection of the self in greater wisdom (Odin acquired, Frazer remarks, "his divine power by learning the magic runes" while hung on the tree) is the mythic essence of Stephen's struggle throughout *A Portrait* and *Ulysses*.

It has already been suggested that Stephen's ritual sacrifice takes place in the "Circe" chapter. Clearly we cannot hope to explore all the relevant ramifications of that very long and compli-

[21] *GB*, v, 289. [22] *GB*, v, 290.

cated chapter. Nevertheless, the major lines of Stephen's archetypal experience can be charted and its dependency on *The Golden Bough*'s themes and perspective established. Central to these is the notion of ritual. Consequently, it is fully appropriate that Stephen should at the beginning of the chapter perform a Christian ritual chant. Yet he does so in an ironic spirit by means of which he moves to a more secular enactment. While flourishing his ashplant he shivers "*the lamp image, shattering light over the world*" (432; author's italics). Not only does this foreshadow his climactic action in the brothel, but it suggests that his ritual combat is also a species of epistemic creation myth. That the action is peculiarly meaningful is underscored by a later remark which shows Frazer's comparative approach to the functions and varieties of ritual: "The rite is the poet's rest. It may be an old hymn to Demeter or also illustrate *Caela enarrant gloriam Domini*. It is susceptible of nodes or modes as far apart as hyperphrygian and mixolydian and of texts so divergent as priests haihooping round David's that is Circes' or what am I saying Ceres' altar and David's tip from the stable to his chief bassoonist about his almightiness" (503-504).

This explicit association of poetry or art with ritual suggests that under the impress of *The Golden Bough* and the climate of opinion it engendered Joyce is here having Stephen recognize the archetypal nature of art and its relation to religion. An ironic intensification of this occurs in Stephen's answer to Mulligan's query as to where they are going: "Lecherous lynx, to *la belle dame sans merci*, Georgina Johnson, *ad deam qui laetificat juventutem meam*" (433). The hallucinatory character of the scene together with Joyce's interest in multi-level ironies combine to suggest there is more to Stephen's comment than mere youthful bravado and cynicism. However fliply, he recognizes that the whore may be a goddess, a creature of a sacred order, and that sexuality is intimately bound up with fertility of all forms.[23]

Shaped by this dual awareness, he later confronts an aspect of his familial myth that he has not alluded to before. It is one that underlines graphically Frazer's stress upon the barbarism of many rites as well as their persistence in more civilized expres-

[23] *GB*, v, 36ff.

sions: "Queens lay with prize bulls. Remember Pasiphaë for whose lust my grandoldgrossfather made the first confession-box" (569). His equating of the labyrinth with the Roman Catholic confessional is a Frazerian device for producing an irony of genesis and origins. It portrays the Christian ritual as a tortuous confrontation with death and the Christian priest (and, by extension, God) as a monster that destroys heroes and victims alike, a creature that is an intensification of the bovine god met by Stephen in *A Portrait*.

The foregoing has shown Stephen steadily moving toward a clear apprehension of the primitive and archetypal nature of human experience as rendered in *The Golden Bough*. Thus, in the midst of his simulated Frenchman's conversation, he gabbles what resembles a sensationalized response to some of Frazer's information: "Perfectly shocking terrific of religion's things mockery seen in universal world" (570). To accommodate such revelations to his own being is Stephen's task, and he accomplishes it with a ritual act and a dialogue with the dead. The act is the wild dance in the brothel joined by people, furnishings, personal ornaments, and the hours of the day. Some of the dancers wear garments with "dark bat sleeves" (576), others are "masked" (577), and still others are "jujuby women" (578), while objects "from gilded snakes dangle" (578), and the "Gadarene swine" (579) and other animals prance. But perhaps most important of all, Stephen himself calls it a "dance of death" and at its culmination after he "whirls giddily" in a dervish-like ecstasy, it is said "he stops dead" (579). This complex seems to owe more than a little to *The Golden Bough* in the way of function. Frazer, of course, has an enormous variety of information about the nature and roles of dance in primitive societies, so much in fact that it would be impossible for anyone to use it all in any one context. Among those items that seem most relevant to the present scene are his stress on dances as rituals of propitiation of the dead, expulsion of ghosts, and initiation, this last being performed in the grave.[24] The relevance of each of these begins to emerge when immediately after the dance's conclusion "*Stephen's mother, emaciated, rises stark through the floor in leper*

[24] *GB*, III, 166, 373-374; IX, 139; XI, 237, 258-259.

grey with a wreath of faded orange blossoms and a torn bridal veil" (579; author's italics). Stephen attempts to propitiate her by pleading that her death was the result of cancer, not of his actions. And he asks initiation into wisdom through asking her to tell him "the word known to all men" (581). Finally, he endeavors to expel the ghost from his consciousness by obscene language, which is frequently part of ritual, and then by the symbolic act of smashing the chandelier.[25]

Frazer's great cruel, voracious mother goddesses like Cybele and Ishtar are identified with her implicitly by Buck Mulligan who, dressed as a fool, has the license to speak freely and indecently: "The mockery of it! Kinch killed her dogsbody bitchbody. She kicked the bucket. . . . Our great sweet mother! *Epi oinopa ponton*" (580). The description of her body as that of a dog and bitch is Joyce's compressed rendering of Frazer's point that the mother of fertility cults is both a deity (Joyce iterates the dog-god equation a number of times so that by this time it is fairly taken as established) and a wanton of prolific sexuality.[26] By this means Joyce suggests the archetypal roots for Stephen's feelings of ambivalence over his mother.

Her persistence in trying to break his spirit through her prayers for his salvation from hell crystallizes his recognition that her love, like that of Frazer's orgiastic goddesses and their human representatives, is ultimately destructive and bound up with death.[27] Her concern with salvation is essentially an effort to have Stephen accept mortality as an imaginative fact. In so doing he would also have to renounce his association, as artist, with the dying and reviving god for whom mortality is a transient not a permanent condition. When he recognizes the nature of her insistence on his repentance, he brands it as death-like in terms whose fullest meaning is rooted in *The Golden Bough*. First, he calls her "The ghoul! Hyena!" and then "The corpsechewer! Raw head and bloody bones!" (581). Since the ghoul was originally a demon of the woods and associated with death, it is clear that it stands to Stephen, the priest-king representative of the dying god, as his perennial antagonist. In addition, Frazer observes

[25] *GB*, III, 154-155.   [26] *GB*, I, 37; IX, 365, 372.
[27] *GB*, IX, 369ff.

that hyenas are thought to contain the souls of the dead, a notion that fuses with their eating of carrion to convey their function of parodying the self-sacrifice of the hanging god.[28] And finally, in the volume on Osiris, Frazer discusses a fabulous Egyptian monster called the "Eater of the Dead" who plays a role in what approximates the Last Judgment.[29] According to Frazer, there is some evidence for supposing that those adjudged unworthy were turned over to this creature to be devoured. The image of "the corpsechewer" seems an adaptation of this figure. With it Joyce has provided a primitive anticipation of a Christian belief that is central to those who seek to break Stephen's spirit and to refute his cry of "Non serviam."

By doing so, Joyce clarifies the mother's relation to Stephen as an artist and dying-god figure. She stands athwart his development of imaginative freedom and as a final gambit equates herself with the crucified Christ: "Inexpressible was my anguish when expiring with love, grief and agony on Mount Calvary" (582). Implicit in this is the idea that Stephen's new and scarcely firm sense of his own role as dying god can be abrogated by her assuming it.

By now, however, having recognized clearly the nature of the threat she poses, Stephen declares the truth and acts the reality of his own being:

Nothung!
    (*He lifts his ashplant high with both hands and smashes the chandelier. Time's livid final flame leaps and, in the following darkness, ruin of all space, shattered glass and toppling masonry.*) (583; author's italics)

His statement refutes emphatically her claim to being the hanged god, thereby preserving his own freedom to prove himself an artist by enacting the role. And by smashing the chandelier he achieves a moment of imaginative apocalypse. With the destruction of time and space he moves wholly into the archetypal and mythical world that is in but not of the phenomenological and historical universe.

[28] *GB*, VIII, 289.   [29] *GB*, VI, 14.

At the same time, Stephen's declaration of "Nothung" applies to himself as well. It is his way of announcing that as the priest-king of the wood he has not yet suffered the mythic defeat that would bring him to the hanged god phase of his existence. How he approaches this state on a simple physical level is seen in the immediately following scene. There Private Carr first circles warily, as in the grove at Nemi, then knocks Stephen down in a highly ironic defeat of the poet-priest by the warrior-priest. This comic version of ritual combat is enacted primarily to show how far the physical, objective issues are from the ritual that most deeply concerns Stephen. Carr's misinterpretation of Stephen's recognition that "in here it is I must kill the priest and the king" (589) touches off a farcical inversion of Stephen's real struggle. This last, of course, is with himself and his unconscious desire to remain the artist priest-king, that is, an artist possessing both secret spiritual power and social status beyond the ordinary man. To achieve a complete vision of the artist, who in Joyce's mind is man dedicated to truth, Stephen must realize it as an enactment of the dying god myth. This alone unites a universal knowledge of mortality with a common participation in the life of mankind.

In effect, this is what he does in the remainder of the book. As a result, by the time he is prepared to depart from Bloom's house it is as someone coming out of Egypt, "from the house of bondage to the wilderness of inhabitation" (697). There he perceives, first, "the heaventree of stars hung with humid nightblue fruit" (698) and then "the mystery of an invisible person" (702). In this and in the catechistic form of the "Ithaca" chapter, Joyce submits Stephen to the ritual of the dying god whereby he departs the known world for the dark realm of the unnecessary and the unconscious. Joyce no longer needs the figure of Stephen as the artist. Therefore he returns to the imaginative matrix where he can participate in the formation of a new artist, Shem, and a new myth, that of the reviving god, HCE. Both of these are, as we shall see, expressions of the comedy of creation rather than of the irony of annihilation.

CHAPTER XIII

James Joyce: *Ulysses*
and the Human Scapegoat

Though recent criticism has stressed Bloom's modestly heroic traits and his role of a twentieth-century Everyman who is the quintessence of the ordinary, it has also suggested clearly the extent to which he is the victim of his world. In Volume 9 of *The Golden Bough*, Frazer explores in a most elaborate manner what he describes as "the use of the Dying God as a scapegoat to free his worshippers from the troubles of all sorts with which life on earth is beset."[1] Obviously not all victims are scapegoats nor all scapegoats dying gods. To the extent, however, that the victim is a traditional selection of his society—chosen in order to free the community at large of its evils and sorrows, associated with a period of license and psychological release, and felt to have some ineffable but real connection with the divine—he may fairly be regarded as an embodiment or representative of the dying god in his role of scapegoat.[2] To insist without qualification that Leopold Bloom is such a figure would be foolish. Nevertheless, an important part of his nature and role in the novel squares most nearly with an adaptation of that primitive sacrifice. Though Bloom is cast in the scapegoat pattern, he is not simply the primitive scapegoat transposed to a twentieth-century milieu. Rather, he is the contemporary homologue to the figure described by Frazer; the changes effected in his manner and constitution by his environment and society are scrupulously rendered so that what emerges is an accurate rendering of modern man as the scapegoat.

As with Stephen, Bloom's archetypal nature develops from his context. In both instances, Joyce's strategy is to surround them

---

[1] *GB*, IX, v.
[2] *GB*, IX, 185ff., 225, 227, 307-312, 345ff.; XI, 24.

with elements and details that establish the primitive and universal properties of their immediately given universe. One of the earliest items by which Joyce links Bloom to a distant past occurs on his return from the butcher shop with his breakfast. Inspired by the Agendath Netaim advertisement as qualified by the cloud-covered sun, he envisages an ancient Mediterranean world that calls up some of Frazer's more graphic descriptions:

> A barren land, bare waste. Vulcanic lake, the dead sea: no fish, weedless, sunk deep in the earth. No wind would lift those waves, grey metal, poisonous foggy waters. Brimstone they called it raining down: the cities of the plain: Sodom, Gomorrah, Edom. All dead names. A dead sea in a dead land, grey and old. Old now. It bore the oldest, the first race. A bent hag crossed from Cassidy's clutching a noggin bottle by the neck. The oldest people. Wandered far away over all the earth, captivity to captivity, multiplying, dying, being born everywhere. It lay there now. Now it could bear no more. Dead: an old woman's: the grey sunken cunt of the world (61).

In its stress on barrenness, greyness, poison, and death it also suggests that Joyce like Eliot may have been influenced by *The Golden Bough*'s description of the area surrounding Ibreez. In addition, the final graphic image captures an initial level of irony about the nature of the civilized world. It affords a scarifying inversion of the historical and anthropological conviction common in Frazer's day that the Near East constituted the cradle and birthplace of world civilization.

These and other references, such as those mentioned already about rain charms, nail- and hair-clippings, and cakes for the dead, establish the lineaments of the primitive world in which Bloom, as a scapegoat, has a vested interest. Similarly, as has been suggested earlier, other features indicate his involvement in Frazer's own sceptical irony about the efficacy or meaning of many early religious customs. One of the most striking and far-reaching of these scenes is that set in All Hallows Church where Bloom muses both on the announced sermon and on the rites of the Roman Catholic faith. His mind moves from the idea of missionary activities in Africa and China, to prayers offered for those of another faith, to a collocation of Buddha and Christ, then back to natives entranced with Christianity. In effect, this renders ironically the ordinary man's approximation to the method and study of comparative religion, which is none the less accurate for being an approximation. This emerges even more clearly in the immediately following response to the communion rite: "The priest bent down to put it into her mouth, murmuring all the time. Latin. The next one. Shut your eyes and open your mouth. What? *Corpus*. Body. Corpse. Good idea the Latin. Stupefies them first. Hospice for the dying. They don't seem to chew it; only swallow it down. Rum idea: eating bits of a corpse why the cannibals cotton to it" (80).

Here, almost exactly like Frazer, Joyce uses a Christian setting to develop the parallels and continuity between pagan primitive rites and those of Christianity. Bloom's identification of communion and cannibalism also involves at least a measure of Frazer's emphasis on the role of the dead in primitive religion. The strength of this last sentiment in Bloom's response is suggested in the "Hades" chapter. There he recalls his dying father's final injunction, juxtaposes it with a phrase from the Lord's Prayer, and concludes reflectively "We obey them in the grave" (90). Bloom combines the response of the primitive mind to its experiential mysteries with the sophisticated appraisal of that response appropriate to a detached bystander. In essence, then, the irony in his position corresponds to that in *The Golden Bough*. For each it results from the interaction of primitive data and experiences with a dispassionately sceptical consciousness of irrational past and progressive present as a single continuum. Thus, Bloom, like Frazer, can see a world in which nail- and hair-clippings, cakes for the dead, and ghosts are important. At the same time he can interpret religious ritual and myth from a broadly Darwinian perspective of survival in which "it's everybody eating everyone else. That's what life is after all" (122).

Largely because of this duality of perspective, as well as Joyce's refusal simply to reenact ancient rituals, Bloom's role as scapegoat is functional and metaphoric rather than literal. Consequently, there is neither need nor purpose to search the novel for minutely accurate renderings of ritual details and customs described by Frazer. Joyce's method is instead to employ isolated elements of a loosely anthropological order that serve as allusive motifs which establish the primitive dimension of the scene or character. These, then, alert the reader to larger ritual approximations homologous to those detailed by *The Golden Bough*. In this way, Joyce elaborates his "mythic method" so that the primeval and the contemporary meet in the concrete situations of the novel with that equality of significance and fidelity to experience out of which the truly archetypal is generated.

The first of these scenes in Bloom's case is provided by the "Hades" chapter in which he attends the funeral of Paddy Dignam and witnesses his interment at Prospect cemetery. As we might expect from the context, Bloom here is brought face to face with the fate his community implicitly seeks for him. His responses show that he has the necessary equanimity about death to play the role of scapegoat in the unsentimental manner of ancient custom. Thus, he sees an enormous rat as a "greatgrandfather" (114) and concludes: "One of those chaps would make short work of a fellow. Pick the bones clean no matter who it was. Ordinary meat for them" (114). Such a quasi-totemistic view perhaps suggests that Joyce may also have been thinking here of Frazer's point about the mingled divine and threatening aspects of the rat in primitive belief. At the same time, Bloom is not a mere passive acquiescent in human mortality. His gritty Odyssean determination to survive at all costs is strengthened by his visit to Parnell's grave immediately after Dignam's funeral. There the first thing asserted is the resurrective nature of Ireland's uncrowned king: "—Some say he is not in that grave at all. That the coffin was filled with stones. That one day he will come again" (112). Such an awe-struck response suggests clearly that Parnell is being likened to Frazer's primitive chieftains who were deified after death and worshipped.[3] Hynes is even careful to use the Irish popular epithet for Parnell to point up the ritual nature of political life, for he speaks of it as "the chief's grave" (112). And in so doing, he underscores Frazer's discussion of tragedy's originating in the worship of the dead as well as Jane

[3] *GB*, VI, 175-187; VIII, 125.

Harrison's notion that the tomb of the dead hero is a place of birth and creation, that is, an *omphalos*.[4]

This interrelation of life and death is one that Bloom is particularly fond of commenting on. When he associates Parnell's grave with a sardonically realistic version of "All souls' day" (113), *The Golden Bough*'s impact emerges clearly. By describing Parnell's grave as standing amid a grove, he implicitly follows Frazer's report that often the soul of a chief was thought to reside in a sacred grove while at the same time reminding us of Parnell's role in life as the lonely warrior guardian of the grove.[5] Similarly, his lower-case reference to "all souls' day," which follows on his notion of handling all the dead at one time, also suggests the Frazerian irony that a pagan festival of the dead underlies the Christian observance.[6] And when we note that immediately prior to this he remarks of the dead "Plant him and have done with him" (113), we see the extent to which the dead political leader is allied with Frazer's vegetative fertility gods like Adonis and Osiris and Dionysus.[7]

Given the presence of the myth of the dying god with its implication of the persistence of life, Bloom is provided with that warrant for playing the scapegoat which alone is sufficient. It is an archetypally meaningful role for the ultimate human condition and is, in a sense, the most fundamental vindication of the ironic view of life available to man.

Both Bloom's sacrificial role and his acceptance of it are emphasized in a variety of manners in subsequent chapters. Thus, in the "Aeolus" section, he, like Stephen in *A Portrait*, is brought into conjunction with "the crossblind" (129) to symbolize his subjection to the institutional sanctions of the community. In this same scene the elements of mockery associated with the ritual of the scapegoat are first brought to bear on Bloom as "the file of capering newsboys" follow him like "a mocking kite" (129). Bloom, however, counters this threat by his attitude in the "Lestrygonians" chapter. He surveys the primitive, cannibalistic feast

---

[4] *GB*, IX, 384, n.2; Jane Harrison, *Prolegomena*, p. 322ff.

[5] *GB*, XI, 161.   [6] See *GB*, VI, 81.

[7] *GB*, V, 236-259; VI, 51-88.

of Dublin at lunch, which issues in the harsh evolutionary perception of "eat or be eaten. Kill! Kill!" (170). Nevertheless, he is able to see the ritual and by implication his own fate in a quizzically comic way:

> Dignam's potted meat. Cannibals would with lemon and rice. White missionary too salty. Like pickled pork. Except the chief consumes the parts of honour. Ought to be tough from exercise. His wives in a row watch the effect. *There was a right royal old nigger. Who ate or something the somethings of the reverend Mr MacTrigger.* With it an abode of bliss. Lord knows what concoction. Cauls mouldy tripes windpipes faked and minced up. Puzzle find the meat. Kosher. No meat and milk together. Hygiene that was what they call now. Yom Kippur fast spring cleaning of inside. Peace and war depend on some fellow's digestion. Religions. Christmas turkeys and geese. Slaughter of innocents. Eat, drink and be merry (171-172).

As this pattern of sacrifice and destruction moves closer to him personally and takes on a more immediate cast, the tone deepens, becomes less jaunty and more threnodic. This is apparent in the "Sirens" chapter where Bloom amid the varied music of the tavern sits silently strumming an elastic band and singing his own unuttered lament: "Let people get fond of each other: lure them on. Then tear asunder. Death" (277). Beneath love there always lies the *sparagmos* of the individual sufferer whom life makes a victim of his own impulses.

Bloom's role as scapegoat in *Ulysses* is a complex one, for he enacts it on a number of levels and with varying degrees of seriousness. On the social plane, the Celtic, Catholic community dedicated to music, sports, and tavern life finds its release in subtle and not so subtle victimizing of Bloom. Stephen's encounter with Mr. Deasy prepares us for the antisemitism visited on Bloom in the course of the novel. This begins with Paddy Dignam's funeral and culminates with the Citizen's furious assault in the "Cyclops" chapter. Bloom's Jewish appearance provides the visual warrant for the ritualized comments about his parsimoniousness, talkativeness, slyness, interest in money, and so on. In their way these function in substantially the same manner as those vituperative and obscene expressions visited on the scapegoat in primitive times. For, according to Frazer, the person selected as the scapegoat is frequently subjected to screams, howls, and curses before being driven with beatings to his death.[8] In Bloom's case the verbal imprecations are both less ritualized and more restrained, as befits the secular, civilized community of which he is the sacrificial representative. Thus, the members of the funeral party obliquely snub him, as John Henry Menton does, or make him feel his alienation from the bonhomerie of Irish gentlemen, as Simon Dedalus does. Similarly, his social right to courtesy is denied in the "Aeolous" chapter. There Lenehan denies it by an exaggeration of the normal forms. Later Myles Crawford, the newspaper editor, denies it by exploding even the minimal expressions of politeness: "—He can kiss my royal Irish arse, Myles Crawford cried loudly over his shoulder. Any time he likes, tell him" (147).

In the "Cyclops" chapter, where Bloom's verbal abuse reaches its climax, Joyce carefully emphasizes the primitive nature of the situation. He does so through a stylistic burlesque of the Homeric giant whose dangerous absurdity is crystallized by his transposition from Greek limpidity to an orotund English. Between the pithy colloquialism of the nameless narrator and the inflated parody of the language of Celtic saga, the mythic method's interrelation of past and present links Bloom more closely to his archetypal role of scapegoat. Thus, though the scene is said to be set in "the land of holy Michan" (293), it is a region of "the wafty sycamore, the Lebanonian cedar, the exalted planetree, the eugenic eucalyptus and other ornaments of the arboreal world with which that region is thoroughly well supplied" (294). The trees effect a fusion of the Ireland of mythic times with the Mediterranean of an even more remote era, in a language that has more than a trace of exaggerating the ripeness of *The Golden Bough*'s style. In subsequent pages, local brewers are said to be as "cunning as the sons of deathless Leda" and their methods to involve "the sacred fire" (299). And Bloom himself is likened to the son of a king and said to be "impervious to fear" and known as "he of the prudent soul" (297). In the very language of the

[8] *GB*, IX, 215, 220, *passim*.

chapter there is an ironic continuity persisting from ancient to modern barbarism. Inherent in the language too is a sense of the way in which legends and myths grow out of the barbarism of the human animal and thereby erect for him at least the lineaments of a civilized and humane being. Just like *The Golden Bough, Ulysses* uses the various kinds of culture existing in the present to illuminate and explain perennial facets of human life observed in the distant past. The limited existences of the Citizen, Bob Doran, Alf Bergan, Joe Hynes, and the rest are cast in the exalted language of ancient saga and legend.

After one of the most elegant and inflated descriptions of tavern life, the Citizen glimpses Bloom outside and pugnaciously titles him "that bloody freemason" (300). From this and other contemptuous epithets on to the final furious attack on Bloom by the Citizen a doubly ironic vision of the scapegoat gradually emerges. This activity involves not only the verbal assaults on Bloom for his high-flown language, pretentious knowledgeability, debatable masculinity, and Jewishness, but the tavern accounts of fights, hangmen, executions, weddings, and miracles. In their several ways, these accounts bring Bloom into conjunction with the basic facts of the scapegoat ritual. According to Frazer, the scapegoat is beaten both as a means of purification and as a way of increasing his reproductive capacities which then were exercised in a brief marriage with a divinely named bride after which he was taken to his death by hanging, drowning, stoning or the like.[9] And in the Aztec custom of killing the god, to which *The Golden Bough* devotes an entire chapter, the supreme miracle of resurrection is even enacted for the scapegoat.[10] As a result, though Joyce makes no effort to tie these significant events specifically to the rituals described by Frazer, the chapter does capture with remarkable accuracy what the actual form of the experience of a twentieth-century scapegoat might be.

This pattern of ritual approximation is pursued not only within the "Cyclops" chapter, which is a kind of microcosm of Bloom's scapegoat experience, but also through the novel as a whole. In this larger structural unit, the "Cyclops" section is homologous

[9] *GB*, IX, 232, 253-254, 255-257, 259-260.
[10] *GB*, IX, 296-302.

with the scapegoat's beating and abuse described by Frazer. Following it, as a fertilizing ritual, we would naturally expect something approximating a marriage or sexual ritual. This is precisely what Bloom enacts, though in devastatingly ironic fashion, in the course of the "Nausicaa" chapter and perhaps in the "Oxen of the Sun" too. Gerty McDowell and Mrs. Purefoy are the twin halves of the scapegoat's ritual relation to woman. Gerty is the temporary liaison sanctioned by the community, and Mrs. Purefoy negatively defines that which the scapegoat can never know, namely, a woman bearing his children. It goes without saying by this time that neither is presented as a figure of solemn religious emotion or awesome social significance. Instead, their absurdities, mental and physical, are developed fully and with terrifying precision. Gerty's silly adolescent romantic fantasies are shown as the virtually total scope of her imaginative existence, and Mrs. Purefoy's annual producing of a child develops *The Golden Bough*'s implications concerning the parodic nature of the recurrent and the cyclical. In both cases, they are fit associates for the scapegoat seen as an ironic emblem of his world and age.

The portion of the scapegoat ritual that consists in execution and death finds its equivalent in the "Circe" chapter. At the beginning of the chapter Bloom appears panting, with a stitch in his side from running, and puzzled as to why he had done so. The implication is clearly that he has just experienced the ritual pursuit and hunt which precedes his execution. In a variety of manners, hallucinatory meetings with his parents and female acquaintances conspire to generate guilt on Bloom's part for social and sexual misdemeanours. This sense of guilt, which is the modern way of singling out the scapegoat, logically eventuates in its ritual, which is that of apprehension by the police, legal trial, and sentencing. All these take place in the next section where Bloom is accused of literary plagiarism and indecent sexual conduct with a variety of women. To this Bloom replies incoherently while beginning the first of a series of metamorphoses. His attorney suggests the modern form of the scapegoat ritual when he declares: "I shall call rebutting evidence to prove up to the hilt that the hidden hand is again at its old game. When in doubt persecute Bloom" (464). Similarly, the Amazonian garbed and mannered The Honourable Mrs. Mervyn Talboys indicates that however metaphoric her language, she is prepared to treat him as ancient scapegoats were treated: "I'll scourge the pigeonlivered cur as long as I can stand over him. I'll flay him alive" (467). And just before he is sentenced one of the police notes: "He is a marked man. Another girl's plait cut" (470). The inference is that Bloom has been involved in this last act, which as The Golden Bough makes clear may be a matter of both purification and sexual sacrifice.[11]

Given these indications that he is the scapegoat, it is no surprise to find him being sentenced to death by hanging. At one stroke, the mythic and literal fates of Bloom are sealed, especially since the subsheriff identifies him with Judas Iscariot. For not only does this render the community's judgment that they are punishing the treacherous betrayer, it also suggests The Golden Bough's implicit alignment of Judas with the scapegoat. Frazer points out, for instance, that effigies of Judas were both driven out of the church and also burnt during Easter—that he in turn is being treated as a scapegoat for his part in the death of the Christian dying god.[12]

Death by hanging, however, is only a threat for Bloom. The hallucinatory world of the chapter swerves away from the ritual death itself, and he finds himself outside Bella Cohen's brothel where Stephen and the rest of the company have already gone. There bells, electors, and torchbearers all join in acclaiming his election as Lord Mayor of Dublin. Clearly, this scene represents Bloom's desires and wish-fantasies just as the earlier one mirrored his anxieties. What is most interesting, however, is Joyce's careful insertion of Frazerian images into the triumph. These images more directly identify Bloom as a scapegoat and at the same time underscore his affinities with the dying and reviving god, who survives all the vicissitudes of the natural and social worlds. Immediately after Bloom's first impassioned political speech, there is an extended parenthetic quasi-stage-direction description which through its welter of detail parodies the whole

[11] GB, III, 283-287; I, 30-31; V, 38.
[12] GB, X, 121, 127-132, 143, 146; XI, 23.

notion of political enthusiasm. At its outset "*Venetian masts, may-poles and festal arches spring up*" (479), and at its conclusion "*Bloom's boys run amid the bystanders with branches of haw-thorn and wrenbushes*" (481). Immediately after this, Bloom's boys join in a ritual song of substantially authentic cast:

> The wren, the wren,
> The king of all birds,
> Saint Stephen's his day,
> Was caught in the furze (481).

All these figure prominently in *The Golden Bough*, and it seems scarcely likely that Joyce was not cognizant of the signifi-cance imputed to them there. The maypole, for instance, is phal-lic in character and ostensibly a fertility charm.[13] Its King and Queen are folk versions of the spirits of vegetation ultimately represented by the dying and reviving god.[14] The pole was also, according to Frazer, frequently set up in front of the house of the mayor.[15] The hawthorn was considered a protective charm against both witches and ghosts—the two things that, in a sense, most threaten Stephen and Bloom—as well as a container of mistletoe, the original golden bough.[16] The song of the wren is part of a ritual described at some length in *The Golden Bough*.[17] Frazer calls the ritual of hunting the wren one that dates from a very early paganism and finds it extremely widespread through-out Europe. According to him, "the wren has been designated the king, the little king, the king of birds, the hedge king, and so forth, and has been reckoned amongst those birds which it is ex-tremely unlucky to kill."[18] Despite this, Frazer goes on, the cus-tom of killing the wren is a well established one and nowhere more than in Ireland:

> Down to the present time the "hunting of the wren" still takes place in parts of Leinster and Connaught. On Christmas Day or St. Stephen's Day the boys hunt and kill the wren, fasten it in the middle of a mass of holly and ivy on the top of a broom-

---

[13] *GB*, II, 52.
[15] *GB*, VIII, 44.
[17] *GB*, VIII, 317-321.

[14] *GB*, I, 84-85, 87-88; IV, 266; IX, 406.
[16] *GB*, II, 55, 127; IX, 153, n.1; XI, 315-316.
[18] *GB*, VIII, 317.

stick, and on St. Stephen's Day go about with it from house to house, singing:—

> "*The wren, the wren, the king of all birds,*
> *St. Stephen's Day was caught in the furze;*
> *Although he is little, his family's great,*
> *I pray you, good landlady, give us a treat.*"[19]

That Joyce would be most attracted to the Irish version of the custom is natural. Yet when we look at Frazer's entire treatment of the topic, it is apparent that Joyce as usual has been eclectic in his choice of materials. The Irish version emphasizes what we might call the local or folk aspects. Others, such as the French, develop features that Joyce appropriates for the social or public dimensions of his scene. Thus, the French ceremony begins with beaters searching the bushes for wrens, while Joyce has them heralding Bloom's arrival.[20] Similarly, this procession is accompanied by a fife and drum band and includes a great many political and religious notables. Among them Bloom appears "*bareheaded, in a crimson velvet mantle trimmed with ermine, bearing Saint Edward's staff, the orb and sceptre with the dove, the curtana*" (481). The French ceremony is remarkably close to this in certain features:

> On the evening of the last day of the year the King and all who had hunted the wren marched through the streets of the town to the light of torches, with drums beating and fifes playing in front of them. . . . On the morning of Twelfth Day the King again marched in procession with great pomp, wearing a crown and a blue mantle and carrying a sceptre. . . . After hearing high mass in the parish church of St. Vincent, surrounded by his officers and guards, the King visited the bishop, the mayor, the magistrates, and the chief inhabitants, collecting money to defray the expenses of the royal banquet which took place in the evening and wound up with a dance.[21]

It is doubtful that Joyce utilized as much of Frazer's material as he does here without wishing also to use Frazer's interpretations and symbology, at least in their broad outlines. In repeating

[19] *GB*, VIII, 320.   [20] *GB*, VIII, 320.   [21] *GB*, VIII, 321.

some of the details of a particular ritual he hopes not only to confer on his scene something of Frazerian specificity but also to point up the extent to which his novel is structured on such Frazerian archetypes as the scapegoat and the dying god.

In this particular chapter the ironic and the comic are so interwoven that Bloom is almost simultaneously a figure of pathos and riotous absurdity. Thus, he develops the phallic significance of the maypole by taking his oath of office with the gesture of *"placing his right hand on his testicles"* (482) and by announcing most augustly that "we have this day repudiated our former spouse and have bestowed our royal hand upon the princess Selene, the splendour of night" (483). Both are brilliantly comic adaptations of primitive ritual, and the same is true of the fireworks honoring his ascension, which *"go up from all sides with symbolical phallopyrotechnic designs"* (482).

From the anthropological standpoint the irony of *Ulysses* is directed more at tracing the death of the god than at social or personal follies. Thus, immediately following the princess Selene's appearance John Howard Parnell announces: "Illustrious Bloom! Successor to my famous brother!" (483). But Parnell's historical fate was disastrous, and Joyce has elsewhere cast him as the tragic hero and dying god. Consequently, this alignment ironically presages Bloom's own downfall. Bloom himself establishes his scapegoat role in the course of enunciating his political platform, for he declares that he stands for "weekly carnival, with masked license" (489), among other things. And as *The Golden Bough* makes clear, the expulsion of communal evil in the form of the scapegoat was either preceded or followed by a period of license which in ancient Italy was known as the Saturnalia and in modern times as the Carnival.[22]

Bloom almost explicitly echoes Frazer here, for, as he remarks, "You call it a festivity. I call it a sacrament" (489). In addition, by way of further stressing its ritual nature, he embodies it in his own *Walpurgisnacht* drama. This emerges clearly when we compare the events with Frazer's comments: "a conspicuous feature of the Carnival is a burlesque figure personifying the festive season, which after a short career of glory and dissipation is

---

[22] *GB*, IX, 225-226, 306, 312.

publicly shot, burnt, or otherwise destroyed, to the feigned grief or genuine delight of the populace. If the view here suggested of the Carnival is correct, this grotesque personage is no other than a direct successor of the old King of the Saturnalia, the master of the revels, the real man who personated Saturn and, when the revels were over, suffered a real death in his assumed character.[23] Bloom's manner and nature make him a figure of fun to many of the characters in the novel. Certainly one of the funniest aspects of his perfomance is his burlesquing of the usual forms of monarchical reigns. In addition, however, he also parodies by implication the archetype of these reigns by his comic rendering of the myth of Saturn and by participating in the Saturnalia of the chapter.

The mythic burlesque nature of Bloom's reign stands out clearly in relation to Frazer's account of the Saturnalia: "This famous festival . . . was popularly supposed to commemorate the merry reign of Saturn, the god of sowing and of husbandry, who lived on earth long ago as a righteous and beneficent king of Italy, drew the rude and scattered dwellers on the mountains together, taught them to till the ground, gave them laws, and ruled in peace. His reign was the fabled Golden Age: the earth brought forth abundantly: no sound of war or discord troubled the happy world: no baleful love of lucre worked like poison in the blood of the industrious and contented peasantry."[24] To the populace initially Bloom is indeed just such a paragon of rulers, constructing the new Bloomusalem, dispensing "free medical and legal advice, solution of doubles and other problems" (487), advocating "the reform of municipal morals and the plain ten commandments" (489), and instituting "free money, free love and a free lay church in a free lay state" (490).

This idyllic world quickly changes, though, and in the eyes of his detractors Bloom assumes something of the sinister quality attributed to Saturn's reign, which, according to Frazer, "was crossed by a dark shadow" of blood sacrifices.[25] After Theodore Purefoy accuses him of using contraceptives "to frustrate the sacred ends of nature" (491), the veiled sibyl is overcome, stabs herself, and dies murmuring "My hero god!" (492). With this

[23] *GB*, IX, 312. [24] *GB*, IX, 306. [25] *GB*, IX, 307.

Bloom's divine nature is made quite explicit. He is linked with Frazer's dying and hanging gods in general and more particularly with Dionysus, who has come to be regarded as preeminently the archetype of human sexuality. Not only the sibyl but a host of other "attractive and enthusiastic women" (492) commit suicide in what Joyce makes into an uproariously comic version of Bacchanalian frenzy. Similarly, the mob's cries of "Lynch him! Roast him!" (492) suggest the god's fate of being torn to pieces by his worshippers. And when the throng goes on to declare him as bad as Parnell and to call him Mr. Fox, the Dionysian role is further underscored. The allusions to Parnell's sexuality and the foxy Dionysus combine to present the god as having a dark and sinister side both in the social, communal world and in the natural universe.[26]

It is in terms of his Dionysian associations that Bloom's assertions of "midsummer madness" (492) and his becoming "a finished example of the new womanly man" (493) are also to be understood. For as a harvest deity his rites are performed just before the crops are collected and in the course of these rites, according to *The Golden Bough*, men dressed as women.[27] A Christian version of the identification of Bloom with Dionysus completes the attribution. The evangelist Alexander J. Dowie unleashes a furious diatribe on Bloom in the course of which he equates him with "this stinking goat of Mendes" (492) as well as with other specifically Christian epithets such as "the white bull mentioned in the Apocalypse" and "a worshipper of the Scarlet Woman" (492). The goat of Mendes, according to *The Golden Bough*, was an Egyptian beast-god worshipped as the productive force in nature.[28] All these factors combine to link it to Dionysus and to the scapegoat, for like so many other animals it was treated as a sacred creature for most of the year and then was sacrificed amid great mourning at a set time.

These essentially maledictive responses to Bloom's king-god role conform, of course, to one of the two contradictory responses ritually appropriate to the worshippers of the dying god, either grievous sorrow or fierce joy and exultation.[29] But since this is a

[26] *GB*, VIII, 282.
[27] *GB*, VI, 258-259.
[28] *GB*, VIII, 172.
[29] *GB*, V, 9, 224-227, 272-273.

world of hallucination, dream, and expressionistic drama, the shifts of attitude are swift and capricious. Thus, the rage of the mob—the modern equivalent to the ritualistic rending of the scapegoat of primitive times—is quickly transformed into compassion by the doctors' announcement that Bloom is "a finished example of the new womanly man" (493) and "about to have a baby" (494). Both the birth and assumed femininity are rooted in ancient practices fully detailed by Frazer. In addition to the customs of men's dressing as women in the rites of Dionysus, this practice was also common at marriage ceremonies, circumcision rites, and ritual efforts to avoid demons or ghosts.[30] Similarly, women near term were frequently mimed by their husbands, who took to their beds in simulated labor. Using these strange rites here suggests the metamorphic character of human consciousness and with it the presence of both male and female components in each individual.

Bloom's role of scapegoat is perfectly in keeping with his basic function in the modern world. To point this up Joyce carefully includes all the ritual items associated with the scapegoat that he can mine from *The Golden Bough*. Thus, there is the use not only of verbal taunts and insults but of covert obscenity as in the song of the Prison Gate Girls, which shrewdly emphasizes the sexual nature of Bloom's sin and guilt.[31] His Judaic affinities with the scapegoat are also made unmistakably in Hornblower's announcement: "And he shall carry the sins of the people to Azazel, the spirit which is in the wilderness, and to Lilith, the nighthag. And they shall stone him and defile him, yea, all from Agendath Netaim and from Mizraim, the land of Ham" (497). Following this, "*All the people cast soft pantomime stones at Bloom*" (497). This act, of course, accords both with the Biblical ritual and with the classical forms discussed by Frazer.[32] It is as if Joyce is trying to make sure that the continuity in the historic observance of the ritual is not overlooked by his readers. This is further borne out by Bloom's being invested with "*a yellow habit with embroidery of painted flames and high pointed hat*" (498). Then he is set on fire by the Dublin Fire Brigade and rendered "*mute, shrunken, carbonised*" (499). Death by fire was central to certain Greek

[30] *GB*, VI, 261-263.   [31] *GB*, IX, 220, *passim*.   [32] *GB*, IX, 253-254.

ceremonies that Frazer details.[33] It was also accompanied by a particular tune's being played on musical instruments. Joyce parodies this by having the fiery demise of Bloom occur with "*a choir of six hundred voices, conducted by Mr. Vincent O'Brien,*" that "*sings the Alleluia chorus, accompanied on the organ by Joseph Glynn*" (499).

In the scene that follows his death by fire Joyce provides a brilliant comic dramatization of the regenerative process in the scapegoat role. He has Bloom appear in Irish emigrant's clothing, leading "*a black bogoak pig*" and declare: "Let me be going now, woman of the house, for by all the goats in Connemara I'm after having the father and mother of a bating. (*With a tear in his eye.*) All insanity. Patriotism, sorrow for the dead, music, future of the race. To be or not to be. Life's dream is o'er. End it peacefully. They can live on. (*He gazes far away mournfully.*) I am ruined. A few pastilles of aconite. The blinds drawn. A letter. Then lie back to rest. (*He breathes softly.*) No more. I have lived. Fare. Farewell" (499). The lugubrious accents of Synge's *Playboy* merge with a Frazerian recognition that his fate has been not merely accidental but determined. Bloom sees himself as a ritual of sacrifice for communal benefit. Yet just as Frazer is ironically sceptical about the rationality or efficacy of many of the most solemn rites he chronicles, so Joyce refuses to let Bloom lapse into his nation's favorite pastime, indulgent self-pity. His imagining of himself as done for, finished, about to die is tartly refuted by the whore Zoe's rejoinder: "Honest? Till the next time" (499). This catches Joyce's ironic awareness of the dramatic and hence partly illusory nature of all rituals, especially those simulating death.

After Bloom's regeneration, however, he still has to grow into full maturity, and in substantial measure this is what he does in the remainder of the "Circe" chapter. Here Joyce continues to adapt primitive rituals of the sort described by *The Golden Bough* to the hallucinatory conditions of the Dublin brothel. According to Frazer, persons undergoing a death and rebirth ritual are frequently obliged to simulate infancy in both its physical and intellectual manifestations.[34] Joyce similarly has Bloom as-

[33] *GB*, IX, 255.　　　　　[34] *GB*, XI, 251, 254.

sume the appearance of a baby *"in babylinen and pelisse, big-headed, with a caul of dark hair,"* who speaks in appropriate accents: "One two tlee: tlee tlwo tlone" (501). Then as he is drawn into the brothel and tempted by the prostitutes, a sign that he is now of the age of manhood, Bloom is joined by Virag, among whose hallucinatory accoutrements is *"an Egyptian pshent"* perched on his head as well as *"two quills"* (511) projecting over his ears. Together the crown and quills suggest that Virag stands to Bloom in the capacity of priest-king and advisor, as the wise old man of the tribe who supervises the initiation of the young men.[35]

Armed with the uncertain but somehow significant knowledge of Virag, Bloom encounters Bella Cohen, the whoremistress and Circe-figure, whose main role is to effect his sexual subordination to woman. Clearly Bloom's fate is a function of his behavior: he becomes a woman dominated by a strong man because that is the role he in essence plays with Molly in the real waking world. Though Joyce is probably still responding to Frazer's treatment of men's disguising themselves in women's clothes, for interpretation of this ancient and recurring phenomenon he appears to rely more on Sacher-Masoch. Thus, he tends to move from an anthropological orientation for his archetype in favor of a psychological or psychoanalytic one.

To the extent that the former is still present, though subterraneously, it may consist in Joyce's conviction that the scapegoat's encounter with woman is, as part of his ritual, also inevitably an encounter with death. In this case, the obvious analogy between sex and death is doubled, for the scapegoat's sexual ritual is succeeded by a self-sacrificial one that is truly final. This prospect is presented starkly and brutally by Bello (the male form of Bella) when he declares to Bloom: "We'll bury you in our shrubbery jakes where you'll be dead and dirty with old Cuck Cohen, my stepnephew I married, the bloody old gouty procurator and sodomite with a crick in his neck, and my other ten or eleven husbands, whatever the buggers' names were, suffocated in the one cesspool. (*He explodes in a loud phlegmy*

[35] *GB*, IX, 225ff.; III, 68.

laugh.) We'll manure you, Mr. Flower! (*He pipes scoffingly*.) Byby, Poldy! Byby, Papli!" (544).

Bloom's is to be as debased a death as ever Frazer's scapegoats suffered. Equally important is the establishment of the man-woman relationship as one of indifferent promiscuity in which the man's personal identity is destroyed. Here Bella the modern whoremistress is the contemporary expression of Semiramis, Astarte, Cybele and the other orgiastic fertility goddesses whose dedication to unbridled lust is matched only by their readiness to put their lovers to death.[36] Some indication that Joyce may have had Frazer and this aspect of *The Golden Bough* in mind is found in the concluding lines. The threat to "manure you, Mr. Flower" ironically associates Bloom with the dying god whose fate and revival frequently were emblemized by miniature gardens of flowers that flourished and died and then were discarded.[37] Similarly, to designate him successively as Mr. Flower, Poldy, and Papli is clearly to identify his major roles in relation to women, that is, lover of Martha Clifford, husband of Molly, and father of Milly. All three of these roles, according to Frazer, were enacted by the dying god or his human representatives with a single woman.[38]

The father-son relationship between Bloom and Stephen is nowhere more subtly or meaningfully limned in than through the similarity of their ultimate revelatory experience in the "Circe" chapter. Stephen, as we have seen, is finally driven to recognize the voracious cruelty of the mother-figure, a cruelty that ultimately consists of the emasculation of the artist-hero's creative potency. Similarly, but with a significant difference, too, Bloom has to penetrate to the heart of feminine reality as it exists for him. This he does in the scene with the Nymph, which immediately follows his Hebraic-dominated miming of death by burial. Significantly enough, this ritual death establishes him as not only the scapegoat suffering to relieve the community of its sins and crimes but also as the dying god or his representative whose re-

[36] *GB*, v, 13ff., 33ff., 268, 278, 279; IX, 365, 369.
[37] *GB*, v, 236, 239ff.
[38] *GB*, IV, 193ff., 214ff.; v, 11ff., 43-44, 47, 224; IX, 386, 401.

vival is a consequence of his death. The ritual nature of his departure is emphasized by the stage directions which describe him as *"broken, closely veiled for the sacrifice,"* with *"his face to the earth"* (544). Its essentially Hebraic nature is then made to suggest something of Frazer's accounts of the death of Adonis, for the Circumcised are said to speak *"in a dark guttural chant as they cast dead sea fruit upon him, no flowers"* (544). After this, voices from the present are juxtaposed with descriptions which make the ceremony Indian in character, thereby pointing up Joyce's implicit adaptation of Frazer's comparative method to the ends of archetypal pattern: *"From the suttee pyre the flame of gum camphire ascends"* (544).

Out of this welter of anthropological emphasis emerges *"a nymph with hair unbound, lightly clad in teabrown art colours, descends from her grotto and passing under interlacing yews, stands over Bloom"* (544-545). She, of course, is the figure from the rotogravure photograph over Bloom's bed, but she has also been humanized into an archetypal figure of the nymph, the virginal form of nature and mankind. By stressing the unbound hair, Joyce may be drawing on *The Golden Bough* to establish the religious nature of the ceremony enacted in the course of the next few pages of the novel and to underscore the sexual nature of it through indicating its post-puberty function as rite.[39] Initially, the nymph emphasizes Bloom's regard for and championing of the virgin. He found her in the evil company of the magazine's contents and rescued her from it, carrying her off to an oak frame above his marriage-bed. And though he kisses her and shades in parts of her body with a pencil, he does so as an act of homage to her as the "beautiful immortal" (546) and his praise of her beauty is "almost to pray" (546). At the same time, it is Bloom who she says "profaned our silent shade" and performed an infamous act "on our virgin sward" (549).

This duality in Joyce's use of ironic myth is brought out even more clearly by Bloom's response to the charge of the nymph and the yews:

I was precocious. Youth. The fauns. I sacrificed to the god of the forest. The flowers that bloom in the spring. It was pairing

[39] *GB*, III, 297-298.

time. Capillary attraction is a natural phenomenon. Lotty Clarke, flaxenhaired, I saw at her night toilette through ill-closed curtains, with poor papa's operaglasses. The wanton ate grass wildly. She rolled downhill at Rialto Bridge to tempt me with her flow of animal spirits. She climbed their crooked tree and I . . . A saint couldn't resist it. The demon possessed me. Besides, who saw? (549)

On the one hand, there is the duality of the setting: the perennially modern world of "natural phenomenon" and the equally persistent and forever ancient realm of ritual myths of the "god of the forest." Joyce cleverly manipulates the two so that the reality of childhood sexuality yields both. The myth defines the desire, while the natural events record the expressions of that desire. The constant and the multiform coalesce through the verbal and scenic juxtaposition.

In terms of myth and ritual of the sort found in *The Golden Bough*, it is difficult to specify what the nature of Bloom's sacrifice is. But on the contemporary human level, it is clearly that of looking, of voyeuristic sexuality, which can be construed as a sacrifice to a fertility deity or force in essentially two ways. First, the capitulation to voyeurism testifies, as Bloom suggests, to the strength of the basic sexual impulse in human affairs. Second, voyeurism is an aberrant act, at least in falling short of the full realization of sexuality. Hence its performance may be regarded as a sacrifice of dedication. On the other hand, Joyce is quick to make it clear that Bloom is not simply the worshipper of the god and the performer of sacrifice. He is also, as the novel ceaselessly dramatizes in a variety of forms, the scapegoat. Thus, immediately after Bloom attempts to provide a rationale for his actions, his symbolic animal form moves ironically through the scene, undercutting with economy and precision his efforts to avoid the fate of his nature: *"High on Ben Howth through rhododendrons a nannygoat passes, plumpuddered, buttytailed, dropping currants"* (550). The goat's final action is a succinct unverbalized appraisal of all that Bloom has been saying in an attempt to rationalize his behavior.

Almost in answer to the bleating of the goat, he gazes down at the sea from Ben Howth and thinks of falling. By linking himself with ironic headlines of other such deaths by falling—"Giddy Elijah" and "Sad end of government printer's clerk" (550)—he suggests his function as an archetype. He does so, however, in the limited, capsulized fashion of modern means of communication, which is mordantly appropriate to both society and its victim. This parodic rendering of the scapegoat ritual is then made explicit by the accompanying stage directions: *"Through silver-silent summer air the dummy of Bloom, rolled in a mummy, rolls rotatingly from the Lion's Head cliff into the purple waiting waters"* (550). The scapegoat's death by water after being hurled from a cliff is merged with the Egyptian device for sustaining or assuring immortality that Frazer describes as a means of prolonging the life of the soul.[40] The result is an ironic fusion of the scapegoat and dying god in a setting of style and image that obviously alludes to the "Lycidas" passage invoked earlier in connection with Stephen.

What Joyce enacts here is both a comic assurance of Bloom's survival and an ironic critique of the verbal pattern of dying god rituals in general. In all likelihood this particular formulation of comic and ironic stances owes a good deal directly to *The Golden Bough*. For instance, in his discussion of scapegoats in classical antiquity, Frazer provides a description that makes the comic nature of ritual an imaginative reality: "From the Lover's Leap, a white bluff at the southern end of their island, the Leucadians used annually to hurl a criminal into the sea as a scapegoat. But to lighten his fall they fastened live birds and feathers to him, and a flotilla of small boats waited below to catch him and convey him beyond the boundary. Probably these humane precautions were a mitigation of an earlier custom of flinging the scapegoat into the sea to drown. . . ."[41] Certainly the scene with its Daedalian echoes and ludicrously appended birds and feathers as well as its Lover's Leap association would have been peculiarly appealing to Joyce in his efforts to forge a myth that encompassed Daedalus, Icarus, and Odysseus as well as Bloom, the one-time wooer of Molly.

[40] *GB*, IV, 4.   [41] *GB*, IX, 254.

By miming the action of the scapegoat, Bloom dramatically adumbrates the verbal equivalent, which follows in the remainder of the scene. In the process, as has been suggested, the nymph's virginal nature is explored in a revealing manner. Her initial response to Bloom's interest in female anatomy is ambiguous. She stresses her remoteness and ethereality at the same time as she coyly reveals a measure of straitened sexual arousal: "(*Loftily.*) We immortals, as you saw today, have not such a place and no hair there either. We are stonecold and pure. We eat electric light. (*She arches her body in lascivious crispation, placing her forefinger in her mouth.*)" (551). But as the remainder of the scene makes clear, this is the extent of the virgin's admission of sexuality. Bloom with his usual common sense recognizes that such a condition denies the concrete, physical, natural ground of existence and so rejects her reduction to the "only ethereal" (553). Her ultimate character emerges, and with it the transformation of Bloom from the sexual scapegoat to the Odyssean hero who wanders in strange places and emerges unscathed and informed, a reviving god of experience. She responds with the secularized religiosity of charges of "Sacrilege" and sullied innocence. Then she launches into a physical attack designed to emasculate Bloom, to make of him a dying god in the mold of Adonis. The virgin, then, stands revealed as a creature ridden with fear, hatred, and the desire to destroy.

It is this that Bloom finally articulates in the course of understanding the full dimensions of his role as scapegoat: "Hoy! Nebrakada! Cat of nine lives! Fair play, madam. No pruning knife. The fox and the grapes, is it? What do we lack with your barbed wire? Crucifix not thick enough? (*He clutches her veil.*) A holy abbot you want or Brophy, the lame gardener, or the spoutless statue of the watercarrier or good Mother Alphonsus, eh Reynard?" (553). Such figures as the pruning knife, the fox, the lame gardener, and the watercarrier suggest that Joyce is here relying on memories gleaned from *The Golden Bough* both for details and for mythic perspective. The virgin is defined in terms of the Druid priest's ritual severing of the golden bough from the oak tree, the animal form of the witch, the maimed fertility deity, and the title bestowed on Athenian maidens, as well as the folk tale.[42] Because she is unable to attain the fertility emblem of the grapes, she becomes a witch who lusts indiscriminately after her religious male equivalent, a crippled cultivator of fertility, or a woman like herself. All these quasi-sexual objects share one feature: the inability, either physical or cultural, to have a complete sexual relation with the virgin, which is precisely the reason she wants them rather than Bloom. Indeed, it is by her effort at emasculation that she shows clearly the state in which he would have to exist to be acceptable to her.

This purges her from Bloom's consciousness and reveals her illusory character. Her plaster cast cracks, and she flees him unveiled, giving off an appropriate "cloud of stench" (553). Bloom has learned that his role as scapegoat is not a by-product of his sexual relation with Molly. Instead it is a direct consequence of his own ordinary, criminal-like (that is, guilty) nature and his capacity to accept victimization. His recoil from Molly's sexuality has led him by a series of stratagems and evasions to think that the virgin, the pure woman, the one who does not insist on the sexual challenge and confrontation, is the ideal. Now, however, he sees that this is not the case, and so he dismisses her forever with "Fool someone else, not me" (554).

As a result, he miraculously finds that he has lost not only misplaced awe and reverence but also misplaced fear. Bella Cohen returns, but now she is incapable of posing her earlier threat. Coolly he appraises her as a woman and declares her sexuality cause neither for alarm nor for demeaning capitulation: "*Passée. Mutton dressed as lamb*" (554). The whore, the polar opposite of the virgin, is equally a chimera now that Bloom realizes the inexpungable nature of sexuality in mankind. Its presence in the virgin not only serves to make it inevitable and inherent in the human condition but also serves to reduce it from the obsessive and special to the ordinary and occasional. That is, it is an important but not uniquely significant part of existence. As he demonstrates in the balance of the book, Bloom now knows that compassion, understanding, and equanimity directed to the preservation of truly human relationships in a relentlessly mortal universe are the vital qualities for the human being acting as the modern

[42] *GB*, VIII, 5; XI, 41, 76-77, 80, 284-285.

epic hero and complete man. With this, Joyce works a powerfully ironic reversal of the scapegoat as an archetypal figure. The sign that Bloom is going to find a *modus vivendi* with Molly and his life is his befriending of Stephen toward the end of the "Circe" chapter. It marks his conscious assumption of the scapegoat role. Insofar as he accepts and understands this role, he returns compassion for contempt and acceptance for rejection. In not only accepting the imposed role but in understanding it and responding to its dynamics, Bloom makes the figure of contempt, the buffoon, into a creature of transcendent worth, into a dying god.

This ancient function clearly has secular and modern possibilities that a mythopoeic ironist of Joyce's capacities could utilize. And *The Golden Bough* played a major role in suggesting this. It gave Joyce the sense of recurrent victimization so important to his irony and comedy. At the same time it indicated by its comparative approach that the victimized figures were secular creatures cast in a religious ritual which in its turn was a psychological projection of the cultural tensions prevalent in society. The intermingling of the secular and the religious, which is so important to the structure of Joyce's imagination, is developed by Frazer as a major motif. From it Joyce learned a great deal both about the principle of almost infinite variation that is central to motif-writing and also about the forms and modes of ordering a welter of details into a coherent and archetypally significant pattern. There is evidence for this, of course, throughout *Ulysses*. It is, however, particularly apparent in that most important of the concluding chapters, the one Joyce called "Ithaca," as if he wished to underline the archetypal, mythopoeic character of his book and its reliance on the "anthropoetic" imagination of *The Golden Bough*.

The entire chapter presents a close correlation between the abstractness of its quasi-religious form as an impersonal catechism and the concreteness of its anthropological matter. The latter has to do substantially with belief and ritual. At times Bloom is caught up in an almost wholly ritualistic perspective, as when he begins "the process of divestiture" (711) or silently recapitulates his entire day's experiences as a sequence of Jewish ritual acts ranging from "burnt offering" (728) to "atonement" (729).

Thus, the ritual antiphonal nature of the catechistical form mirrors and complements the novel's penultimate perspective, which is one of dispassionate contemplation and static ordering of the immediate human condition. Joyce here suggests that the ultimate form of the dialogue mode is the catechism directed not at the essentials of religious dogma but at the immediacy of secular existence.

The last chapter, Molly's "Penelope" excursus on her life and role as woman, is complementary. There Joyce presents the dynamic of life's matrix, which ritual is designed to order and render meaningful. Molly's role as fertility goddess, as emblem of generative vitality, is on such a fundamental level that little is presented other than the seething drive of life as a persisting phenomenon. Consequently, the "Penelope" chapter does not demonstrate directly Joyce's reliance on Frazer for the shape and character of the fertility figure as an orgiastic deity of life. Instead, her character is defined together with Bloom's and Stephen's in the preceding "Ithaca" chapter. Just before the opening of Molly's chapter, as Bloom recounts to her the events of the day, she is described as lying in bed "in the attitude of Gea-Tellus, fulfilled, recumbent, big with seed" (737). The classical image of earth as a female possessing power over marriage, death, and the underworld is given a final Frazerian caste virtually on the novel's last page when Molly recalls the "one true thing he [Bloom] said in his life" (782). She remembers his remarking that "I [Molly] was a flower of the mountain yes so we are flowers all a womans body" (782).

Similarly, Bloom in addition to ritualizing his life also signals his involvement with *The Golden Bough* by discovering as many connections between the moon and woman as does Frazer. Further, one of the points that emerges most clearly from *The Golden Bough* is the recurrent importance of sexuality to the persistence of life. Frazer demonstrates both the need for surrounding it with ritual solemnity and also the inevitability of ritualized sex's assuming an ironic significance. Bloom points up both the recurrence and the irony when he enters his bed, becomes aware of Boylan's prior presence, and puts it in an almost Frazerian universal perspective: "If he had smiled why would he have smiled?

To reflect that each one who enters imagines himself to be the first to enter whereas he is always the last term of a preceding series even if the first term of a succeeding one, each imagining himself to be first, last, only and alone, whereas he is neither first nor last nor only nor alone in a series originating in and repeated to infinity" (731).

And finally, as if to make the novel's reliance on *The Golden Bough* virtually unequivocal, Joyce has Bloom envisage as part of his "ultimate ambition" (712) a series of intellectual pursuits which includes the "comparative study of religions, folklore relative to various amatory and superstitious practices" (715). If this does not encompass the entire content of Frazer's work, nevertheless it serves as an excellent approximation to the main issues in the course of *The Golden Bough*. And when we take into account the ironic note Joyce plays over this "syllabus of intellectual pursuits" (715), it is clear that something of Frazer's own arabesques of amusement are being woven around the solemn, dreaming, struggling figure of Bloom in a manner that makes him a worthy representative of the mankind that Frazer saw moving slowly and painfully toward some ultimately brighter world no matter how distant.

CHAPTER XIV

James Joyce:
Finnegans Wake and the
Rituals of Mortality

[I]

In *Finnegans Wake* Joyce's experimental techniques of organization, selection, and perspective are, of course, brought to an apex of sophistication. It also exhibits by far the most sustained and unequivocal evidence of Joyce's familiarity with *The Golden Bough*. From "oaks of ald" to "icy and missilethroes" its pages are crowded with images, figures, and motifs drawn from Frazer.[1] Phrases like "our bright bull babe" (562:22), "the rowantree" (588:31), and "the herblord" (254:36) encapsulate some of the leading figural nodes that recur in Frazer. In so doing they confer on *Finnegans Wake* much of *The Golden Bough*'s cyclical, sacrificial, and vegetative aura. Joyce also glances with a blandly ironic eye at some of Frazer's leading ideas and the language in which they are couched. Thus, fairly early in the *Wake* he observes with something like Frazer's portentous rhetorical balance that "the use of the homeborn shillelagh . . . shows a distinct advance from savagery to barbarism" (114:12-13). In this he ironically renders one of Frazer's chief beliefs, namely, that human history is the record of a slow and painful ascent from savagery to civilization. He also with trenchant economy undercuts in a revelatory manner Frazer's penchant for solemnly uttering views of an intellectually simple order. And at the close of the third chapter when HCE's death and resurrection are being sketched, they are presented, like the illustrative instances of *The Golden*

---

[1] James Joyce, *Finnegans Wake* (New York: Viking Press, 1947), pp. 4:15, 616:32. For convenience, line references are included following the colon. Subsequent references will be included in the text.

Bough, as forming "a theory none too rectiline of the evoluation of human society and a testament of the rocks from all the dead unto some the living" (73:31-33).

A similar stress on Frazer's pervasive sense of the past's intrusiveness in the present is rendered by the remark that "ancients link with presents as the human chain extends" (254:8-9). The same is true of the marginalia in the children's school lesson chapter, where one comment reads: "Primanouriture and Ultimogeniture" (300: marginalia). Frazer's emphasis on man's food supply and sexual reproduction as religion's early foci is caught in a manner that cleverly echoes his elaborate analyses of primitive means of determining familial succession by primogeniture and ultimogeniture. Such a movement "from cannibal king to property horse" (600:1) ultimately yields a full-scale parody of the scholar's effort to summarize the whole intricate course of human history:

> Signifying, if tungs may tolkan, that, primeval conditions having gradually receded but nevertheless the emplacement of solid and fluid having to a great extent persisted through intermittences of sullemn fulminance, sollemn nuptialism, sallemn sepulture and providential divining, making possible and even inevitable, after his a time has a tense haves and havenots hesitency, at the place and period under consideration a socially organic entity of a millenary military mariotry monetary morphological circumformation in a more or less settled state of equonomic ecolube equalobe equilab equilibbrium (599:9-18).

Frazer's work constitutes a central aspect of *Finnegans Wake*, which might easily merit its inclusion among the structural books of the *Wake*. Clearly, the characters HCE, ALP, Shem, Issy, and the rest continue the archetypal function of *Ulysses*. The endlessly dying and reviving god, the scapegoat of the community, and dutiful, patient, questing, Isis-like wife, to mention but the most important, enact their roles throughout recorded history as well as in the narratives of dream, legend, and myth. Instead of the classical, Judaic, and Christian cultures of *Ulysses* a pan-cultural complex is generated as Scandinavian elements jostle with Oriental, Germanic, Celtic, Romanic, and numerous others. Here the stress upon a comparative perspective found in Frazer is realized with a vengeance, as Joyce suggests when he observes: "How far-flung is your fokloire" (419:12-13).

The idea of the emergence of aesthetic form from the detritus of language is, as Joyce saw, intrinsically comic. Consequently, the dying god is not allowed to retain his usual Frazerian sonorities of travail and death. The metamorphosis of his traditional ritual *sparagmos* into a comparative religion joke is caught in the declaration that "they have waved his green boughs o'er him as they have torn him limb from lamb" (58:6-7). And with his death the event acquires resurrection's divinely comic note when he likens it to "the sprangflowers of his burstday" (59:11), and also mortality's black humor when he suggests it "was a viridable god-inpotty for the reinworms" (59:12). Here *The Golden Bough*'s accounts of the ritual sowing and flowering of gardens of Adonis in small pots as emblems of the god's death and resurrection are given a resolutely comic inflection.[2]

When we survey the passages from the *Wake* that reflect *The Golden Bough*, we are struck by how closely they render the major emphases of Frazer's concerns. On one level, *The Golden Bough* is an encyclopedic effort to show that man's religious expressions throughout history revolve around the ideas of sex, death, immortality, and law. Thus, his world revolves around phallic symbols, fertility rituals, solemn sacrifices, signs of resurrection, and taboos or prohibitions against crime. Substantially the same focus obtains in *Finnegans Wake*. It abounds in scenes of and references to love-making, organs of generation, and other signs of sexuality as well as HCE's recurring ritual demise and revival, together with the celebrated crime in the park, which seems to symbolize the violation of man's most dread taboo. The chief difference from Frazer's treatment of these motifs of the religious impulse in man is that while *The Golden Bough* takes a cultivated and urbane but resolutely ironic attitude, *Finnegans Wake* assumes an exuberantly bawdy and vulgar, yet highly comic, stance. It is, in effect, a human comedy on man's religious consciousness, dramatizing a secularized and so comic version of

---

[2] *GB*, v, 236ff., 253ff.

the struggle between religious guilt and fear and imaginative satisfaction and sexual joy.

Informing the fear is the fact of mortality. By stressing the ritual forms of death, *Finnegans Wake* follows closely the lead of *The Golden Bough* and is particularly sedulous in using its images and figures.[3] After the wake for Finnegan the four old men declare as the third of its four constant features "(Tammuz.) An auburn mayde, o'brine a'bride, to be desarted. Adear, adear!" (13:26-27). Goldsmith's virginal girl mourns the death of Frazer's god in the fashion prescribed since the days of ancient Jerusalem.[4] Frazer's associating him with Adonis, the handsome young lover of the wanton fertility goddess Ishtar, makes his mourning by "a brazenlockt damsel" (14:7) particularly appropriate. In the same way *The Golden Bough*'s information that Tammuz means "true son of the deep water" explains why she is called a bride "o'brine."[5] When the narrator suggests we look away from the book to the natural scene, the first thing seen amid a sentimentalized pastoral setting is "lean neath stone pine the pastor lies with his crook" (14:32). Even here the aura of death and crime hangs about the serene, peaceful scene. The Christian note of gentle protection seen in the pastor and his shepherd's crook is offset by the pine, emblematic of the emasculated dying god Attis, and the ironies of criminality resident in "crook."[6] The use of the stone pine further suggests a time when the Christian pastor is recumbent beneath a different stone, equally symbolic of death.

The interrelation of Christian and Frazerian motifs is continued in the immediately following conversation between Mutt and Jute. The latter offers Mutt a bribe for betrayal and in doing so draws Parnell into the archetypal pattern of ritual mur-

[3] The reliance on *The Golden Bough* for the *Wake*'s sexual pattern is equally heavy, but since the evidence does not significantly qualify the fact or nature of Frazer's impact, it is foregone in this study. For its details, see my "'Finnegans Wake' and Sexual Metamorphosis," *Contemporary Literature*, XIII (1972), 213-242.

[4] *GB*, V, 11, 17, 20; IX, 400.

[5] *GB*, V, 6, 8, 246; IX, 371, 373, 399, 406.

[6] *GB*, V, 264-267, 271, 277-285. The crook is also an emblem of Osiris. See *GB*, VI, 108, 153.

der: "One eyegonblack. Bisons is bisons. Let me fore all your has-
itancy cross your qualm with trink gilt. Here have sylvan coyne,
a piece of oak. Ghinees hies good for you" (16:29-32). When
Mutt is paid in "sylvan coyne, a piece of oak," both Judas and the
King of the Wood at Nemi become involved. To be given part of
the oak forest is to be made responsible for it, to have to guard
it as the priest-king of Nemi did.[7]

As if to underscore their linking Finnegan's death with the
Frazerian dying and reviving god, the four old men are called
upon to quiet Finnegan, aroused by the whisky spilled on him.
At the outset, one with comic condescension treats him as if he
were what in fact he is, the image of human death and revival:
"Now be aisy, good Mr Finnimore, sir. And take your laysure like
a god on pension and don't be walking abroad" (24:16). Here
Joyce uses comedy where Frazer uses irony but to the same end,
namely, the humanizing of deities. The Frazerian impact of the
injunction is intensified also by the underlying significance of his
being told to take his "laysure like a god." The ease of leisure is
certainly urged on him, but so is sexual intercourse. "Sure" is
both the Irish expression which here suggests the easy, assured
casualness of divine copulation, as with Zeus frequently, and the
more common term indicating the certainty of the act. The latter
is a comic deflation of that portion of the ritual performed by the
temporary king or scapegoat, the human representative of the
dying god, in which he is provided with a woman for intercourse
before suffering death.[8] The old man continues to urge quiet on

[7] GB, I, 42. Additional support for this view appears in the same passage.
For instance, "eyegonblack" seems to be a combination of the Greek
"agon" and the German "Augenblick," which would suggest a ritual combat caught in a moment of perception. The "agon," of course was one of the
crucial features of Greek tragedy and its ritual basis was outlined by Gilbert
Murray, one of Frazer's most influential followers. "Bisons" obviously are
"bygones," but that The Golden Bough indicates that they also achieve
resurrection may just possibly suggest that Joyce is emphasizing that the
ritual death of the dying god also issues in his revival (see GB, VIII, 256).
Similarly, while "Ghinees" is clearly Guinness, the brewery, it may barely
conceivably also reflect Frazer's point about the existence of priest kings in
Guinea (see GB, III, 5). The inhabitants' profound belief in dreams and
their annual performance of expulsion rituals would have given Joyce additional reasons for working in such a reference (see GB, III, 37; IX, 131).
[8] GB, IX, 278, 309.

Finnegan, and in the process reveals unmistakably that he is to be treated like a god because he is one rather than simply as a humoring gesture. Now he is not in a modern coffin but "under your sycamore by the keld water" (24:30-31). He belongs there because he is now Osiris, a point clear from *The Golden Bough*'s identification of the sycamore as sacred to the Egyptian god and associated with his effigy.[9]

The identification of the dead man with a god is matched by the ritual acts promised by the old man. Not only will his grave be cared for in the modern fashion but he will be brought offerings, as Frazer's primitive tribes did for their gods.[10] He will receive "offerings of the field" (25:3-4) including honey, "the holiest thing ever was" (25:6), and goat's milk, offerings precisely of the sort described in *The Golden Bough*.[11] In addition, his worship is spreading rapidly and even the gravestones recall him from a time when Frazerian nature-worship was rife and "every hollow holds a hallow" (25:13-14).

Even more significantly, his worshippers speak the vegetative language of *The Golden Bough*. They understand precisely why the god must die and the part that human fertility played in his perpetuation: "If you were bowed and soild and letdown itself from the oner of the load it was that paddyplanters might pack up plenty and when you were undone in every point fore the laps of goddesses you showed our labourlasses how to free was easy. The game old Gunne, they do be saying, (skull!) that was a planter for you, a spicer of them all" (25:18-23). Because he accepts his ritual death with the harvest and like Adonis sees its sexual nature, he provides for both vegetative and human fertility and is recognized as its prime occasioner. Consequently, he is elevated above all others, including Irish, Oriental, and Frazerian monarchs and chiefs: "There was never a warlord in Great Erinnes and Brettland, no, nor in all Pike County like you, they say. No, nor a king nor an ardking, bung king, sung king, or hung king" (25:27-29).

When the emphasis shifts from Finnegan to HCE, something of the same order can be found, though if anything the humor is

---

[9] *GB*, VI, 88, 110. [10] *GB*, VI, 194; IX, 26-30.
[11] *GB*, I, 311; IV, 86; V, 85, 87; VI, 194; VIII, 288; IX, 26ff.

increased. At the opening of the third chapter, various views of HCE's fate are advanced. In the course of one of these, he is described as having died painlessly on Hallowe'en night and been expelled into the great Beyond with blows "upon his oyster and atlas on behanged and behooved and behicked and behulked of his last fishandblood bedscrappers" (49:26-28). Clearly the prankish quality of Hallowe'en is appropriate to "this Eyrawyggla saga" (48:28-29). At the same time, the point of much of Joyce's humor resides in his comic appreciation of Frazer's observation about the historical diminution of the spiritually important to secular amusement. Very likely he knew that Hallowe'en and Beltane night were the two chief fire-festivals of the ancient Celts, and if he did not know it, he could easily have learned it from *The Golden Bough*.[12] Hallowe'en was the festival of the Celtic New Year as well.[13] Hosty is the figure of the dying god and the old year and expires just at the moment when the new year enters. Support for this appears earlier when the dying but reviving god Tammuz is brought into conjunction with Baalfire's night, which according to Frazer is the popular derivation for Beltane or May Day.[14] The reviving god is linked with the day of fertility just as the scapegoat predeceases that of the new year.

This scapegoat motif is anticipated just before the "Ballad of Persse O'Reilly" in Chapter II. It is sung before a huge throng including "a deuce of dianas ridy for the hunt" (43:11), a phrase which renders one of the goddess' characteristics presented at the very beginning of *The Golden Bough*.[15] Later on the same page, however, we find the ballad of the scapegoat ritual being sung to the accompaniment of "the flute, that onecrooned king of inscrewments" (43:31-32). According to Frazer, the flute was traditionally employed in ritual music for dying gods like Tammuz and Adonis and was held to have a particularly exciting, stimulating effect in comparison to other instruments, a point perhaps hinted at in Mr. Delaney's "anticipating a perfect downpour of plaudits among the rapsods" (43:33-34).[16]

---

[12] *GB*, XI, 40ff.   [13] See *GB*, X, 224ff.
[14] See *Finnegans Wake*, 13:26, 36 and *GB*, X, 146, 149, n.1, 150, n.1.
[15] *GB*, I, 6.   [16] *GB*, V, 9, 54, 225, n.3.

The ballad's musical attack and ritual expulsion and death of HCE is matched on the level of reported action by Hosty's death. To emphasize the sexual aspect as a means of underscoring Parnell's involvement in the scene, he is identified as follows: "Greatwheel Dunlop was the name was on him: behung, all we are his bisaacles. As hollyday in his house so was he priest and king to that: ulvy came, envy saw, ivy conquered. Lou! Lou! They have waved his green boughs o'er him as they have torn him limb from lamb. For his muertification and uxpiration and dumnation and annuhulation" (58:3-9). Here "behung" is a description of genitality as well as mortality. In this Joyce resembles Frazer in that the dying god too has his phallic and fertile aspect in addition to his suffering and disappearing form. The suggestion that "we" are all cyclical versions of "Greatwheel Dunlop" further develops the universal, archetypal nature of HCE and the drama he enacts in the *Wake*. Thus, Parnell is not merely an Irish scapegoat victimized by society's expulsion of its own impulses to illicit passion. He is also Frazer's dying god embodied in human form from its earliest times. This is testified to by the collocation of holly, priest, king, ivy, and green boughs.[17]

At the very end of the chapter HCE's accuser demands, among other things, that he "come out, you jewbeggar, to be Executed Amen" (70:34-35). Instead of complying, HCE makes a list of the 111 names he has been called by his antagonist. The accuser describes him explicitly as a Frazerian archetype: "Earwicker, that patternmind, that paradigmatic ear, receptoretentive as his of Dionysius, longsuffering although whitening under restraint in the sititout corner of his conservatory" (70:35-71:2). His paradigmatic capacity to encompass all the names derives from his being an embodiment of the dying god whose dismemberment is the culmination of a violent assault upon him. His connection with *The Golden Bough*'s dying god is further underscored by some of the names he recites. "Wheatears" (71:11) obviously suggests the vegetative qualities of Adonis and Osiris, and "Godsoilman" (71:14) seems to carry something of their connection with the earth. "Moonface the Murderer" (71:15), on the other hand, may be a composite of myth and ritual, alluding to

[17] *GB*, II, 122, 251; V, 66, 72ff., 278; VI, 88, 110, 112; VII, 1ff., 30ff.

the moon's association with Osiris and to human sacrifices performed in honor of the moon by primitive peoples.[18] Two others stress the sexual nature of the Frazerian fertility deities and their eastern Mediterranean origin. Thus, in being called "Sower Rapes" (72:10), HCE is, among many other things, being associated with the custom described in *The Golden Bough* of orgiastic ceremonies at planting time to assure the fertility of the fields.[19] And in identifying him as an "Easyathic Phallusaphist" (72:14), Joyce elides into a single phrase Frazer's points about the dying god's Asiatic origins, role as fertility symbol, and status as a philosophical force in the primitive mind.

Not all the death images, however, focus on HCE's hanging, dismemberment, and burial. Early in the fifth chapter, the dead HCE is linked with "broody old flishguds" (73:6) and buried "three monads in his watery grave" (78:19). Like Frazer's Adonis and Osiris, he is the god whose body is committed to the waves in order to assure his return to his needy people. But in Joyce's hands this ceases to be an earnest of the harmonious relationship between the god and his worshippers. It becomes instead a comic record of the trials attendant on being the revived, life-sustaining deity who endures the ritual sacramental meal in his own person.

The comic qualities with which Joyce invests even the dying and reviving god become even more apparent in the next chapter in which Shem asks Shaun twelve questions designed to provide a series of pictures of the archetypal human family. The first question is very long and is, among other things, a sequence of descriptions of the god's or hero's powers and characteristics. It closely resembles the mythic accounts of efforts to gain power over the deity through guessing his name. Hence it has more than a slight connection with Frazer's discussion of the primitive belief that one's name was a vital part of one and its disclosure would leave one susceptible to hostile magic.[20] At another point it is remarked: "as far as wind dries and rain eats and sun turns and water bounds he is exalted and depressed, assembled and asundered" (136:5-7). Clearly one major aspect of the riddle in-

[18] *GB*, V, 73; VI, 129ff.; VII, 261; IX, 282.
[19] *GB*, II, 98-101, 103-104. [20] *GB*, III, 318ff., 374ff.

volves Frazer's human embodiment of natural recurrence and vegetative fertility and the ritual by which his composition and dissolution is enacted. Here Joyce moves away from the note of primitive awe and civilized contemplation with which *The Golden Bough* surrounds the cyclic periodicity of nature and man. For him the unvarying round carries a note of comic absurdity in its reduction of the human figure to the dictates and movements of wind and rain, sun and water. The dying god whose dismemberment purports to be a freely elected sacrifice is in reality a puppet of the elements elevated and cast down, constituted and annihilated according to their dictates.

In another part of the same question Shem remarks: "theer's his bow and wheer's his leaker and heer lays his bequiet hearse, deep" (137:5-7). The query buried in the middle of the excerpt is a burlesque of Osiris' dismemberment and Isis' search for the parts of his body. As Frazer emphasizes, the only part not recovered were his genital organs.[21] What this does, of course, is as it were, to de-Olympianize the dying god and his consort. The exalted metaphor of the god's lost potency is shrunk to a comic image of a mislaid personal item, and mystery is replaced by mirth. The same note is continued in the question about the old maidservant Kate. Her answer contains the observation that "I thawght I knew his stain on the flower" (141:31-32). The allusion is to *The Golden Bough*'s account of Adonis and/or Hyacinth, whose mythic deaths were memorialized by a change in the color or markings of the flower traditionally associated with them.[22]

As we have seen, Joyce refuses to allow HCE an easy escape into the role of society's victim and the noble, self-sacrificing hero. At the same time he is sensitive to the reality and value of the scapegoat and the longsuffering hero. In the fable of the Mookse and the Gripes, the explosive, dogmatic Mookse declares: "Blast yourself and your anathomy infairioriboos! No, hang you for an animal rurale! I am superbly in my supremest poncif! Abase you, baldyqueens! Gather behind me, satraps! Rots!" (154:10-13). In this Joyce draws on *The Golden Bough* for a custom easily associated with the scapegoat ritual and yet capable of revealing that contempt rather than reverence ordains the

[21] *GB*, VI, 10, 102.   [22] *GB*, V, 226.

Mookse's use of it, as when he says, "No, hang you for an animal rurale!" (154:11). In that portion of *The Golden Bough* which concentrates on the various dying gods, Frazer records the custom of animals being sacrificed by being hanged.[23] The Latin form "rurale" indicates in a loosely Frazerian idiom that the sacrifice is of a wild rather than an urban, domestic creature. The image of hanging even more emphatically links with Frazer's hanged god and scapegoat, thereby making of the Gripes a sympathetic victim but one whose divine connection will assure his survival and triumph. At the same time, the language and tone used by the Mookse reveals that he is not regarding the Gripes reverently as a religious sacrifice but contemptuously as essentially a political enemy. In short, he demonstrates one of *The Golden Bough*'s most subtly emphasized points, namely, that the gradual politicizing of society's power by priest-kings results in the secularization of society and the consequent forgetting of the victim's religious significance.

Shaun's penchant for eliminating opposition by the most ruthless of means is developed more fully in the next chapter. There he recounts the nature and career of Shem, the artist as seen by his prime antagonist. He casts Shem in the Frazerian role of the ritually slain king: "perhaps, agglaggagglomeratively asaspenking, after all and arklast fore arklyst on his last public misappearance, circling the square, for the deathfête of Saint Ignaceous Poisonivy, of the Fickle Crowd (hopon the sixth day of Hogsober, killim our king, layum low!)" (186:10-14). He feels, of course, that Shem is not actually the dying god, but he hopes that by a process of imaginative agglomeration he may be quasi-magically induced to share the god's fate. Hence he is assimilated to the "aspenking" or King of the Wood, who, as we have seen, is also represented by Parnell. What was verbal assault and symbolic sacrifice of Parnell will, Shaun hopes, become literal for Shem just as it was for the mythic figures of *The Golden Bough* like Attis, who also is invoked by the references to ivy and hogs.[24] The drift of his desire and intent is clear enough from his final speech and ritual gesture. He first declares Shem mad and then "points the deathbone and the quick are still" (193:29). In utiliz-

---

[23] *GB*, v, 289-292.   [24] *GB*, v, 278; viii, 22.

ing this aboriginal custom, which Frazer describes in several places in *The Golden Bough*, Joyce seeks to delineate Shaun as a comic figure of death and black magic.[25] His magic is weak and inadequate and the only stillness he can wreak on the truly living is that which the fool and dunce have always engendered in others, an inability to stay awake: *"Insomnia, somnia somniorum. Awmawm"* (193:29-30).

In the second chapter of Book II, the three Earwicker children are concerned with their school lessons. These must, according to Joyce, deal both with their immediate family's history and also with the archetypal events of the human race. Thus, they attend to what appears to be the male father-figure "dirging a past of bloody altars" (276:4). In doing so, they catch a concentrated glimpse of their natural, classical, and primitive heritage. The human sacrifices of the Irish Druids, the slaughter of Greek innocents, and the tribal appeasing of powerful gods of nature, all dealt with exhaustively by *The Golden Bough*, are implicit in this phrase, which is redolent with the regret and observances of man since the beginning of time.[26] But, as we might expect, the children must learn that there is more to the alphabet of human existence than generalized sacrifice and bloodshed. It also includes ritual destruction of persons filling a specific role in the order of society: "When men want to write a letters. Ten men, ton men, pen men, pun men, wont to rise a ladder. And den men, dun men, fen men, fun men, hen men, hun men wend to raze a leader" (278:18-21). What is humorous to Joyce, however, is unsettling to the children: "We have wounded our way on foe tris prince till that force in the gill is faint afarred and the face in the treebark feigns afear" (278:25-279:1). As Frazer indicates, Adonis was born from a myrrh tree and later suffered his fatal wound from an enemy disguised as a boar.[27] Here the children recognize that they too, as members of the human race, have attacked the god in his form of the sad young prince Tristan. At the same time, they have wound back through time from the sophisticated legend of Tristan to the primitive myth of Adonis, a jour-

[25] *GB*, IV, 60; X, 14.
[26] *GB*, I, 386-387; IV, 161ff.; IX, 210ff., 409 *passim*; XI, 32ff.
[27] *GB*, V, 6ff., 55, 227; VI, 110.

ney whose result they still find somewhat puzzling: "Strangely cult for this ceasing of the yore" (279:2-3). Issy, though engrossed in the romantic sexual forms of life and myth such as the Adonis story, also senses their more somber dimensions. She remembers the dog day when she "sat astrid uppum their Drewitt's altar" (279:n.1, 11. 27), urges "sago sound, rite go round, kill kackle, kook kettle" (279:n.1, 11. 25), and muses that "it most have been Mad Mullans planted him" (279:n.1, 11. 23-24). Clearly she grasps least the dying god's ritual sacrifice and burial so copiously rendered by *The Golden Bough*.

When the action moves, in the next chapter, to HCE's pub and the plays performed there, something of what they have learned is seen. Both plays are supposedly about the overthrow of the father, which is the Freudian or domestic version of the ritual slaying of the dying god. At one point therefore Taff says: "The fourscore soculums are watchyoumaycodding to cooll the skoopgoods blooff" (346:25-26). He makes this comment "*whiles they all are bealting pots to dubrin din for old daddam dombstom to tomb and wamb humbs lumbs agamb*" (346:16-18). That is to say, everyone is engaged in the ritual noise-making that Frazer suggests may accompany both the burial of the god and the efforts to purify the area and encourage fertility.[28] Butt responds by declaring that he ranges from the extreme past to future and so has many memories of those dead who are living elsewhere and whom he identifies implicitly with the Frazerian dying god by calling them "me alma marthyrs" (348:10-11). The reference is not to the fostering mother, as the phrase "old boyars" (348:10) indicates, but to all males who like Attis are beloved by the fertility goddess and sacrifice their virility in an act of martyrdom to her honor.[29] His salutation to their memory further bears out the comedy wrought by the transmogrifying mythopoeic imagination: "I dring to them, bycorn spirits fuselaiding" (348:11). In celebrating those bygone spirits, he is honoring both the Celtic figure emblematic of liquor itself, John Barleycorn, and the Frazerian cereal deities from whom he descended.[30]

[28] *GB*, IX, 109, 111, 113, 116, 118, 120, 126, 146-147, 196, 204, 252, 256ff., 272ff.
[29] *GB*, V, 263, 282-283.   [30] See *GB*, V, 230, 233, 279; VI, 34, 48, 89ff., 96ff.

As the chapter moves on toward the children's attack on HCE and his symbolic death through drunkenness, the stress upon *The Golden Bough*'s central images of sacrifice and ritual death becomes heavier and more explicit. One tavern customer observes: " 'Tis golden sickle's hour. Holy moon priestess, we'd love our grappes of mistellose!" (360:24-25). One of Frazer's chief points is that the golden bough, the mistletoe, constitutes the life or external soul of the dying god Balder and so is to be cut but once a year, on either the first or sixth day of the moon, and then only with a golden sickle as a symbolic ritual sacrifice of the vegetative form of the god.[31] Clearly what is being announced is the time for HCE's symbolic ritual demise. The customers, however, question his authenticity and accuse him of cohabiting with a known prostitute at a time "when all the perts in princer street set up their tinker's humn, (the rann, the rann, that keen of old bards)" (363:4-5). As the earlier discussion of the wren as the king of the birds made clear, Frazer identifies this folk custom as the sacramental sacrifice of the dying god in animal form.[32] The criticism of HCE, then, is not so much a moral as a ritual one. He is ignoring the message of the song, which speaks of death, not fertility or sexuality. For as Frazer points out, the mistletoe and the wren are associated by the placement of a mistletoe wreath on the pole to which the dead wren is fastened.[33] Yet to disregard the song and emblem of the dead god is also to bypass the sign of health, fertility, and protection against evil that *The Golden Bough* finds in the mistletoe.[34]

At the same time, Joyce is aware of the archetypal ritual of death as necessary for revival. He shows it by fusing the song of John Brown with *The Golden Bough*'s emphasis on the burial's occurring in the deity's sacred grove: "Shaum Baum's bode he is amustering in the groves while his shool comes merging along!" (364:8-9). Then, toward the end of the chapter, the three children incite one another to fresh indignities, urge him to participate gladly in his hanging, and then stand back to rejoice in its achievement: "Isn't it great he is swaying above us for his good

[31] *GB*, XI, 77-78, 80, 279, 283, 315ff.
[32] *GB*, VIII, 317ff.   [33] *GB*, VIII, 321.
[34] *GB*, XI, 77-79, 82-83, 85ff., 282-283, 294.

and ours. Fly your balloons, dannies and dennises! He's door-knobs dead! And Annie Delap is free! Ones more. We could ate you, par Buccas, and imbabe through you, reassuranced in the wild lac of gotliness. One fledge, one brood till hulm culms evurdyburdy" (377:36-378:5). Here too Joyce takes his cue from *The Golden Bough*. He has HCE suffer the death by hanging in order to point up his scapegoat role as the hanged god. Then, with his death announced, Joyce modulates him into a more specific form of the dying god, Bacchus or Dionysus.[35] In turn, Dionysus' association with Osiris, as pointed out by Frazer, may cast some light on the final sentence in the above passage in which Joyce suddenly associates the communion god with a flock of birds.[36] According to *The Golden Bough*, the bird was a creature known as "the soul of Osiris" and in addition was traditionally regarded as the seat of a dead person's soul as well as representing the corn spirit and serving as a scapegoat.[37] Clearly the image of the bird allows Joyce to draw into a single complex figure HCE's components as dead man, dying god, scapegoat victim, and guardian of intoxication.

As befits a book of cyclical and simultaneous structure, images of and allusions to death and the dying god continue throughout the remainder of *Finnegans Wake*. They are, however, neither so numerous nor so central to the main thrust of the narrative.

[35] He does for several reasons. One, of course, is to link the human HCE, the drunken tavern-owner, with the mythic guardian of the vine in order to show simultaneously the perdurability and the metamorphosis of the archetype. Another reason is that in assuming the form of Bacchus, HCE also blends, as Frazer points out, with Dionysus (see *GB*, VII, 2). Bacchus' legendary association with an Athenian festival of swinging may also contribute to Joyce's linking of him with a hanged god "swaying above us" (see *GB*, IV, 281-283). This association also renders accessible the comic vision of the traditional communion meal, a vision which like that of *The Golden Bough* emphasizes the continuity existing between primitive pagan and Christian versions of the observance. Dionysus, of all Frazer's dying gods, was the one whose ritual preeminently involved not only dismemberment but devouring of the god or his representative (see *GB*, VI, 98; VII, 13-14, 17-18, 25; VIII, 16). That these sacrifices sometimes included children would help to explain also why in anticipating the ceremonial drinking of the god's blood, the celebrants should speak of it as an "imbabe through you" (see *GB*, IV, 166 n.1).

[36] *GB*, VI, 113, 127; VII, 3.

[37] *GB*, VI, 110; VII, 295ff.; VIII, 296; IX, 35ff, 51ff.

They sometimes suggest the scope of time and the order of human creation, presumably through the constant of mortality, as when Shaun in the process of becoming Christ tries to love all "from the King of all Wrenns down to infuseries" (431:13). Or they invoke the ritual combat of the priest at Nemi as well as something of Frazer's antipathy to religion for the purpose of anti-clerical satire, as Shaun inadvertently does in urging the young girls to read the Archdeacon's book subtitled "*Viewed to Death by a Priest Hunter*" (440:2-3). Or they are used to suggest that the ritual death is not confined to HCE alone, as when Shem is identified as "my said brother, the skipgod" (488:22). Or they serve to reassure frightened children by being associated with the natural world of sex as when HCE tries to quiet Shem and Shaun by equating Phoenix Park and his own private parts with "the mound where anciently first murders were wanted to take root" (564:29). Or they hold out the tempting ambiguous truth about the imaginative function of death, as ALP shows when she declares: "Once you are balladproof you are unperceable to haily, icy and missilethroes" (616:31-33). To be bulletproof is to be physically immune to hail, ice, and spears of all sorts. To be immune to song and story, however, is to be unperceivable by the holy, whether Isis the savior of the dying god or Loki his slayer. And since the two alternatives are enshrined in the one sentence, one cannot choose the one without the other, Joyce avers. Thus, as *Finnegans Wake* has been insisting all along by its dramatic metamorphoses, to recognize death and mortality and to live fully with that awareness is to know the only true idea of the holy available to man in this or any other century.

Index

Because of the frequency of their appearance references to Frazer and *The Golden Bough* are indexed only when they are of central importance and so of particular use to the reader.